German Empires and Decolonial Fantasies, 1492–1942

Social History, Popular Culture, and Politics in Germany
Kathleen Canning, Series Editor

Recent Titles
German Empires and Decolonial Fantasies, 1492–1942
    Patricia Anne Simpson
Women in German Expressionism: Gender, Sexuality, Activism
    Anke Finger and Julie Shoults, Editors
Queer Livability: German Sexual Sciences and Life Writing
    Ina Linge
Moderate Modernity: The Newspaper Tempo *and the
    Transformation of Weimar Democracy*
    Jochen Hung
African Students in East Germany, 1949–1975
    Sara Pugach
The Arts of Democratization: Styling Political Sensibilities in Postwar West Germany
    Jennifer M. Kapczynski and Caroline A. Kita, Editors
Decolonizing German and European History at the Museum
    Katrin Sieg
Spaces of Honor: Making German Civil Society, 1700–1914
    Heikki Lempa
Bankruptcy and Debt Collection in Liberal Capitalism: Switzerland, 1800–1900
    Mischa Suter
*Marking Modern Movement: Dance and Gender in the Visual Imagery of
    the Weimar Republic*
    Susan Funkenstein
Anti-Heimat Cinema: The Jewish Invention of the German Landscape
    Ofer Ashkenazi
Dispossession: Plundering German Jewry, 1933–1953
    Christoph Kreutzmüller and Jonathan R. Zatlin, Editors
*Sex between Body and Mind: Psychoanalysis and Sexology in the
    German-speaking World, 1890s–1930s*
    Katie Sutton
Imperial Fictions: German Literature Before and Beyond the Nation-State
    Todd Kontje
White Rebels in Black: German Appropriation of Black Popular Culture
    Priscilla Layne
*Not Straight from Germany: Sexual Publics and Sexual Citizenship
    since Magnus Hirschfeld*
    Michael Thomas Taylor, Annette F. Timm, and Rainer Herrn, Editors
Passing Illusions: Jewish Visibility in Weimar Germany
    Kerry Wallach
Cosmopolitanisms and the Jews
    Cathy S. Gelbin and Sander L. Gilman

For a complete list of titles, please see www.press.umich.edu

German Empires and Decolonial Fantasies, 1492–1942

Patricia Anne Simpson

University of Michigan Press
Ann Arbor

Copyright © 2025 by Patricia Anne Simpson

This work is licensed under a Creative Commons Attribution-NonCommercial 4.0 International License. *Note to users*: A Creative Commons license is only valid when it is applied by the person or entity that holds rights to the licensed work. Works may contain components (e.g., photographs, illustrations, or quotations) to which the rightsholder in the work cannot apply the license. It is ultimately your responsibility to independently evaluate the copyright status of any work or component part of a work you use, in light of your intended use. To view a copy of this license, visit http://creativecommons.org/licenses/by-nc/4.0/

For questions or permissions, please contact um.press.perms@umich.edu
Published in the United States of America by the
University of Michigan Press
First published March 2025

A CIP catalog record for this book is available from the British Library.

Library of Congress Cataloging-in-Publication Data

Names: Simpson, Patricia Anne, 1958– author.
Title: German empires and decolonial fantasies, 1492–1942 / Patricia Anne Simpson.
Description: Ann Arbor : University of Michigan Press, 2025. | Series: Social history, popular
   culture, and politics in Germany | Includes bibliographical references and index.
Identifiers: LCCN 2024046682 (print) | LCCN 2024046683 (ebook) | ISBN 9780472077373
   (hardcover) | ISBN 9780472057375 (paperback) | ISBN 9780472904976 (ebook other)
Subjects: LCSH: Germany—Colonies—History. | Europe, German-speaking—Civilization—
   Foreign influences. | National characteristics, German. | German literature—Foreign
   influences. | Imperialism in literature. | Colonies in literature. | Decolonization.
Classification: LCC JV2027 .S475 2025 (print) | LCC JV2027 (ebook) | DDC 325/.343—dc23/
   eng/20241216
LC record available at https://lccn.loc.gov/2024046682
LC ebook record available at https://lccn.loc.gov/2024046683

DOI: https://doi.org/10.3998/mpub.12901912

The University of Michigan Press's open access publishing program is made possible thanks to additional funding from the University of Michigan Office of the Provost and the generous support of contributing libraries.

CONTENTS

List of Illustrations   vii

Archival Sources   ix

Acknowledgments   xi

Introduction: The "German" Globe, 1492   1

Part I: Imperial Entanglements

Chapter One.   Prussia's First Fortress   31

Chapter Two.   Enlightened Colonialism   50

Chapter Three.   Enslaved Souls, Perfect Freedom, and Savagery   78

Part II: Transatlantic German Worlds

Chapter Four.   The New World Wilderness   111

Chapter Five.   German Pioneers   150

Chapter Six.   Upon the Water: Immigration as Destiny   174

Part III: Global Imaginaries

Chapter Seven.   Global German Frontiers   213

Chapter Eight.   *Wohin?* The Ungovernable   247

Chapter Nine.   First Footprints and Recolonial Fantasies   272

Conclusion: Decolonial Fantasies   290

Works Cited 301

Index 323

Digital materials related to this title can be found on the Fulcrum platform via the following citable URL: https://doi.org/10.3998/mpub.12901912

ILLUSTRATIONS

Figure 1. Martin Beheim *Erdapfel* (1492)   2
Figure 2. Equestrian statue of the Great Elector   33
Figure 3. Exterior wall of Groß-Friedrichsburg in 2020   39
Figure 4. Dungeon of Groß-Friedrichsburg, directly below the Chapel   40
Figure 5. Chapel of Groß-Friedrichsburg, directly above dungeon   41
Figure 6. German Colonial Administration, Kpando   47
Figure 7. German Colonial Administration, Kpando   47
Figure 8. Corridor, German Colonial Station, Kpando   48
Figure 9. Door in the German Colonial Administration, Kpando   49
Figure 10. Antoine Pesne, 1711. "Prinz Friedrich Ludwig in Preußen (1707–1708) im Gartenwagen mit schwarzem Kammerdiener, um 1711   54
Figure 11. Letter signed by Anton Ulrich   76
Figure 12. *The Purchase of Christian Captives from the Barbary States* (Anonymous)   83
Figure 13. Sugar sculpture, Pedro II + Tereza Cristina (1859–1864)   113
Figure 14. Rotermund-Heuer *Fibel*, "Zaun" (fence)   143
Figure 15. Rotermund-Heuer *Fibel*, "They like to do damage to the corn"   144
Figure 16. Guiherme Litran (1840–1897), *Carga de cavalaria Farroupilha*, 1893   147
Figure 17. Mauricio Rugendas, *El rapto de la cautiva*, 1845   153
Figure 18. "wie Federmann in Venezuela und Staden in Brasilien, so hat am Silberstrom Ulrich Schmidel seine Erlebnisse aufgezeichnet"   157
Figure 19. Butcher advertisement, including imported meats from Germany   160
Figure 20. Playing Pieces 2, "Germany's Game of Colonies," ca. 1890   251
Figure 21. "A thief in chains," from *Deutsche Kolonien in Wort und Bild*, "Kamerun"   259

Figure 22. *Chained women prisoners with their overseer,* "Deutsch-Ostafrika" 261
Figure 23. Kolonial-Ehrentafel, cigarette cards ca. 1936 276
Figure 24. Book cover, Ernst Ludwig Cramer *Die Kinderfarm* (1941) 287
Figure 25. Book cover, Ernst Ludwig Cramer *Kinderfarm-Briefe* (1942) 288
Figure 26. "Germany's Game of Colonies," ca. 1890 294

ARCHIVAL SOURCES

Biblioteca Nacional de Chile, Santiago
Biblioteca Nacional Mariano Moreno, Buenos Aires
Biblioteca y Archivo Histórico Emilio Held Winkler, Santiago de Chile
Bibliothek des Kupferstichkabinetts, Staatliche Museen zu Berlin
El Centro de Documentación de la Inmigración de Habla Alemana (Centro DIHA), Buenos Aires
Ibero-Amerikanisches Institut, Berlin
Joseph P. Horner Memorial Library, German Society of Pennsylvania
Leo Beck Institute, New York
New York Public Library
Special Collections, Love Library, Lincoln
Staatsbibliothek zu Berlin, Preußischer Kulturbesitz, Berlin
Unitätsarchiv, Moravian Archives, Herrnhut

ACKNOWLEDGMENTS

The writing of this book has taken several years and led me on even more circuitous routes; the length of time and uncertainty of destination have caused me to backspace over multiple disjointed beginnings, but I proceed by first expressing thanks to colleagues and interlocutors who have read versions of chapter drafts and book proposals: Robert Kelz, Benjamin Bryce, Eve Moore, thank you. For questions and responses to conference presentations and lectures, thanks to Jennifer Valko, Lora Wildenthal, Mary Helen Dupree, Imke Meyer, Heidi Schlipphacke, Willi Goetschel, John Noyes, Anke Finke, and Adjaï Paulin Oloukpona-Yinnon. Even, or especially, the skeptical queries prompted productive reasoning and (I hope) clearer writing. With regard to the writing practice itself, to the DDGC (Diversity, Decolonization, and the German Curriculum) Collective Slack channelers, I am indebted to you all for your inspiration, consolation, and motivation; thank you for the encouragement, commiseration, and virtual community, and occasional Zooms.

For insightful editorial comments on related projects, I am grateful to Daniel Purdy, Bettina Brandt, Elisabeth Krimmer, Chunjie Zhang, Cristian Cercel, James T. Koranyi, Carl Niekerk, Michael Saman, Nell ter Horst, and Sarah Vandegrift Eldridge. Additionally, colleagues, friends, and students whose names are too numerous to mention asked pointed questions at every stage of this book's progress, for which I offer collective thanks. More guidance came my way over a coffee in library cafes, over empanadas in the street, or to my inbox, so thank you, too, Glenn Penny, Regula Rohland De Langbehn, Nurudeen Mohammed, Adam Blackler, and K. Molly O'Donnell.

My gratitude extends to colleagues at the University of Michigan Press, especially to Katie LaPlant and series editor Kathleen Canning for your help and encouragement during the process of shepherding this book into print (and other formats). Additional thanks go to Madison Allums and Mary Hashman for assistance in the final stages. And, of course, I appreciate the critical feedback from two or more anonymous readers. Your comments helped strengthen the weaknesses, thank you. Shortcomings are my own.

I am beyond grateful to the many librarians and archivists who practiced patience with my many requests and reborrowings, among them Ulrike Mühlschlegel, Olaf Nippe, and Bettina Hess. Their expertise and recommendations, often in response to not completely articulated arguments, posted signs along this journey.

Funding granted by the College of Arts and Sciences, University of Nebraska-Lincoln, and the Department of Modern Language and Literatures has enabled archival research and conference participation, without which this book would be considerably shorter and less ambitious. Insights from my UNL colleague Luis Othoniel Rosa and his ongoing series of philosophical essays, *Lo ingobernable / On Unruliness*, inspired my more utilitarian interpretation of that which is "ungovernable" in the context of (German) colonial rule.

For assistance with images and obtaining or granting permissions to reprint, thank you to Elizabeth Mattos, Albino B. De Olveira, Dudu Schnaider, and Doris Couto. Sections of chapter 7 appeared with the title "Farming Frontiers: The German Woman Pioneer," in Elisabeth Krimmer and Chunjie Zhang, eds. *Gender and German Colonialism: Intimacies, Accountabilities, Intersections* (New York: Routledge, 2024), 29–48; and sections from chapter 2 were published in a *Goethe Yearbook* 30, "Black Actors: Eighteenth-Century Cultures and Decolonial Fantasies" (2023): 119–24. Parts of chapter 3 appeared as "Poetry of Empire: 'Der Wilde,' Indenture, and Indigeneity around 1800," *Goethe Yearbook* 31 (2024): 143–50.

At numerous places along the way, I have appreciated the many artisanal lattes, cortados, matcha lattes, and writing vibes at Treeline, the Coffee House, Meadowlark, Cultiva, Wim, Bonanza, Espresso 77 (laptops at the center table only), the Coffee Project, Café Catmandoo, Second Cup, and even the occasional Starbucks, from Berlin and Santiago to Lincoln and Jackson Heights.

Finally, love and gratitude to the family, all of you.

Introduction

The "German" Globe, 1492

In 1492, tradesman and cartographer Martin Behaim completed a commission to produce what became known as the *Erdapfel* (figure 1), the oldest extant globe reflecting European knowledge of the world just prior to European landfall in the Americas. Its surface recapitulates myth and magic on the same latitude and longitude with products and people, the topography of raw materials, and the respective kings and rulers presiding over the landscape of natural resources. The *Erdapfel* embodies a world made knowable through European eyes. Despite the sketchy details of Behaim's biography, his authorship of this artifact remains undisputed. Generations of geographers and scholars have questioned the veracity of Behaim's claims to have traveled with Diego Cão on a voyage under the sponsorship of the Portuguese crown to the west coast of Africa in 1484–85. Dubiously, Behaim himself gives divergent accounts of this alleged voyage.[1] Indeed, the truth value of his many exploits diminishes under objective examination. While legal records do attest to Behaim's having been charged with and sentenced to jail for the heinous infraction of dancing at a Jew's wedding during Lent, few historical documents verify his and subsequent claims to fame, based on expertise as a navigator and *Seefahrer*. Few of his "firsts," from landfall in Africa to the discovery of the Americas, have passed the test of time or scholarly scrutiny.

Despite boasts about his accomplishments that elude the verifiable, a memorial in Nuremberg was erected in 1890.[2] Myth making around his life and globe aside, Behaim's significance coincides with efforts to recuperate,

---

1. See Ernst Georg Ravenstein, *Martin Behaim: His Life and His Globe* (London: G. Philip & Son, Ltd., 1908), 20.

2. See Peter Bräunlein, *Martin Beheim: Legende und Wirklichkeit eines berühmten Nürnbergers* (Munich: Bayerische Verlagsanstalt, 1992), 117–34.

Figure 1. Martin Beheim *Erdapfel* (1492) https://www.gnm.de/museum-aktuell/global-seit-1492.

or invent as needed, a hallowed German colonial past, motivated in part by a desire to rival the empires of other European powers. The stories and stones that monumentalize Behaim's world—eddies in the stronger current of interest in all things global—serve to posit a much longer legacy of "German" or German-adjacent imperialism, beginning in 1492, with emphasis not on the "discovery" of the Americas or European landfall in the Caribbean— the *Erdapfel* does not depict the Americas or the Pacific—but with Behaim's white footprint on the coast of Africa. The triangular transatlantic story shapes the empires and fantasies of this study. The purpose of this book is

Introduction 3

to decolonize the spaces constructed by the colonial logic of this "German" globe and its power to center 450 years of historical narratives.

Behaim's alleged achievements continue to generate studies of his sketchy itinerary. Historian David Blackbourn asks a crucial question: why was he "a German hero of the age of discovery?"[3] More than four hundred years after the Behaim globe, the claim that he put his foot down on Africa becomes a reference point for a 1942 settler memoir about a lost German colony and his return to the fatherland. *German Empires and Decolonial Fantasies* explores the diverse narratives of being and becoming "German" between 1492 and 1942. In that interim, a range of historical actors featured in this book collectively write a narrative of imperial entanglements with colonialism, of transatlantic "German" worlds legitimatized by bloodlines and bloodshed, and finally by German-inflected global imaginaries drawn from histories and fantasies of a logical itinerary from one fictional footprint to brutal historical fact. The intertextuality between historical and literary sources is often overlooked. The purpose of this book is to examine that interrelationship and its powers of persuasion; to read the latter not for canonical status nor aesthetic accomplishment, but rather for the underwriting or undermining of historical narratives of colonial engagement.

Behaim's orientation in the late fifteenth century was eastward. Blackbourn speculates: "The likely purpose of the globe was demonstrative—to show Nuremberg's merchants the commercial opportunities that existed in an expanding world, from the gold of the West African coast to the spices of the east."[4] European landfall in the Americas would eclipse the influence of the Hanseatic League and turn European attention toward other Indigenous empires. Behaim's globe opens this study because it tells a single story, albeit a persuasive one, based on incomplete, unsubstantiated knowledge, "alternative facts," all the while purporting to represent the world, the global, and the universal. Another aim of this book is to emphasize the ways German-speaking Europe's historical and cultural narratives encompass centuries of entanglement with a colonial world order. From the Holy Roman Empire, to the Holy Roman Empire of the German Nation, with its seat in Vienna, to the Hohenzollern-dominated legacy of Prussian-centric power, through the pan-Germanic European surge around 1900, imperial narratives coexist with

---

3. David Blackbourn, *Germany in the World: A Global History 1500–2000* (New York: Liveright, 2023), 34.

4. Blackbourn, *Germany in the World*, 41.

counternarratives that oppose colonial expansion and absolute power. They encompass contemporary critiques of absolute power; acts of passive, cultural, or armed resistance; and the assertion of moral superiority over other European powers as well as over the conquered, converted, or subjugated. Yet kings could safely ignore arch poems; uprisings could be used to justify genocide long before the term was coined; and immigrants in the Southern Cone and settlers in German Southwest Africa could lambaste other Europeans while calling for racial alliances based on whiteness. Such accounts refuse to stay still.

Without official state-sponsored colonialism, German-speaking Europeans have circulated themselves, families, knowledge, goods, services, and ideologies, creating global networks for centuries. In his *German History Unbound*, Glenn Penny moves beyond historical metanarratives organized by the nation-state in an effort to see beyond its borders.[5] He contends that it "can and should be written with greater attention to mobility and a greater emphasis on the explanatory power of modes of affiliation, affinity, and belonging."[6] This history of mobility, necessarily polycentric, generates multiple, movable archives and multidirectional regimes of knowledge, and not all roads lead to National Socialism, though the writing of history, Penny argues persuasively, driven by the organizing principles of the nation-state, tends to tell a single story. His work to "unbind" German history also puts pressure on the question of how global German can be. Sebastian Conrad, too, contemplates the possibilities of global history and the ability to decenter the "methodological nationalism" of any Eurocentric approach.[7] Modern European enthusiasms for the "genre of world and universal history"[8] presuppose a definable world and universe, despite the impossibility of comprehending totalities with confidence. Conrad notes the consequences: that it "tends to downplay the fundamental differences between the various forms of colonial

---

5. H. Glenn Penny, *German History Unbound: From 1750 to the Present* (New York: Cambridge University Press, 2022), 8. In the introduction, Penny defines the "cunning teleology of national histories," 3. Penny's public lecture, "Unbinding Germans' Transnational Histories" (September 14, 2021) provides a glimpse into his work on the ways "unbinding" these histories can resemble "decolonizing the western histories of the world." See https://networks.h-net.org/node/35008/discussions/8207186/unbinding-germans-transnational-histories. He develops the topic expansively in *German History Unbound*.

6. Penny, *German History Unbound*, 8.

7. Sebastian Conrad, *What Is Global History?* (Princeton, NJ: Princeton University Press, 2016), 3.

8. Conrad, *What Is Global History?*, 28.

rule, which range from extractive empires of the early modern era to complex structures of informal empire building in the present day."[9] Raising the "German" question complicates linear narratives of empire.

The question can be admittedly thorny. The five-hundred-year timeframe in Blackbourn's *Germany in the World* does not disappoint as a narrative with the potential to revise or at least destabilize any sense that history can only happen with the national state. Blackbourn argues for a German transatlantic world, one that demands recognition of involvement in the slave trade;[10] their role in establishing other empires; and also the ways in which Germans "were often chameleons, or shape-shifters, as they passed through or settled in the empires of others." This, accompanied by renaming or transliterating, leads further: "But the fact that Germans often became invisible points to something important. They disappeared into the empires of others because there was no German empire."[11] *Germany in the World* is a long-range, wide-angle, global reading of a "national" history, and the nearly aphoristic logic of the declaration is convincing at first glance. Still, the agents of empire with whom my study engages themselves demonstrated awareness of the forces that resisted them from within and beyond Europe. "Germans often became invisible," but not inaudible. To reimagine a history of the unarchived, I pay attention to the sources—literary, historical, material, and philosophical— that resist invisibility, that recuperate or reinvent a past toward leveraging the conditions of indenture and enslavement to fuel a discourse about ethnic entitlement, amplified by political extremes of the early twentieth century. Some Germans told the story of their becoming invisible with a vengeance, actively erasing the presence of others. To the extent possible, *German Empires and Decolonial Fantasies* acknowledges that presence.

The Age of Empire (1884–1918) retroactively constructs colonial history as global, relying on narratives of early modern noble expansion and unsung heroism. Behaim would play a starring role. The plot thickens in the early twentieth century, accelerated by the realization of colonial fantasies and realities. In one example, the first sentence of Gustav Meinecke's 1901 journal proclaims: "Das deutsche Volk ist ein uraltes Kolonialvolk" (The German people is an ancient colonial people).[12] Director of the German

---

9. Conrad, *What Is Global History?*, 56.
10. Blackbourn, *Germany in the World*, 18.
11. Blackbourn, *Germany in the World*, 18.
12. Gustav Meinecke, *Die deutschen Kolonien in Wort und Bild*. 2nd expanded edition (Leipzig: J. J. Weber, 1901), 1. Based on publications from 1893 to 1897.

Colonial Museum and author, Meinecke makes this assertion under the auspices of imperial history: "Die brandenburgisch-preußische Kolonialpolitk" (Brandenburg-Prussian colonial politics).[13] Meinecke's name receded from historical awareness, but his colonial writings and fiction make legible the subtext of a central argument in German-speaking Europe's engagement with the colonial world: entitlement to territory and a moral high ground above it.

German Empires and Decolonial Fantasies examines case studies that deterritorialize these spaces of "German" history. My study attempts not to reinscribe German cultural and historical artifacts into a totalizing message of its place in global history; but rather to analyze the apparatus of world making and the frictions that would disrupt it, the latter made up of resistance in multiple forms with varying intensity, from satirical poetry, to responsible research honed to shatter myths, to armed rebellion. The multiple forms are untidily contained by migration and immigration studies of one nation at one time,[14] for many of the agents of this history envision themselves and their projects in colonialist terms. Even a productive application of categories that reflect mobility, such as transnational or transcultural, imply a reciprocity; they can suggest a power symmetry that can be misleading. Moreover, the features of mobile Germanness gaze at their reflection within a colonial framework. Teutonic tribes vanquish the armies of Rome; serfdom was slavery, and through an inherent will to be free, they themselves broke the chains of servitude; French occupiers around 1800 were colonial masters; the innate superiority of German-speaking immigrants meant they should rise above the conditions of enslaved labor.

From the imperial fortress of early modern Brandenburg on the West African coast, to the rhetorical reclamation of German Southwest Africa as a Nazi-era colony, this study brings together texts and contexts from predominantly German-language cultures of mobility, produced by prominent and little-known actors. These "agents of history" include the famous, among them Friedrich II (Frederick the Great) and Johann Wolfgang von Goethe, to men and women on missions, writers in the *Kolonien* of the Southern Cone, poets at court, doctors in their journeymen years, farmers on the "frontier," economic immigrants, journalists recruited to educate and integrate ethnic

---

13. Meinecke, *Die deutschen Kolonien*, 1.

14. For a cogent overview of scholarship on German-speaking stages in Argentina, see Robert Kelz, *Competing Germanies: Nazi, Antifascist, and Jewish Theater in German Argentina, 1933–1965* (Ithaca, NY: Cornell University Press, 2019), 10–13. Kelz also explores this material through the lens of exile studies.

enclaves, patriotic colonists, colonial administrators, and catalogue publishers, all of whom contribute to networks that sustain multiple discourses about the objects and projects of empire.

Material cultures matter; objects interact with subjects to produce narratives. The work of historian Leora Auslander, who, in "Beyond Words," elevates the status of material culture, generally defined as human- and machine-produced objects, artifacts, and material things, to an active role in history: "In their communicative, performative, emotive, and expressive capacities, they act, have effects in the world."[15] Objects of history have a role to play, from maps and monuments to board games and equestrian statuary. Why this assemblage of source material? From my subject position as a literary scholar and cultural theorist, the interplay between marginal texts, even those by canonical authors, material objects, such as the Behaim globe, and their respective histories tends to fall between disciplinary cracks. Theoretical models for literary studies, imported from the social sciences, including philosophy, history, and sociology, spotlight the presence of interstitial cultural constructions, otherwise overlooked or invisible. One takeaway from the Behaim globe: universal knowledge is always partial. In that emblematic object, it is limited by a European perspective. Multiple material cultures interact with ontologies (what exists), and with epistemologies (how do we know it), to produce and reproduce narratives about the subjects and objects of empire. To resist reinscribing a metanarrative of a modern German nation in colonial motion, *German Empires and Decolonial Fantasies* looks back at Eurocentrism.

Decentering Eurocentrism

Sociologist Aníbal Quijano's critical concept of the *colonialidad de poder* (coloniality of power) helps reframe modernity as inextricably tied to colonialism. He writes that "coloniality of power is based upon 'racial' social classification of the world population under Eurocentered world power. But coloniality of power is not exhausted in the problem of 'racist' social relations. It pervaded and modulated the basic instances of the Eurocentered capitalist colonial/modern world power to become the cornerstone of this coloniality

---

15. Leora Auslander, "Beyond Words," *American Historical Review* 110, issue 4 (October 2005): 1015–45, here 1016. https://doi.org/10.1086/ahr.110.4.1015.

of power."[16] In another seminal essay, he echoes this definition, which reverberates within the history of the transatlantic world, thus bringing together the idea of coloniality of power, which survives in the aftermath of colonialism, and the essentially European epistemology of binary thought. Quijano does not so much reject a replacement of a Eurocentric metanarrative of history—he acknowledges the persistence of binary logic—as enact a decolonial analysis of European dominance, predicated on whiteness. Neither does he advocate supplanting one structure of hegemonic dominance with another; rather Quijano disrupts the totalizations of race-based epistemologies that construct memory, imagination, and knowledge with decolonial writing. Much of postcolonial theory acknowledges the reliance of colonial logic on the dualisms propagated by European thought, the presumed oppositions between self and other that devolve so seamlessly into power hierarchies based on socially constructed categories of race, gender, ethnicity, nationality, religion, and linguistic, mental, and corporal strength. In other words, the attributes of intersectionality (Kimberlé Crenshaw) rotate in and out of binarity of European thought, exacerbated by dislocating mobility, for exploration, colonization, conversion, or economic emigration.

Quijano sketches a way forward in broad strokes. First, decolonizing knowledge and the mechanisms that maintain inequality in society requires recognition of decolonial revolutions: first and foremost is Haiti. Further, he argues for worldwide re-Indigenization, acknowledgment and acceptance of multiple epistemologies, implemented through epistemic revolution.[17] My narrative argument retraces these steps from the perspective of German-language histories about their own empires, revolutions, and colonies. Their early modern antecedents stay the course into the twentieth century. Their world making annexes contiguous land from other European empires. Looking back to the power core, he observes that the nation-state in Europe begins as "a process of colonization of some peoples over others."[18] Case studies on this process in and from Brandenburg and Vienna make up part 1 of my book. The missions, maps, and travelogues of the long eighteenth century connect in the syntax of a relentless colonial logic in which Africa and the Amer-

---

16. Aníbal Quijano, "Coloniality and Modernity/Rationality," *Cultural Studies* 21, no. 2: 168–78.

17. Aníbal Quijano, Keynote, III Congreso Latinoamericano y Caribeño de Ciencias Sociales, August 25, 2015, Quito. FLASCO Ecuador. https://www.youtube.com/watch?v=OxL5KwZGvdY.

18. Aníbal Quijano, "Coloniality of Power, Eurocentrism, and Latin America," trans. Michael Ennis, in *Neplanta: Views from South* 1, no. 3 (2000): 533–80, here 558.

Introduction

icas are separated by a comma or a coordinating conjunction rather than an ocean. They are associated also in the European political imaginary by Blackness. In the context of Latin America, Quijano works within a specific Europe: Power is represented by and held most visibly by Spanish and Portuguese, and Blacks and Indigenous people and "mestizos" supplied labor in proximity to whiteness. Slavery serves as the connection between Africa and the Americas: "This racist distribution of labor in the interior of colonial/modern capitalism model was maintained throughout the colonial period."[19] Stories of German-speaking Europeans within this model are the focus of part 2. Finally, the coloniality of power as a Eurocentrically defined model of hegemony retains and replicates the racial axis Quijano identifies as the most important aspect of the power matrix. It is "more durable and stable"[20] than colonialism, and "the binary dualist perspective on knowledge, particular to Eurocentrism, was imposed as globally hegemonic in the same course as the expansion of European colonial dominance over the world."[21] The stories of German-speaking Europeans' role in enforcing—or rejecting—this binary model are treated in part 3.

In his introduction to a volume dedicated to the topic, inspired by Quijano's essay, Walter Mignolo traces the intellectual provenance of the decolonial thinking in response to the question: "what are the differences between existing critical projects and de-colonization of knowledge."[22] To answer the question, he reports on the consensus: "We decided to focus on Max Horkheimer's formulation of 'critical theory' for several reasons. The first was that the project of the Frankfurt School and the early works of Horkheimer in particular were meaningful for some of the participants in the project modernity/coloniality."[23] Mignolo elaborates on the importance of critical thought in the Frankfurt School and, not least, Jewish criticism of the racism and coloniality in the German context. He problematizes certain terminologies of the postcolonial; he even posits certain models of Marxist thought as hegemonic, but for my purposes, recourse to Horkheimer's sustained attempt to think through his critique of empiricism, "the opposition between materialism and

---

19. Quijano, "Coloniality of Power, Eurocentrism, and Latin America," 536.
20. Quijano, "Coloniality of Power, Eurocentrism, and Latin America," 533–80.
21. Quijano, "Coloniality of Power, Eurocentrism, and Latin America," 542.
22. Walter Mignolo, "Introduction: *Coloniality of Power and De-colonial Thinking*," *Cultural Studies* 21, no. 2-3, (2007): 155-67, here 155.
23. Mignolo, "Introduction," 155.

idealism,"[24] leads the way back to early modern logics about the relationship between perception of the world, knowing that world, and defining the world in terms of oppositions. Historical problems ensue. In the "Culture" section of his essay "Authority and the Family," Horkheimer questions the validity of periodization, which "arose out of the growing conviction that the history of mankind as a whole or at least of large groups of European peoples along with certain parts of Africa, Asia, and America presents even to the more penetrating eye a structured unity and not a disorganized and chaotic series of occurrences."[25] Thus recognizing the totalizing narratives of Eurocentrism, Horkheimer models an eccentric reading of those narratives. My approach, interpreted through Quijano, hopes to bring the model into a decolonial reading that not only refuses to see a structural unity, but attempts to reconstruct the occurrences as anything but random. The perception of those moments as unrelated would be akin to modeling transatlantic history on the Behaim globe. Even though Horkheimer sets up the homology between Europe and its others, his argument elides colonial connections—fails to see the imperial agency—that imposed selective Enlightenment models of humanity on the "elsewheres" of Europe.

Understanding imperial agency in the long, collective history of colonialism and the even more encompassing coloniality of power necessitates a philosophical and practical approach to the interaction between thoughts and things, an understanding Horkheimer develops in radical, though seemingly understated ways. In contrast, Horkheimer argues the interdependence of the concrete and abstract: "Materialism . . . maintains the irreducible tension between concept and object and thus has a critical weapon of defense against belief in the infinity of the mind."[26] That irreducible approximates, in another theoretical and philosophical register, the undecidable in poststructuralism, the unreadable or undecidable in deconstruction. Extending the insight to a reading of Hegel, he concisely states the essential problem with Hegel's system: it is philosophical contactless delivery. The resistance produced by any colonial enterprise continually replicates and projects this model, excising any thing and/or body that is unthinkable and therefore unknowable, as in

---

24. Horkheimer, "Materialism and Metaphysics," in *Critical Theory: Selected Essays*, translated by Matthew J. O'Connell et al. (New York: Continuum, 2002), 13.

25. Max Horkheimer, "Authority and Family," trans. Matthew J. O'Connell, in Max Horkheimer, *Critical Theory: Selected Essays*, trans. Matthew J. O'Connell et al. (New York: Continuum, 1972), 47–131, here 48.

26. Horkheimer, "Materialism and Metaphysics," 28.

Introduction

those colonized. Similarly, the totality of knowledge implicit in the term globalization, for instance, can only be partial, despite protests to the contrary. Yet the unknowable, the unthinkable, and the "ungovernables"[27] persist. To decolonize theory, grounded in the process of constructing identity, it is imperative to historicize the construction of those marginalized, subdued, or erased realities and fantasies that do not factor into colonial logic.

Rereading the World

Literary scholars have widened the lens with foundational works in postcolonial studies, such as Susanne Zantop's *Colonial Fantasies*. These works perform acts of deterritorializing explicitly "colonial" histories. Unlike Zantop, the colonial narratives in this book predate the 1770s; and the fantasies of sexual encounter as empowerment do not remain imaginary; that aspect, the performative nature of the interaction between epistemology and national history constitutes their appeal. Postcolonial interventions, such as Chunjie Zhang's *Transculturality and German Discourse in the Age of European Colonialism*,[28] non-European epistemologies decentralize a model that embeds the knowledge of place—and the knowledge about the production of knowledge—in a Eurocentric worldview. Further, Zhang puts pressure on Zantop's argument in recognition of a need to differentiate between eighteenth-century thought and later eras of imperialism to mitigate the risk of imposing twentieth-century perspectives on earlier periods. For reasons of practicality and disciplinary responsibility, though, we tend to categorize objects of study by language, epoch, genre, method, all of which have come to be dominated by Penny's "cunning teleology" of the nation-state. The critical insights into colonial-era scholarship on the importance of ethnographic discourses, the "symbolic competition" among colonial administrators and officials, and the plurality of responses and reactions from the colonized, demonstrate continuities between pre- and colonial administrations throughout official German colonies.[29]

---

27. The work of Latin American scholar and novelist Luis Othoniel Rosa inspires my use of this term, which I elaborate on in subsequent chapters.

28. Chunjie Zhang, *Transculturality and German Discourse in the Age of European Colonialism* (Evanston, IL: Northwestern University Press, 2017).

29. See George Steinmetz, *The Devil's Handwriting: Precoloniality and the German Colonial State in Qingdao, Samoa, and South Africa* (Chicago: University of Chicago Press, 2007), 2. The

Anthropology provides models that inform this work. The "durabilities" of the colonial enterprise engage the complex forces of "imperial formations," as Ann Laura Stoler formulates the forces of empires.[30] *Duress* encompasses Stoler's long-standing interests "in the distributions of inequities that concepts condone, inscribe, and inhabit; in the challenges of writing new colonial histories that press on the present; and, not least, in unlearning what we imagine to know about colonial governance and why those understandings and misrecognitions should continue to concern us now."[31] Stoler redirects colonial legacies, recasting specific formations across case studies from France and the Middle East to Dutch East India to identify their imperial function. Some have reverse-engineered the approach through examining precolonial anthropology's influence on colonial law.[32] George Steinmetz and others are doing the work of decolonizing German theory. In his succinct formulation, theory occupies a shared space among philosophy, social theory, and cultural theory; he calls attention to the complex itinerary of German theory and those who produced its archive. In so doing, Steinmetz echoes Quijano's work to enlarge the framework of history outside the nation: "But Germans were involved in exploration, colonialism, and slaving, often in the service of another flag, throughout the seventeenth, eighteenth, and nineteenth centuries."[33] Others have marked the starting point in early modern philosophies of human difference based on the scientific study of the natural world. Justin Smith writes, "It is no exaggeration to say that early modern globalization was one of the most important impetuses behind the radical transformations that occurred within philosophy between the sixteenth and the eighteenth centuries."[34] Indeed, my parsing Quijano's use of the term "European" to reterritorialize national difference within a hegemonic power structure sets up my

---

localized competition among colonial officers during the "scramble" and Age of Empire is present, I claim, in the ontology of emigration as well as settler colonialist self-definition.

30. See her introduction to the journal issue based on a 2005 conference; this essay concludes the book "Imperial Debris: Reflections on Ruin and Ruination." *Cultural Anthropology* 23, no. 2 (2008): 191–219. Rather than empire, the focus on "imperial formations" registers "the ongoing quality of processes of decimation, displacement, and reclamation." 193.

31. Ann Laura Stoler, *Duress: Imperial Durabilities in our Times* (Durham, NC: Duke University Press, 2016), 8.

32. See Steinmetz, *The Devil's Handwriting*.

33. George Steinmetz, "Decolonizing German Theory: An Introduction," *Postcolonial Studies* 9, no. 1 (2006): 3–13, here 3.

34. Justin E. H. Smith, *Nature, Human Nature, and Human Difference: Race in Early Modern Philosophy* (Princeton, NJ: Princeton University Press, 2022), 10.

Introduction   13

argument for legitimate criticism. Yet the marginalizing or limiting of German coloniality serves to perpetuate the avoidance of a narrative that nonetheless constructs historically significant processes, among them migration and immigration, citizenship and human rights, and religious freedoms, all of which derive from the imagined communities of the nation. Closer to the "German" question my study raises, the legacy of Marxist thought illuminates an often occluded interplay between philosophy and history.

Susan Buck-Morss's work on Hegel, the Haitian Revolution, and universality intervenes into the disciplines of philosophy and history, recognizing the essential first step Hegel takes in his Jena texts and lecture notes (1805–1806; including the *Phenomenology of Spirit*) with an implicit argument about consumer desire and the bourgeois subject: "Hegel is in fact describing the deterritorialized, world market of the European colonial system, and he is the first philosopher to do so."[35] As a self-defined philosopher with a "materialist bent,"[36] Buck-Morss intensifies this insight, reframing the reality of the Haitian Revolution, the emergence of the master-servitude dialectic as a figure of thought, and the material conditions under which "freedom" became the calling card of European Enlightenment philosophy, if not politics. According to Buck-Morss, "Conceptually, the revolutionary struggle of slaves,[37] who overthrew their own servitude and established a constitutional state, provides the theoretical hinge that takes Hegel's analysis out of the limitlessly expanding colonial economy and onto the plane of world history, which he defines as the realization of freedom, a theoretical solution that was taking place in practice in Haiti at that very moment."[38] Hegel's effective racialization of "freedom" cast a long shadow; his own views of Africa, and the characterization of the African, who "exhibits the natural man in his completely wild and untamed state,"[39] remains notorious. The wide-ranging impact of this position is evident in scholarly works that interrogate the presumptuousness of universality,

---

35. Susan Buck-Morss, *Hegel, Haiti, and University History* (Pittsburgh: University of Pittsburgh Press, 2009), 7–8.

36. Buck-Morss, *Hegel, Haiti*, 6.

37. Throughout this study, I quote accurately from a range of sources, but use "enslaved people" to preserve the humanity and avoid conflating this imposed identity or nonidentity onto human beings. To avoid the repetition of offensive and derogatory terms, asterisks replace certain vowels.

38. Buck-Morss, *Hegel, Haiti*, 11–12.

39. G. W. F. Hegel, *The Philosophy of History*, prefaces by Charles Hegel and the translator, J. Sibree (Kitchener: Batoche Books, 2001), 111.

among them Denise da Silva's *Toward a Global History of Race*.[40] Justin E. H. Smith takes an additional step, refracting the focus of her argument that early modern nineteenth-century science and philosophy define humanity racially to protect it.[41] Both projects resonate with my claims, but with the difference that multiple ways of knowing coexisted with universalizing narratives.

Interdisciplinary scholars are engaged in the elaboration of German colonialism as a historical process with far-reaching implications beyond the period between 1884 and 1918. In a volume on German colonialism in a global era, Naranch introduces with great clarity the historiography, noting "conceptual constraints that limited the story that German colonialism could tell."[42] Naranch refers to "the complexities and contradictions of Germany's distinctively discontinuous colonial path."[43] His introductory remarks pertain to German colonialism in a global age, not restricted to the actual colonial ambitions of the nation-state. Still, the imperative to recognize gender, race, and ethnic and racial difference as categories of inquiry itself participates in a considerably longer history, one that significantly predates German national unification in 1871.[44] The self-identification of German-speaking Europeans in the enterprise of empire and unapologetic desire for imperialist conquest begins with figuration: the self as sovereign, the world as home. Latter-day narratives of belonging elsewhere, in Africa or the Southern Cone or North America, sought ways to connect the points of the "discontinuous colonial path."

The durability of empire, the hegemony of *colonialidad de poder*, the tenacity of binary oppositions overcome only in the assertion of race-based superiority present a seemingly insurmountable obstacle to decolonial practice. Whenever and wherever possible, this study turns to sources relegated to the margins as a source of friction. The eighteenth-century philosophical model by the Ghanaian-German philosopher Anton Wilhelm Amo emerges from a "contact" zone the predates Pratt's. His focus on the relationship between

---

40. Denise da Silva, *Toward a Global History of Race* (Minneapolis: University of Minnesota Press, 2007).

41. Smith, *Nature, Human Nature, and Human Difference*, 19.

42. Bradley Naranch, "German Colonialism Made Simple." In *German Colonialism in a Global Age*, ed. Bradley Naranch and Geoff Eley (Durham, NC: Duke University Press, 2014), 2.

43. Naranch, "Introduction: German Colonialism Made Simple," 9.

44. For an early examination of this constellation in the British Empire, from the Victorian era to post-Apartheid South Africa, see Anne McClintock, *Imperial Leather: Race, Gender, and Sexuality in the Colonial Context* (London: Routledge, 1995).

body and mind recapitulates Cartesian dualism, but with the critique that knowledge is based in physical materiality. His examination of human spirit and body in his *Inaugural Dissertation on the Impassivity of the Human Mind* (1734) poses a question about the dual nature of the human being. Though his legal thesis *De jure Maurorum in Europa* (On the right of m**rs in Europe), according to editors and translators Stephen Menn and Justin E. H Smith, "is no longer extant (and may never have existed in written form at all),"[45] and details of his biography are frustratingly sketchy, his argument that sensation and the power of sensing depend on "contact," and thus to the body, suggests a tantalizingly non-Cartesian interpretation of early modern empiricism.[46] Amo's philosophy has begun to receive more serious scholarly attention from an international cadre of researchers in the social sciences and humanities. I run the risk of overemphasizing this academic credential, but I speculate that Amo's positive thesis posits agency, a possible preface to the foundational Enlightenment logic of sovereignty and its extension from abstract knowledge to physical, material bodies. This signifies in a context of reading racist philosophy. Smith argues that "while a commitment to the existence of a body-independent rational soul was in certain important respects a bulwark against the rise of modern racism, the interactions between this commitment and the rising naturalism of the modern period helped over the *longue durée* to generate the modern, racially charged dichotomy between two basic varieties of people: the people of reason and the people of nature, so to speak."[47]

Smith's cogent analysis of the mind-body duality throughout his study showcases Amo's influences and his own philosophical contributions as an African to Enlightenment thought. Smith expands on the slender store of biographical details that makes the twenty-first-century Germanist ache for more information and mourn the racism that relegated traces of this history to the farthest margins. Smith's chapter on Amo highlights the underlying argument of Amo's (lost) *On the Rights of M**rs*: that as subjects of the Roman Empire African kinds were recognized under Roman law, thus endowing all African descendants with legal status in Europe.[48] Smith expounds on Amo's challenge to Descartes and proponents of a dualism that was the hot-button

---

45. Stephen Menn and Justin E. H. Smith, "Introduction," in Anton Wilhelm Amo, *Anton Wilhelm Amo's Philosophical Dissertations on Mind and Body* (New York: Oxford University Press, 2020), 2.
46. Menn and Smith, "Introduction," 101.
47. Smith, *Nature, Human Nature, and Human Difference*, 18.
48. Smith, *Nature, Human Nature, and Human Difference*, 210.

issue of the day. Amo's critique of Descartes serves as an antecedent to Pratt's contact zones. In his *Inaugural Dissertation on the Impassivity of the Human Mind* (1735), he makes the radical claim of corporeal agency. The mind does not sense, in Amo's explanation. It constitutes "spirit," and therefore does not "admit passion within itself," as "this would have to occur either by communication, or by penetration, or, finally, by contact."[49] While Smith constructs an intellectual context in which Amo's work features prominently, I depart from his theory to supplement a method of interpreting contact zones: Contact occurs, Amo writes, "when two surfaces mutually touch one another in some physical or sensible point."[50] Since the early Enlightenment, Amo's work has challenged a dominant Cartesian model predicated on the separation of mind from body, resulting in a filtered empiricism, the selective use of human sense perception from which the binarism of subject-object identifiers that undergird Western epistemology derives its stubborn force. This opposition, never a relationship of equality, privileges the subject position as the "doer of the action" on behalf of the objectified. As Pratt writes, "European bourgeois subject simultaneously innocent and imperial."[51]

That innocence is interwoven into the stories told by German-speaking agents of imperialism, immigration, colonization, and recolonization. These narratives are often recounted from the perspective of the empire-adjacent, the belated nation, and the myth of innocence, which was sustained by claims of noncomplicity in chattel slavery; or of kinder, gentler settlerism, each of which reinscribes an essential opposition based eventually on race. Histor-

---

49. Amo, *Inaugural Dissertation*, 161. Chris Meyns recognizes this as a "core premise" of Amo's, interested more in the departure from Descartes than in the application of this philosophy as a critical tool. See Meyns, "Anton Wilhelm Amo and the Problems of Perception," in *The Senses in the History of Philosophy*, ed. Brian R. Glenney and José Filipe Pereira da Silva (London: Routledge, 2019), 169–84. I quote from the nonpaginated online PDF. See also Meyns. "Anton Wilhelm Amo's Philosophy of Mind," *Philosophy Compass*, 2019;14:e12571, https.//doi.org/10.1111/phc3.12571MEYNS13. In literary studies of work around 1800, several scholars have made significant contributions. See, for example, Reinhold Grimm and Jost Hermand, eds., *Blacks in German Culture* (Madison, WI: *Monatshefte Occasional Papers*, 1986); Birgit Tautz, *Reading and Seeing Ethnic Differences in the Enlightenment: From China to Africa* (London: Palgrave Macmillan, 2007), specifically on Amo, 145–46; also Tautz, ed., *Colors: 1800/1900/2000: Signs of Ethnic Difference*, Amsterdamer Beiträge zur Neueren Germanistik 56 (Amsterdam: Rodopi, 2004).

50. Amo, *Inaugural Dissertation*, 163.

51. Mary Louise Pratt, *Imperial Eyes: Travel Writing and Transculturation* (London: Routledge, 1992, 2008), 33.

ically, the resolution of such abstract thinking enters into public discourse with G. W. F. Hegel and his considerable influence. Briefly, the process of determinate negation makes the stolid opposition between subject and object dynamic. In the *Vorrede* (Preface) to the *Phenomenology*, Hegel lays out the thought process in abstract terms.[52] Essentially, the predicates of thought appropriate otherness (*Anderes*) through negation, and in so doing render it positive, the interdependence subsumed into the subject position. This sketch informs centuries of passionate debate about the politics of Hegel and Hegelian philosophy. In political science and political philosophy, the dispute continues.[53] For the sake of brevity and coherence, my argument relies on Susan Buck-Morss's intervention of history into theory. It is a daunting task to arrest the totalizing power of the universal-particular dialectic, and I do not purport to do so.

Narrating Race

Instead, I work through the rhetorical reversals that tell the story of race as a transferable attribute and the anxieties these involve. The German-specific, latter-day nation/colonization model lends itself to this analysis because freedom of the subject and sovereignty of the body are always already at stake; racialized institutions, such as slavery, pass through historical filters, enabling stories of white subjection to leverage entitlements at home and abroad. Freedom becomes a moral, rather than a political empowerment. While a concept of political freedom and autonomy was racialized, and enslavement deterritorialized, the corollary was a deracialization of slavery. As I demonstrate in the chapters that follow, in each case study of German-language networks that transverse the world, a "decolonial" discourse and/or practice

---

52. The passage reads: "Es ist die Reflexion in das leere Ich, die Eitelkeit seines Wissens. – Diese Eitelkeit drückt aber nicht nur dies aus, daß dieser Inhalt eitel, sondern auch, daß diese Einsicht selbst es ist; denn sie ist das Negative, das nicht das Positive in sich erblickt.... Dagegen, wie vorhin gezeigt, gehört im begreifenden Denken das Negative dem Inhalte selbst an und ist sowohl als seine *immanente* Bewegung und Bestimmung wie als *Ganzes* derselben das *Positive*. Als Resultat aufgefaßt, ist es das aus dieser Bewegung herkommende, das *bestimmte* Negative, und hiermit ebenso ein positiver Inhalt" (*Phänomenologie des Geistes*, Vorrede).

53. Highlights range from Adorno and Horkheimer and French Hegelians to Judith Butler, Ernesto Laclau, and Slavoj Žižek. In terms of the nation-state dialectic, see Moran M. Mandelbaum, *The Nation/State Fantasy: A Psychoanalytical Genealogy of Nationalism* (London: Palgrave Macmillan, 2020).

existed contemporaneously with the single stories of power. In the case of German-speaking Europe, my use of the term decolonial does not consistently reflect historical decolonization processes; but often we encounter a concurrent awareness of—and yes, at times a fantasy about—discovering and/or identifying with a persecuted, enslaved, marginalized, or otherwise historically disadvantaged people.

Decolonial projects can decenter the socioeconomic and cultural architectures and infrastructures of colonialism, which themselves rely on a Eurocentric construction of race as an epistemological and material category.[54] The decolonizing project has far-reaching implications that impact individuals and institutions alike. In contemporary debates, one need look only to the global Berlin exhibit at the Humboldt Forum, or workshops that ask how to decolonize the museum, with the possession of objects so closely intertwined with colonialism.[55] For much of the nineteenth and twentieth centuries, for example, accounts of national, specifically German, interventions revolve around the exploits of early modern investigators and adventurers who were German speakers: They were scientists and artists, explorers and members of the royal honor guard of a Habsburg princess who enter into economic and communicative transatlantic networks to broadcast their experiences with Indigenous peoples, most often with the expressed intention of conquest, exploitation, and conversion, all of which project fixed power hierarchies onto the spaces of noncontiguous lands. The contact zones, so eloquently elaborated by Pratt, yield stories that inscribe themselves into history. She defines contact zones as "social spaces where disparate cultures meet, clash, and grapple with each other, often in highly asymmetrical relations of domination and subordination—such as colonialism and slavery, or their aftermaths as they are lived out across the globe today."[56] Pratt's focus on literary and cultural longevity of inequality characterized in travel writing highlight the endurance of a dominant-subordinate model explicated across the social sciences. In her work on the persistence of colonialism, these insightful and retrospective arguments culminate in Quijano's sweeping realignment of modernity as coloniality of power predicated on race.

In his address on Anton Wilhelm Amo's significance in contemporary

---

54. Quijano, "Coloniality and Modernity/Rationality."
55. See for example the forum on this question: https://www.eaberlin.de/seminars/data/2022/pol/wie-laesst-sich-ein-museum-dekolonisieren/.
56. Pratt, *Imperial Eyes*, 7.

Introduction

African philosophy, Prof. Josephat Obi Oguejiofor argued for the importance of the first Black scholar to earn a degree from the University of Halle. He noted that it would be more than two centuries before the second. Professor Oguejiofor also honored the legacy of Amo in African philosophy, lamenting that his name has yet to become widely known. Further, he affirmed the hybridity of Amo's life and work as Afro-European and Ghanaian-German and acknowledged the importance of studies by W. Abraham V. U. Emma-Adamah, and also translations. "We do not need Amo and his success to tell us that slavery and racism, that these two practices are horrendous." He continued, "It is likely that Kant knew of his exploits. Why did it not change him?"[57] The question remains resonant and unanswered.

To "reconceptualize German identity in global terms,"[58] I examine the attributes of Germanness identified in its exported form. This approach leads out of the dichotomous choice between "Enlightenment" and "Empire," a model that has served scholarship well.[59] Periodically, the intervention of German-speaking Europeans into other colonial projects constitutes a form of cosmopolitanism while elevating the German-specific as wholesomely provincial. As Glenn Penny and Matti Bunzl have observed, the possibility of "worldly provincialism" exists in their sustained examination of nineteenth-century German anthropology.[60] The discipline itself had been shored up by popularizations of "scientific" racism, derived from Enlightenment race theory. In other words, colonial racial profiling has a cultural patrimony with seventeenth-century justifications about power across shared borders. Quijano identifies this type of acquisition/appropriation in a way that forges connections between the epistemological and the material: "Cultural Europeanisation was transformed into an aspiration. It was a way of participating and later to reach the same material benefits and the same power as the Europeans: viz, to conquer nature—in short for 'development'. European culture became a universal cultural model. The imaginary in the non-European

---

57. Wilhelm Amo Symposium, Prof. Josephat Obi Oguejiofor, "The Significance of Anton Wilhelm Amo on Contemporary African Philosophy," December 9, 2021, University of Ghana, https://www.ug.edu.gh/mias-africa/content/anton-wilhelm-amo-lecture-symposium.

58. Krista O'Donnell, Renate Bridenthal, and Nancy Reagin, "Introduction," *The Heimat Abroad: The Boundaries of Germanness* (Ann Arbor: University of Michigan Press, 2005), 4.

59. Russell A. Berman, *Enlightenment or Empire: Colonial Discourse in German Culture* (Lincoln: University of Nebraska Press, 1998).

60. H. Glenn Penny and Matti Bunzl, eds., *Worldly Provincialism: German Anthropology in the Age of Empire* (Ann Arbor: University of Michigan Press, 2010).

cultures could hardly exist today and, above all, reproduce itself outside of these relations."[61] He illuminates the processes that instill competitive forces across European/Indigenous contact zones. Penny's subsequent work in the history of ethnography and museum collections emphasizes the work of Adolf Bastian in his efforts to tell a human story through objects, a more inclusive model than the racialized evidence of superior whiteness that drove his peers.[62] The competitive model among collectors and colonizers to police the line between the civilized and barbaric had a far reach.

Disciplinary differences, sometimes productively resolved, have contributed significant analyses that launched multiple approaches to the study of German-specific colonialisms, and I engage these works in individual chapters in greater detail.[63] From the discipline of history, Lora Wildenthal's *German Women for Empire* (2001) lays the groundwork for subsequent studies of female identity, citizenship, masculinity, and national identity during the Age of Empire. My work hopes to expand the scope by including the colonial imaginary as a shared dynamic among "Germans" in Europe, the Americas, and Africa.

Chapter Overview

Part I explores the imperial entanglements of German-speaking Europe during the early modern period, drawing on literary, historical, musical, and monumental sources. Each chapter sets Prussian power on a world stage and calibrates its force through an ability to enslave and to free. The chapters sketch the "world-making" drive to gain a foothold in the lucrative transatlantic slave trade; enlightened absolutism and its corollary, enlightened colonialism: to know the world is to own the world; and the ennobling of (white)

---

61. Quijano, "Coloniality and Modernity/Rationality."
62. H. Glenn Penny, *In Humboldt's Shadow: A Tragic History of German Ethnology* (Princeton, NJ: Princeton University Press, 2021).
63. See for example Eric Ames, Marcia Klotz, and Lora Wildenthal, eds., *Germany's Colonial Pasts* (Lincoln: University of Nebraska Press, 2007). This work looks beyond the African colonies, as do Sara Lennox and Sara Friedrichsmeyer in *The Imperialist Imagination: German Colonialism and Its Legacy* (Ann Arbor: University of Michigan Press, 2005). See also Krista O'Donnell, et al. With regard to the significance of the image and print media, see David Ciarlo, *Advertising Empire: Race and Visual Culture in Imperial Germany* (Cambridge, MA: Harvard University Press, 2011).

Introduction

slavery as the political prerequisite to enable human sovereignty selectively. Throughout, I include sources that speak back to the linear narrative of progress and prosperity. Throughout, I provide evidence from a range of sources that document resistance to the "coloniality of power."

The narrative argument follows a general chronology from the early modern to the early twentieth century. Chapter 1, "Prussia's First Fortress," sets the start date of German colonialism to align with a Hohenzollern Elector's first foothold in the transatlantic slave trade. The journey opens with a reading of the imposing equestrian statue of the Great Elector that originally presided over the Lange Brücke (Long Bridge, now the Rathausbrücke). The significance of the statue and its pedestal connects the complicated networks of "New Guinae," enslavement in antiquity and in metaphor, Berlin as political center, and transportation infrastructure throughout Prussia. This chapter analyzes the forces that drive Brandenburg expansionism after the devastation of the Thirty Years' War (1618–1648) into the logic of early modern imperialism. The contact zones connect the Hohenzollern fortress on the Guinean coast to the Americas, transoceanic geographies united by coloniality and driven by commerce. The decolonial investment, an unintended consequence of the Great Elector's failed attempt at planting a foothold in the transatlantic slave trade, culminates in his purchase of enslaved Guineans to adorn and serve the Prussian court. The diplomatic strategy from the emperor of the Kingdom of Dahomê, during the Age of Empire, puts an end to any idea of racial equality between empires during the German colonial period. The erstwhile African empire hosts the ruins of German colonialism across redrawn territories of postcolonial nation-states.

Chapter 2, "To Own the World: Enlightened Colonialism," examines the imperial options of Friedrich II (Frederick the Great), who did not join the grab for colonies abroad; instead, he turned his sights to the acquisition of contiguous land from other European empires. The Enlightenment ideals of autonomy and reason, ostensibly the counsel Frederick kept, proved to belong more solidly in the realm of political theory than Prussian reality. Chapter 2 begins with a consideration of select theoretical writings, the influence of Voltaire, and a creative work, the opera libretto *Montezuma* (1755), with music composed by Carl Heinrich Graun (1704–1759). There Frederick portrays the brutality of the Spanish against the deceived, defeated, yet ennobled emperor of the Aztec empire. Erstwhile admirer turned detractor, Gotthold Ephraim Lessing, inscribed what is among the earliest German-language decolonial texts about European colonization of the Americas.

From his post in the Duke of Braunschweig's archive, Lessing continued his practice of lambasting tyranny, with an anticolonial voice. This chapter centers on his decolonial writing, including a few short poems, excerpts from his freemason dialogue, a fable about a dancing bear, and finally his comments on the *Beschreibung des portuguesischen America* (Description of Portuguese America). There he makes the aphoristic pronouncement: "Nur die Völker sollten die Welt besitzen, die die Welt der Welt doch wenigstens bekannt machen" (Only those peoples should own the world who at least make the world known to the world); this, I contend, posits a provisional model of enlightened colonialism. The king of Prussia focuses on an emotional enlightenment, embodied in the ability to empathize as constitutive of humanity, a regime of feeling that does not necessarily inform his own political practice; whereas Lessing advocates the dissemination of knowledge. Both the king and the librarian rely on the interconnections between the historical context of empire and enslavement in the Americas.

In "Enslaved Souls, Perfect Freedom, and Savagery," Enlightenment philosophies of universality are projected through genres of public lectures, poetry written into canonical marginalia, and the literature of German-language settler recruitment. To contrast the various incarnation of multiple German-language Europeans as imperial, mercantile, proselytist, and anticolonial tropes, this chapter examines the ways abstractions, such as freedom, universality, and humanity, construct tropes of the uncivilized, the enslaved, the savage, and the cannibal as racialized. The racializations emerge from contact zones produced by material and textual cultures. Immanuel Kant's racist trope of the self-induced savagery prefaces a reading of Friedrich Schiller's contention that enslavement is self-imposed, agentic, implicitly above race. To push back against this position, I look to the "whitening" of enslavement in poetry, the whitewashing of enslavement in prose, and the ennobling of the cannibal in translation. They are respectively exemplified, by Ludwig Christoph Heinrich Hölty (1748–1776) in a poem about Barbary pirates; a recruitment treatise, *Brasilien als unabhängiges Reich in historischer, mercantilischer und politischer Beziehung* (1824; Brazil as independent empire in historical, mercantile, and political terms), by Ritter von Schäffer Dr., who was a major in the imperial Brazilian Honor Guard and dedicated servant of Maria Leopoldine, Empress of Brazil; and two Brazilian poems by Johann Wolfgang von Goethe (1749–1832). The decolonial fantasies considered in these three chapters align more closely with concepts of critique. Real colonies did not exist; footholds were sold off to the Dutch. Economic affiliations sufficiently

Eureopeanize the Americas to re-examine the savagery of Black Africans and the Indigenous. While the first section of this book attends to the colonizing attempts, failures, theories, and practices of early modern to Enlightenment discourses, the second part focuses on the migration stories that defy the histories of official colonization; instead, they inscribe German-speaking Europeans' insertion into the persecuted profile of the enslaved.

Part 2, "Transatlantic German Worlds," engages more granularly in nineteenth-century discourses about mobility and identity, which around 1900 tend to subsume immigration and colonization under one expansive exit strategy about the intersectional attributes of identity. In this section, colonial logics of nation, class, gender, race, and religion circulate to establish national entitlements derived from "German" traits. Decolonial fantasies articulate a subject position that identifies with the formerly colonized, the enslaved, the subjugated, in ways that tend to minimize racial difference. Though official colonization is separate from other displacements and emplacements, the contemporary discourses featured in this section, circulating in letters, entertainment literature, and the print media, positioned themselves vis-à-vis colonial expansion. Contact zones multiply; a concept of the German or Teutonic race begins to underwrite German-specific tropes of the white settler, pioneer, and mobile male professional. The trope of the tropical wild, which South America epitomizes for the readership of nineteenth-century German-speaking Europe, commutes between the literary imagination and "contact" enabled by a future "upon the water."

The fourth chapter, "The New World Wilderness" focuses on stories of conflict between the the "wild," the South American *Urwald*, and the adaptation of the German-speaking European as self-appointed steward of the land and professional settler. Here, I examine the work of Wilhelm Rotermund (1843–1925), who served as a pastor in São Leopoldo (1874–1919); he published the *Deutsche Post* (1880) and the *Kalender für die Deutschen in Brasilien*. In addition, he wrote stories, compiled in *Südamerikanische Literatur*. His work advances a narrative about Germanness abroad that hinges on the decolonial fantasy of emigrant life endangered by the conditions of enslavement. The "wilderness" reconnects Europeans with their inner "savage"; only the intervention of a local politician can leverage the industry at their ethnic core. By contrast, the work of W. Helmar, a pseudonym for the writer Maria Hellemeyer, who published stories and fairy tales directed primarily at a younger German-language audience, adds gender difference as a constitutive element of the "wild," tamed in remigration. Her *Vom Urwald zur Kultur.*

Erlebnisse eines Mädchens (From the jungle to civilization: Experiences of a young girl, 1898) defines her protagonist in tension with prevailing models of "wild" and "civilized" behaviors and follows the remigration of Juanita (Anni) from the forest to a German city in search of her Teutonic roots. With a Tupi friend in her distant past and an ever-faithful Black servant, a stand-in maternal figure, Hellemeyer's protagonist undergoes a process of re-Indigenization in the gender-fatigued German metropolis circa 1900. The destiny of male professional Germans and female farmers, some of whom would remigrate while others would remain *im Ausland*, lay in immigration. The corollary of immigration destiny is established in the notion of Germans on frontiers. The remigration process captured in young-adult fiction resonates with the historical experiences of German immigrants to the Global South, again prior to and during the Age of Empire and Germany's acquisition of official colonies and protectorates. The sustained presence of Germans and their projection of whiteness onto non-European spaces inspires strategies of legitimization that further elicit genealogies of justifications, recourse to early modern German footprints. Evocations of servitude and enslavement recycle tropes of ethnic immigrant entitlement.

In chapter 5, "German Pioneers," I focus on the construction of immigrant identity among competing European communities in mid-to-late nineteenth-century Argentina, followed by an examination of select examples from print media. In the final section, I analyze an 1879 novel by Friedrich Spielhagen (1829–1911) that bridges German settlers in the transatlantic world by positing them as underdogs, even as victims. My reading of James Scott's work on the weapons of the powerless, such as foot dragging, frames the argument in this and subsequent chapters that deal with official colonies and protectorates. In order to generalize effectively about the social structures of dominance and subordination, he intentionally elides categories—with caveats—to make a point about the commonalities among institutions and implements of power: "These similarities in the cases of slavery, serfdom, and caste subordination are fairly straightforward. Each represents an institutionalized arrangement for appropriating labor, goods, and services from a subordinate population."[64] Scott continues with the observation that such institutions deprive subordinate populations of political and civil rights; they are born into their conditions: "Social mobility, in principle, if not in practice,

---

64. James C. Scott, *Domination and the Arts of Resistance: Hidden Transcripts* (New Haven, CT: Yale University Press, 1992), x.

is precluded."[65] In the language of nineteenth-century migration stories, the conflation of immigration with enslavement willfully elides the opportunity of social and economic advancement among the former, predicated on the whiteness of their protagonists. These conditions determine the trope of the German pioneer, conferring a settler identity that proves contingent upon identification between immigration and the conditions of slavery.

"Upon the Water: Immigration as Destiny" follows, with analyses of reports and personal accounts of immigration and remigration in the context of empire and national mobilities. The title modifies Kaiser Wilhelm's proclamation that the German future "liegt auf dem Wasser" (lies upon the water). Chapter 6 begins with the connection between European exploration and colonization, aided and abetted by an Ur-German ancestor whose legacy and bloodlines interpellate the experience of emigration during the Age of Empire. In the context of postcolonial Chile, the legend of an explorer, his Indigenous mistress, and their illegitimate daughter who inherits "his" earth provides sufficient ancient history to shape Chile as German around 1900. After this preface, the chapter examines several of the personal and professional medical letters of Karl Theodor Piderit (1826–1912), a doctor and psychologist who worked in Valparaiso (1851–1859) among German speakers and settlers. In contrast, Frau Magdelene Barbara Hörz (geb. Aichele) wrote letters, used as recruitment literature, about the life of female immigrant sent ahead from Swabia to reconnoiter for the family at home. The interaction between the politics of the homeland and the "zweite Heimat" are negotiated frequently in the German-language press in the region. To conclude this chapter, I turn to articles in the *Deutsche Post*, later, the *Deutsche Zeitung für Süd-Chile*, self-defined as the "Organ für alle Deutschen in Chile," in which the editors debate questions about citizenship, naturalization, and their relationship to whiteness and African colonial politics. The transatlantic German language takes center stage in the struggle for cultural identity intimately connected to white "fragility" in the increasingly precarious global contact zone.

Part 3 explores the interconnections among the global imaginaries produced and reproduced during the Age of Empire. In this section, I examine works of little-known colonial activists who work at the nexus of theory and history, fantasy and reality. They acquire expertise through their personal travels and tribulations; they eagerly create audiences for their research and writings by aligning it with the global colonial project, even though the bor-

---

65. Scott, *Domination*, x.

ders of this "globe" remain the transatlantic world, an empire interrupted. In the literature of colonial reality and fantasy, however, plans unfold for pushing and defending German frontiers, subduing the "ungovernable," determined by race, but authorized by the ability to subdue the "ungovernable" forces within, and finally, that alleged first footprint returns, memorialized to fuel the fervor of recolonial fantasies.

Chapter 7, "Global German Frontiers," follows the connection forged by the German-language call to white alliances from the Southern Cone to the American "frontier" of the Lutheran American states; through immigration and colonization manuals; to the tropical frontier of German Southwest Africa (GSA). With gendered identities shifting within a colonial or immigration paradigm—though firmly ensconced in heteronormativity—tropes generated by "contact" with Black and Indigenous populations pushed the limits of German-language dominant cultures of solidarity. The interconnections among these texts and contexts come into focus through an examination of young-adult fiction, produced by the Ohio-Missouri synod. The eponymous protagonist, Jager Afrikaner, embodies a rebellious African who ultimately repudiates his violent ways to become "Christian Afrikaner." The conversion story plays off missionary competition for justice and mercy; simultaneously, the plot turns on degrees of barbaric colonizers. The ontology of immigration recedes in the practical catechism published by a colonial administrator who balances recruitment of all Germans to do the patriotic thing and relieve population pressure on the Fatherland. The logic of immigration versus colonization illuminates the portrayal of "contact zones" as spaces for investment and settlement. During the Age of Empire, the presumed male German pioneer is joined to the trope of the *Farmersfrau*. Loyal through marriage and farming both to a Motherland and a family, the trope and person of the *Farmersfrau* emerged around 1900 from encounters between German and Anglophone colonizers. These adjacencies inscribe female identity into ancillary roles, but historical exigencies of social mobility through immigration and ideological services rendered by colonizing for the German nation-state reinscribe them into political allegories, accessing specific myths of empowerment. The "*Farmersfrau*" encompasses the South American immigrant woman as pioneer; the North American as fighting frontierswoman; and the German of colonial Südwestafrika as the self-sacrificing, hard-working, and gender-fluid caregiver. Cramer's 1913 memoir *Weiß oder Schwarz* amounts to a "public transcript," one that nonetheless recounts the "private transcript" of African resistance to German farmers. Cramer mobilizes racial difference against a colonial administration in German Southwest Africa (GSW), pitting the latter against the former in the postwar era during which German laws regulating the treatment of Black Africans drove a wedge between the representatives of German authority and the colonial patriots themselves. They see themselves locked in a battle for survival against the *Eingeborenen*.

Chapter 8, "*Wohin?* The Ungovernable," elaborates on the colonial-era fiction and nonfiction that constructs a single framework for settler colonialism and emigration. Around 1900, administrators and activists take and switch sides to reconfigure the world as German-centric. From west to east Africa, and the Americas, several key texts pose and attempt to answer the question *wohin*, which tended to overshadow the question of *warum*. When Arjun Appadurai writes about the "unruliness of the world of things," he articulates a "tension between the rule of the commodity and the unruliness of the thing itself."[66] In sending the "German" as export, not exile, the qualifier has to be quantified, its value converted into exchangeable currency. In this process, the "German" self confronts both the unruliness of things and contains the resistance of the ungovernable. In each of the imperial texts pertinent to my reading of colonial-era nonfiction and fiction, the writer inscribes these uncontainable moments; the inventories attempt to govern them through a process of performative repetition of enumeration, all in the effort to measure, regulate, and appropriate Indigenous forms through force. The allegorical "Germans" and their interrelated existence from Africa to the Americas encompasses an entire spectrum of colonial subjects and objects, from desired raw materials, inhospitable climates, scientific research, and strategies of discipline and punish to subjugate the ungovernable, the resisters who cannot (or will not) regulate themselves nor conform to the labor ethic exacted/extracted from them. The ungovernable become part of the picture beyond contemporary ethnographic curiosity and collection; they are commodified. Commodification in keeping imperial inventories devolved along dividing lines of race and gender.

To conclude the final section, chapter 9 considers several visual and verbal artifacts that reprise the narratives of imperial legitimacy and transform failed histories into recolonial fantasies. A GSW settler experiences life on the farm, the loss of the colony, and redemption in Nazi-era imperialism. He imagines the first footprint of a white man on the African continent as rightfully, nationally, essentially German. This is his forefather. The resurrec-

---

66. Arjun Appadurai, "The Thing Itself," *Public Culture* 18, no. 1 (2006): 15–21, here 21.

tion of early colonial leaders and dreamers revise a German history as global that occurred only discursively. Martin Beheim's pre-Columbus *Erdapfel* (1492; globe) stakes a global claim touted by Ernst Ludwig Cramer, Ada Cramer's son, in his Nazi-era memoir *Die Kinderfarm* (1941). His 1942 sequel, *Kinderfarm-Briefe*, retrospectively engages colonial racism in the white supremacist logic of the Nazi era. In response to the death of his young son, Cramer's life writing about his existence as a farmer in Africa, his struggles and self-reliance, and his Ur-Germanic resourcefulness, resonates with the genre of mourning, not only for his child, but for the colony. His is a narrative of recolonial fantasy that reflattens the world.

PART I

Imperial Entanglements

CHAPTER ONE

Prussia's First Fortress

Envisioned and modeled by baroque sculptor Andreas Schlüter (1659–1714) and cast by Johann Jacobi (1661–1726), the imposing equestrian statue of the Great Elector (figure 2) that originally presided over the Lange Brücke (Long Bridge, now the Rathausbrücke), tells a complex colonial story in metal and stone. Equally important is its placement. Work on a draft of this monument had begun in 1696, according to art historian Guido Hinterkeuser, a prolific expert on the art and architecture of Berlin. He recounts the elaborate and labor-intensive production process, from the arrival of the iron, to the casting of a mold, to the production of a gold-leaf covered plaster. The bronze statue and marble pedestal, completed in 1709, depicts the great-grandfather of Frederick II at the nexus of Prussian expansionist ambitions. Moreover, it variously embodies themes of dynasty and slavery to advance an imperialist agenda, despite the historical failure of its implementation. Known not only for his advancement of the Prussian economy and recovery from the devastations of the Thirty Years' War, but also for his military prowess, the Great Elector on horseback references Roman antecedents, enshrining the Prussian monarch in an imperial lineage. Friedrich III, who reigned from 1688 to 1713 and leveraged his position to assume the title Friedrich I, participated in the project with himself in mind as model, but ultimately demonstrated filial piety by dedicating it to his father. According to Hinterkeuser, the monument belongs in the "great tradition of western European equestrian statues"; he contests the idea that its location on a bridge invites an "interpretation of the Great Elector as the legendary hero of Roman virtue, Horatius Cocles," the sixth-century Roman legend who famously defended Rome from the Etruscans by holding a strategic bridge until it could be destroyed.[1] The monument's composition, origin, and initial placement set multiple interpretive

---

1. Guido Hinterkeuser, "Visions of power: Andreas Schlüter's monuments to the Great Elector and Friedrich III and I," *Sculpture Journal* 22, no. 1 (2013): 21–35, here 26.

engines in motion. My reading follows the visual narrative of the Great Elector as icon of the Prussian claim to a postcolonial past and its entanglement in an early modern system of colonization.

The equestrian statue rests on a pedestal; four enslaved male figures represent allegories of Prussian history elevated and emancipated under the Great Elector's reign. Frederick William I's active acquisitions and building on the West African coast, discussed below, demonstrate his desire to establish a Prussian foothold in the slave trade. He also devoted himself to the building of infrastructure that would connect Berlin with the sea. In his history and catalogue of equestrian statues, Kees van Tilburg writes that the Great Elector was responsible for constructing the Frederick William Summit Canal, the purpose of which was to link "his capital to ocean traffic. He was frustrated in building up naval power, lacking ports and sailors."[2] Around 1700, political and economic actors in German-speaking Europe fostered desires for empire, networking transportation infrastructure to larger markets, as well as pursuing the acquisition or defense of contiguous lands in Europe and beyond. Prussian politics, informed primarily by adjacent empires of Austria and Russia, but also Denmark and the Netherlands, were driven by aspirations to be a force in the European world.

Friedrich Wilhelm on horseback stood at a crucial juncture: on the bridge over a canal he had built to connect Berlin to world trade routes. A ship, too, was named for him. Friedrich Wilhelm's commitment to transportation infrastructure is evident in his investment in seafaring vessels. Built by G. C. Peckelhering, the ship built in his name was launched in 1681. Financed by letters of reprisal (*Kaperbriefe*) against Sweden and trade on the Gold Coast, the Elector's fleet enabled a Prussian expedition to the coast of Guinea, which forged strong connections between the Crown and the shipyard in Pillau. In July 1682, it sailed for the Churfürstlich African-Brandenburgische Compagnie to West Africa to load a cargo of enslaved people destined for St. Thomas.[3] The interconnections among early modern Brandenburg, the transatlantic slave trade, and the legacy of imagined and/or incomplete colonial empires are the subject of this chapter's case studies. Prussia's fort, built on the Gold Coast, attests to its complicity in the colonial enterprise, even though the

---

2. Kees van Tilburg, "Equestrian Statues." 2017. https://equestrianstatue.org/friedrich-wilhelm-kurf-rst/.

3. https://www.modelships.de/Museums_and_replicas/Maritimes_Museum_Hamburg/Frigate_Friedrich_Wilhelm_zu_Pferde.htm.

Figure 2. Equestrian statue of the Great Elector Frederick William (1620–1688) of the House of Hohenzollern, located on the Lange Brücke in Berlin, 1888, historical image. (ImageBROKER.com GmbH & Company KG/ Alamy Stock Photo.)

effort was unsustainable. In 1721, he sold it to the Dutch. Prussia continued to position itself vis-à-vis European maritime powers, and in the Age of Empire, the early modern past reanimates colonial desires with imperial realities, evident in a narrative poem titled *Groß-Friedrichsburg*, which hits the high notes in the "German" colonial register; it revised and repurposed fragments and ruins from the transatlantic world to position Germans as worthy, benevolent, and uplifting masters, themselves postcolonial subjects of history. Documents written by King Glèlè (1814–1889) give the lie to that benevolent narrative. King Glèlè communicates emperor to emperor, in a strategic move to argue for color-blind negotiations between equals. This archival evidence proves the existence of a decolonial act in the face of German colonial expansion, albeit eclipsed. Despite contemporary counternarratives of decolonial strength, transatlantic Germans leverage race to map their dominant status across the Americas, the Atlantic, and the African continent.

Transatlantic logics of the early modern world originate overwhelmingly in Eurocentric narratives about imperial economics, exploration and science, and religious exports. At the nexus of these, early modern transatlantic tropes form around the contact zones among Europeans, Africans, and Indigenous peoples. In this way, the prominence of European epistemologies, erected on a foundation of knowledge with all things and thoughts established in comparison to market values, the state of science, and religious denominations, circulates throughout and beyond a European *terra cognita*. Often omitted from examinations of these narrative accounts is the recalibration of "European" itself as an early modern trope, widely disseminated through materially mediated communicative networks. In the Germanic-languages accounts of travel and encounters with African and American cartographies and peoples, ambiguities devolve into "curiosities" and invite closer examination. These ambiguities trigger intra-European competition and contestation that accommodate centuries of imperialist expansion and the attendant atrocities of slavery, indenture, and exploitation. The complexities of early modern mercantilism, specifically those enabling the secular reproduction of the Eurocentric experience in the world through communicative networks connected through transportation and trade infrastructures, are captured in the competition for dominance, both economic and narrative. Driven by the desire for clarity and knowledge, early modern Europeans assert their subject positions as accurate versions of the world for the purpose of ownership. For my purpose, persistent ambiguities further indicate a complex constellation of agency among colonial powers from the early modern transatlantic world that includes German-speaking Europe in sometimes surprising ways.

Discursive colonialisms enable the intractable preservation of European agency while moralizing about other imperial atrocities. The topic covers a lot of territory and time. German colonial enterprises flower briefly at the end of the nineteenth century, with acquired protectorates in Africa and select locations in the Pacific region ceded to other European powers by 1918. Zantop charted this cultural territory in her now classical work on Germany's colonial fantasies; she takes into account the early modern reality of a Welser intervention in Africa to establish a foothold in the slave trade, which is unleashed in the context of the defense of Indigenous peoples by Bartolomé de las Casas, who famously claimed their humanity and proposed, to his later regret, the enslavement of Africans.[4] As she writes, "The Brandenburgers had bought blacks from slave hunters in their African outpost Gross-Friedrichsburg and sold them in St. Thomas. This dirty past became a dirty secret, which was only reluctantly unearthed and confronted by a few accounts later in the century."[5] Zantop joins others—and guides subsequent scholarship—in asserting the culpability of the claim to a moral high ground in the German colonial modality. To understand the strength and legacy of this trope, it is important to consider texts across contexts and continents. Jeff Bowersox, on the site Black Central Europe, contextualizes the founding and modest flourishing of the Brandenburg African Company (BAC) with a report from the entrepreneur Otto Friedrich von der Groeben about the "negotiations" with the local leaders (*capsicir*). The latter, however, negotiate with more finesse than von der Groeben's report suggests. Nonetheless, though on a smaller scale than the Dutch competitors, the BAC transported nineteen thousand Africans to the Caribbean into enslavement.[6] The "dirty secret" became, in fact, a point of celebration, having launched a lust for territory beyond all borders. These collective narratives swirl around contested sites; some authors inscribe counternarratives that have thus far been underestimated. The tenacity of this legacy enables a narrative not only of

---

4. The provenance of this work and its translation is significant, beyond the elaborate, detailed titles of the era: the snapshot of content, of bearing witness to atrocities, inscribes intent. See Bartolomé de las Casas, *Brief Account of the Destruction of the Indies Or, a faithful NARRATIVE OF THE Horrid and Unexampled Massacres, Butcheries, and all manner of Cruelties, that Hell and Malice could invent, committed by the Popish Spanish Party on the inhabitants of West-India, TOGETHER With the Devastations of several Kingdoms in America by Fire and Sword, for the space of Forty and Two Years, from the time of its first Discovery by them*. From the English translation: "Composed first in Spanish by Bartholomew de las Casas, a Bishop there, and Eye-Witness of most of these Barbarous Cruelties; afterward Translated by him into Latin, then by other hands, into High-Dutch, Low-Dutch, French, and now Taught to Speak Modern English." *Brevisima relacion de la destruccion de las Indias*, by Bartolome de las Casas, originally published in Seville in 1552. London: Printed for R. Hewson at the Crown in Corn, 1689.

5. Suzanne Zantop, *Colonial Fantasies: Conquest, Family, and Nation in Precolonial Germany, 1770–1870* (Durham, NC: Duke University Press, 1997), 28.

6. Jeff Bowersox, "Founding a Slave-Trading Company in West Africa," Black Central Europe, https://blackcentraleurope.com/sources/1500-1750/founding-a-slave-trading-colony-in-west-africa-1682-1683/. The von der Groeben source is *Guineische Reise-Beschreibung. Nebst einem Anhang der Expedition in Morea* (Marienwerder: S. Reinigern, 1694), 80–83.

German moral and intellectual superiority, but, as I contend in this study, a storyline that oscillates between German victory and victimhood. This theme of whiteness frequently varies between a rhetoric of past or present scarcity and future prosperity.

Prussian Footholds

In 1681, two ships from Brandenburg landed on the Gold Coast; built between 1683 and 1685, Fort Groß-Friedrichsburg, named after the prince elector Friedrich Wilhelm, established a foothold on the west coast of Africa in the Ahanta region. Zantop discusses nineteenth-century sources that indicate Brandenburgers "may have dealt with blacks more humanely than other nations, since they allowed infants to stay with their mothers."[7] According to source material and contemporary Ghanaians, the Brandenburg Company agreed to protect the village from the Dutch; the Brandenburgers functioned as allies in trade and partners against a common enemy. Contemporary sources in Princes Town claim that women and children, by agreement, were spared from the slave trade. Original plans to colonize the Guinea Coast, as it was also known, were formulated in 1680; these included the building of nearby Dorotheanschänze, named after the Kurfürst's wife. (Today, the ruins are covered in refuse.) The plans included the construction of at least five forts in the region; these did not come to fruition. Both military and engineering history intersect in this vision of Brandenburg on the Gold Coast.[8] Ultimately, the Dutch, who followed Brandenburg's plans with skepticism from the beginning,[9] came to dominate the area for two centuries. The Prussian footholds, however, would cast a long shadow.

German-language reports of scientific exploration, religious proselytizing, and economic adventuring shaped the imaginative geography in European cosmopolitan desires. The dissemination of such narratives intersects with the increase in print media, as well as developments in transportation infrastructure. First, economic motives drove competition for colonial hold-

---

7. Zantop, *Colonial Fantasies*, 28–29.
8. Ulrich van der Heyden, *Rote Adler an Afrikas Küste. Die brandenburgisch-preußische Kolonie Großfriedrichsburg in Westafrika* (Berlin: Selignow, 2001), 13.
9. Van der Heyden, *Rote Adler an Afrikas Küste*, 15.

ings, endorsed by executive power. Dubbed the "Großer Kurfürst," Friedrich Wilhelm I of Prussia (1620–1688) took the throne in 1640, during the Thirty Years' War (1618–1648).[10] He would not be the first nor the last monarch to leverage the devastations of war with territorial and economic expansion.

The alliance between the monarchy and the enterprising Benjamin Raule of the Brandenburg Company is attested by documents that display the transatlantic logic of the early modern colonial era. The successful return of one ship prompted the elector's enactment and agreement to establish a company. The language exceeds the formalities associated with such decrees, revealing the motivated relationships among topography, economics, and divine sanction:

> Demnach Wir erwogen, wie daß der höchste Gott einige Unserer Landen mit wohlgelegenen Seehäfen beneficiret, und dannenhero Vorhaben sein, unter andern Mitteln, so Wir zur Verbesserung der Schiff-Fahrt und des Commercii, als worin die beste Aufnahm eines Landes bestehet, einzuführen bedacht, vermittelst Göttlicher Hülfe und Segens, eine nach der in Africa belegenen so genanndten Guineischen Küste handelnde Kompagnie aufzurichten und zu Publiciren, welche unter Unserer Flagge Autorität und Schutz, und mit Unseren See-Pässen versehen, den Handel an freye Orte daselbst treiben sollen und mögen.[11]

> Accordingly, We, in considering that the Supreme God endowed some of our lands with well-situated seaports, and then plans to undertake other means, so that We consider the improvement of shipping and commerce activities as to what constitutes the best interests of a country, by means of divine help and blessing, to establish a company acting on the so-called Guinea Coast in Africa, and to publish it under the authority and protection of Our flag, and is provided with Our sea passports and should conduct business there in all free places.

The authorization for land appropriation on the African coast derives from divine sources, a justification for absolutist expressions, but because of the intermediary endowment of the proposed motherland with accommo-

---

10. Van der Heyden, *Rote Adler an Afrikas Küste*, 8.
11. Quoted in Van der Heyden, *Rote Adler an Afrikas Küste*, 20.

dating harbors. The materiality of the *Land* itself, its bodies of water and its soil, provides sufficient reason for imperial economic expansion. Power inscribed in the contract cited above sets acquisition in motion. Under the leadership of Major Von der Groeben, who became the first commandant of Groß-Friedrichsburg, the Brandenburg Company returned to Africa with gifts from the elector (including his portrait) and planted the flag on January 1, 1683. While the fort depended on material imported from Brandenburg, ground shells and local oils also were used in the construction, as was African labor. The Brandenburg enterprise extended for approximately fifty kilometers.[12] In addition, it took possession of Arguin Island, a commercially advantageous site, which lent the Brandenburg Africa Company temporary dominance in the world rubber trade.[13] In addition to Arguin, they took Whyday in Benin around 1700. Okafor inventories the possessions in the Americas: "Saint Thomas by lease from a Danish company (1685–1720), Island of Crabs by annexation (1689–1693), Tertholen by occupation (1696)."[14]

The focus of Brandenburg's colonial reality remained Groß-Friedrichsburg (figure 3). The structure remains intact, if difficult to access. Adjaï Paulin Oloukpona-Yinnon reads the intervention as the beginning of German colonial literature, which he explores further in *Unter deutschen Palmen*: It is situated "[a]m Anfang der Belletristik," a point to which I return below.[15] The fortress faces the ocean, with an interior courtyard and storehouse. Important to the existence of the economic hub, a Protestant chapel (figure 5) provided space for worship. Directly below the chapel, the dungeon (figure 4) held captives to be sold. The ruins of this foothold, sold to the Dutch in 1721, remain. The foothold itself in its monumental, material existence, takes on a life of its own in the reinventing of a colonial past that comes to inform the colonial present during the Age of Empire.

---

12. Local guides at the fort provided the information about the materials used from the locale. For more background on the building process, and the beginnings of Dorotheenschanze, see van der Heyden, *Rote Adler an Afrikas Küste*, 23–32.

13. Van der Heyden, *Rote Adler an Afrikas Küste*, 42.

14. Uche Onyedi Okafor, "Mapping Germany's Colonial Discourse: Fantasy, Reality and Dilemma (PhD dissertation, University of Maryland, 2013), 62–63.

15. Adjaï Paulin Oloukpona-Yinnon, *Unter deutschen Palmen. Die "Musterkolonie" Togo im Spiegel deutscher Kolonialliteratur (1884–1944)* (Frankfurt a/M: IKO—Verlag für Interkulturelle Kommunikation, 1996), 68.

Figure 3. Exterior wall of Groß-Friedrichsburg, built in 1683, in 2020, Princes Town, Ghana. (Photo by the author.)

Imperial Realities

Early modern German geographies of the colonial world foreground the cosmopolitan project of knowledge expansion. The entitlements, abstracted through the structure of faith and decentering of Indigeneity form the foundation of the later imperial project. The legacy of Friedrich Wilhelm posits a close connection between his colonizing efforts and the later narratives of empires. Further associations between trade and empire feature the Großer

Figure 4. Dungeon of Groß-Friedrichsburg. (Photo by the author.)

Kurfürst as the primary source of imperial inspiration. Though he sold the fortresses, effectively conceding to more powerful European colonizers and abandoning the expansionist ambitions of Brandenburg at the time, his legacy served the purpose of nationalist posterity and later colonial projects.

The German-speaking advocates of reclaiming the colonial past around 1900 started to tell a revisionist history. Interest in the Brandenburg forts piqued the curiosity of scholars beyond the realm of colonial nationalists. Historical engagement on the African coast prompted, for example, the

Figure 5. Chapel, directly above dungeon. (Photo by the author.)

publication of *Deutsche Seebücherei* (1907).[16] Otto Richter introduces the "Erzählung aus der Wende des 17. Und 18. Jahrhunderts" (story from the turn of the seventeenth and eighteenth century) into a political context, revealing his motivation to restore maritime power by mining Prussian colonizing his-

---

16. Professor Dr. Julius Wilhelm Otto Richter (Otto von Colmen), *Deutsche Seebücherei. Erzählungen aus dem Leben des detuschen Volkes für Jugend und Volk. 14. Band. Die brandenburgische Kolnie Groß-Friedrichsburg und ihr Begründer Otto Friedrich von der Groeben* (Altenburg: Stephan Geibel Verlag, 1907).

tories. Richter names the devastation of Brandenburg as the Great Elector's motivating force, "seinen durch den Dreißigjährigen Krieg zerrütteten Staat durch Seefahrt und Seehandel wieder zu heben"[17] (to again raise up his state, which had been shattered by the Thirty Years' War). *Belletristik* brought forth repeated attempts to raise colonial consciousness from the history hidden in plain sight. In 1911, Emil Sembritzki reprinted excerpts from von Festenberg's 120-page narrative poem, *Groß-Friedrichsburg*.[18] Von Festenberg foregrounds the kinder, gentler German rule, reaching into the genealogy of power and folding it into a contemporary politics of coloniality in which Prussia trumps the Portuguese, Spanish, and Dutch in the treatment of Blacks:

> Und zu milden Sitten wurden
> Auferzogen jetzt die M*hren
> Die mit schneller Fassungsgabe
> Wohl den Unterschied bemerkten
> Zwischen ihren neuen Herrn
> Und den schlimmen Niederländern,
> Die, wie Portugies' und Spanier
> Räubern gleich nur Beute suchten
> An den Küsten Afrikas,
> Ohne sich das Wohl des schwarzen
> Eingeborenen Volks zu kümmern.[19]

> And to gentler custom were
> The M**rs raised who with
> Quick comprehension noticed well
> The difference between the new masters
> And the bad Netherlanders,
> Who, like the Portuguese and Spanish
> Predators only looked for prey
> On the coasts of Africa,
> Without a care for the well-being
> Of the Black natives.

---

17. Richter, *Deutsche Seebücherei*, 1.
18. Hermann V. Festenburg, *Groß-Groß-Friedrichsburg*, in Emil Sembritzki, ed., *Kolonial-Gedicht- und Liederbuch* (Berlin: Deutscher-Kolonial Verlag, 1911), 9–13.
19. Von Festenberg, "Hie gut Brandenburg allewege," 9–13.

The moral superiority of the "new masters" thus established, von Festenberg describes flourishing trade in the "1683" section. He enumerates the treasures brought by caravans from the "dark interior" of the continent: palm oil, pepper, salt, ebony, leopard skins, ivory, stones, and gold dust, among others. The well-being of the local inhabitants prefaces the prosperity around the new fort Groß-Friedrichsburg. The excerpts that appeal to Sembritzki's colonial fervor include the historical sections 1681, 1683, 1717, and 1884. For him and fellow Germans, the mid-1880s mark the reincarnation of empire.

The colonial competition enacted by Germany with other European powers intersected with the racial politics of empire in Africa. In 1884, Togo was becoming a German colony.[20] The kingdom of Danhomê sought European allies—or at least support—to fend off the French-sponsored attacks locally (in Porto Novo, for example), while it was protecting German businessmen and interests. Generally, Béhanzin considered the Germans to be his friends.[21] His predecessor and father, King Glèlè (1814–1889), purportedly considered all Europeans his friends even though he felt compelled to wage war against the French, and the German Kaiser felt compelled not to intervene after his death in 1889. Kondo, his son, took the name Béhanzin when he ascended to the throne, and he explained the hostile relationship to the French in 1890, when Cotonou grew to a significant commercial center.[22] Through diplomatic channels, specifically the Imperial Commissioner Puttkamer in Zébé (approximately forty kilometers east of Lomé), the king was informed he would be held responsible for the lives of German businessmen in country. Using the language of friendship (with the two businessmen, for example), Béhanzin maintained correspondences with Berlin, Zébé, and the archives.

While Britain and France had outlawed slavery early in the nineteenth century, their economic interests and colonial enterprises displaced the practice to Africa. In its ascendance to nationhood and aspirational empire, Germany, too, vied for territories and commerce equal to that of its European rivals. In this historical epistolary exchange, evidence of German ownership of enslaved people—in Africa—arises. Oloukpona-Yinnon writes of document 7, the copy of a draft letter from Freiherr von Gravenreuth to the king of Danhomê, that the latter spent time in Ouidah as a captain in the Imperial German Infantry. There

---

20. Adjaï Paulin Oloukpona-Yinnon, ed. and introduction, *Gbêhanzin und die Deutschen. Politische Korrespondenz zwischen dem Königreich Danhomê und dem Deutschen Reich (1882–1892). Deutsch-französische Dokumentation* (Berlin: Edition Ost, 1996), 9.
21. Oloukpona-Yinnon, *Gbêhanzin und die Deutschen*, 11.
22. Oloukpona-Yinnon, *Gbêhanzin und die Deutschen*, 26.

he purchased several Africans to enslave from the Danhomê king, through the middleman, the German salesman Ernst Richter of the Hamburg firm of Wölber & Brohm. These were to serve him in Africa.[23]

In January 1892, King Bénzim (Béhanzim, 1845–1906), ruler of the Empire of Dahomey, wrote to Kaiser Wilhelm II, emperor to emperor. Negotiating wars and alliances among the French, Germans, and local rivals, the king's correspondence documents his diplomatic efforts to protect his power on the west coast of Africa. He writes,

> So God created both white and black and put the Europeans Government to reign over the Eureopans [sic] likewise I the King of Dahomey have to reign over the West-Coasts of Africa since that we still keep up our Friendschip continualy [sic], as what cannot be necessary to you I will not allow such things to be done to any of the European Government and I also believe that what cannot be necessary to me, you also cannot allow such things to be done to me in any of your Protectorates. You are a powerful and respectable Emperor in Europe like wise [sic] I am a powerful and responsible king in the West Coast of Africa.[24]

Von der Groeben, in the 1690s, would jokingly trade gulps of alcohol and contractual signatures with the local leaders near Groß-Friedrichsburg. They secured promises of protection, of themselves and their families, against the Dutch. The level of disingenuousness of Von der Groeben—he and his lieutenant married nine-year-old girls to secure the deal—exceeds the private transcript of the *capiscir*, whose authority is disparaged.[25] The leveraging of credulity against African authority has a long history. In this region, Togo eventually gained the moniker of Germany's model colony, attributable to a range of factors, not least of which includes that it did not cost the Reich money. In the early 1890s, this letter from Gbêhanzin attempts a negotiation on equal footing with the kaiser. Adopting a national identity to engage with a German ruler, Béhanzin predicates a relationship to the German Empire on equality of power, disregarding the reality of unequal resources and desires. Béhanzin ignores any disequilibrium based on racial difference.

Distinct from the real existing colonies claimed by the German Reich,

---

23. Oloukpona-Yinnon, *Gbêhanzin und die Deutschen*, 32, 63.
24. Quoted in Oloukpona-Yinnon, *Gbêhanzin und die Deutschen*, 34.
25. See Bowersox, "Founding a Slave-Trading Company."

other enclaves of immigrants redefined the borders of the homeland. Both in South and North America, the unformalized "colonies" produce a narrative that writes German identity into the legacy of persecution. To the *Schutzgebiete* (protectorates) of the African continent and elsewhere, the story illuminates the impact of German geographical projections on nationalist thinking that drives the pan-Germanism of the Second Empire in Europe and continues into the 1930s, after the loss of the war and with it, all remaining noncontiguous land. Meanwhile, German "colonists," emigrants, and settlers in the Americas chimed in on the nature of African royalty, their rivalries, and their spheres of influence.

From West to East Africa

Colonial logics are embedded in syntax that triumphs over time and space. Repeatedly, the vectors connecting German-speaking subjects with points on a map erase or elide facts of distance; they join far-flung territories with the use of a coordinating conjunction or preposition. Media networks enabled the circulation of ideas about race and empire accessible across national and imperial boundaries, arbitrary though these may be. West African coastal territories simply segue across the continent. The West African erstwhile protectorate known as Togoland stretches across the Ghana-Togo border as a result of British colonization and struggles for independence.

In the case of Germany, the acquisition of African colonies, though comparatively short-lived, casts a long shadow over institutional memory in the Togoland and Trans-Volta region of Ghana. Under the entry on Togo, Meinecke attests to the origin and function of the Kpando site, a station he describes as having great economic value because of its location on the trade route from Sudan south to Lomé, Kitta, and Accra.[26] The modest structure seems far from the "icons of a romantic loss" Stoler takes to task in "Imperial Debris."[27] Yet these ruins leave markers of imperial aspirations used to leverage revisionist histories throughout the twentieth century. The textbooks for Germans abroad, the memoirs from Southwest Africa, the ideologues

---

26. Gustav Meinecke, *Die Deutschen Kolonien in Wort und Bild. Geschichte, Länder- und Völkerkunde, Tier- und Pflanzenwelt, Handels- und Wirtschaftsverhältnisse der Schutzgebiete des Deutschen Reiches* 2nd, expanded edition (Leipzig: Verlag von J.J. Weber, 1901), 14.

27. Ann Laura Stoler, "Imperial Debris: Reflections on Ruin and Ruination," in *Cultural Anthropology* 23, no. 2 (2008): 191–219, 194.

of expansion mourned the loss of colonies; instrumentalized after the First World War, that longing was weaponized. During the Age of Empire, the early modern conquest provided grist for the narrative mill of colonial entitlements. In the Volta Regional Museum, located in Ho, the collection houses the chair of state of the last German colonial governor, local paintings, artifacts, and pottery. Nearby, in Amedzofe, the legacy of colonialism is inscribed into the landscape: Mount Gemi (second highest mountain in Ghana) is an abbreviation for German Evangelical Mission, which came to the region in 1847 and established the Ewe Church (there is a school nearby as well). In Kpando, the ruins of the nineteenth-century German colonial administration, and the surrounding houses for officials, bear no markings of their history (figures 6–9). On the coast of Ghana, near Axim—Amo's birthplace—the Great Elector's fort remains; farther inland, in the mountainous region of Volta, the ruins of other empires stand as neglected agents of German colonial history. The contemporary debate about German colonial possessions, their acquisition and their return, forces a re-examination of the historical and literary stories that connect the first fortress with the first footprint.

One colonial-era periodical demonstrates the ways occasional poetry and satirical verse nonetheless wove connections across emigrant and colonial epistemics. Titled "Neueste Erlebnisse aus Ost Afrika"[28] (Latest experiences from East Africa), this poem was meant to be sung to the tune of "Krambambulli," a nineteenth-century student song. To escape the stagnant West, the trope of decline circa 1900, the poetic "I" makes his way to Africa, where he meets a prince, naked but for a loincloth. Immediately, they are "auf du und du," on equal, informal terms. Drunk on schnapps, "Fürst Owakakuh" bestows gifts of ivory and palm essence and access to his harem with 250 women. The "administrative" poetic voice offers an official report; they play *Räuberskat*. In the event another prince comes along and pokes fun at Owakakuh's power, he is murdered and cooked ("Und kam ein andrer N*ggerfürste / Und ulkte wider seine Macht"; and if another n*prince came along / And made jokes against his power), then he was slayed and cooked to a stew. "Doch Alles naht sich seinem Ende" (yet everything must come to an end): Owakakuh's people rebel and devour him, "Doch hatte [er] leider stark Hautgout" (But unfortunately [he] had a strong gamey taste). Published in a Berlin colonial periodical in 1907, during the Age of Empire, the anonymous poem appeared to ridicule African monarchs and keep the cannibal trope alive.

---

28. Anonymous, *Koloniale Zeitschrift*, ed. A. Herfurth (Berlin: Verlag der Kolonialen Zeitschrift, 1907), February 28, 1907, Nr. 3: 8. Jahrgang, 86.

Figure 6. German colonial-era administration station, built ca. 1897, Togo. Kpando. (Photo by the author.)

Figure 7. German colonial station, Kpando. (Photo by the author.)

Figure 8. Corridor, German colonial station, Kpando. (Photo by the author.)

The American origin can be corroborated by the use of "i" in the N-word; the asterisks replace "e" elsewhere in the publication. The multidirectionality of German-language reports, critiques, sermons, and racist satires retained the category of the national for themselves. The logic of colonial national borders, drawn by the contingencies of competition among Europeans, had as a corollary the common project of German administration abroad, articulated by the poem above. Though a disappointment to some, the Great Elector's legacy persists through the devastation of the First World War and the gusto for reclaiming entitlements.

Always embedded in structures of power, narratives of superiority, persecution, and industry justified the conversion of Indigenous epistemologies into European property—abnegating subaltern agency in Spivak's exploration of postcolonial logic—and stories into knowledge, and knowledge into power. The colonial German subject, however, accesses historical moments and recodes them to assert identification with the colonized. The rhetorical transformation of the German ancestor into landowner, enslaved Africans into European victims, and German immigrants into the enslaved enact that agency. The narratives of coloniality posit a close alignment between the

Figure 9. Exterior door, German colonial station, Kpando. (Photo by the author.).

trope of the noble colonizer and German masculinity. Each installment in "progress" toward a German global imaginary recycles selective stories.

The Great Elector, once disparaged for abandoning the colonial project and selling Groß-Friedrichsburg to the Dutch figures as the capstone, surrounded by colonial governors and generals. The renewal of German global desires in the interwar period, fueled by National Socialist ideologies, seems in retrospect more a juggernaut than a debate. I am not suggesting any ambivalence, but the immigration narratives put forth a decolonial model that also took recourse to a national subtext. Thus the legacy of African empires precedes and outlives the colonial period, which nonetheless obscures the German colonial footprints and blueprints of its purportedly enlightened colonialism.

CHAPTER TWO

Enlightened Colonialism

By the mid-eighteenth century, critical reports of slavery in the West Indies circulated widely in a variety of print media, which included religious treatises, semipublic letters, travel writing, contracts with companies representing specific national and imperial interests, and literature. Along with communicative networks, economic and scientific exploration conveyed artifacts and material objects, often botanical or mineral, in addition to various specimens and treasures assigned a wide range of value. These include purchased human beings. At this time, competing ideas of who counted as human engaged skin color as part of a colonial "logic" that justified enslavement. Considered by some to be the first ethnography of the West Indies, Christian Georg Andreas Oldendorp (1721–1787) records the history of the Moravian mission to the Danish colonies in his *Geschichte der Mission der evangelischen Brüder auf den caraibischen Insels S. Thomas, S. Croix und S. Jan* (History of the mission of the evangelical brethren on the Caribbean islands of St. Thomas, St. Croix and St, John).[1] Reporting on his own experiences during a 1767–1768 voyage, Oldendorp relays in the first volume the geographic, political, and natural history of the islands; the second rehearses the history of the *Brüdergemeine*'s mission (1732–1768).[2] Familiar under the name Moravian Brethren or Unitätskirche, the church sent missionaries to the Caribbean in the 1730s to evangelize the enslaved but also to alleviate human suffering. Oldendorp, himself a member of the church, eschewed the dehumanization of the enslaved; he opposed the institution of slavery and believed humanity was not defined by skin color. Jacqueline Van Gent expounds on Oldendorp's position in the context of the history of emotions. Oldendorp

---

1. C. G. A. Oldendorp and Johann Jakob Bossart, *Geschichte der Mission der Evangelischen Brüder auf den Caraibischen Inseln St. Thomas, St. Crux und St. Jan* (Leipzig: C. F. Laux, 1777).

2. Karin Schüller, *Die deutsche Rezeption haitianischer Geschichte in der ersten Hälfte des 19. Jahrhunderts. Ein Beitrag zum deutschen Bild vom Schwarzen* (Cologne: Böhlau, 1992), 71.

recognizes "savagery" in both slaveholders and the enslaved, acknowledging the regime of violence that produces it. She writes, "'Savagery' as a knowledge system is for Oldendorp not synonymous with 'savages' as people, often explicitly identified as those living at the geographical periphery of Europe or beyond, as was the more common understanding in the 18th century."[3] Such testaments push back against the homology between non-Europeans and the condition of savagery. Oldendorp's report from the Danish-Caribbean "contact zone" challenges the European reader to view colonialism through the lens of Enlightenment thought. In this chapter, Prussia under Frederick the Great negotiates its borders with colonialism, Enlightenment thought, and the transatlantic political imaginary to investigate the possibility of enlightened colonialism.

Under the expansion wars led by Frederick after his accession to the throne in 1749, the focus turned to establishing Prussia as a contender among empires. Peripherally, the more distant world was represented at the court. In the celebrated case of Frederick II, he summoned Voltaire to his side; imported porcelain from Silesia; engaged with political imperial theory; imposed his Francophile literacy on Prussian institutions; welcomed refugees, among them Huguenots, to Berlin; eschewed the provincial; and engaged in artistic production and performance, seemingly the only monarch to have a play list on Spotify. The major European powers married, fought among themselves, conscripted and sold mercenaries, and bargained their way into each other's sovereignty. At a time when such entanglements prevailed, Prussia's marginal position as a smaller state was well-established. By examining these entanglements in an age of enlightened absolutism under a philosopher-king, this chapter engages the idea of enlightened colonialism as a corollary to enlightened absolutism. Both concepts are predicated on the performative capacity of epistemological models that equate knowledge with power. These equivalent expressions, however, involve variables and produce criticism that at least acknowledges the value of the unknown and perhaps unknowable in the colonial project.

---

3. Jacqueline Van Gent, "Rethinking Savagery: Slavery Experiences and the Role of Emotions in Oldendorp's Mission Ethnography," *History of the Human Sciences* 32, no. 4: 28–42, here 40. https://doi.org/10.1177/0952695119843210. See also Schüller, *Die deutsche Rezeption haitianischer Geschichte*, 72. Certain assumptions about the enslaved persisted. For example, it was the *Branntwein* that robbed the enslaved of all their feeling of social responsibility, while slavery took away their right to any equality. Schüller refers to the original: [slavery] "habe das vorweggenommen, was der Tod schließlich bei allen Menschen bewirke, Gleichheit."

Theorizing about Prussia and its power structures intersects with prevailing discourses about hegemony, such as drafts of perpetual peace, waging cabinet wars, and the defense of empires. In 1713, for example, during negotiations to conclude the Wars of Spanish Succession between England and France, the Treaty of Utrecht inspired the Castel de Saint-Pierre (1658–1743) to conceptualize a blueprint for perpetual peace. He opines about ways to achieve a balance of power and diplomacy, rather than engage in chronic warfare. The political essay, however, lends insight into the contest for sovereignty not only among the greater, but also the lesser powers, including the German-speaking states. Saint-Pierre additionally attempts to extend his model to include all the states of the world. In making this rhetorical gesture, he meets with resistance that sheds light on the status of Prussia at the time and the contemporary European rejection of Asian and African sovereignty. Theories of perpetual peace trickle down into strategies of waging war.

Kant's intervention, too, which will undergird my argument in the next chapter, posits perpetual peace as achievable. Both examples of this genre function within a European concept of sovereignty based on the marginalized presence of Africans. Tensions between theories of power and colonial expansion overlap during the eighteenth century in illuminating ways. Efforts to imperialize Prussia to compete more effectively with other European powers were also informed by the presence of Blacks—however decorative and peripheral—purchased into enslavement by the Great Elector. I hope to make visible and legible the fragmented colonial contexts that ground Frederick's "enlightened absolutism" and enlightened colonialism. My purpose is not to engage the question of how great was Frederick, but instead to bring into focus the network of forces that he had to negotiate on behalf of Prussian prominence, and to suggest the cumulative effect of colonial thinking on a Prussian center of gravity. To do so, I first sketch the plight of small states and their futile attempts to establish extensive colonies in competition with England, France, Spain, Portugal, and Holland. I next turn to Frederick's writings to elucidate his position. Finally, to provide evidence that critical and anticolonial voices existed, I examine Gotthold Ephraim Lessing's critique of Prussian hegemony within the logic of "imperial formations" (Stoler) tempered by theorizing the possible contours of an enlightened colonialism. This chapter constructs an overview of colonial contexts that, while seeming at first contingent, in fact exert significant influence of strategic land annexation. Followed by case studies of texts penned by the self-appointed "philosopher of Sanssouci" and Lessing's

Enlightened Colonialism

critique of tyranny under Frederician Prussia, I draw together the center and peripheries of enlightened colonialism.

Prussia's Colonial Unconscious

Pesne's oil painting (figure 10) invites the viewer to linger on the nearly beatific countenance of the young crown prince. The composition evokes adoration and mourning. Posed in wheeled carriage, Friedrich Wilhelm's body is bisected by a royal red sash and held by red upholstery to draw the viewer's eye, and it is flanked by his servant, who gazes at his youthful master. The child's identity is limited to his servitude, like many in this position whose stories failed even to make the footnotes of royal histories. This child was likely among those the Great Elector ordered from the Guinean coast and brought to enslavement in Berlin. Historian Jürgen Overhoff intervenes productively in the public debate about the renaming of "M*hrenstrasse" in Berlin; he brings the history of colonial aspirations to the foreground in an article about the presence of Blacks in the Prussian court. Basing his analysis on the later painting, he brings into focus the young Black rendered barely visible in the far right portrait of Frederick and Wilhelmine.[4] Overhoff further contextualizes the genre of painting "Hofm*hren" or "Kammerm*hren." The Great Elector ordered several "M*hren" from the provisional colony (discussed in the previous chapter), naming the first one after himself (1686), as was the practice, to be joined later (1715) by three young males, Cupido, Pampi, and Mercurius, and a girl, Marguerite. The enslaved Prussians on the monument to the Great Elector demonstrate not only a connection to Roman antiquity, but to contemporary Prussian men in chains, while enslaved Blacks performed in court and were transported by Brandenburg's vessels. Overhoff's research challenges notions of a comparatively modest involvement of Prussia in the slave trade. Prussia sent twenty thousand enslaved Africans to the Caribbean: contemporary Prussia had twenty thousand inhabitants. Admittedly, the challenges to writing biographies of the enslaved Blacks at court are many, with names and identities erased and replaced, and records lost to twentieth-century bombs. Some traces of history survive in literature and the arts. By contrast, this sketch captures a bond between the two children—and

---

4. Jürgen Overhoff, "Preußens verborgene Sklaven," *Die Zeit* online, August 19, 2020. https://www.zeit.de/2020/35/kolonialismus-preussen-afrikaner-sklaven/komplettansicht#print.

Figure 10. Antoine Pesne, Prinz Friedrich Ludwig in Preußen (1707–1708) im Gartenwagen mit schwarzem Kammerdiener, um 1711, GK I 3424. Stiftung Preußische Schlösser und Gärten Berlin-Brandenburg. (Photo by Daniel Lindner.)

the servant stands above his royal ward. As his royal children came of age, however, the *Soldatenkönig* (1688–1740), who reigned from 1713–1740, beat any and all childhood fantasies out of the Crown Prince and held both him and Wilhelmine strictly to his wishes for strategic marriages. The dominant goal of solidifying Prussia's power further trumped any colonial desires.

As power aggregated around Prussia after the Crown Prince ascended to the throne, he surprised fellow monarchs with his ability to wage strategic wars of land acquisition. While perhaps not the backwater of Europe, Prussia had not been a player. Castel de Saint-Pierre first describes the relationships among the major European powers, then turns to the multiplicity of the German states, implying a need for consolidation: "The same grounds and means that managed in the past to shape a permanent Society between the sovereignties of Germany are available to the Rulers of today, and could serve to form a permanent association of all the Christian sovereignties of Europe."[5] Unarticulated yet presumed is the dominance of Habsburg Austria. In the second part of his project, Saint-Pierre broadens his vision to encompass the world, but

> my friends pointed out that in the coming centuries most sovereigns of Asia and Africa will request a reception into the Union. This vision seemed so very distant, and encumbered with so many difficulties, that it overshadowed the whole project with an air, an appearance of impossibility that repelled every reader, with the result that some came to believe that even limited to a Christian Europe, the project would be impossible to achieve.[6]

The sketch of his project posits a hegemonic German-speaking state in Europe that would cast Prussia in a supporting role. It also anticipates an Asia and Africa with sovereign rulers who would apply for membership, but reader revulsion and disbelief prompted him to discard that ambition. Here religious difference trumps race, though the two intersectional aspects of Asian and African identities coincide in this exclusionary vision of Europe. The variability of religious identity presents the post-Enlightenment German global imaginary with a dilemma, leaving the imperialism in the later nineteenth century in a moral panic. While the clear aim of proselytizing

---

5. Castel de Saint-Pierre, "Europe: A Project for Peace," in *The Idea of Europe: Enlightenment Perspectives*, texts selected by Catriona Seth and Rotraud von Kulessa, translated by Catriona Seth et al. (Open Book Publishers, 2017), 12–14, here 13. https://books.openbookpublishers.com/10.11647/obp.0123.pdf.

6. Saint-Pierre, "Europe: A Project for Peace," 14.

and religious conversion redeem souls, African, Asian, and American bodies need to be racially recoded. From this inaugural moment of religious gerrymandering, the despotic emerges under the guise of limited tolerance toward non-Christian religions.

German-speaking nobility—and Francophiles like Frederick—took their cues from proximate and powerful neighbors. In terms of colonial aspirations, these remained modest, with smaller states vying for what footholds they could. For example, Duke Jacob I of Courland (*Kurland*) (1642–1681), a duchy with a German elite and Latvian population, sought to acquire territory in South America. Like Frederick William, the Great Elector, he had spent time in the Netherlands. The historian Heinrich Volberg has written extensively on Brandenburg's efforts to grow an overseas empire, observing that both the Duke of Courland and the Elector had spent time in the Netherlands, "wo beide sich für Seefahrt und Überseehandel begeisterten (where both were enthusiastic about seafaring and overseas trade)."[7] Volberg's research documents the intricate efforts of *Kurland* and Brandenburg, sovereign lands related by ambition and marriage, to establish footholds in South America and the Caribbean islands. Disputed or unknown ownership of the territories often complicated negotiations. *Kurland*'s presence in Tobago began sometime between 1634 and 1654, but ended on December 11, 1659.[8] It was then that Sweden attacked *Kurland* and captured Herzog Jakob, who signed over the island to Holland. Once released (1660), he reasserted entitlements with a vengeance, sent new ships, and built a new fort, but he ultimately proved no match for Holland, France, and England.[9] The smaller states faced challenges and defeats, their attempts to compete with their stronger European neighbors thwarted. The aspirational geographies encompassed Africa and the Americas. By the time Brandenburg had divested itself of any African possessions and sold all to the Dutch, Prussia was otherwise occupied.

Despite the absence of colonial possessions and a more pressing desire for contiguous territory, Prussia's aggressions demanded vigilant diplomacy that worked through and around secretive alliances; these, in turn, drove delicate negotiations, if not balances. Several attempts to implicate Prussia in minor colonial enterprises illuminate the complex interrelationships among bellicose heads of state bargaining for men, land, and colonial possessions. In his multivolume biography of Frederick, Scottish historian Thomas Carlyle

---

7. Heinrich Volberg, *Deutsche Kolonialbestrebungen in Südamerika nach dem Dreißigjährigen Krieg* (Cologne: Böhlau-Verlag, 1977), 23.
8. Volberg, *Deutsche Kolonialbestrebungen in Südamerika*, 27 and 30.
9. Volberg, *Deutsche Kolonialbestrebungen in Südamerika*, 30.

Enlightened Colonialism

shines a light on the colonial entanglements of Prussia, even in the absence of colonies. During the Seven Years' War, a French ambassador, unaware of Frederick's clandestine arrangement with England, tried to make the king an offer he could not but did refuse. Riverois attempted to barter with a Caribbean island in exchange for military support against their war with England. The duke proffered Tobago. The response: "Die Insel Tobago? Sie meinen wohl die Insel Barataria, für die ich aber nicht den Sancho Pansa machen kann"[10] (The island Tobago? You probably mean the island Barataria, but I cannot be its Sancho Panza). The well-read Frederick alluded to the fictional island, the governance of which Don Quixote promised as a practical reward for his squire. A duke and duchess pretend to give him rule of the Insula Barataria; they proceed to stage a series of parodic abuses, and Sancho returns to the adventure, having ruled with some down-to-earth common sense. Recognizing the fanciful trap that an island colony could represent, Friedrich declined. When, in 1755, Holland tried to persuade Frederick the Great to purchase the French part of the Caribbean island St. Maarten, he refused, his attention fixed on maintaining his claim on Silesia and consolidating Prussia's weight as a player in the European balance of power. Restraint the better part of valor, at least in this case, Frederick focused his energy not on the acquisition of colonies, but on the annexation of contiguous land to expand Prussian territory and political power.

In his youth, Frederick conceived a type of enlightened colonialism, articulated primarily in his "Anti-Machiavel." The philosopher of power—here I refer to Frederick—engages in a textual dialogue with Machiavelli's Prince, and though the king of Prussia's model of a monarch, of himself both as head of state and servant of the people, has been widely criticized, he did eschew the acquisition of noncontiguous territories; in this prioritization of Prussia in Europe, he avails himself of Machiavelli's work within the states of Italy and its imperial legacies. For example, in elaborating the playbook for a conqueror, Machiavelli recommends sending groups of loyal subjects or colonies to the new territories. Frederick pushes back:

> Let us see if these colonies—for the establishment of which Machiavel gives license to his students to commit so many injustices—are as useful as the author says. Either you send strong colonies into the newly-conquered country, or you send weak ones there. If these colonies are strong, you depopu-

---

10. Quoted in Franz Mehring, *Die Lessing-Legende:: Zur Geschichte und Kritik des preussischen Despotismus und der klassischen Literatur*, 2nd edition (Stuttgart: J.H.W. Dietz nachf., 1906), 166.

late your State considerably, and you drive out a great number of your new subjects, which decreases your forces. If you send weak colonies into these conquered countries, they will not fulfill their duties very effectively there. You will have made those whom you drive out unhappy, without much compensating profit.[11]

While Frederick here insists on the primary meaning of the signifier "colony" as an enclave, a homogeneous, cohesive group that constitutes a minority in a noncontiguous territory, his reasoning resonates throughout subsequent efforts to forge a German-speaking presence up and into the late nineteenth century. The establishing of administrative enclaves as an imperial exercise of centralizing power and extracting resources intersects with climate theories and racialized labor hierarchies in ways that leave an indelible mark on the Age of Empire, which featured colonization as a logical corollary to a unified nation-state. Though Friedrich II consciously rejects all offers and turns away from the acquisitiveness of the Great Elector, he nonetheless engaged with the Americas at a variety of levels. To pose problems for those bound for America, he decreed in 1753 that Prussia would not allow America-bound travelers to pass through it.[12] The artist and musician in him celebrated spirits and acts of resistance to colonial Spain's brutality in Mexico with the libretto *Montezuma*, music composed by Carl Heinrich Graun (1704–1759). Friedrich, recuperating his love of the arts after his father's punitive brutality to deprive his son of any pleasure or indulgence, famously supported a wide range of cultural activities and institutions. This opera, however, provides us with insights into political theory and a critique of uncontained colonial power that exceeds the psychological and musicological interpretations of the work, though these unarguably illuminate multiple aspect of Frederick the Great's life and family dynamic. John Rice, for example, has written eloquently about the autobiographical: "*Montezuma* vividly reflects Frederick's enigmatic personality and the unique musical culture he created in Berlin."[13]

---

11. Friedrich II, *The Refutation of Machiavelli's Prince or, Anti-Machiavel*, chap. III, "Mixed Principalities," 8. 1740. https://archive.org/details/AntiMachiavelFriedericktheGreat/page/n7/mode/2up?view=theater.

12. See Bernd Brunner, *Nach Amerika: Die Geschichte der deutschen Auswanderung*, 2nd ed. (Munich: C. H. Beck, 2017), 92.

13. John A. Rice, "Opera at the Court of Frederick the Great: Graun's *Montezuma* as Royal Autobiography," Expansion of a colloquium talk at Princeton University (October 2009), the University of Pittsburgh (February 5, 2010), and the University of Iowa (May 2010); updated April

The librettist imbued the protagonist with a sense of enlightened love for his people and endowed him with a fictional wife who fights for freedom.

Friedrich may have eschewed acquiring New World colonies and fantasy islands, but his aesthetic production included themes of colonial struggle, and he takes the side of the colonized. Better known for his flute performances, compositions, musical court culture, and improvisation with J. S. Bach, the king of Prussia also wrote the libretto for an opera composed by Graun. First performed in 1755, *Montezuma* depicted the Spanish conqueror Cortes and his defeat of the Aztec emperor. Inspired by Voltaire's play, Friedrich portrays the "barbaric" Montezuma, now also known as Moctezuma II, as a victim of Cortes's brutality. In contrast to his political writings and expansionist wars, Friedrich projects a model of colonial barbarism onto the Spanish invaders and a paradigm of enlightened, ennobled humanity onto the Aztec emperor.

The libretto is divided into three "*Handlungen*" (acts), each punctuated with a ballet. *Montezuma* amplifies human emotions, intrinsic to much eighteenth-century European opera. Here, though, the emotional response, the ability to evoke the fear and pity (*Furcht und Mitleid*) of Aristotelian tragedy, is manifest in the performance itself. In composing the historical characters of Cortes and Montezuma, Friedrich attributes the emotional capacity for *Mitleid* or *Mitleiden* to the purportedly barbaric *Mexicaner*; while the Spanish care only for their god, their emperor, his gold, and his glory, not necessarily in that order. In the first act, Montezuma is prepared to welcome the shipwrecked Cortes and the Spanish according to the principles of hospitality and against the advice of aides: "Er soll als ein Fremder aufgenommen werden Dem ich Beystand und Hülfe schuldig bin"[14] (He shall be received as a stranger / To whom I owe support and assistance). He further assumes a common humanity: "Wenn sie endlich nur als / Fremde zu uns kommen; so verbindet uns / Die Menschlichkeit. (I:8, 41; Even if they come to us / Just as strangers; still we are bound / By our humanity).

In the second act, Cortes reveals his intention to deceive the Aztec emperor; he storms the palace and puts Montezuma in chains. Friedrich inverts the enlightened racial hierarchy: Montezuma repeatedly hurls the

---

2014. https://www.academia.edu/7135439/Opera_at_the_Court_of_Frederick_the_Great_Grauns_Montezuma_as_Royal_Autobiography.

14. *Montezuma, ein musikalisches Trauerspiel* (Berlin: Bey Haude und Spener, 1770), I:7, 37. Quoted from https://www.loc.gov/resource/musschatz.17908.0/?sp=3&st=image&r=-0.631,-0.099,2.263,1.002,0. Further references appear in parenthesis followed by act, scene, and page number(s).

epithet "Barbar!" (II:6, 63; barbarian) at the invader, to whom he has extended hospitality and succor. Predictably, Cortes plays the human sacrifice card (II:6, 65) and extols his religion. Montezuma counters with his religion: "Sie lehrt uns, mit einem jeden, der anders denkt als wir,/ Mitleiden haben" (II:8, 67; It teaches us to have sympahty for everyone who thinks differently than we do). Eupaforice and Erirene dialogue about the plight of the queen and her beloved husband: the latter wonders what kind of heart could lack feeling: "Daß es nicht Mitleiden empfände / Und dir zu helfen bereit wäre?" (II:13, 95; that it does not feel sympathy for you). The third act rushes toward the tragic end, with Eupaforice also leveling accusations of humanity at Cortes, but futilely: "Du siehst unsere Thränen, / Ohne bewegt zu werden . . . Die wahren Helden / Haben menschliche Empfindungen" (III:5, 123–25; You see our tears, / Without being moved . . . True heroes / Have human feelings). Her suicide elicits a cold and conquistadorial comment: "Jetzt sehe ich, / Daß man dieses Volk vertilgen muß, / Wenn man es überwinden will" (III:5, 129; Now I see / that you have to destroy this people, / if you want to conquer them). The motto of conquest promises genocide. This is the king's villain; Friedrich's creative production, epitomized by the fictional version of Montezuma, drafts a view of the noble Indigenous emperor defeated by the barbaric Spanish.

Consistent with the logic of a possible enlightened colonialism, Friedrich rejects some, but not all, slavery. Jürgen Luh has written extensively on the life of the Prussian king, recently including a view into his attitudes toward enslavement. Luh situates Frederick's own position within the context of Voltaire's characterization of the Turks as barbarians. Citing the French philosopher's reaction to the war between Russia and the Ottomans, Luh elucidates the politics and epistemology of the Prussian king. Voltaire, who sided with Catherine II and attempted to enlist Prussian support in the war, derides the Turks, under the leadership of Sultan Mustaphe III, for their rejection of art and treatment of women. Frederick opposed the condition of slavery, as Luh clarifies this opposition with reference to a 1777 treatise of forms of government and power: "Sicherlich ist kein Mensch dazu geboren, der Sklave von seinesgleichen zu sein" (Certainly no human being is born to be a slave to his own kind).[15] He also provides further interpretation of this antislavery

---

15. Quoted in Jürgen Luh, "Friedrich der Große und Said Ali Aga oder Des Königs Verhältnis zur Sklaverei," *Texte des Research Center Sanssouci für Wissen und Gesellschaft (RECS)* #55 (06.03.2023): https://recs.hypotheses.org/10110.

position, observing that the condition of serfdom was foremost in Friedrich's mind. But when the king received a human "gift" in 1772, along with a horse, from a Russian field general, he sent the man back to Turkey via Vienna. The king's correspondence alludes to Said Ali Aga's return with a mention of Belgrade (then under Turkish rule) in March 1772. According to other sources, Said Ali Aga was ultimately received by the sultan, but his fate is uncertain. From several sources, then, Friedrich II lays the foundation for the logic of enlightened colonialism. First, reject extraterritorial possessions. His economic rationale, positioned vis-à-vis Machiavelli, justifies the rejection of distant islands in the Caribbean as phantasms, imagined territories that would only distract from the pursuit of Prussian hegemony in Europe. Finally, he theorized an antislavery, specific to serfdom but which he extended in practice to the "M*hr" and "N*ger" given to him as a gift, enslaved in the spoils of war. On the one hand, this selective reading could indicate a theoretical project for "enlightened colonialism." There is another hand.

To Own the World?

Frederick had critics, among them Lessing. Perhaps the best-known of German Enlightenment authors, Lessing left a legacy of political and aesthetic opposition to tyrannical absolutism. Lessing bore witness to the wars Prussia waged and their effects. In his plays, he thematizes the status of the Prussian veteran in the absence of war: a comedy. The abusive and predatory patriarchy comes under fire in *Emilia Galotti*. Though Lessing traveled little, he gained a reputation as *Weltbürger* largely through reading and writing. With his most prominent literary creations, foremost among them the valedictory *Nathan der Weise* (1779), Lessing established the foundation for a critique of tyranny—manifest in religion—culminating in the sage Nathan, who counterbalances overbearing religious orthodoxies to establish the gold standard of tolerance, though some have raised objections.[16] The play, which earned a justifiable place in posterity for its advocacy of religious pluralism, evinces a tradition of tolerance that has not been without controversy.[17] He does artic-

---

16. Uche Onyedi Okafor, "Mapping Germany's Colonial Discourse: Fantasy, Reality and Dilemma (PhD dissertation, University of Maryland, 2013), 3. This legacy of Lessing's reading can be met with skepticism, for the result is: "This effort consequently contributed to the self-image among Germans of being more humane and cultured than other Europeans."

17. H. B. Nisbet, "On the Rise of Toleration in Europe: Lessing and the German Contribution,"

ulate a civilian, secular pathway to perpetual peace. The Seven Years' War and its impact on Prussia and Frederick's detractors cast a long shadow over a European geography of power that elicited a range of cultural responses to colonial tensions (between England and France) in their competition for dominance. Beyond these major works, Lessing devoted considerable professional energy to the critique of Frederician censorship and centralized power and also to European imperialism as an impediment to knowledge.

In the final year of his life, for example, Lessing immersed himself in a translation project based on his work for the duke of Braunschweig at the library in Wolfenbüttel. From within the confines of German-speaking urban and less urban centers, Lessing also resists the type of religious and racial profiling in his assessment of humankind that so many of his contemporaries indulged. A significant and diverse scholarly archive, however disparate and adept in approaches and ideologies, achieves unusual consensus about the contributions of Lessing's Enlightenment project.[18] In reframing a series of references to Prussian power, Roman mythology, and the colonial rivals laying claim to the Amazon—and to the river's name—I attempt to conjure Lessing's attack on European colonial efforts to expand national public spheres beyond their shores. As an archivist, he exhibited little tolerance for research inaccuracies, but he makes an exemplary error worthy of examination.

His critical gaze falls on Brazil and an impressionistic geography of Portuguese, Dutch, and Spanish "possessions" that share regional characteristics as well as contiguous, if disputed, lands. Several European powers contested the rule of Suriname, for example, until the Dutch established their presence in the late seventeenth century. The Dutch additionally competed with the Portuguese for northern Brazil (Nieuw Holland) between 1630 and 1654.[19] A complicated history, interweaving trade, war, and plantation economies, resulted in the Dutch ultimately surrendering to the Portuguese in 1654, but

---

Modern Language Review 105, no. 4 (October 2010): xxviii–xliv. Nisbet mentions Henryk M. Broder's *Kritik der reinen Toleranz* (Berlin: WJS Verlag, 2008). For an attack on tolerance from a twenty-first-century feminist perspective, see Zana Ramadani, *Die verschleierte Gefahr: Die Macht der muslimischen Mütter und der Toleranzwahn der Deutschen* (Berlin: Europa Verlag, 2017).

18. On his relationship to religion, see Henry E. Allison, *Lessing and the Enlightenment: His Philosophy of Religion and Its Relation to Eighteenth-Century Thought* (Albany: State University of New York Press, 2018).

19. See Michiel van Groesen, *The Legacy of Dutch Brazil* (New York: Cambridge University Press, 2014).

Enlightened Colonialism 63

they remained dominant in Suriname through the efforts of the Dutch West India Company.

Against this backdrop, Lessing found a manuscript in Wolfenbüttel about Brazil; he sought help from a colleague to correct a particular problem. The seventeenth-century travel narrative about Brazil, which turned out to be an administrative report, was republished in 1780 under Braunschweig's auspices. The *Beschreibung des portuguesischen America* (Description of Portuguese America), by Cudena, appeared with an introduction by Lessing, with further notes and additions by Christian Leiste, rector of the ducal school in Wolfenbüttel.[20] Lessing's aphoristic pronouncement, "Nur die Völker sollten die Welt besitzen, die die Welt der Welt doch wenigstens bekannt machen" (Only those peoples should own the world who at least make the world known to the world), posits a provisional model of enlightened colonialism. Lessing's introduction covers the potential problem in the naming of the Marañón River. For Lessing, the failure to circulate knowledge about colonized spaces redounds poorly on the colonizing nations. His concerns rise above the Iberian rivalries in the Amazon region, joined by the Dutch and the British. In this instance, the attack on colonialism is reserved for those powers unable to contribute to the world account of knowledge.

The naming of the river allegedly followed from the man who explored and thus "conquered" the region. Even in the remove of Braunschweig, Lessing intervened in a land dispute, expressed in the need to eliminate ambiguity and credit the discoverer with the discovery and attendant tensions between European and Indigenous provenance. Intersects with Jesuit history and cartography were present as well. Camila Loureira Dias traces the path of Bohemian Jesuit Father Simon Fritz (1654–1725, 1728, or 1730), who produced two versions in 1707 and 1717 with varying border demarcations that became important for sociopolitical discourses about religious and colonial rights to occupy the region.[21] He correctly identifies the Marañón River as the main source for the Amazon, and his demarcations proved useful in the conflict between Portuguese Brazil and the Spanish Peru, but also in establishing Jesuit hegemony. Dias describes the former version as "a tool of territorial expansion," while the 1717 version simplified the representation of the

---

20. Ernst Feder, "Lessing entdeckt Brasilien," *Sonderdruck aus dem Serra-Post Kalender* (Rio de Janeiro, 1952), 3–4.

21. Camila Loureira Dias, "Jesuit Maps and Political Discourse: The Amazon River of Father Samuel Fritz," *The Americas* 69, no. 1 (July 2012): 95–116.

territory and left no trace of the war between colonizing powers that ended just three years prior; this version was reproduced in the most important report of Jesuit activities to a European audience, translated from French into Spanish, German, Italian, and English.[22] By the late 1700s, the name of the Marañón River, which raises Lessing's hackles, had been stabilized, so his interest in the lexical dispute raises some questions answered by his position, a decolonial attempt at Enlightened colonialism. In what follows, I relocate the critique of colonial epistemologies within Lessing's decrying of despotism in Prussia as part of a decolonial Enlightenment moment.

Such moments can be found in the connections between Lessing's critique of the despotic, embodied by European absolutism, and the foundations of a decolonial model of Enlightenment thought, derived from subtexts in several of his works, particularly Lessing's poems: "Das Pferd Friedrich Wilhelms auf der Brücke zu Berlin (Frederick William's horse on the bridge to Berlin)," "Unter das Bildnis des Königs von Preußen (Beneath the image of the King of Prussia)" and "Der 24ste Jenner in Berlin." The first epigram, published in 1771, along with other poems and the poetic fable "Der Tanzbär (The dancing bear)," open into a critique of absolute power that is underwritten by a communicative network of visual and verbal significations that reproduce power. In each, whether explicitly or indirectly, Lessing opposes the condition of slavery to tyranny. His literary work evokes absolutist models of power that Frederick inherits and abuses, under the guise of reason. For example, the iconic Frederick Wilhelm on horseback functions as a transitive verb in the syntax of a coloniality of power; it embodies a moment in a genealogy of Prussian hegemony. The dynastic intricacies subsequently write themselves as linear narratives, self-referentially gathering the legacy of Brandenburg in the slave trade and the prioritizing of infrastructure to the negotiations of acquiring contiguous land. Next, the self-representation of Friedrich der Große as philosopher-king empowers Lessing's vocabulary of critique; he forges a direct link between the philosopher monarch and a wayward colonial travel writer. In his preface, Lessing reinscribes a colonial grammar that structures the relationship between the subject and indirect object, one that simultaneously acknowledges the hegemony of European colonial power and decenters it, tilting that totalizing "Welt" on its axis. But he did make mistakes, and I rely on them for my reading. So I turn briefly to the contingent power of

---

22. Dias, "Jesuit Maps," 111 and 112. Dias refers to volume 12 of the *Lettres édifïantes et curieuses écrites des missions étrangerès par quelques missionnaires de la Compagnie de Jésus.*

signification in *Ernst und Falk: Gespräche für Freimäurer* (Ernst and Falk: Dialogues for Freemasons, 1778) to demonstrate his awareness of colonial exploits in the Americas. These references capture Lessing's opposition to the despotic with a subtext of critique leveled at the colonial enterprise.[23] His dialogue about the origins of Freemasonry and its truths segues into the writing of Nathan[24] and the parable of pluralism.[25] As Dorothea von Mücke has argued, Lessing's work itself contributes to constituting a reading public: "In the case of Lessing," she writes, "a much wider context and spectrum of publications comes into play. For Lessing inhabited and transformed various public spheres."[26] That public encompasses the readership of the world.

Ambivalent Empires

Lessing had a short fuse for fuzzy thinking and the abuse of power. According to H. B. Nisbet, "The main difference between Lessing's perspectivism and that of Leibniz is that Lessing's version incorporates a higher degree of scepticism with regard to obtaining certainty in the truths we believe we possess, not least those of religion."[27] That perspectivism, interpolated with skepticism, extends to Lessing's critique of absolutist abuse of power. In his *Lessing-Legende*, Mehring elaborates on the Enlightenment author's hatred of anything despotic, an antipathy that extended to the Prussian monarch. He writes, for example, "Frederick deeply despised the 'roture,' whose advocate Lessing was, and with his own hands expelled every bourgeois element from the ranks of his officers. Lessing, in absolute agreement with his spiritual

---

23. See my remarks in the introduction on Quijano and the "coloniality of power" to reframe the three-hundred-year cultural and literary narratives from and beyond German-speaking Europe about the imperial enterprise. With particular attention to eighteenth-century models constructed from the relationship between materiality and epistemologies, I locate Lessing's interventions in a discourse about enslavement and freedom. Also, Buck-Morss, in *Hegel, Haiti and Universal History*, as outlined in the introduction, demonstrated the interaction between the historical reality of enslavement and the development of European elevations of freedom and autonomy as concepts.

24. From this crucible of thought, anonymously he published the *Gespräche*, and with freemasonry's origins on his mind, he wrote *Nathan*. On his relationship to religion, see Allison, *Lessing and the Enlightenment*.

25. Nisbet, "On the Rise of Toleration in Europe," xxviii–xliv.

26. Dorothea von Mücke, "Authority, Authorship, and Audience: Enlightenment Models for a Critical Public," *Representations* 111, no. 1 (Summer 2010): 60–87, here 63.

27. Nisbet, "On the Rise of Toleration," xxxvii.

kinsmen Herder and Winckelmann, loathed Frederick's state as 'the most servile country in Europe.'" *Roture* refers to the seigneurial system of prerevolutionary France of tenuring land in exchange for collecting rents, rather than feudal obligations and personal service. Roturiers were essentially made up of the lower classes, the petit bourgeois for whom Lessing advocated. The ownership of land is the essential connection to my larger argument. Further, boundaries, both literal and figurative, characterize the despotic. According to Mehring, "But essentially petty despotism remained everywhere what it was and was bound to be. There was no punishment for its grotesque and ghastly crimes," and with regard to *Emilia Galotti*, "the play is rooted in the economic structure of the society in which Lessing's figures lived. And the author could not go beyond those barriers."[28]

Other scholars maintain that Mehring goes too far in portraying Lessing as a rebel. In the 1930s, German professor William R. Gaede reads Lessing's comments on the Prussian king alongside the former's biography: his dashed hopes for a position in Berlin, Saxon origins and Prussian officer friends, disappointment in Braunschweig, where he deferred marriage until he could afford it. Gaede contextualizes the post-1871 critics who saw Frederick and Lessing "als Einheit" (as a unit).[29] His analysis quotes the second stanza of the dancing bear fable to underscore Lessing's distaste for court intrigue and self-advancement, and justifies the dismissal of the *Lobgedichte* (praise poems).[30] The larger Lessing project, however, takes a position on slavery and colonialism, as I argue, that may be invested in more marginal texts, but my reading hopes to drive a wedge in that image of unity.

Lessing's advocacy of the bourgeois in Europe and aesthetic innovations inspires a model of reading that has recently expanded the horizons of his work. Obenewaa Oduro-Opuni, for example, analyzes Lessing's bourgeois tragedy *Emilia Galotti* in the context of her close examination of *Sklavenstücke* (slave plays) and their connections to abolitionist awareness, pre-

---

28. Mehring, The Lessing Legend, A. S Grogan translation, https://www.marxists.org/archive/mehring/1892/lessing/chap2. htm; and https://www.marxists.org/archive/mehring/1892/lessing/chap4. htmIts etymology: "From Middle French, French roture status of an estate held by a commoner, estate held by a commoner, status of a commoner, estate for which rent is paid." *Oxford Dictionary* on lexico: https://www.lexico.com/en/definition/roture.

29. William R. Gaede, "Wie dachte Lessing über Friedrich II.?" *Journal of English and German Philology* 35, no. 4 (October 1936): 546–65, here 546.

30. Gaede, "Wie dachte Lessing," 550, 551.

sumed absent from German eighteenth-century literature.[31] Targeting the despotism of the aristocracy resonates with antislavery convictions.[32] In his preface to the *Beschreibung des portuguesischen America*, Lessing unpacks the mechanics of colonization in Brazil. The notes and additions by Leiste more explicitly parse the performatives of "discovery" and "exploration,"[33] while Lessing's introduction disputes the naming of the Marañón River. He opens with a lexical explanation to avoid any confusion or further faulty translations and transcription of the manuscript in the library's holdings: German printers could not reproduce the diacritical ñ from Spanish. Convinced he was correcting a mistake, and postulating that the name of the land informed the name of the river, rather than the inverse, Lessing died before his colleague Leiste was able to sort the problem, with the help of a different publisher and a Jesuit priest, who corrected many of Leiste's errors, which the latter appreciated. In this preface, however, Lessing delivers an indictment of coloniality predicated on knowledge that equates naming with ownership. In this instance, the attack on European acquisitions is reserved for those powers unable to contribute productively to the circulation of knowledge. Prussian power models the abuse.

Lessing displayed an ambivalent relationship to Berlin and the power of the Prussian king, whom he disparaged for ignoring German-language culture and literature. In the genre of the *Sinngedicht* (epigram), Frederick as regal signifier and the signified of power constitute a semiotic alliance Lessing disrupts. Frederick was particular about his self-presentation and knew well to control the production and reproduction of himself. He kept a series of portrait painters occupied throughout his life. Prominent among them is Johann Georg Ziensis, allegedly the only portrait he sat for (1764). Two women who engaged in history painting also rendered a Rococo interpretation of the king, one of whom is Anna Dorothea Therbusch.[34] His image

---

31. Obenawaa Oduro-Opuni, "Modes of Transnationalism and Black Revisionist History: Slavery, The Transatlantic Slave Trade and Abolition in 18th and 19th Century German Literature" (PhD diss., Arizona State University, 2020), 4.

32. Oduro-Opuni, *Modes of Transnationalism and Black Revisionist History*, 303–4.

33. Feder, "Lessing entdeckt Brasilien," 3–4.

34. After the second Silesian war, he made an attempt to establish a porcelain manufacture to rival Meissen's. When that effort failed, he founded his own, KPM, in 1763. A quick study in the ways of luxury and diplomacy, Frederick began using porcelain sets as diplomatic gifts—royal swag. https://www.smb.museum/ausstellungen/detail/porzellane-fuer-die-schloesser-friedrichs-des-grossen/.

was reproduced as a porcelain bust, approximating marble. Though Frederick eschewed displaying images of himself in his residences, he circulated the portraits as gifts. His later portrayals irked him, but he did love his horse. (Iconic is Daniel Nikolaus Chodowiecki's "Friedrich II. Zu Pferde," from 1777.) Frederick's possessions transform into attributes of his power, from the beloved greyhounds Alkmene and Hasenfuß to Condé, his favorite horse, whose skeleton was preserved and displayed. A brief sketch of Lessing's disruption of the imagistic dissemination of power reveals associations between the ship of state, genealogies of greatness, and connections to Prussian interventions in the enslavement of Africans.

Berlin displayed its status as capital of an ambitious European power. Lessing employs the genre of poetry to comment on the visual inscriptions of monarchic presence in the Hohenzollern genealogy. In "Das Pferd Friedrich Wilhelms auf der Brücke zu Berlin," Lessing anthropomorphizes the horse of the Great Elector: "Ihr bleibet vor Verwundrung stehn, Und zweifelt doch an meinem Leben?!"[35] (You stop and stare in amazement, and yet you doubt my life?). This *Sinngedicht* remarks on the ability of the equestrian statue to impose the presence of the Great Elector into the future. The legacy of power is perhaps the inspiration for the multiple poems dedicated to the projection of a monarch's image. In "Der 24ste Jenner in Berlin" (The 24th of January in Berlin, Frederick the Great's birthday), he invokes the muses of classical antiquity in an almost ekphrastic description of contemporary power viewed through an imperial lens: "Welch leichter Morgentraum ließ, auf den heilgen Höhen, / Der Musen Fest um *Friedrichs* Bild" (What gentle morning dream allowed, on the holy heights, / Of the muses' festival [to dance] around Frederick's image).[36] The influence of classical aesthetics on the equestrian bronze and marble pedestal posits equivalence between contemporary Berlin and the antecedent, imperial Rome. Lessing's poems highlight the myth-making power of art. A close reading of the "praise poems" opens an apercu on the poet's ambivalence toward the monarch, a possible short-circuit in the ritual meaning of public birthday celebrations. The muses, for example, will never dance around the king, only his image. The interplay of presence and absence, the performative power of naming, connects Lessing's aesthetics of praise/blame with the colonial presence/absence, as I will demonstrate below.

---

35. Lessings *Gesammelte Werke*, 2 vols. (Leipzig: G. J. Göschen'sche Verlagsbuchhandlung, 1865), 1:9.
36. Lessings *Gesammelte Werke*, I:28.

In the epigram that locates the poet passing beneath the image of the king of Prussia, Lessing uncouples the self-identified philosopher (portrait of his with books) from the politician.

"Unter das Bildnis des Königs von Preußen"
Wer kennt ihn nicht?
Die hohe Miene spricht
Den Denkenden. Der Denkende allein
Kann Philosoph, kann Held, kann beides sein.[37]

Who does not know him?
The high aspect speaks
To the thinking. The thinking man alone
Can be a philosopher, can be a hero, can be both.

The curators of a Frederick-based research project point out in the description of a painting by Anton Friedrich König, 1769, that it reflects "how Frederick the Great wanted to be seen during his lifetime, namely as an intellectual surrounded by the books in his library, and as an author historian, and philosopher."[38] The library was the most beloved room in the refuge of Sanssouci; Frederick signed his work as "The Philosopher of Sanssouci."[39]

In his Prussian phase, Lessing celebrates the simultaneous philosopher and king through this poem. The intertwining of knowledge and power leads Lessing into a different, more critical register. Facing the realities of wars—at Frederick's behest—Lessing changes course as he elaborates, in marginal texts, a semiotics of colonial power. Increasingly, he turns his critical eye toward the circuits of dependence between Europe and the Americas. Moving away from praise, he tells fables of debasement. In an animal allegory, Lessing associates the ostensible refinement and politesse at court with the enactment of slavery. In the poetic fable "Der Tanzbär" (the dancing bear),

---

37. Gotthold Ephraim Lessing, *Werke*, ed. Herbert G. Göpfert in Zusammenarbeit with Karl Eibl, Helmut Göbel, Karl S. Guthke, Gerd Hillen, Albert von Schirmding, and Jörg Schönert, vols. 1–8 (München: Hanser, 1970), 49. This poem is not included in the 1864 edition.

38. Curators Dr. Jürgen Luh, Dr. Irene Kosmanová, Truc Vu Minh, MA (SPSG, Research Center, Sanssouci). Artsandculture.google.com/exhibit/images-of-frederick-schloss-sanssouci/kwJSLcu12YrVJQ?hl=en.

39. https://artsandculture.google.com/exhibit/images-of-frederick-schloss-sanssouci/kwJSLcu12YrVJQ?hl=en.

we meet a trained bear who breaks his chains and, among other bears, he performs his master dance for the wild audience. He has learned to entertain, insisting that it is art: "Das lernt man in der Welt" (One learns this in the world). An old bear responds that the "art" "Zeigt deinen niedren Geist und deine Sklaverei" (Shows your lower mind and your enslavement).[40] The wild bear in Lessing develops this blunt dismissal of a performance in his work at the duke of Brunswick's archive. An expression of his wide-ranging interests, centered in scholarly rigor and the practice of tolerance, Lessing identifies a path toward enlightened colonialism through mediation between the geographical peripheries of empire and their epistemological center.

Toward the end of his life, Lessing frankly assessed a travel book in a search for reliable place names in the New World. The text is Antonio de Ulloa's (1716–1775), a contemporary Spanish officer and author of a travel book among the library's holdings. In particular, Lessing objects to the sloppiness of de Ulloa's reporting on the topography: "Dieses Raisonnement scheint mir ein wenig sehr spanisch, und der aufgedunsenen leeren Beredsamkeit eines Dominicaners würdiger, als der Reisebeschreibung eines Philosophen" (This reasoning seems to me a little bit very Spanish, and more worthy of the long-winded, empty rhetoric of a Dominican rather than the travelogue of a philosopher).

Lessing further disparages Spanish colonizers by praising the reasonable expansion of knowledge in the manuscript. At the very least, the touted author acknowledges the native provenance of the river, its name, and its plural meanings:

> Man weiß auch nicht, wie ihn die Indianer genannt haben; ob es wohl, glaublich ist, daß sie ihm einen, und manchmal auch wohl mehrere Namen beygelegt haben müsen. Da verschiedne Nationen an seinen Ufern wohnten: so war es ganz natürlich, daß eine jegliche ihm einen besondern Namen beylegte, oder denjenigen beybehielt, den ihm eine andere Nation gegeben hatte. Allein die ersten Spanier, welche hierher gekommen sind, haben sich entweder nicht genugsam darunzbekümmert, oder sind gleich damals, durch die übrigen Namen, die man diesem Strome beylegte, in Verwirrung gesetzt worden, so daß das Andenken derselben in der Geschichte nirgends aufbehalten worden ist.

---

40. Lessing, "Der Tanzbär," *G.E. Lessings Gesammelte Werke*, 2 vols. (Leipzig: G. J. Göschen'sche Verlagsbuchhandlung, 1865), I:31.

Nor does anyone know what the Indians called it; whether it is possible, probable, that they called it by one, sometimes even many names. Because different nations lived on the banks, thus it was highly likely that one gave it a special name, or that it retained the name another nation had given it. But the first Spaniards who came here either did not care about it sufficiently or even then were so confused by the other names given to the river that their memory is nowhere retained in history.

Lessing has undertaken a search for the source, much like the "explorers" themselves, but he concedes the limits of knowledge about origins. The Indigenous name or names cannot be known after European landfall. As archivist and truth teller, Lessing formulates a decolonial critique aimed at the subsequent struggles among politically motivated Spanish and Portuguese authors about what else remains inaccessible because erased or otherwise also unknown ("Man weiß auch nicht"). He acknowledges the plurality of names and nations and that all else remains speculation in Lessing's semiotics of power and its abuse.

In *Ernst und Falk*, Lessing argues that national identities within Europe rival each other as well. References to knowledge, revolution, and transatlantic infrastructure haunt the subtext. The recent war of independence filters into the masonic dialogue: a global conflict which reverberated locally, for the duke of Brunswick sold men as mercenaries to fight on the side of the English in order to fill his state's coffers at home.[41] Moreover, the dialogue between Falk, Lessing's mouthpiece, and Ernst turns to the competing identities between European nation-states that preclude any idea of a unitary humanity.

> Das ist: wenn itzt ein Deutscher einem Franzosen, ein Franzose einem Engländer oder umgekehrt begegnet, so begegnet nicht mehr ein *blosser* Mensch einem *blossen Menschen* die vermöge ihrer gleichen Natur gegeneinander angezogen werden, sondern ein *solcher* Mensch begegnet einem *solchen* Menschen, die ihrer verschiednen Tendenz sich bewusst sind, welches sie gegeneinander kalt, zurückhaltend, misstrauisch macht, noch ehe sie führ ihre einzelne Person das geringste miteinander zu schaffen und zu teilen haben.[42]

---

41. I rely on Channinah Maschler's work on the translation for much of this section. See her "Lessing's Ernst and Falk, Dialogues for Freemasons. A Translation with Notes," in *Interpretation: A Journal of Political Philosophy* 14:1 (1986): 1–50.

42. Lessing, *Ernst und Falk*.

When a German meets a Frenchman or a Frenchman an Englishman, he does not meet him simply as a human being, a fellow man to whom he is drawn because of their shared nature. They meet as German and French, French and English. Aware of these national differences, they are cold, distant, suspicious even before they have had any personal dealings.[43]

The contingencies of misunderstanding, the false assumption of a singular state and a unitary power, and the hegemonic structures of statecraft can hinge upon a rhetorical turn; a metonymy, an adjacency. Humanity devolves along the lines of national identities.

Those rivalries inform Lessing's position in his preface, where he takes issue with Cudena's sloppiness in crediting the name of the river to a Spanish captain whose existence seems questionable. The auspices of the name evoke the three rings parable. According to the Cudena, each of the "Weltteile" (parts of the world) has its mighty river: Europe has the Donau; Asia the Ganges, Africa the Nile, and America the Amazon. The river in question is known by three names as well: the Maranjon, the Amazon, and the Orellana. Lessing takes issue with the assertion that the original name is claimed to be Marañón. He disregards possible Indian names; instead, he points out that the original text and the German translation are marred with egregious errors. Lessing is further incensed by the negligence implicit in the colonial project that shares information only for exploitation, withholding contributions to the bank of world knowledge.

> Es ist kaum glaublich, wie weit wir in der Kenntniß der Amerikanischen Länder, die unter Spanischer und Portugiesischer Bothmäßigkeit stehen, seit anderthalbhundert Jahren zurück sind: und doch ist es wahr. Nur die Völker sollte die Welt besitzen, welche die Welt der Welt doch wenigstens bekannt machen!

> It is hard to believe how far back we are in knowledge of the American lands that have been under Spanish and Portuguese rule for a century and a half; and yet it is true. Only those peoples should own the world who at least make the world known to the world!

In Leiste's extensive commentaries, he takes up the gauntlet Lessing casts, after the librarian's death in 1781. Leiste speculates that the Spanish captain

---

43. Lessing, *Ernst und Falk*, Maschler translation, 23.

in fact named himself after the lands he captured. Feder sorted out the issue in 1952, correctly identifying the original author as Pedro Cadena de Vilha; Leiste received help from the Jesuit priest Anselm Eckart to correct further infelicities in his remarks, though the publication never materialized. Feder focuses on the brief gloss that the origin of the name "Maranjon" is "unbekannt" (unknown).[44] The significance of the debate is overshadowed by the fact that the Wolfenbüttel library had in its collection the first German-language report on Brazil. Lessing's role becomes peripheral. Yet it makes sense to recall that the relationship between naming and measuring land constituted discovering, conquering, and owning it. In the poems, Lessing briefly pays tribute to, then questions the monarch's power. In *Ernst und Falk*, he insists on the contingent histories of power and truth, which originates in etymological error. Finally, his insistence on diacritical marks, untranslatable between Spanish originals and German reproductions, illuminates Lessing's belief in accountability, a lexical error with repercussions for the power struggle among European powers in the Southern Cone. In each instance, Lessing exposes the coloniality of power as both absolute and aberrant. Lessing—though through an act of misreading—models the project of decentering imperial power as the only form of enlightened colonialism.

Throughout this chapter, I have argued that the copresence of historically and metaphorically enslaved in German-speaking Brandenburg and beyond demonstrates the coexistence of colonial and critical discourses that would decolonize Prussian imperialism, though these do not constitute a dialogue. Both rely on an Enlightenment model of knowledge and its dissemination; both factor national and regional rivalries into the process of selecting what is worth knowing about Africa and the Americas. Enlightened colonialism opened channels (and canals) in Berlin to global trade, diplomatic negotiations for Caribbean holdings to leverage cabinet wars, the collection of "Hofm*hren," the acquisition of manuscripts, the import of curiosities, and objects of scientific study. From Berlin, he identified tyranny in the monarch. From Braunschweig, Lessing cast his reading eyes across the world.

The vicissitudes of German national history chronically reinvent the place of literary and cultural luminaries in the wider world. Lessing and Goethe, among such luminaries, wrote and worked across the Atlantic, without themselves traveling. Their engagement with the colonial transatlantic world, however tenuous or marginalized, inspired twentieth-century Ger-

---

44. Feder, "Lessing entdeckt Brasilien," 14.

man speakers to read through the cultural archives of exile and immigration. One scholar and journalist, Ernst Feder, uncovered connections between eighteenth-century German-language culture and what became his home in exile, Brazil. Feder, a German Jew forced to flee Nazi Germany, lectured about Lessing's late work (and also on Goethe's involvement with the explorer and geologist Wilhelm Ludwig von Eschwege). Feder, unlike some others I discuss in this book, was not looking toward a genealogy of Germanness to legitimize entitlements or justify white settlerism. His prize-winning 1952 text "Lessing entdeckt Brasilien"[45] (Lessing discovers Brazil) praises Lessing for his convictions about the circulation of knowledge and its ability to maintain selective ignorance about the transatlantic world.

The desire to inscribe Lessing into a national narrative from a twentieth-century perspective of exile is understandable in the historical context. Lessing's investment in enlightened colonialism extends to the connection among tyrannical European power practices and their entanglements in the Americas. From Leipzig to Berlin to Braunschweig, Lessing recognized abuses and named them. He showed contempt for the self-enslaving performance of the dancing bear, and he got to the core of what it means to be human in the voice of the "wild" one who scoffs at the self-debasement. But he also acknowledged the difference between courtly preening and the mercenary trade. He was not alone in forging these connections. Lessing's freemasonry dialogue appeared in 1778. He died in 1781, just prior to the indenture of translator, author, and teacher Johann Gottlieb Seume (1763–1810). Born into modest circumstances, Seume lost his father in battle. He embarked on an education in theology, but found it limiting. On his way to begin military training, Seume was pressed into service as a mercenary for the Landgrave of Hesse-Kassel, ostensibly an "enlightened" despot.

Seume recounts his life and experiences in poetry and prose; he tells of the miserable voyage to the Americas (1782–1783), and after returning to Europe he was taken by Prussians and imprisoned until 1787. After that, he traveled and wrote. His volume of poetry, published in 1800, went into two further editions by 1809, an indication of its popularity. In prefaces, Seume disparages the works, hesitating even to label them poems.[46] One poem, "Der

---

45. Feder, "Lessing entdeckt Brasilien," Feder's work on Goethe has received considerably more attention. See Sylk Schneider, *Goethes Reise nach Brasilien. Gedankenkreise eines Genies* (Weimar: Weimarer Taschenbuch Verlag, 2008).

46. The prefaces appear in the volume *Gedichte von Johann Gottlieb Seume* (Leipzig: Reclam, 1801, 1804, 1809), 5–10. The author notes that many of the poems had already appeared in print.

Wilde," echoes the decolonial moments in Lessing's fable of the dancing bear. Though Lessing indicts the court performer as self-enslaved and celebrates the wisdom of his wild counterpart, the critique of power and the hegemonic force of compulsory civilizing remains in the realm of animal fantasy. Seume, however, insists his poem tells a true story. "Der Wilde" (The savage) tells of a "European" settler (Pflanzer) in Canada, presumably French as the poem takes place near Quebec, and his engagement with a "Kanadier," a Huron, who, on a journey to sell wares, is caught in a storm. He seeks shelter from the European, who slams the door in his face. The situation is reversed: the settler is hopelessly lost in the woods and seeks shelter and aid from the Huron. Only after the latter shows the European generous hospitality and points him in the right direction does the European recognize the Jäger (hunter). A stammered apology elicits the response:

> Ruhig lächelnd sagte der Hurone:
> Seht, ihr fremden klugen, weißen Leute,
> Seht, wir Wilden sind doch beßre Menschen!
> Und er schlug sich seitwärts in die Büsche.[47]

> Quietly smiling the Huron said:
> Behold, you foreign clever white people,
> Behold, we savages are indeed better humans!
> And he slipped sideways into the woods.

Seume adds the footnote:

> Diese Erzählung habe ich, als ich selbst in Amerika und in der dortigen Gegend war, als eine wahre Geschichte gehört. Sie interessierte mich durch ihre ächte reine primitive Menschengüte, die so selten durch unsere höhere Cultur gewinnt. Ob man gleich ähnliche hat, so habe ich sie hier doch nicht unterdrücken wollen.[48]

> I heard this narrative when I myself was in America and in that region, as a true story. It interested me through its authentic, pure, primitive humanity

---

The third, expanded, revised edition: *Gedichte* (Wien und Prag: Franz Hans, 1810).
   47. Seume, "Der Wilde," in *Gedichte*, 57–60, here 60.
   48. Seume, *Gedichte*, 253 note 2.

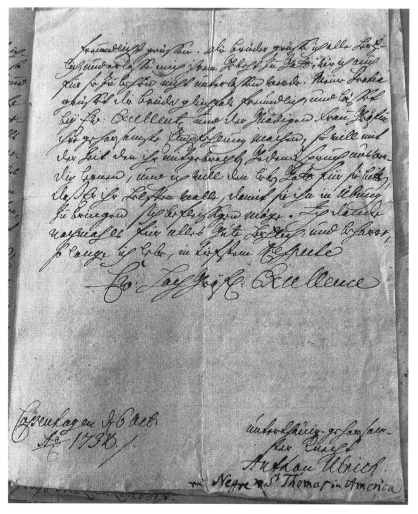

Figure 11. Letter from Anton Ulrich, Copenhagen, 1730. Unitätsarchiv Herrnhut, R.15.B.a.12.e.

that so seldom benefits from our higher culture. Although there is also a similar one, I still did not want to quash it here.

Seume's footnote to the story raises questions about sources and stories, filtered through predominantly white institutions, from the military to the spectrum of religious sects; archives rarely provide complete answers, but as I began this chapter with reference to Oldendorp's antislavery treatise on Danish possessions in the West Indies and the conversion mission of the Unitätskirche, I return to one source in its closing.

The Herrnhut Moravian Archive houses a collection of church correspondence that includes multiple letters from Blacks in the Danish colony to the king of Denmark.[49] "In her work on "Protestant Supremacy," Katharine Gerbner acknowledges the agency assumed by converted Blacks who presumed to write to the Danish king: "Take, for example, the letters that black Moravians wrote to the Danish monarchs in 1739 after they were beaten for attending worship services. The white slave owners 'burn our books, [and] call our baptism the baptism of dogs,' they wrote."[50] Protest against limits to Black religious practice took place, telling truth to power, albeit a distant one. Still within the perimeters of a separatist Protestant sect (Pietist), conversion presumes the capacity for empowerment, the claiming of identity. In another example, the enslaved Anton Ulrich signs his name, an exonym, with his race: "Negre" and place, "St. Thomas in America" (figure 11).

Black agency in the West Indies was hard-won, framed in Christian practices, yet uncompliant. At the same time, poets and philosophers in German-speaking Europe were segregating political freedom. Yet we can detect a fundamental disconnect in convoluted colonial logics. Religious conversion confers agency, thus enabling rights to worship without persecution, at least in theory. Yet the freedom remains spiritual and presumptive; it does not mean emancipation. Consequently, freedom as a European political condition becomes part of a decolonial fantasy that occludes the historical facts of the transatlantic slave trade. The next chapter explores the interplay between philosophical and literary discourses on enslavement, autonomy, and savagery.

---

49. They are: "Ein Schreiben von 50 N*gern an den König von Dänemark, aufgesetzt und unterschrieben von Pieter Mingo, 15. Februar 1739"; "Schreiben von 250 N*gern an den König [mehrfach]"; the "Schreiben einiger N*gerbrüder an die Westindische Kompanie. Eigenhändiges Konzept des mitunterschriebenen Negers David"; and "Das Schreiben der N*ger an den König."

50. Katherine Gerbner, "Protestant Supremacy: The Story of a Neologism," *Church History* 88, no. 3 (September 2019), 773–80, here 779. A freed African woman wrote to the queen about her syncretic Christianity, Gerbner adds (780 note 45).

CHAPTER THREE

Enslaved Souls, Perfect Freedom, and Savagery

Enslaved bodies need not, according to Enlightenment theory, host enslaved souls. This colonial logic implies agency, which, as demonstrated in the previous chapter, becomes increasingly racialized through scenes of persuasion, enacted in the transatlantic world through religious conversion. Though this discourse does not unfold chronologically—rather, colonial narratives are inflected and resuscitated to revise national histories—it spreads from theological to political debate, the latter reflected in philosophical and literary texts devoted not to the color of the soul, but of the skin, and its influence on human rights. Enlightenment scholar Andrew S. Curran opens his stunning work, *The Anatomy of Blackness*, with an example of probing, literally, for the depth of Blackness. Curran writes, "In 1618, the influential Parisian anatomist Jean Riolan the Younger became the first person to seek out the precise source of the blackness within African skin."[1] He elaborates on the specification of the *rete mucosum*, the genealogy of empirical, experimental inquiry to determine with anatomical correctness and the source of pigmentation, and incorporates anatomy into the climate theories and scriptural speculations about the origin of racial differences. This chapter elaborates on influential and lesser-known texts that thematize philosophical and literary racial profiling. References to Immanuel Kant's racist theory frame Friedrich Schiller's concept of freedom to define universality, advancing the lofty idea that freedom itself is a universally available choice. These ideas—that freedom is universally available to all who choose it—persists in the contemporary poetry of political protest against tyranny and barbarity. Enslaved whiteness on European shores overshadows the transatlantic slave trade; Blackness and

---

1. Andrew S. Curran, *The Anatomy of Blackness: Science and Slavery in an Age of Enlightenment* (Baltimore: Johns Hopkins University Press, 2011), 1. Further references to this volume are followed by page numbers in parenthesis.

Indigeneity of the Americas enter the discourse as measures of European colonizers' ability to civilize the world.

Kantian Savagery and the Will to Freedom

Widely debated in contemporary scholarship on race theory and the Enlightenment, Kant's three major interventions on race have elicited a range of polemical responses. Of his "On the Different Races of Human Beings" (1775); "Determination of the concept of a human race" (1785); and finally his "On the Use of Teleological Principles in Philosophy" (1788), the 1775 essay informs my argument. Kant believes climate and its influence on chemical processes determine skin color. True to form, the imperative of reason can counter the degeneration of the human species. While he insists on the criterion of "universally and unfailingly hereditary" to establish traits that define human race,[2] his logic exposes anxiety about any deviation from white paternity in every example he gives: defective women mating, experimentally mixing races, and the uncontainable boundlessness of the human imagination, all of which need to be disciplined by the instrument of his reason. Others have elaborated on Kant's racism. I alight on it briefly to emphasize the naturalization of masculinity, whiteness, and reason in the hegemony of Kantian savagery. My argument acknowledges the insights of philosopher of science Huaping Lu-Adler, who has published on Kant's use of testimony in developing his theory of race,[3] and also on Kant and what she calls "lazy savagery, racialized."[4] In a

---

2. Immanuel Kant, "Determination of the concept of a human race," in *Immanuel Kant: Anthropology, history and education*, edited by Holly Wilson and Günther Zöller, introduced and translated by the editors (Cambridge: Cambridge University Press, 2013), 147-59, here 149.

3. Huaping Lu-Adler, "Kant's Use of Travel Reports in Theorizing about Race—A Case Study about How Testimony Features in Natural Philosophy," *Studies in History and Philosophy and Philosophy of Science* 91 (2022): 10–19. See also Wendy Sutherland, *Staging Blackness and Performing Whiteness in Eighteenth-Century German Drama* (New York: Routledge, 2016), 15–19. Sutherland engages the seminal work, Emmanuel Chukwudi Eze's, "The Color of Reason: The Idea of 'Race' in Kant's Anthropology," in *Postcolonial African Philosophy: A Critical Reader*, ed. Emmanuel Chukwudi Eze (Cambridge: Blackwell, 1997), 103-40. Here I accept as given that these are "raced" sites; my interest is rather in the politicization of enslavement to advance European concepts of freedom.

4. Lu-Adler identifies the use of travel and testimony in Kant to corroborate his arguments. He relies on a motivated relationship between human race and the four *Weltteile* (parts of the world) with the Ur-Africans ensconced in Gambia. Informing his rationale is the 1768 report by

twisted logic, laziness causes enslavement, which produces Blackness. We find a corollary to this equation in the definition of universal humanity.

In 1789, Friedrich Schiller formulates his academic address at Jena as a question: "Was heisst und zu welchem Ende studiert man Universalgeschichte?"[5] He intervenes in the contemporary discourse about the totality of world history and the most fruitful path toward completion of knowledge, toward an immutable notion of truth. To conjure up a straw man, a lamentable human being who has science and art at his disposal, who nonetheless aspires to nothing more than wealth. Schiller writes,

> Beklagenswerter Mensch, der mit dem edelsten aller Werkzeuge, mit Wissenschaft und Kunst, nichts höheres will und ausrichtet, als der Taglöhner mit dem schlechtesten!—der im Reiche der vollkommensten Freiheit eine Sklavenseele mit sich herum trägt![6]

> Deplorable human, who, with the noblest of all tools, with science and art, who desires and achieves nothing more than the day laborer with the worst!—who in the realm of the most perfect freedom carries within him the soul of a slave.[7]

Schiller's moral message posits the conditions of absolute freedom, presumed to exist in the realm of thought. Even here, Schiller's rhetoric relies on a Kantian moment of agency: the individual chooses his enslavement. Though his formulation is not a direct allusion to the language of "selbstverschuldete Unmündigkeit" made famous in Kant's answer to the question of what

---

James Lind, "An Essay on Diseases Incidental to Europeans in Hot Climates." She quotes several important passages on the nature of Black blood; the impact of air and sun, briefly, on the role of climate in determining race and its hereditability; and the bodily functions, such as breathing to expel an excess of acids and sweating to perform the same work, as significant for the implicit and explicit racial hierarchy Kant imputes. See her "Kant's Use of Travel Reports," 17.

5. Friedrich Schiller, "Was heisst und zu welchem Ende studiert man Universalgeschichte? Eine akademische Antrittsrede," in Friedrich Schiller, *Werke und Briefe in 12 Bänden*, edited by Harro Hilzinger et al. Vol. 6, "Historische Schriften und Erzählungen," ed. Otto Dann (Frankfurt: Deutscher Klassiker Verlag, 1988-), vol. 6: 411–31, here 411.

6. Schiller, "Was heisst und zu welchem Ende studiert man Universalgeschichte?" 413–14.

7. My translation, with consultation of the English version, "What Is, and to What End do We Study Universal History," trans. Caroline Stephan and Robert Trout, in *Friedrich Schiller: Poet of Freedom* Vol. II. The Schiller Institute, https://archive.schillerinstitute.com/transl/Schiller_essays/universal_history.html. No pagination.

is Enlightenment, Schiller needs slavery as metaphor. The body of the civil servant, the *"Brotgelehrter,"* can choose to carry around the soul of a slave.

Schiller seeks to transform the ambitions of the bread-fed civil servants, with their narrow focus and rigid thinking, into global citizens, to invoke contemporary parlance. With the category of universality informing his theory, he cites examples of world exploration to expand the historical horizons of the minds he aims to turn toward philosophy. In effect, the study of universal history enhances the worldview of the new student cohort. Presumably eschewing to carry within him the enslaved soul, the ideal student rises above the local and connects with his "other brothers"; and "he meets them where all enlightened minds find them together."[8] Having set the core position, study of all things from the perspective of the center, Schiller elaborates on the immediate topic. Beginning with the discoveries of "European mariners" of distant shores and their inhabitants, he laments the primitive childhood of mankind reflected there. Schiller thus projects a common chronotope onto any non-European people. Striking in this inventory is his knowledge of the transatlantic slave trade. He writes, for example, in a register that inflects an exculpatory argument about enslavement:

> War, however, was with them all, and the flesh of the vanquished enemy was not seldom the prize of victory. Among others, acquainted with various leisures of life, who had already achieved a higher level of culture, slavery and despotism presented us a dreadful picture of them. Once we find a tyrant in Africa trading his subjects for a gulp of brandy; another time they would be slaughtered on his grave to serve him in the underworld."[9]

Schiller ascribes blame for the slave trade to the African tyrants and despots who abuse their subjects, moving quickly from the practice of enslaving defeated enemies as the spoils of war to the selling and slaughtering of one's "own" subjects.

These works capture the tensions between universality and particularity that govern German colonial discourses and practices. Alongside the political transferability of enslavement—as agentic—across racial difference, German-language intellectuals and later colonial activists wrote extensively on the equivalence of *Leibeigenschaft* or indentured servitude as slavery; the

---

8. Schiller, "What Is, and to What End," no page.
9. Schiller, "What Is, and to What End," no page.

plight of white slaves[10] was portrayed as horrific, worse than conditions of plantation labor. In the early 1820s, colonial recruiters highlighted the more humane treatment of enslaved Africans in the Americas, where Blacks fared better than they would in their native lands; immigrants who left German-speaking Europe for a range of reasons throughout the nineteenth and into the early twentieth century were memorialized in popular literature as themselves enslaved, transported like freight, subject to tyrannical masters, and self-identified among the persecuted.[11] As I demonstrate, ethnographic tropes of Amerindians, the enslaved, and the ideal European settler-recruit persist across time and genres of fact and fiction. While Brazil was never a colony, German-speaking emigrants in the late nineteenth century either self-identified as "colonists," or hoped it eventually would be. To maintain an entitled subject position, however, a colonial narrative emerges around 1800 about white enslavement and slavery as metaphor, as a political choice.

Enslaved Whiteness

More specifically, the competitive victimization principle used to claim equal risk for Christians unfolds in the verbal and visual arts that document the experience of whites enslaved by Muslim pirates. As Justin Smith summarizes, the sixteenth- and seventeenth-century representation of slavery had not yet "taken on a rigidly racial dimension for Europeans, but was as likely to be associated in their minds with the Ottoman slave trade or with the economic system of ancient Rome."[12] These histories are recycled in the visual

---

10. The enslavement of Europeans exists historically, from feudal serfdom to sex trafficking, but the escalation of the transatlantic slave trade inflected the trope of the "white slave," positioning European identity as a more deserving victim. Further, the white slave features in immigration histories, especially German speakers in the Americas. See Bernd Brunner, *Nach Amerika: Die Geschichte der deutschen Auswanderung* 2nd ed. (Munich: C. H. Beck, 2017), 56.

11. More familiar literary texts about slavery and the colonial fight for the Caribbean, such as Heinrich von Kleist's "Die Verlobung in St. Domingo" (1811; "The betrothal in St. Domingo") and Caroline Auguste Fischer's "William der N*ger" (1817; William the N*gro), have received significant scholarly attention. For an illuminating reading of these works with Herder, see Joanna Raisbeck, "Race and Colonialism around 1800: Herder, Fischer, Kleist," *Publications of the English Goethe Society* 99, no. 2 (2022): 140–56. See also my "From Miracles to Miscegenation: Enlightening Skin," in *Colonialism and Enlightenment: The Legacies of German Race Theory*, ed. Daniel Leonhard Purdy and Bettina Brandt (Oxford: Oxford University Press, forthcoming 2025).

12. Justin E. H. Smith, *Nature, Human Nature, and Human Difference: Race in Early Modern*

Enslaved Souls, Perfect Freedom, and Savagery 83

Figure 12. *Rédemption des Pères de la Merci à Tunis* ("The Purchase of Christian Captives from the Barbary States") (Anonymous). Photograph by Christian Zonza. Cover image of *Le commerce des captifs: les intermèdiaires dans l'échange et le rachat des prisonniers en Méditerranée, XVe-XVIIIe siècle*, Wolfgang Kaiser, ed. (Rome: École Française de Rome, 2008). Public Domain, https://commons.wikimedia.org/w/index.php?curid=6790595.

and verbal arts of the Enlightenment in ways that become more exculpatory than contingent. In the print "The Purchase of Christian Captives from the Barbary States" (figure 12), the Religieux de la Mercy pledge to buy the slaves' freedom; the caption indicates they would, if required, take their place. Further, they repeat the event, freeing one hundred from Algiers in 1662; more in Tunis in 1666, and again from Algiers in 1667. The role of the Catholic Church is pivotal, with the Fathers of Mercy credited for the emancipatory intervention, ransoming the souls and skins of the faithful. This image and the emotional response it evokes combine to render ancillary the historically dominant trade in African slaves between European powers and the

---

Philosophy (Princeton, NH: Princeton University Press, 2015), 5–6. Smith notes Charles Verlinden's classic study, 6 note 16.

Americas. The unifying ideologies of Christian religion and white worthiness realign the sympathies of the contemporary audience.

In the eighteenth century, proponents of the transatlantic network that fostered trade, scientific advancement, and cultural dissemination all demonstrated a preoccupation with the epistemological status of race. In a constant process of differentiation, driven by the lofty ideals to promote human progress and the teleology of Enlightenment universality, historical actors told a German story of the heroic journey toward civilization. At the same time Europeans sought, some through experimentation, to "discover the physical cause of the color of N*groes,"[13] equating skin color with suitability to enslavement and toil in the tropics, poets and philosophers contemplated the nature of freedom and servitude. Buck-Morss elaborated the complex relationship between G. W. F. Hegel's master-slave dialectic with regard to the press coverage of the Haitian Revolution.[14] A period of revolutionary fervor in German-speaking Europe preceded the upheaval of the late 1780s. Prior to the press coverage of African slavery and the material reality—of precious metals and chained bodies—that enables the dialectic of idealist philosophy, a different geography of human trafficking captured the attention of European populations. For example, associated with the intellectuals and lyric poets of *Göttinger Hainbund* and the *Sturm-und-Drang*, Ludwig Christoph Heinrich Hölty (1748–1776) abandoned the study of theology and pursued a life of letters. Known in his lifetime for his celebration of the *Volkslied* and his ballads, Hölty produced a poem in 1773 that posits an equivalence between the repressed politics of the educated, disenfranchised bourgeois male subject and the condition of enslavement. Through the lyrical voice of a freed slave, Hölty projects a political statement that indicts not the transatlantic, but the Mediterranean slave trade, dominated by Muslims. This short poem underwrites Buck-Morss's argument about the semantics and politics of freedom and slavery, albeit with the villain an alterity closer to Europe's shore. In the poem, "Der befreite Sklave," Hölty writes,

Gottlob, daß keine Kette mehr
An diesem Arme klirrt,

---

13. Londa Schiebinger, *Secret Cures of Slaves: People, Plants, and Medicine in the Eighteenth-Century Atlantic World* (Palo Alto, CA: Stanford University Press, 2017), 30. See also my discussion in chapter 1. Throughout I quote source material accurately to reflect the historical use of racist terminology.

14. Susan Buck-Morss, *Hegel, Haiti, and University History* (Pittsburgh: University of Pittsburgh Press, 2009), see my discussion in the introduction.

Kein Teufel mit gezückter Wehr
Mich Rudernden umirrt!

Der ganze Himmel schwebt um mich,
Die Schöpfung ist mir neu;
Dich hab' ich, süße Freiheit, dich!
Gott! frei bin ich, bin frei!

Der Bliz des Christen fraß dein Boot,
Du wütiger Korsar;
Sein Donner brüllte Höll' und Tod
Auf deine Räuberschaar.[15]

Praise God, that no longer do chains
Clank around this arm,
No devil with a weapon drawn
Strays around me, rowing.

All the heavens hover around me,
Creation appears new to me;
You I have, sweet freedom, you!
God! Free I am, I am free.

The Christian attack devoured your boat,
You raging Corsair;
His thunder brought hell and death
Upon your band of robbers.

The poem makes a metaphor of slavery. Relying on the condition of capture as the preface, Hölty focuses on the moment of emancipation from chains and the expressive celebration of freedom in the world. The figure of the corsair most likely refers to the Barbary Corsairs or pirates who plagued merchant ships and prompted all manner of protective alliances and who embody satanic evil. Still, the pirate as trope in the musical culture of the European

---

15. Ludwig Heinrich Christoph Hölty, "Der befreite Sklave," in *Gedichte* (Hamburg: Bohm, 1783), 168. DTA. https://www.deutschestextarchiv.de/book/view/hoelty_gedichte_1783?p=208. My translation.

cultural consumer would not gain purchase until later, with Mozart's *Singspiel*, based on the libretto by Gottlied Stephanie, based on Christoph Friedrich Braezner's *Belmont und Constance oder Die Entführung aus dem Serail* (1781). In his *Kriminalroman Der Geisterseher. Ein Fragment* (The ghost-seer: A fragment), Friedrich Schiller piques European anxiety about the Barbary Corsairs, but channels that fear to cover up a fratricide in the story of young Marquis Jeronimo, whose murdering brother tells of a failed rescue attempt of his sibling from an Algerian. How does the fictional world of abduction, enslavement, and regaining freedom inspire the Göttinger Hain?

The preoccupation in this poem with the condition of Christian, European slaves at the hands of the Muslim pirates refocuses the narrative of victimization. It further evokes the religious zeal of the Crusades, of autonomous Europeans pitted against any competing claims to the territories of the Christian "east." This particular instance, which may refer to the victory of Chevalier Acton in 1773 against Moroccan pirates from Salé, glorifies the emancipation of the individual, protected by a maritime power allied with Christian rule, against the Corsairs. The geopolitical conflict between Christian Europe and the Islamic world occludes the local rivalries and economic protectionism that sustained piracy. Further, the declaration of freedom from the *Kette*, or chain, elides the history of particular internecine struggles among European powers who worked with, not against, the Barbary Corsairs and the North African rulers who engaged and protected them.[16] Wendy Sutherland's work calls attention to ways of reading the literary and cultural contemporaries that stage Blackness, also present in eighteenth-century imports to German-speaking Europe. Of Karl Gotthelf Lessing's play *Die Mätresse* (The mistress, 1780), she writes, "Eighteenth-century German connections to the global trade presuppose German involvement in the major driving force of emerging capitalism, that of slavery, the slave trade, and the trade in colonial goods."[17] She notes as well the poetic portrayal of the enslaved African brutalized by a white man in a 1775 poem published in a newspaper, the *Wandsbecker Bothe*, to which Gotthold Ephraim Lessing and other luminaries also contributed.[18] As late as 1795, in his road map to perpetual peace, Kant thematized the pre-

---

16. See Stanley Lane-Poole and Lt. J. D. Jerrold Kelley, *The Story of the Barbary Corsairs* (New York: Putnam, 1890).

17. Sutherland, *Staging Blackness*, 43.

18. The poem "Der Schwarze in der Zuckerplantage" is by Matthias Claudius (1740–1815), who was hired by Heinrich Carl Schimmelmann (1724–1782) to edit the newspaper. See Sutherland, *Staging Blackness*, 81–83.

sumed opposition between civilization and barbarism, himself vilifying in the third definitive article the "inhospitable practice in vogue on some sea coasts, as of the Barbary States, of robbing ships in the neighboring seas, or of making slaves of shipwrecked people."[19] In other words, the philosophic and literary public sphere demonstrated a knowledge of enslaved Blacks, but referred to capturing Europeans as examples of uncivilized practices. By contrast, Hölty invokes slavery as a temporary condition. The mechanisms that sustain competing colonialisms generate a hierarchy that accommodates slavery for some while taking a principled stance against it as a violation of human autonomy, with race and racialized geographies as the primary criteria. The post-Enlightenment rallying cry of the *Sturm und Drang* opposed tyranny at home, with little concern for slavery in the Atlantic world.

In the early 1820s, colonial recruiters highlighted the more humane treatment of enslaved Africans in the Americas, where Blacks fared better than they would in their native lands; immigrants who left German-speaking Europe for a range of reasons throughout the nineteenth and into the early twentieth century were memorialized in popular literature as themselves enslaved, transported like freight, subject to tyrannical masters, and self-identified among the persecuted. These tropes become central to mobility narratives, even performative, in the Age of Empire, when eyewitness experience replaced the reliance on testimony from subjects of other colonial powers.

Goethe's Brazilian Turn

The condition of the cosmopolitan is grounded in European epistemologies, the universality of which has been persuasively interrogated, exposed as Eurocentric, and dismantled. The examination of competing colonialisms through cultural analysis helps understand the tenacity and longevity of the trope and its dire effects on the world. In other words, this approach offers us a way to historicize the experience of globalization. Clearly, the hierarchies disseminated through colonial expansion were never uncontested; recessive critical discourses succumbed to historical metanarratives. Still, the power imbalances sustained by internecine colonial struggles generated a range of responses, some of which were in themselves contradictory. Lessing's asser-

---

19. Immanuel Kant, quoted from translation, Black Central Europe.

tion of religious equipoise did not immunize him against valorizing the quest for knowledge. By way of counterexample to Lessing, Goethe experiences a non-European cultural landscape through the lens and objects of transatlantic trade, Indigenous cultural appropriations, and scientific inquiry. Additionally, he set his sights beyond the Western horizon, for a range of reasons.[20] Goethe understood the complex, multidirectional circulation of knowledge and things. Scholars, among them Karl S. Guthke, Sylk Schneider, Gabrielle Bersier, Nancy Boerner, and Peter Boerner, have treated Goethe's interest in Brazil primarily through the enabling trope of a journey of the mind.[21] With specific connection to the nation, Ernst Feder, whose work on Lessing I discussed in the previous chapter, also paid attention to Goethe's "love of Brazil."[22] From his place among German-speaking peers, Feder sought cultural connections that potentially elevate the experience of exile and integrate it into the extended horizons of a literary landscape. Additionally, there is a substantial and rich archive of scholarship on Goethe as a natural scientist, and here too Brazil figures prominently in the naming of this plant: Goethea. There is an equally significant body of work on Goethe and objects and, recently, a careful and creative study of Goethe's *Sammlungsschränke*."[23] While Lessing did not identify with Brazil, but rather with the topography

---

20. See Daniel Purdy, *Chinese Sympathies: Media, Missionaries, and World Literature from Marco Polo to Goethe* (Ithaca, NY: Cornell University Press, 2021). The scholarship is vast, and the focal points differ widely. See also the important study, Katharina Mommsen, *Goethe und die arabische Welt* (Frankfurt a/M: Insel, 1988). In this chapter, I engage the Brazil-specific leverage on *Weltliteratur*.

21. Karl S. Guthke, *Goethes Reise nach Spanisch-Amerika. Weltbewohnen in Weimar* (Göttingen: Wallstein Verlag, 2018). Guthke stresses Goethe's dialogues with Alexander von Humboldt and Georg Forster (8); the contents of his library ("als Beigaben zu Werken von Humboldt und anderen, auch Karten von Mexiko, Guatemala, Kolumbien, Brasilien, Chile, Peru, den 'Vereinigten Provinzen von Süd-Amerika' (Argentinien), Kuba, Haiti, und den Antillen" (10). In addition, he owned translations of ethnographic journals and volumes from the series "*Neue Bibliothek der wichtigsten Reisebeschreibungen zur Erweiterung der Erd- und Völkerkunde*" (10–11). There is interest in a canal (Durchfahrtsrinne); silver mining in Mexico; and further geological and mineralogical interests (13).

22. Ernst Feder, *Goethes Liebe zu Brasilien. Mit vier Bildern und einem Vorwort von Professor Roquette Pinto* (Ijuí: Ulrich Löw, 1950).

23. Diana Stört, *Goethes Sammlungsschränke. Wissensbehältnisse nach Maß*, in cooperation with Katharina Popov-Sellinat, Parerga und Paratexte. Wie Dinge zur Sprache kommen. Praktiken und Präsentationsformen in Goethes Sammlungen, vol. 3. Series editors Johannes Grave, Wolfgang Holler, Christiane Holm, and Cornelia Ortlieb, Bundesministerium für Bildung und Forschung (Dresden: Sandstein Verlag, 2020).

and place-naming politics of the Americas, Goethe lives to see the Habsburg queen consort rule over a republic independent from Portugal. Both Lessing and Goethe shared an interest in accessing Indigenous knowledge; they used it differently.

In 1782, Goethe transcribed two songs: "Todeslied eines Gefangenen" and "Liebeslied eines amerikanischen Wilden," both of which carry the subtitle: "Brasilianisch." Based on his reading of Montaine's essay on cannibals, which appeared in German translation in 1753–1754, Goethe projects a rebellious voice into the sacrificial victim and the lover of snakeskin. Later in his professional life, he returns to the latter song, the 1825 substitute titled simply "Brasilianisch." The short poem, read through the dominant mode of Goethean *Weltliteratur*, bespeaks not only the acquisition of things, but also forecloses on a moment of insight into the understanding of non-European humanity and the potential to include the "barbaric" and unenlightened cultural practices into a definition of universality.

In the decades between the translation and the revision, Goethe encountered Brazil in his work. In Weimar, Goethe welcomed "Brazilian interlocutors" and the scientific knowledge they shared. His poems and their divergent fates give insight into Goethe's cultural curating of that which can be "worlded." Goethe of the 1780s projects a rebellious yet ennobled voice into the subject positions of the sacrificial victim. He leaves that moment behind him. Instead, he reinscribes the snakeskin belt, an object of exchange and value between the poetic voice and the lover. In other words, Goethe makes a choice to revise or not to revise. Selectively, he upcycles one object from Amerindian culture to *Weltliteratur*.

The poems, united in their subtitle, took divergent trajectories. The "Todeslied eines Gefangenen" speaks in the voice of a captive about to be sacrificed and consumed. Several scholars highlight the uncanny subject matter for Goethe: cannibalism. He only published the poem once, in the *Tiefurter Journal*, while the "Liebeslied" he reincarnated after his encounter with South American scientific writing and after he did the duke's bidding to acquire Brazilian diamonds.[24] In his work on Goethe as *Weltbürger*, Volker Hesse notes the poems in the European context mediated knowledge about Brazil, which was considered an "unkultiviertes und zum Teil gefährliches Land, in dem selbst der Kannibalismus nicht ungewöhnlich gewesen sein soll" (unciv-

---

24. Gabrielle Bersier, Nancy Boerner, and Peter Boerner. *Goethe: Journeys of the Mind* (London: Haus Publishing, 2019), 68–72.

ilized and in part dangerous country where even cannibalism was said to be not unusual).[25] The focus on Goethe's interest in geographical and geological exploration aside, his interaction with objects and these poems speaks to the appropriation of distanced captivity and execution as a European trope of freedom.

The "Brazil" lyrics of 1782 compose poetic renditions of translation ostensibly derived from authentic Indigenous voices. This authentic voice is multiply mediated, first through eyewitness reports from a traveler; then through the humanist French philosopher Montaigne, before being translated into German in the period of Enlightenment. The projecting of this voice makes its audible in the network of early modern communicative structures about Indigeneity in the transatlantic world. While Goethe first inscribes Montaigne's implicit "argument for relativism based on the supposed cultural practices of New World natives"[26] in the early "translations," his later aesthetic choices suggest a more selective universality for poetry. With the "Todeslied," Goethe renders cannibalism contemporary. Like so many of his contemporaries, he focuses not on the grisly reality, but on the scene of self-empowerment in spiritual emancipation, even though this poem asserts human dignity and common humanity on the verge of a cannibalistic act. The voice of the captive proclaims his agency with audacity; he commands the captors and victors, "Kommt," which occurs five times throughout the sixteen-line poem:

> Kommt nur kühnlich kommt nur alle
> Und versammelt euch zum Schmause
> Denn ihr werdet mich mit dräuen,
> Mich mit Hoffnung nimmer beugen.
> Seht hier bin ich, bin gefangen,
> Aber doch nicht überwunden.
> Kommt verzehret meine Glieder
> Und verzehrt zugleich mit ihnen
> Eure Ahnherrn eure Väter,
> Die zur Speise mir geworden
> Dieses Fleisch das ich Euch reiche,

---

25. Volker Hesse, "'Ich habe [. . .] selbst eine Landschaft phantasiert'—Goethes Interesse an der wissenschaftlichen Entdeckung Südamerikas," in *Weltbürger Goethe: Schriften der Berliner Goethegesellschaft*, ed. Monika Estermann and Uwe Hentschel (Berlin: Berliner Wissenschaftsverlag, 2019), 128.

26. Smith, *Nature, Human Nature*, 11.

Ist, ihr Toren, euer eignes
Und in meinen innern Knochen
Stickt das Mark von euren Ahnherrn.
Kommt nur kommt mit jeden Bissen
Kann sie euer Gaumen schmecken.[27]

Just come boldly, just come all,
And assemble for the feast.
For you will never bend me,
Not with threats, not with hope.
Behold, here I am, captive,
And yet not overcome.
Come, consume my limbs,
And consume with them also
Your ancestors, your fathers.
That have become my food.
This meat that I give you,
You fools, is your own,
And within my bones
Is the marrow of your forefathers.
Come, just come, and with each bite
Your palate can taste them.

Each direct address occurs in the imperative mood. The crucial couplet reads: "Seht hier bin ich, bin gefangen, / Aber noch nicht überwunden" (Behold, I am here, am captured, / And yet not overcome). At this juncture, Goethe seems to be intervening in the early modern ethnographic debate about the trope of the cannibal "as a challenge to the universality of moral principles,"[28] indeed, on the side of the cannibal. The proclamation of moral victory in the face of a victorious adversary evokes the tone of Goethe's earlier "Prometheus" (1774), a pendant piece to his "Ganymed," which together constitute

---

27. The German-language press has taken an interest in this topic, given the iconic status of the poet. See Mathias Mayer, "Johann Wolfgang Goethe: 'Todeslied eines Gefangenen,'" in the Frankfurter Anthologie section of the *Frankfurter Allgemeine Zeitung*, June 12, 2015. https://www.faz.net/aktuell/feuilleton/buecher/frankfurter-anthologie/frankfurter-anthologie-johann-wolfgang-goethe-todeslied-eines-gefangenen-13644033.html. I quote the poem from this essay.

28. Smith, *Nature, Human Nature*, 14.

a multivalent relationship to patriarchal authority figures.[29] Though the two poets diverge in terms of talent and reputation, Hölty and Goethe share a moment of inserting a distinctly masculine, white, European voice into a historical framework of captivity for the purpose of mobilizing emotions against the captors.

Goethe's "Brazilian" return is launched in 1817, with his contact to mineralogists. Bersier et al. discuss his reading of John Mawe's work. A British diamond dealer, Mawe published *A Treatise on Diamonds and Precious Stones* and *Travels in the Interior of Brazil, Particularly in the Gold and Diamond Districts of that Country*, projects resulting from his exploration of Minas Gerais.[30] That same year, he became acquainted with the work of Wilhelm Ludwig von Eschwege (1777–1855), a mineralogist and geographer with extensive experience in South American field work. Cataloguing efforts prove that Goethe owned a copy of Eschwege's later work as well.[31] Eschwege and Goethe visited several times in person in 1822 and 1823.[32] That same year, Goethe read Eschwege's *Journal von Brasilien, oder vermischte Nachrichten aus Brasilien*.[33] The negotiation may have been finalized, but Goethe's continued interest in things Brazilian focused largely on developments in nature science.[34] With his "Liebeslied," he demonstrates an acceleration in the circulation of knowledge. The eight-line poem of 1782 projects the voice of the lover in direct address to a snake, the coveted skin of which will be crafted into a gift for the beloved:

> Schlange, warte, warte Schlange,
> Daß nach Deinen schönen Farben,
> Nach der Zeichnung Deiner Ringe,

---

29. Essential in this discourse is the collection edited by Alice Kuzniar, *Outing Goethe and His Age* (Palo Alto, CA: Stanford University Press, 1996).

30. Bersier, Boerner, and Boerner, *Journeys of the Mind*, 67.

31. Wilhelm Ludwig von Eschwege, *Geognostisches Gemälde von Brasilien und wahrscheinliches Muttergestein der Diamanten mit einem Kupfer* (Weimar, im Verlage des Gr. H. S. priv. Landes-Industrie-Comptoirs, 1822). See Bersier, Boerner, and Boerner, *Journeys of the Mind*, 67–70, here 68.

32. Bersier, Boerner, and Boerner, *Journeys of the Mind*, 67.

33. Eschwege, *Geognostisches Gemälde von Brasilien* See Bersier, Boerner, and Boerner, *Journeys of the Mind*, 67–70, here 68.

34. Bersier, Boerner, and Boerner, *Journeys of the Mind*, on botany and Maximilian zu Wied-Neuwied, 70–71; on the flora and fauna of Brazil, interpreted with help from the paleobotanist Kaspar Maria von Sternberg, see 74–78; on palm tree research and Carl Friedrich Philipp von Martius, see 78–86.

Meine Schwester Band und Gürtel
Mir für meine Liebste flechte.
Deine Schönheit, Deine Bildung
Wird von allen andern Schlangen
Herrlich dann gepriesen werden.[35]

Snake, wait, wait snake,
That like your stunning colors
Like the drawing of your rings
For my beloved, my sister
May braid a belt and ribbon.
Your beauty, your composition
Will then from all other snakes
Be gloriously praised.

Goethe destines this sacrificial reptile for praise above all others, its manipulated skin to live on in a band and belt. A caesura occurs in the middle of each line, creating a sense of pause, evoking the pursuit. In 1825, Goethe crafted from this a ten-line poem in which he varies the prosody but maintains the content, the story of the snakeskin belt as a token of love. Simply entitled "Brasilianisch," the poet associates the proper adjective with the sum of his mediated experience of the republic, which was declared in 1820. He then recapitulates early-modern representations of Brazil into the poem: *Weltliteratur*, placing that signifier on par with other premodern locales. Purdy draws attention to the shared interest of Goethe and Schiller in cross-cultural influence: they were "looking for good material to adapt to their own writing." This hinges on "the translatability of aesthetic and ethical forms."[36] With reference to China, this rings true. Back to Brazil: What of the "Todeslied"?

In this example, I contend, Goethe encountered that which is or was no longer translatable. In *Translating the World*, Birgit Tautz convincingly redirects eighteenth-century German literary cultures away from the orientation of the nation; she calls attention to the global and Atlantic turning and the literary and historiographic challenges that accompany that re-envisioning.[37] Goethe, in my reading, turns away from translation, even as he appropriates

---

35. Quoted in Ernst Feder, *Goethes Liebe zu Brasilien*, "Vorwort" by Roquette Pinto (Rio Gr. Do Sul: Verlag Ulrich Löw-Ijuî, 1950), 11.

36. Purdy, *Chinese Sympathies*, 14.

37. Birgit Tautz, *Translating the World: Toward a New History of German Literature Around 1800* (University Park: Penn State University Press), 10.

it. The focus on Goethe's interest in geographical and geological exploration aside, his interaction with objects and these poems speaks to the appropriation of distanced captivity and execution as a European trope of freedom: an overpowered captive ennobled by his resistance to the tyrannical and insistence on the universality of the human. Yet Goethe turns away from the poem, while turning toward the Brazil that produced luxuries and the privilege of knowledge, reproduced in Weimar. The scant scholarship on the cannibal captive repeats this gesture of nonknowing.[38] Just an example: the exhaustive *Goethe-Wörterbuch*, under "Brasilien" and "brasilianisch," makes no mention of the poem, albeit a "translation" of sorts—though "B-es Gedicht an die Schlange" (B-ian poem to the snake)—is recorded.[39]

Goethe's continued interest in things Brazilian focused largely on developments in nature science.[40] For the most part, the presumption of multidirectional circulation of knowledge needs to be re-examined. As historians have noted, not until the royal court decamped from Lisbon to Brazil, landing in Rio de Janeiro in 1808 to escape Napoleon's forces, were closer information circuits forged between Europe and South America. Moreover, the marriage of the Habsburg Maria Leopoldina of Austria to the prince regent in 1817 opened up extensive exploration and opportunity. Maria Leopoldina sponsored scientists, some of whom joined her on the voyage to meet her husband—he was in absentia at the wedding ceremony—in Brazil. Goethe identifies "Brazil" with the snakeskin belt as commodity, an object of exchange in a sexual and aesthetic economy. Separately, the postcolonial republic of Brazil was establishing connections across the Atlantic that sought to foster other types of exchange.

Rhetorics of Recruitment I: Royal

Between the 1782 and 1824 versions of Goethe's Brazil poems, the European continent bore witness to historic upheavals in the form of revolutions in the transatlantic world; the impact of racism, slavery, and human rights discourses was felt on both sides of the Atlantic. This was accompanied by a rising tide of abolitionist activism that could be motivated by authen-

---

38. Chunjie Zhang considers cannibalism in a different context, see *Transculturality and German Discourse in the Age of European Colonialism* (Evanston, IL: Northwestern University Press, 2017), 36–39.
39. https://woerterbuchnetz.de/?sigle=GWB&bookref=2,856,12#2.
40. Bersier, Boerner, and Boerner, *Journeys of the Mind*, see note 33.

tic humanism as well as economic expedience. John Stedman's narrative of his experience in Suriname, his presence primarily motivated by orders to put down slave revolts and the warring maroons, served as one source of information about the treatment of enslaved people. The genre, as Klarer has argued, can be described as "humanitarian porn," as the narrating Stedman, himself in a sexual relationship with a mulatto woman he left behind, lingers on the scenes of sex-specific torture and execution.[41] While Goethe may allude to the treatment of slaves in *Faust II*, as some have claimed, the German-language poetry discussed here averts its gaze, abstracting the real conditions into representation and avoiding the near prurience Stedman's history conveys. In the same year as the revision of "Liebeslied" appeared, another German-language tome addressed itself to another type of writing, geared toward overcoming the savage images of precolonial Brazil and of slavery's brutality. *Brasilien als unabhängiges Reich in historischer, mercantilischer und politischer Beziehung*, by Georg Anton Schäffer (1779–1836), was published in Altona by the J. F. Hammerich press. His signature line includes his titles Ritter (knight) and "Major der K. brasilischen Ehrengarde" (major in the Brazilian Honor Guard). Dedicated to Maria Leopoldine, empress of Brazil, Schäffer takes a plural approach to polishing the image of the newly independent country to attract German interest and perhaps investment in immigration. In his efforts to praise the empress and span the distance between Europe and Brazil, Schäffer touts her commitment to research, the loyalty of her people, and the richness of the land itself. Further, one aspect of his rhetorical strategy relies on casting the treatment of Indigenous peoples and Africans in a humane light, thus attempting to assuage the European conscience. The language he uses, however, suggests that this benevolence, which would confound the idea of hierarchy in a "contact zone," remains rhetorical.

Schäffer praises the "royal child" of Europe in an opening encomium, which further elucidates the bond between herself and the emperor, and the appeal of Brazil for the nations. In the first stanza, he alludes to the history of exploration that rationalizes the presence of Maria Leopoldina in Brazil: "Europa forscht nach seinem Furstenkinde / Und nach dem Lande, wo es hingeschunden— / Wo es ein wunderseltnes Glück gefunden; / Vergönn' es

---

41. Mario Klarer, "Humanitarian Pornography: John Gabriel *Stedman's Narrative of a Five Years Expedition against the Revolted N*groes of Surinam* (1796), *New Literary History* 36, no. 4 (2005): 559–87.

mir, dass ich's der Welt verkünde"[42] (Europe is searching for its royal child / And for the land where it ventured— / Where it found miraculous happiness; / Permit me to announce it to the world). With the gravity of an archangel, Schäffer introduces the realm with clear intent. His purpose seems to function retroactively, meeting Lessing's standard of conscientious colonialism that tells the world about the world. With sparse classical references, chiefly Latin, Schäffer inserts himself into the register of the epic and the invocation of the muse. He compares Leopoldina's love for the emperor to the vanilla that embraces the bark of the laurel tree; and she serves as the heroic reward for Alciden, Hercules in Virgil's *Aeneid*.[43] Dom Pedro's actual political achievements notwithstanding, Schäffer proclaims, "Horch! Völker jubeln, die sein Arm befreite, / Auch Deutsche drängen sich, Ihm treu zu dienen, / Weil Er des Kronos golden Zeit erneute" (VI; Listen! Nations rejoice, freed by his arm, / Even Germans hasten to serve him with loyalty). The short, and admittedly amateur poem, nonetheless reprises the purpose of the tome: praise of the political figure whose marriage connects Europe to Brazil. Later in the treatise, he elaborates on the political events and their unfolding that led to Maria Leopoldina's crowning as empress (176–96) and a discussion of Portuguese tyranny (158). In the foreword, Schäffer recounts the history of the world as an *Offenbarung* (vii; revelation), with Asia, from which all culture issues, remaining constant and unchanging as the West progresses. In his survey of the four parts of the world, he characterizes Africa as follows: "In wilder Wuth stellt sich hingegen im heissen Africa der Mensch als Raubthier dar, das, seiner Muskelkraft froh, sich selbst zerreist, nach Blut dürstet und nur zerstören will" (viii; In wild rage, by contrast, the human being in hot Africa presents himself as a predator, who, delighting in his physical strength, tears himself up, thirsts for blood and wants only to destroy). Europe produces human beings born to individual strength, skill, and self-sufficiency (viii). The text targets a German-speaking audience, and segues from continental essentialism to issues of immigration: overpopulation prompts some to seek foreign lands to find that, "wofür Alles zu haben ist—edle Metalle" (viii; for which everything can be had—precious metals). This, he concludes,

---

42. Ritter von Schäffer, *Brasilien als unabhängiges Reich in historischer, mercantilischer und politischer Beziehung*, Dr., Major der K. brasilischen Ehrengarde (Altona: J. F. Hammerich, 1824). Further references to this volume appear in parenthesis throughout the section.

43. Schäffer's stanza reads, "Wie die Vanille um des Laurus Rinde, / Umschlingst, erhab'ne, Du, in schönen Stunden, / Den Kaiser, den die Liebe Dir verbunden, / Dass er Alcidens Heldenlohn empfinde."

drives a nearly accidental discovery, comparing the emergence of the continent to Aphrodite rising from the sea: "und daher als el Dorado (Goldland) berühmt ward" (ix; and so it came to be known as el Dorado [Land of Gold]). Here, he asserts, Europeans, because they are skilled in war, trade, and land cultivation, quickly established a "zweites Vaterland" (ix; second fatherland). Connecting the encomium to the foreword, Schäffer delivers an allegory of German entitlement to Brazil.

Rhetorics of Recruitment II: Indigenous Brazil and Slavery

The discourse about Brazil encompasses the Americas, and to talk about Brazil Schäffer divides the populace into three *Stammrassen* (68; roughly, tribal races). The first, those who rule because they are in the majority, are presumed white. The second, "die braune Rasse" (68; the brown race), he posits as a transitional people who will be mixed with whites eventually. The third "sind die N*ger" (69; are the n*groes), the majority of whom are enslaved people. In Brazil, he begins with the description of contact zones with the Indigenous people, who work with the colonists. In describing his search for a place to settle, he remarks on the winning behavior of the Europeans near Frankenthal, the Germany colony:

> In der Nähe hausen in den Wäldern wilde Patachos und Machacaris. Mit Keulen, Bogen und Pfeilen bewaffnet, schlichen sie aus ihren Schlupfwinkeln hervor; meine Freunde gingen ihnen mit Feuergewehren entgegen, legten aber in einer gewissen Entfernung ihre Waffen nieder, und gaben den Eingebornen durch Mienen zu verstehen, dass auch sie die Waffen ablegen möchten. Die thaten es. Die Colonisten gingen auf die nackten Menschen zu und es wurden Zeichen der Freundschaft und des Friedens ausgetauscht; unbewaffnet folgten nun jene in die Hütten der Colonisten, assen, was gerade vorhanden war und jeder Wilde erhielt ein Glas Branntwein. (14–15)

> Nearby, wild Patachos and Macharis live in the forest. Armed with clubs and bows and arrows, they crept out from their hiding places; my friends met them with their firearms, but, at a certain distance, they lay down their weapons, and mimed to the natives with gestures that they might do the same. They did it. The colonists approached the naked people and signs of friendship and peace were exchanged; unarmed, the latter followed the colonists

to their huts, ate whatever was available and each savage was given a glass of brandy.

The encounter Schäffer relates between his armed friends and the Patachos and Macacaris in the forest conveys the triumph of reason and communication; with miming and small gestures, and at the friends' initiative, weapons are set aside and, over a ration of spirits, cooperation ensues:

> Die Wilden boten ihre Hülfe bei der Urbarmachung an und dieses Anerbieten wurde mit Freuden angenommen. Sie hauten eine Strecke Urwaldung nieder, was eine recht saure Arbeit ist, rodeten die Wurzeln aus, reinigten den Boden, trafen, unter Leitung meiner Freunde, alle Vorkehrungen zur Anlegung einer Kaffeepflanzung, halfen ein Haus bauen und für alle diese Arbeiten, die sie mit der grössten Willigkeit vollbrachten, erhielten sie blos Kleinigkeiten, ein Stückchen Tabak zum Kauen, Messer, Nadeln, Nägel, Scheeren, Maultrommeln, Fischangeln, ihre Kinder Kupfermünzen, die sie ihnen durchbohrt an den Hals hängen und etwas Branntwein. Kein Tag verging, dass sie nicht köstliche Braten: wilde Schweine, Beutelthiere etc. in die Küche lieferten. Kurz, die Wilden bewiesen sich so gefällig, dass ihnen unser herzlicher Dankt gebührt. So ward Frankenthal angelegt, ohne dass ein Schweisstropfen, oder die Thräne eines Sclaven, auf meinen Boden gefallen wäre. (15)

> The savages offered their help with the cultivation of the land, and this offer was joyfully accepted. They cut down a stretch of primeval forest, which is a fairly acidic job, pulled out the roots, cleared the ground, made all the preparations, under the direction of my friends, necessary for the planting of coffee, helped build a house, and, for all this work, which they performed with the greatest willingness, they received merely a few little things, a piece of chewing tobacco, knives, needles, nails, scissors, harmonicas, fishing hooks, for their children copper coins, which they pierced and hung around their necks, and a little brandy. Not a day went by that they did not deliver delicious roasted meat to the kitchen; wild boars, bagged animals, etc. In brief, the savages proved themselves so willing to please that our heartfelt thanks go out to them. And thus was Frankenthal established, without a single drop of sweat or the tears of a slave would fall on my land.

Central to his story, he established residency in the colony of Frankenthal with the help and work of Indigenous labor. No mention of land ownership or fair wages graces the narrative, but he takes pride in the fact that no slave labor, no sweat nor tears of a single slave, saturated his land. Because he worked with the Indigenous, he seamlessly integrates his subjectivity into the immigration story. In his account, labor, land, and privilege are connected.

Such positive views toward the condition of slavery are unique: Schäffer holds up exemplary treatment of slaves as the key to success, and he credits good managerial style and German industry. Almost unbelievably, he writes, "Die Sclaven werden, wie fast überall in Brasilien, milde und menschlich behandelt, leben mit dem Gutsherrn wie Hausgenossen, vertraulich zusammen, und sehen daher äusserst gesund und fröhlich aus" (22; Like almost everywhere in Brazil, the slaves are treated mercifully and humanely; they live with the lord of the manor as household companions in an atmosphere of trust; and for that reason they appear to be extremely healthy and cheerful). This description, uncorroborated by any other evidence, suggests an overcoming of racial hierarchy in the name of productivity. The plantation economy that drove Brazil's development for centuries, and displaced the capital from north to south before Brasilia, relied on a system of fazendas made famous in Gilberto Freyre's *Casa Grande e Senzala* (1933; The mansion and the shanties, 1936). Though Freyre's work underwrites the myth of a racially plural and harmonious society, his arguments about the separation between the big house and the slaves' quarters do not quite align with the contrasting portrayal of Schäffer's property. Perhaps Schäffer extrapolates from his own experience and projects the image onto the entirety of Brazil, but my interest lies in his publicizing of benevolence rewarded between the Germans and the Indians.

One prime motivator for immigration is the lure of profit and prosperity. Schäffer begins with the flexible value of precious metals. He alights on the mines and the attendant slave markets, and he discusses natural resources and returns frequently to the racialization of labor. In the middle of an extended answer to the question "Was heisst jetzt Geld?" (255; what does money mean now?), in which he elaborates the condition of the economy and trade, he turns to slavery and human rights. With brief mentions of the locations that supply Brazil, Angola, Cabinda, Benguela, and the coast of Congo (278), he turns to human trade: "dort gegen Tabak, Eisenwaaren, Schiesspulver u. dergl. schwarze Sclaven eintauschen und diese nach Brasilien bringen" (278; there, black slaves are traded for tobacco, iron wares, gunpowder, and the like and they are brought to Brazil). He names this commodification *menschenrechtwidrig* (278; violation of human rights), then outlines the legal terms of the slave trade below the equator.

Still, he writes, "Allerdings ist es entsetzlich für einen gebildeten, aufgeklärten Europäer, wenn er sieht, wie seine Mitmenschen, gleich einem Stück Vieh, auf den Markt geführt und öffentlich verkauft werden. Man muss aber dabei nicht vergessen, dass diese Menschen, bei allen Lasten und Einschränkungen, die sie zu erdulden haben, doch ein besseres Loos theilen, als man es sich in Europa gewöhnlich denkt" (279; Nonetheless, it is horrifying for an educated, enlightened European to witness the way his fellow human beings, like a head of cattle, are led to the market and publicly auctioned). Schäffer, clearly aware of abolitionist sentiments and moral panics, identifies with the reader as enlightened, writing of slavery as a violation of human rights and of the enslaved as human beings. His argument does not end there.

His position includes a justification of slavery through recourse to the complicity of Africans in the slave trade. Those sold in Brazilian markets to kinder masters were already leading a miserable life as prisoners of war, slaves, or subjects of tyrannical chiefs: "so schlägt man sie gewöhnlich todt, gleich einem Vieh, welches das Futter nicht werth ist. Dieser Schmach und einer grausamen Behandlung werden sie dadurch entrissen, dass man sie aus ihrem Vaterlande, wohin sich kein N*ger zurücksehnt, sondern woran er vielmehr mit Schrecken denkt—nach Brasilien führt" (279; thus they are beaten, usually to death, like an animal that is not worth its feed. They are taken to Brazil, torn away from this shame and a gruesome treatment, they are taken from their fatherland, to which no n*gro longs to return, rather they think of it with horror). Again, Schäffer compares the lot of an enslaved African to that of an abused animal, the same comparison he made through European eyes witnessing a slave auction. He invokes situational ethics through these relativizing of human lives. For a larger comparison, he turns to white slavery.

Fifty-one years intervened between the publication of the Hölty poem and Schäffer's introduction to Brazil, but the specter of white slavery still functions as a trope in the hierarchy of indenture. Schäffer insists that no threat inspires more fear in a slave than to return him to the fatherland: "Nein, weit lieber wollen sie bei Massa—ihrem amerikanischen Herrn—bleiben. Sie werden in Brasilien menschlich behandelt; man sucht sie zum Christenthum zu bekehren und möglichst zu bilden" (278; No, he would much rather stay with Massa—their American master. In Brazil, they are treated humanely; one tries to convert them to Christianity and to educate them if possible). Further descriptions of privilege paint a rosy picture of slave conditions in Brazil before Schäffer concludes:

Enslaved Souls, Perfect Freedom, and Savagery 101

> Kurz, das Loos dieser N*ger ist weit beneidenswerther, als das Schicksal der unglücklichen *weissen* Sclaven (der sogenannten Auslöslinge, *Redemptioners*) in den Vereinigten Staaten von Nordamerika, welche sich, um die Fracht für ihre Ueberfahrt abzuverdienen, Jahre lang, ja vielleicht ihr ganzes Leben hindurch unter der Peitsche eines Treibers abquälen müssen. Die N*ger sind in einer besseren Lage, als die Unglücklichen, die sich durch einige Seelenverkäufer im Jahre 1822 heimlich nach einem Hafen in der Nähe von Bahia schleppen liessen, wo jene Gewissenlosen sie als weisse Sclaven auf erschlichenen Ländereien, die gleichsam einen Status in statu bilden sollten, zu gebrauchen beabsichtigten. (279)

> In brief, the lot of these n*groes is far more enviable than the fate of those *white* slaves (the so-called triggers or *Redemptioners*) in the United States of North America, who, in order to pay back the cost of their voyage, must work for years, indeed, sometimes their entire lives, tortured by the whip of a driver. The n*groes are in a better situation than those unfortunates who, in the year 1822, were secretly transported to a harbor near Bahia by several *Seelenverkäufer* [soul vendors, human traffickers, also vessels unworthy to sail], where those men without conscience planned to sell them as white slaves to suspicious land holdings, that formed at the same time the status in state.

Schäffer argues and persuades through comparisons of the slave's fate, relying on the identification between the German reader and the white victims in North and South America. The historical truths about slavery's brutality and the African slave trade, which was abolished only in 1888, are elided in the deference to white victimization. The author creates a racialized hierarchy with which he compares and suggests a moral competition among Indigenous people (cooperative); Africans, enslaved (empathized with but better treated than some others; and enslaved whites who spend their lives in North American captivity.

In addressing issues regarding the cultivation of the land, Schäffer picks up the motif about the "savages" who assisted the clearing of his plantation. With the observation that nearly all the agricultural work is left to the enslaved Blacks, he indicates that they are incapable of actually becoming farmers as they lack the necessary instruction (306). Here he connects slavery, ostensibly justified through deficiency, and again introduces the need for

German-language whiteness in this economy. This condition applies not only to the agricultural enterprises, but to extraction industries as well. He argues further that in Minas Gerais, there is an abundance of food, wood, water, and "goldreiche Minen" (306; gold-rich mines); "es wird aber aus Mangel an Arbeitern und Sclaven wenig aufgesucht" (306; but it is scarcely sought after due to a lack of workers and slaves). Schäffer connects this need for labor with European competition for influence and further links epistemological justifications for the white presence and dominance in Brazil with the land itself. He supplies exculpatory narratives to justify enslavement.

While he is dedicated to the service of the Portuguese empress, Schäffer does not hesitate to ascribe responsibility for wrongdoing to Portugal. In terms of Brazil's early colonial history, he insists that Portugal behaved in a not "fraternal" way (47), and the conceit of the family romance unfolds: Brazilians thought of the country of their origin "nicht als eine Mutter, sondern vielmehr als eine recht böse Stiefmutter" (47; not as a mother, but rather much more as a really evil stepmother). He lists many of Portugal's mistakes in Brazil (58–59) and characterizes Portuguese tyranny as an abuse of power visited on the natives, the European colonist, and the African slave alike. In identifying "die Portuguiesische Tyranney" (158; Portuguese tyranny), he writes, "Der wilde Eingeborne und der Europäische Colonist mussten, auf gleiche Weise genöthigt, dieselbe Laufbahn des Elends und der Sklaverei durchwandern" (158–59; The savage native and the European colonist, coerced in the same way, had to take the same path of misery and of slavery). Portuguese tyranny, he argues in this overdetermined logic, equates the status of the natives and colonists, and equates these with slavery. Schäffer does locate this abuse of power in the past (171) and concludes that Brazil is now ready to receive Europeans: "Die rechtlichen Europäer, unsere Mitbürger, werden nicht undankbar gegen das Land seyn, das sie wie Kinder aufnimmt, sie ehrt und bereichert" (171; The legally entitled Europeans, our fellow citizens, will not be ungrateful to the land that accepts them like children, honors and enriches them).

After a statistical comparison of Russia, Austria, the British Empire, and France, Schäffer takes the larger context of rights and privileges in the new Brazil and compares some aspects to Prussia (244). As indicated above, he consistently appeals to the German-speaking immigrant, who implicitly has the skills, intelligence, and ethical backbone to succeed in Brazil: "Deutsche sind ohne Zweifel für diesen Zweck die passendsten Subjekte" (244; Germans are without doubt the best suited subjects for this goal). The colonial logic, combined with a colonial imaginary, relativize the distribution of labor across the racial spectrum: "Die N*ger kosten nicht nur Geld, sondern sind auch theuer zu unterhalten; sie leisten, verglichen mit dem, was der deutsche Bauer z.B. am Main, im Magdeburgischen und in Holstein arbeitet, nur wenig. Zehn fleissige Bauersleute arbeiten in zwölf Stunden mehr, als funfzig N*ger in derselben Zeit" (310; The n*groes do not only cost money, they also are expensive to keep; they perform, compared with what the German farmer, for example, on the Main, in Magdeburg and in Holstein, merely a bit. Ten industrious farmers work more in 12 hours than 50 n*groes in the same time). From a foregrounding of white slavery, Schäffer places Germans above all other Europeans. In summary, he justifies why whites should not do the same work as slaves; as with the indentured servants in Russia. It is best, he writes,

[I]n den Ackerbau-Ansiedelungen wenig oder gar keine N*gersclaven zu dulden. Der Europäer, der sich schämt, selbst eine Arbeit anzugreifen, passt nicht für Brasilien.—Als Gehülfen sind dort keine so empfehlungswerth, als die wackern Indianer, die Capoculos, die Machacaris, die Puris, die Patachos und selbst die Botocuden; weiss man diese mit Freundlichkeit anzulocken, so hat man für möglichst geringe Unkosten eine höchst wirksame Hülfe bei der Arbeit, welche Hülfe für das Heil des Landes weit ersspriesslicher ist, als die Nothbehelf der schwarzen Sclaven. Auch freie Schwarze und Mulatten werden sich Ansiedlern, die mit ihnen umzugehn wissen, bereitwillig als Mitarbeiter zugesellen. Lernen sie, dass man durch deutsche Handgriffe und mit deutschen Werkzeugen mehr ausrichten und erwerben kann, so greifen sie gewiss rüstig zu, weil sie für sich selbst arbeiten. Allein der Sclave bleibt bei seinem Schlendrian, da ja überhaupt die Sclaverei nur ein Schlendrian ist. (311)

[T]o tolerate few or no N*gro slaves in the arable farming settlements. The European, who is ashamed of doing work himself, does not belong in Brazil. As helpers there are none so worthy of praise as the brave Indians, the Capoculos, the Machacaris, the Puris, the Patachos, and even the Botocuden. If one knows how to lure them with friendliness, one has, for the least possible expenses, a most effective assistance at work, assistance that is far more profitable for the salvation of the country, than the emergency help of the black slaves. Even free blacks and mulattos will be willing to associate with settlers who know how to deal with them. If you learn that you can do more with German hands and with German tools, you will certainly be vigorous, because you work for yourself. Only the slave stays with his drowsiness, since slavery is after all itself just drowsiness.

German hands, German tools, and managerial savvy can function as the means to cultivate the land, civilize the natives, and motivate the enslaved.

The economic logic put forth by Schäffer intersects with an ecological logic that characterizes competing colonialisms: the projection of European epistemological models onto the people and the land naturalizes exploitation. He writes, "Die sauerste Arbeit für den Ansiedler ist die Ausrodung der durch Schlingkraut wild verwachsenen Urwälder, so, Stamm an Stamm gedrängt, im Innern ewige Nacht herrscht. Wohl dem Landmann, der bei dieser Arbeit von Indianern unterstützt wird; diese wissen, wenn man sie mit Werkzeugen versieht, sehr gut damit umzugehn" (314–15; The least appealing work for the settler is the clearing of the primeval forests, wildly overgrown with creeping weeds, so pressed trunk-to-trunk that in the interior an eternal night reigns. Lucky is the plantation owner who is supported in this work by Indians; they know when to use tools and how to use them). There is poignancy in this assertion that will strike a minor chord in a contemporary reader. The exploitation of Indigenous knowledge, of Indigenous labor to deforest recapitulates the colonial logic in a way that the competition among European powers is always already lost. The texts that map the connectivity among German-language literature and media produced in and about Europe, the Americas, and Africa themselves generate subsequent narratives of legitimacy, of a specifically German story about the past that connects ancestry and adventure to later immigration identities that focus on legitimizing the exploitation of human labor in the service of acquiring raw and cultivated materials. This narrative process relies on the exclusion of decolonial knowledge.

Modernizing the Cannibal

Above, I outlined knowledge of Brazil in the *Goethezeit*. Another travelogue, written in Dutch and translated into German, yields greater insight into the cultural practices of cannibalism in context. Published in Berlin in 1784, the first part of Johann Jakob Hartsink's *Beschreibung von Guiana oder der wilden Küste in Südamerika* (Description of Guiana or of wild coasts in South America) contains a foreword by M. J. E. Fabri, the Inspektor der königlichen Freitische und Sekretär der hallischen naturforschenden Gesellschaft (with etchings and maps). In his introductory remarks (he is not the translator), Fabri mentions the readers' likely familiarity with Hans Staden's sixteenth-century work, painting a South American landscape "der wilden, nacketen, grimmigen Menschenfresser."[44] The *Adelung*, while not geographically specific, provides the operative definition of people who eat people as practiced "unter manchen wilden Völkern in den ungesitteten Welttheilen"[45] (among some savage peoples in the uncivilized parts of the world). The definitional language maps cannibalism onto distant parts of the world. Eighteenth-century anthropology, as practiced and disseminated in travelogues, disrupts the hegemonic image of partially colonized Guyana. The reader of Hartsink's volume would encounter ethnographic portrayals of Indigeneity: "Wenn man sie gut behandelt, so sind sie sehr willig; da sie aber die Freyheit lieben, so wollen sie sich nicht befehlen lassen, noch auf eine sclavische Art regiert seyn, und thun das Gegentheil von allem, was man ihnen befiehlt"[46] (If one treats them well, then they are quite willing; because they do love freedom, they do not want to be commanded, nor governed in a slavish way, and thus do the opposite of everything they are ordered to do). A fairly innocuous example follows: if you insist they hunt, they go fishing; order them to fish, they go hunting. If asked in a friendly manner, however, they cooperate willingly. He closes with the observation that they take their children to the river every morning to bathe and swim. Crucial here is the emphasis on "Freyheit," the operative term that would go straight to the hearts and minds of a German-speaking European.

Hartsink's portrayal of the Amerindians in Guyana differentiates among the "Stämme," though some customs he attributes to the region's inhabitants more generally. In the seventh section, on the language, travels, wars, treaties, and music, he differentiates the tribes from those elsewhere in South America based on the absence of an "allgemeine Sprache"[47] (common language). Elsewhere he describes them as different from each other as are Europeans. Such a comparison was strictly taboo. The savagery for which they are known, cannibalism, is put into perspective. The section on wars describes the practices

---

44. Fabri, "Vorrede." Johann Jakob Hartsink, *Johann Jakob Hartsink's Beschreibung von Guiana oder der wilden Küste in Süamerika. Aus dem Holländischen übersetzt. Erster Theil. Mit einer Vorrede und Zusa4tzen von M. J. E. Fabri*, no translator named (Berlin: Johann Friedrich Unger, 1784), iii–vix, here v.
45. Bd. 3, Sp. 178. https://woerterbuchnetz.de/?sigle=Adelung#2.
46. Hartsink, *Beschreibung*, 19.
47. Hartsink, *Beschreibung*, 44.

of ferocious attack; the capture of women and children for enslavement and/ or sale to Europeans[48] and the torture of male captives as justice for those fallen or captured from the victorious tribe. Avoiding an exculpatory tone, Hartsink nonetheless observes as a corrective that the consumption of the executed is by no means a "tägliche Speise" (daily food); rather the ritual satisfies the victors' "Rachedurst" (thirst for revenge) and is intended to inspire dread among their enemies.[49] Well in advance of the institutionalization of anthropology, he insists on a distinction between ritual exocannibalism and anthropography. In other words, he refrains from projecting a European epistemology onto the ritual practice, which challenges tropes of universality.

In the poem "Weltliteratur," Goethe reinscribes the "Brazilian" moment into a pantheon of cross-cultural borrowings, inspiration for the capaciousness of European poetry. Goethe inventories King David's harp, the Persian Bulbul's rosebush, cross-cultural wine and song, sometimes classified as "Volkspoesie":

Wie David königlich zur Harfe sang,
Der Winzerin Lied am Throne lieblich klang,
Des Persers Bulbul Rosenbusch umbangt,
Und Schlangenhaut als Wildengürtel prangt,
Von Pol zu Pol Gesänge sich ernenn–
Ein Sphärentanz harmonisch im Getümmel–
Laßt alle Völker unter gleichem Himmel
Sich gleicher Habe wohlgemuth erfreun![50]

As David royally sang to the harp
The winemaker's song sounded sweet at the throne
The Persian Bulbul's rosebush entwined
And snakeskin emblazoned as a savage belt.
From pole to pole songs anoint themselves—
A dance of spheres harmonic in the turmoil—
May all peoples beneath the same sky
Enjoy good-naturedly the same belongings!

48. Hartsink, *Beschreibung*, 46.
49. Hartsink, *Beschreibung*, 48.
50. Quoted from Projekt Gutenberg. https://www.projekt-gutenberg.org/goethe/gedichte/chap409.html.

According to Marcus Mazzari, who deftly analyzes references to Brazilian nature in major texts, such as *Faust*, the paying forward of the snakeskin belt ennobles the poet's relationship to the nation. Goethe celebrates the best possible version of well-meaning universality about things culturally shared, without dwelling on the asymmetry of wealth, freedom, or labor. It is possible to take a high road, as Mazzari clearly does. He writes, "How much appreciation he showed to this manifestation of the Brazilian Indians by including it in another poem of his old age along with David's psalms and Persian poetry."[51] As to the "diamonds," Goethe functioned as middleman. Only one "diamond," a small, highly polished stone but ultimately a "diamond" survives (Prescher-No. 0001; SI 11), and its whereabouts is unknown.[52] As the first in the systematic mineralogical collection ("oryktognostisch"), it is significant. For my purposes, the stones themselves connected Goethe to the sciences deployed in the imperial "mining" of Brazil, from its minerals to its morals, geology, and botany to anthropology. In Goethe's poetry, his choice of objects to curate into the circulation of cultural capital sheds light on the selective universality of *Weltliteratur*. Though he rejects it, the "Todeslied eines Wilden" survives as an unwritten decolonial text, one that imagined humanity beyond European epistemological models. The "wilderness" within the white bourgeois subject turns relentlessly toward cultivating the world.

---

51. Marcus V. Mazzari, "Nature or God: Pantheistic Affinities between Goethe and Martius 'the Brazilian," in *Estudos Avançados* 24, no. 69 (2012): 183–202, here 188.

52. I thank Dr. Thomas Schmuck, Curator of the Natural Science Collections at the Goethe National Museum (Klassik Stiftung Weimar), who assisted with this research. In an email (November 3, 2021), he writes, "In der geowissenschaftlichen Sammlung Goethes ist nur ein „Diamant" erhalten geblieben (Prescher-Nr. 0001, S I 1 1). Dieser sehr kleine, geschliffene „Diamant" (Fundort unbekannt) ist allerdings nicht echt. Mit ihm beginnt—insofern kommt ihm eine herausgehobene Stellung zu—der systematisch-mineralogische (sog. „oryktognostische") Teil der Goethe-Sammlung, wie es auch in vielen anderen zeitgenössischen Sammlungen üblich war."

PART II

Transatlantic German Worlds

CHAPTER FOUR

The New World Wilderness

The communicative project to encourage identification with German-specific cultivating of the "wilderness" produces lasting and devastating tropes that preside across genres and landscapes from Africa to the Americas and between them. In this and subsequent chapters, I turn to the interplay between immigration and colonization as the former increased and the latter became a reality. The figurative wilderness of the New World, the unwritten pages of prairies, the untamed, unowned jungles ready for cultivation, the empty pampas, all entered discursive, transnationally sanctioned space. The acquisition of land by settlers in the American West, sanctioned by the Homestead Act in 1862, sets the stage for conflict and more in the United States; in settler narratives, it legitimizes entitlements and homogenizes whiteness and national identity. The nations of Latin America share only sections of this trajectory. Citizenship rights, land ownership, and cultural autonomy in the South follow diverse itineraries that intersect with international law and policy. Other scholars have examined, in particular, the German emigrant communities of southern Brazil as a colonial space; specifically, the ethos of industry and labor as constitutive of German civilization and cultural superiority feed into this discourse. As Cassidy writes, "Slavery was at the heart of the alleged Brazilian incapacity to work; the institution made work dishonorable. German nationalists in Europe and Brazil claimed that settlers would remedy this and remake the country and its people."[1] Closer examinations of cultural and literary history, however, pose challenges to the hegemony of economic and diplomatic history.

In this chapter, I focus on stories that represent physical and metaphorical returns to culture, via the experience of the "wild," the primeval forest of Brazil, that foreground the incorporation of the pioneer, farmer, or professional

---

1. Eugene S. Cassidy, "Germanness, Civilization, and Slavery: Southern Brazil as German Colonial Space (1819–1888)" (PhD diss., University of Michigan, 2015), 2.

settler in an implicitly hostile environment, and the wilderness within. Wilhelm Rotermund's (1843–1925) role as Lutheran pastor, writer, and publicist demands he set examples that resolve hostilities among Germans, by emphasizing not their regional rivalries but their diasporic identities. The German space of São Leopoldo originates earlier in the century, with Ritter von Schäffer's recruitment treatise, which reached a target audience. Founded in 1824 by German immigrants, São Leopoldo in Rio Grande do Sul was named in honor of Maria Leopoldine. Rotermund advocates for an ethnic principle of unifying German speakers in their settlements. He leverages the politics of racism to forge provincial pride in Brazil. By contrast, the young protagonist Anni of W. Helmar's *Vom Urwald zur Kultur. Erlebnisse eines Mädchens* (From the jungle to civilization: Experiences of a young girl, 1898) moves from the wilderness to the German metropole. The author behind the pen name is Maria Hellemeyer, who may or may not have had direct experiences of the Global South, but who sets multiple works of fiction and fairy tales in contact zones between white settlers and Black and Indigenous peoples. In the jungle, her character Juanita/Anni serves as interlocutor for the good whites with the Tupi. Her wild ways must be overcome once she finds herself married and among Germans after remigration. Finally, a German-language primer, part of Rotermund's legacy, conveys the essential Germanness needed to be cultivated in Brazil to maintain European logics. Ultimately, these texts adjust and revise the relationship between the New World wilderness and the Old World civilization. Gender differences vary the model without disrupting it.

The reliance on agricultural production in Brazil to recruit and attract German-speaking immigrants integrates the early modern discursive entitlements, but it also rewrites the stories of power and reciprocity between Europe and Brazil. One artifact embodies the fusion of political identity with material reality. Produced in 1859, the sugar sculpture of Pedro II and Tereza Cristina (1822–1889), now displayed in the Museu do Homem do Nordeste in Recife, at once celebrates imperial power and reveals its fragility (figure 13). Sculpted with the traditional attributes of the laurel wreath and an angel, the last couple of the Brazilian empire as a monarchy required glass protection. Additionally, Pedro I encouraged German immigration while Pedro II's wife Tereza Cristina, a princess of the House of the Kingdom of Two Sicilies, promoted Italian immigration. The end of their reign marked the end of European power in Brazil. Theirs is also a story of return. In exile, the news of the overthrow contributed to the emperor consort's death. In situ, the sculpture is displayed alongside the iron instruments of torture used to enslave. The juxtaposition of beauty and delicacy with brutality speaks volumes. The link-

The New World Wilderness

Figure 13. Sugar sculpture, Pedro II and Tereza Cristina (1859–1864), used with permission of the Museu do Homem do Nordeste. (Photo by Dudu Schnaider.)

ages between material culture and epistemology are forged in the process of transculturation, define by Pratt as a way "to describe how subordinated or marginal groups select and invent from materials transmitted to them by a dominant or metropolitan culture." She further observes that at the end of the eighteenth century, "South America and Africa, long linked with Europe and each other by trade, became parallel sites of new European expansionist initiatives."[2] In the previous chapter, the linkages extended to Europe to North and South America. The return to Europe frames what is to come.

Unarguably, as Leora Auslander contends, objects are not only products of history, "they are also active agents in history."[3] As a corollary, they migrate along with narratives of national identity. The ideological and material matters coalesce around cultural education and patrimony. In the period between the fall of the monarchy and World War I, identity borders undergo an elaborate process of renegotiation. To untangle aspects of this process, I look first at a persistent religious discourse, filtered through the writings of a Lutheran pastor, journalist, and publicist. Among his works, a German-language primer designed for use in Brazil, provides particular evidence of his attempts to integrate the Brazilian context into the German language. To open, I contextualize his stories of immigration in the continuum of discovering German identity between the epistemological and the material. Next, I examine the work of an elusive author who penned a two-volume work that takes the reader from the jungles of Brazil back to the culture of Germany around 1900. The rupture of world war seems to hold these reins lightly, but competing models of gendered identities invite closer scrutiny. To conclude the chapter, I return to the signifiers of Brazilian German identity generated by language instruction and its illustrations.

One aspect of intellectual migration advanced with great consistency across borders and oceans is the focus on education. Even as German-speaking communities eschewed their native language to achieve seamless integration, others, as we saw with the Missouri Saxon Germans, resisted this level of assimilation more vigorously.[4] Despite socioeconomic changes in Brazil that led to enhanced opportunities—or contracted those options in the prelude to World War I—religious discourses continued to provide instruction that augmented civic engagement as well. Born near Hanover, Rotermund was raised Lutheran, studied in Jena, and served as a pastor in

---

2. Mary Louis Pratt, *Imperial Eyes: Travel Writing and Transculturation* (London: Routledge, 2008 [1992]), 7 and 11 respectively.

3. Leora Auslander, "Beyond Words," *American Historical Review* 110, issue 4 (October 2005): 1015–1045, here 1017. https://doi.org/10.1086/ahr.110.4.1015.

4. Patricia Anne Simpson, *The Play World: Toys, Texts, and the Transatlantic German Childhood* (University Park: Penn State University Press, 2020), 189–99. There I discuss the publisher and German-language activist Ernst Steiger and his commitment to bilingualism, that English not erase German in the American generations.

São Leopoldo (1874–1919).[5] An advocate of Ludwig Feuerbach and Ernst Haeckel, Rotermund published the *Deutsche Post* (1880) and the *Kalender für die Deutschen in Brasilien*. Beyond his occasional and journalistic writings, he published stories, compiled in *Südamerikanische Literatur*.[6] Unlike Hellemeyer, who wrote under a pseudonym and published with German houses, Rotermund sought a German-speaking audience in Brazil. As Neumann points out, Rotermund began publishing and producing journalism in 1877, which did not always endear the "new Germans" to the inhabitants of São Leopoldo.[7] The almanac grew in circulation and popularity; in 1906, six thousand copies circulated; by 1923, the number increased to thirty thousand.[8]

Neumann and earlier scholars, albeit with considerably different agendas, note the importance of the *Kalender* and periodicals in the establishing of German colonies and cohesive identities in southern Brazil. Manfred Kuder, for example, published a lengthy article about the transition from *Eigenständigkeit* to *Bodenständigkeit* (independence to autochothony) among the German speakers in Brazil.[9] For his purposes, writing in the late 1930s about publications through 1933, the aesthetic value of the literature yields the right-of-way to its "volkstumspolitische" significance.[10] Explicitly, he states that the textual production by German Brazilians should be characterized by "ihre biologische Erscheinungen" (their biological appearances).[11] He, too, traces the history of conflict between Rotermund and Karl von Koseritz (1830–1890), an 1848er, liberal, and reader of Feuerbach who repudiated religion and embraced theoretical materialism.[12] Unsurprisingly, Rotermund crafts characters who rediscover their German worth in Christian values and behavior. His respect for a galvanizing political figure, Silveira, inspires a fictional version in one story, "Die beiden Nachbarn" (The two neighbors), which I discuss at greater length below. Before moving to the literary analysis,

---

5. For background on Rotermund, see Frederik Schulze, *Auswanderung als nationales Projekt. 'Deutschtum' und Kolonialdiskurse im südlichen Brasilien* (Göttingen: Böhlau, 2016), 74–75.

6. Wilhelm Rotermund, *Südamerikanische Literatur*, vol. 15 of *Gesammelte Schriften von Dr. Wilhelm Rotermund* (São Leopoldo, Rottermund Verlag, 1918.

7. Gerson Roberto Neumann, "'Os dois vizinhos, cenas da colônia,' de Wilhelm Rotermund," *Contingentia* 4, no. 2 (2009): 2.

8. Neuman, "Oso id vizinhos," 2.

9. Manfred Kuder, *Die deutschbrasilianische Literatur und das Bodenständigkeitsgefühl der deutschen Volksgruppe in Brasilien* (Berlin: Ferdinand Dümmler, 1937).

10. Kuder, *Die deutschbrasilianische Literatur*, 396.

11. Kuder, *Die deutschbrasilianische Literatur*, 397.

12. See Neumann, "Oso id vizinhos,"; Kuder, *Die deutschbrasilianische Literatur*, 406–8.

however, I want to draw attention to the religious network that tightens connections between the American North and South with Germany's African colonies.

The processes by which spaces in Brazil become "German" topography interact with histories of migration, the centrality of the nation-state, and ideological constructions of national identity. These are further compounded by historiographic imperatives. María Cecilia Gallero provides an overview of scholarship devoted to German migration to Brazil, Paraguay, and Argentina. Of interest is her characterization of two types: "como colono ideal" or "como elemento poco asimilable."[13] Additionally, historiographies tend toward reinforcing metanarratives of the national as the constitutive category of human experience. Gallero cites the work that emerged in the 1990s of UNISINOS, noting the translations into Portuguese of stories and memoirs from the nineteenth century originally written in German, Rotermund's among them.[14] Marcos Antônio Witt considers Rotermund's pastoral interventions in São Leopoldo in his work, which challenges classic historiographies of German migration in ways that complicate the standard vocabulary of European immigration: "civilized," "orderly," and "worker."[15]

Instead, Witt destabilizes the myths, prominent among them the apolitical spaces of the colonies. Focusing on the network around São Leopoldo, Witt demonstrates the ways in which German-speaking immigrants asserted political agency and claimed political space.[16] He devotes attention to the infighting among Germans, elaborating conflicts based on religion (90), ordained vs. nonordained pastors and the extent to which they should engage in economic enterprises (91 ff.), and other factors. Rotermund enters his analysis as the founder of a synod (1886) and commentator on the feud between two other religious leaders. I would like to look more closely at the ways Rotermund's stories unfold in the textual space of a "German" Brazil; they add texture and turbulence to the efforts at a grand-synthesis story of migration.[17]

---

13. María Cecilia Gallero, *Con la patria a cuestas: La inmigración alemana-brasileña en la Colonia Puerto Rico, Misiones* (Buenos Aires: Araucaria editora, 2009), 322.

14. Gallero, *Con la patria a cuestas*, 325.

15. Marcos Antônio Witt, *Em busca de um lugar ao sol: Estratégias políticas. Imigração alemã Rio Grande do Sul—Século XIX* (São Leopoldo: Editora Oikos, 2015), 32.

16. Witt, *Em busca de um lugar ao sol*, 42.

17. Gallero, *Con la patria a cuestas*, 324. She describes the research trend in the 1980s on immigration and colonization and the effort to compile histories of "blancos no-portugueses," 324. I do not dispute the homogenizing forces of whiteness, but I do want to examine the argu-

The pastor and publisher's story of feuding neighbors leverages local politics and old tropes of subjugation to facilitate belonging as secondary neo-nationalism, achieved through identification with victims of forced displacement and enslavement in the Southern Cone. With this newly minted ethnic national identity, the novella resolves dissonance between German regional and emigrant identities, but at what cost?

The shared religion of German-speaking immigrants may forge bonds across multiple networks, while causing rifts in others. In particular, the assonance between Lutheran communities and the production of print media generates religious networks that blend past conversions with contemporary colonization. A Missouri synod publishing enterprise comes into focus in the source material for the story "Christian Afrikaner," which I discuss in a subsequent chapter. This institution and its agents cast a long shadow across the continents. In his summative study, Kuder mentions the synod not only for its religious leadership in the regional United States, but for its outreach to Brazil. Toward what would mark the end of World War I, Brazil imposed a ban on German-language publications. In 1923, the Rotermund press initiated the *Luther-Kalender*, under the auspices of the Casa Publicadora Concordia in Port Alegre. The *Luther-Kalender für Südamerika* appeared "under dem Zeichen der Missouri-Synode" (under the sign of the Missouri synod). Kuder adds the footnote: "Eine nach Nordamerika ausgerichtete Tochtergründung kam 1901 nach Rio Grande und machte im Jahre 1923 vielleicht 1/12 der gesamten protestantischen Bevölkerung aus" (An affiliate of the North American branch came to Rio Grande in 1901 and constituted approximately 1/12 of the total Protestant population in 1923).[18] The affinities, mediated by the Missouri synod, between Brazilian and North American Lutherans played a role in the publication of religious, didactic literature designed to have a transcultural and transnational appeal, delivered in a national language.

In Rotermund's work, the pastor treats a range of topics embedded in the immigrant experience in accordance with a Protestant socioeconomic ethos. Instructively entertaining in nature, Rotermund frequently writes in an avuncular narrative tone. In the story "Täuschungen" (Deceptions), for example, the narrator visits a friend who has been deeply affected by reading letters from Brazil. The plot, revealed in recently unearthed letters between

---

ments that led to the consolidation of power among immigrant groups.
  18. Kuder, *Die deutschbrasilianische Literatur*, 415 note 57. "100 Jahre Deutschtum in Rio Grande do Sul."

a prodigal daughter and her parents and sister, revolves around an elopement, immigration, a faithful wife and drunken, disappointed husband. It ends badly. In the story "Brilhantine," we encounter a woman abused as a household servant. The narrator concludes, "Wir Deutschen müssen unsere Kraft bewahren; wir haben gar große Aufgaben in diesem Lande zu erfüllen. Dazu aber können wir die Mithülfe der Frau nicht entbehren" (We Germans must preserve our strength; we have great tasks to fulfill in this land. To do so, however, we cannot do without the help of women).[19] In "Das Glück" (Happiness), the shared experience again focuses on immigration. The writer asks, "Wer bist du, wenn du die Heimat, wenn du das Vaterland verläßt?" (Who are you, if you leave the homeland, the fatherland?).[20] Happiness remains elusive, pending a reconciliation with faith. In "Der Schein trügt" (Appearances deceive), published in 1881, he proceeds from the truism that everything has a bright and dark side. These are figured respectively by local nature references in his recounting the story of a young friend who allowed himself to be conned in the purchase of his first horse.[21] We find ourselves in the realm of the ordinary, replete with its own extremes as the emigrant characters and their families in the homeland follow the tales of exposure to the vicissitudes of a new world, with the chronotope of the "wilderness" yet to be tamed and made profitable. But the contiguous spatial relations between emigrants and the wild exert considerable influence over the construction of settler identity. In this example, the importance of narrative, even the disparaged *Belletristik*, resonates for understanding the immigrant experience as part of a larger story. Schulze's *Auswanderung als nationalistisches Projekt* (Emigration as national project) dismisses Zantop's work as too dependent on lit-

---

19. Rotermund, "Brilhantine," 7. *Kalender für die Deutschen in Brasilien* (Rotermund-Kalender), São Leopoldo, Rotermund Verlag, 1898, 123–29; also in *Südamerikanische Literatur*, 15. Band. *Gesammelte Schriften von Dr. Wilhelm Rotermund* 2. Band, São Leopoldo, Rottermund Verlag, s.a. 103–12. Text transcribed from Gothic by Zuleica L. Kraemer.

20. Rotermund, "Das Glück," in *Kalender für die Deutschen in Brasilien* (Rotermund-Kalender São Leopoldo: Rotermund Verlag, 1882), 29–39. See also *Südamerikanische Literatur.* 15. Band. *Gesammelte Schriften von Dr. Wilhelm Rotermund* 2. Band (São Leopoldo: Rottermund Verlag, s/d.), 65–80. Text transcribed from Gothic by Zuleica L. Kraemer.

21. Rotermund, "Der Schein trügt," in *Kalender für die Deutschen in Brasilien* (São Leopoldo: Rottermund Verlag, 1897, 96–101). Also: Rotermund, Wilhelm. Das Glück. In *Südamerikanische Literatur.* 15. Band. *Gesammelte Schriften von Dr. Wilhelm Rotermund* 2. Band (São Leopoldo: Rottermund Verlag, s/d.,) 65–80. Texto transcrito do gótico por Lício Cesar Bischoff. *Südamerikanische Literatur. Gesammelte Schriften von Dr. Wilhelm Rotermund.* 15. Band (São Leopoldo, Rottermund Verlag, s.a.), 94–102.

erary forms.[22] Accessing literary authorities, Rotermund cites poetry within the prose; he references Heinrich Heine and Fritz Reuter, among others. The novella "Die beiden Nachbarn. Bilder aus der Kolonie" (The two neighbors, images from the colony), the most accomplished of his works, deserves closer attention. More than the emigrant exempla, this novella aspires to write Brazil into the genre of the *Dorfgeschichte* (Village story), consonant with the tropes of realism dominant in German-language literature of the nineteenth century. Small lives of provinciality achieve greatness, to scale. Moreover, the two neighbors novella incarnates the narcissism of minor differences at the core of colonial competition; it plays out regional, even municipal rivalries and leads a path beyond fragmented German identity via the *Urwald* of southern Brazil.

The novella, best characterized as an example of Brazilian literature of the German expression, appeared in two installments between 1883 and 1884.[23] The action unfolds in a fictional Picade Isabelle in the northern province of Rio Grande do Sul. Scholars connect it to the life in a German colony. Neumann, who wrote a dissertation about Rotermund and has worked extensively on the Brazil Germans, focuses on the use of a *Muttersprache* (mother tongue) and its preservation.[24] Indeed, the characters in the novella themselves debate the value of preserving the language of the homeland.[25] Neumann follows this lead, recognizing an insular quality often highlighted in discussions about Germans in Brazil.[26] Social media has accumulated instructional videos and eyewitness accounts of Brazilians of German descent, among them fifth-generation Brazilians, who speak Hunsrückisch, a German dialect some grew up with at home. Undeniably, the German language was a component of colony life and heritage; its preservation in the Southern Cone often drove

---

22. See Schulze, *Auswanderung als nationales Projekt*. I appreciate Schulze's argument about immigration as a national project with repercussions for colonial discourses. Our focus differs, as I do incorporate the study of media, entertainment, and educational literature as part of the process. He writes, for example, "Wenig überzeugend ist die Studie [of Zantop] allerdings bei der Quellenauswahl, die sich fast nur aus Belletristik speist. Kaum einer der ausgewählten Autoren war in Lateinamerika, die Auswandersthematik kommt gar nicht und Brrasilien nur am Rande vor. Die Idealisierungen etwa von 'deutschen' Vermischungswünschen mit Indigenen, die Zantop herausbeitet, spielen daher für die in dieser Studie rekonstruierten Diskurse über deutsche Einwanderung keine Rolle" (31–32).
23. Neumann, "Oso id vizinhos," 3/8.
24. Neumann, "Oso id vizinhos," 4/8.
25. Neumann, "Oso id vizinhos," 5/8.
26. Neumann, "Oso id vizinhos," 6/8.

literary and journalistic activity. The possibility of political and economic advancement for the *Kolonien* depends though on innate Christian values that triumph over provincialism.

Neighbors and the Narcissism of Minor Difference

In consulting Grimms' dictionary, the signifier itself shares a history of proximate hostilities. The noun *Nachbar* is a composite:

> nachbar ist zusammengesetzt aus dem adv. nach nahe und bauer, das in dieser composition noch die alte bedeutung von bauen 'sich niederlassen, wohnen' festhält: der nahewohner, anwohner. LOGAU 2 zweite zugabe 52 löst das wort richtig auf in nahebauer, giebt dem bauen aber die bedeutung von aedificare.[27]

> neighbor is composed of the adv. after, near and farmer, which still maintains the old meaning of building "settle, live" in this composite: the local people, residents. Logau 2 second addition 52 resolves the word correctly in Nahebauer, but gives the building the meaning of aedificare.

Literally grounded in agrarian early modernity, the substantive contains the mutually dependent psychological profile between supposed equals. Upsets to the balance generate legends of blood feuds that follow German-speaking explorers, evangelists, and emigrants across oceans and continents, and across fences. In other words, the provincial precedes and accompanies the cosmopolitan.

With the kernel of ambivalence integral to the relationship across fences, the presence of he who builds near me, the Grimms offer illustrative examples, usually from canonical literature. In this case, they begin with a couplet from Friedrich von Logau (1605–1655), a member of the language society (*Fruchtbringende Gesellschaft*), and poet: "nachbar heist ein nahebauer; gar zu nahe bauet der, / der bey nacht ins nachbars bette bauet eines andren leer" (neighbor means a farmer near; who builds too nearby, / who by night in a neighbor's bed builds the other's empty). Sara Eigen Figel, in her work on warfare in the era of Frederick the Great, incorporates definitional language from Zedler's lexicon, which extends the reach of land ownership to "acres,

---

27. Jakob and Wilhelm Grimm, *Deutsches Wörterbuch* online, Sp. 22 bis 25.

fields, forests, vineyards, and other plots of land, also entire estates together."[28] Her sustained reading of the noun "Nächster" in the long eighteenth century carries Luther's catechism forward; it embraces the neighbor and the next of kin, whose house shall not be coveted.[29] In Logau, we do not need to consult the ten commandments, nor historicize the misogyny, to grasp the open secrets of corporeality and contiguity, of bodies and borders.

At a time when his works were turning from the individual to the collective neuroses, inspired by developments in contemporary anthropology, Sigmund Freud updated the proximate rivalries in his theory of the "narcissism of minor differences" that erupt from shared borders and tensions arising from proximity of identity and difference in *Civilization and Its Discontents* (1930).[30] It is worthwhile to acknowledge the influence of then contemporary anthropology on Freud's writing. Robert Kenny has highlighted a shift in Freud's thinking after his trip to America and celebrated participation at the Clark University Conference.[31] Moreover, Kenny draws conclusions about the possibilities of direct impact on both Freud and C. J. Jung, acknowledging the intervention of Franz Boas (1858–1942) and the paper he delivered on the "psychological problems in anthropology." The nuances of evolutionist anthropology and lines of influence concern my argument less than the impact of cultural specificity and material conditions on human behavior, a challenge to the hegemony of Eurocentric subjectivity and by extension definitions of humanity. Freud sampled liberally across the globe to establish purportedly universal truths about conflicts between "savage" and "civilized" man. With regard to the "narcissism of minor differences," practitioners and critics of psychoanalytic theory point out that Freud used the term earlier, for example, in *The Taboo of Virginity* (1917), and that it designates both individual and group behavior. David S. Werman foregrounds the potential for a "pernicious escalation of hostile and destructive actions on a widespread

---

28. Sara Eigen Figel, "The Point of Recognition: Enemy, Neighbor, and Next of Kin in the Era of Frederick the Great," in *Enlightened War: German Theories and Cultures of Warfare from Frederick the Great to Clausewitz*, ed. Elisabeth Krimmer and Patricia Anne Simpson (Rochester: Camden House, 2010), 21–40, 29.

29. Figel, "The Point of Recognition," 34.

30. Sigmund Freud, *Civilization and Its Discontents*, trans. James Strachey (New York: Norton, 1962).

31. Robert Kenny, "Freud, Jung and Boas," *Notes and Records of the Royal Society* 69, no. 2 (2015): 73–190.

scale" in his reassessment of Freud's social diagnosis.[32] The "European" signifier governs that which is known, even if inflected. In his groundbreaking study of psychoanalysis in India, Ashis Nandy identifies the complex mechanisms through which Western models of critique, Marxism and psychoanalysis, recycle rather than disrupt the power hierarchies that produced them. What unites them, Nandy argues, despite their ambivalence about their own genesis, is a capacity for gaining allies but relegating them to lesser status; the "racial arrogance was not obvious to their native converts." Thus allied, Marxist and psychoanalytic paradigms could produce "bidirectional criticism—of the contemporary European society and of the savage world."[33]

While Freudian concepts have informed readings of colonial sexual desires and fantasies, this study looks toward the social theory informed by contemporary developments in the field of anthropology circa 1900. The "narcissism of minor differences" theory has considerable explanatory force; it has the potential to project the immediacy of hostile blood feuds among European neighbors onto a global scale: Freud rediscovers the "savage" in the ostensibly "civilized" white European male. In other words, Freud medicalizes white rivalries and internalizes as anthropological white-white hatreds at a time of tectonic imperial shifts. Against the collapse of the Austro-Hungarian Empire and the expansionist politics of a pan-German Berlin-centric power axis, Freud brackets the colonial origin stories (English over Scottish), rendering whiteness invisible. This diagnosed, treated, and therefore presumably contained "savagery" undergoes a process of deterritorialization in the European metropolis, but its potential as a trope of uninhibited strength in an all-out battle for control against external enemies can be unleashed in the wilds of elsewhere. We see this struggle increasingly depicted in settler narratives, both in (or about) official colonies or emigre *Kolonien*.

Hate Thy Neighbor

Rotermund's novella, though not as accomplished in structure or literariness, invites comparisons with Gottfried Keller (1819–1890) and his *Romeo und*

---

32. David S. Werman, "Freud's 'Narcissism of Minor Differences': A Review and Reassessment," *Journal of the American Academy of Psychoanalysis* 16, no. 4 (1988): 451–59, 451.

33. Ashis Nandy, *The Savage Freud and Other Essays on Possible and Retrievable Selves* (Princeton, NJ: Princeton University Press, 1995), 82.

Julia auf dem Dorfe, from the cycle *Die Leute von Seldwyla* (1875). The tragic tale of young love, thwarted by feuding parents—in this case, over land— loses any connection to poetic realism in Rotermund's version. The feuding neighbors, Lips-Peter, a Birkenfelder, and the enterprising *Wirt*, a Pomeranian, do have offspring, Luise and Christian respectively, who initially reject their paternal burden of antipathy. That conflict, however, derives from trespass and transgression of a two-part directive: if my livestock comes onto your land, drive it off and close off your land; if yours comes onto mine, I do the same and fix the hole in the fence.[34] The persona of the *Wirt* bears some resemblance to the head of a clan, Pastor Carlos Leopoldo Voges (1801–1893). A nonordained pastor, Voges expanded his influence primarily through economic enterprises. Some tried to justify the commercial ambitions of Voges's family. Harking back to the generation of immigrants who heard Schäffer's call to Brazil, many expected rewards for their service, in the military or in the church. Voges came to Brazil in 1824, headed for São Leopoldo (1825), where he supplanted another pastor, and moved to Três Fourquilhas in 1826. Rotermund, Witt reports, criticized Voges.[35] In any case, the emphasis on money and material things earns the narrator's disapprobation. That negative character trait dominates the *Wirt*'s character, even as those around him abandon his sphere of influence and his manipulative ways. The figure of the son, however, seems to have inherited the dominant traits from the paternal end of the gene pool. Rotermund's narrator asserts, "Gute und getreue Nachbarn sind eine seltene Sache auf der Kolonie" (6; Good and trustworthy neighbors are a rare thing in the colony). His novella provides a script for engendering the right kind of neighbor.

The father-child conflicts focus on the masculine experience of immigration, though Rotermund reserves margins for female-specific contributions to the survival of the Germanized community in Brazil. The turbulently tempered Christian, a strong only child and his father's pride and joy, falls in love with Luise, and initially she reciprocates. Even though the narrator acknowledges mutual attraction, he portrays a suitor with an ulterior motive; Christian learns that marriage might protect him from military service, which seems to cast a shadow over his character. The *Wirt* only assents to

---

34. Rotermund, "Die beiden Nachbarn," 6. *Kalender für die Deutschen in Brasilien Südamerikanische Literatur* (São Leopoldo, Rottermund Verlag, s/d., 1883): 33–69; 1884: 33–70. Also in *Gesammelte Schriften von Dr. Wilhelm Rotermund*. 1. Band (São Leopoldo, Rottermund Verlag, Band 5.

35. Witt, *Em busca de um lugar ao sol*, 85–90.

the marriage proposal to his arch-nemesis's daughter when he realizes how much it will cost him to buy his son out of conscription. Regardless, Lips-Peter insults the young man who asks for his daughter's hand, and then Luise fails to meet Christian for a planned rendezvous. The narrator remarks, "In dieser Nacht sog er bittren, grimmen Haß ein gegen die ganze Menschheit" (That night, he fed on a bitter, grim hatred toward the entire human race).[36] Christian's personality turns. He keeps company with the Black servant Mico, whom he grew up with. I examine the fate of Mico and the ways Rotermund positions the disparaging influence of Blackness, excessive "freedom" in Brazil, and white settlerism in greater detail below, but as the story unfolds, Christian displays behavior that is evidence of his moral decline. In a Pfarrer's sermon, he laments the flaws of his flock: "Das in Brasilien heranwachsende Geschlecht sei leider zum größten Teil zu flach und äußerlich" (20; The race growing up in Brazil is unfortunately too dull and superficial for the most part). Christian seems to embody that stunted growth.

Rotermund plots the novella in two parts, both of which revolve around a public event in the colony. The first is a church celebration, the second a political rally. In part one, a church festival, *Kerbtag*, draws German speakers from the city as well as the colony. Here, the parallel love stories unfold. Christian's father, the *Wirt*, also *Vendamann* or *Vendemann* (salesman, a mix of Portuguese and German), as the storekeeper, plays host as the proprietor of the meeting place. The tensions among inhabitants of the city (*Städter*) and jungle dwellers (*Urwälder*) play out along with other sources of tension and division, from preferences for beer over wine to degrees of education and influence. In conversation with the visitor Peter, the *Wirt* holds forth about the virtues he preaches without practicing: "Ja, der Mensch ist kein Stück Vieh, das bloß arbeitet und frißt; der Mensch muß auch fortschreiten [. . .] O, wir Urwälder sind auch nicht bloß Dreckbauern. Bildung muß sein; ja ohne Bildung geht's nicht" (15; Yes, the human being is not a head of livestock that just works and feeds; the human being must also move forward [. . .] Oh, we jungle dwellers are more than just dirty farmers. You have to have education; yes, without education, nothing works). Peter, the smith from the city and the Birkenfelder Jakob's son, tolerates the *Vendemann*'s insults. The self-important *Wirt* gives him a sign that he is a freemason and is visibly annoyed when Peter fails to recognize it. The *Wirt* flaunts material wealth, bullies

---

36. Rotermund, "Die beiden Nachbarn," 10. Further references to this text appear as page numbers in parenthesis. The transcription should probably read "zog" (rather than "sog").

everyone including his son, and sees himself as part of a powerful inner circle. Freemasonry was embedded in Brazil's history. Dom Pedro I was a freemason; he named a fellow freemason first grand master of Grande Oriente do Brasil after independence in 1822. The lodges played key roles in disseminating certain liberal politics. Rotermund's characterization of the *Wirt* as the villain signals the author's disdain for his membership in the secret society.

The *Kerbtag* provides a stage for a number of conflicts, including tensions among the suitors. The innocent Peter, having promised Sulmire a dance, keeps his word. Christian, eager to move on to a new conquest, Sulmire, indulges a fit of jealous rage and starts a fight. With his father egging him on, Christian hits Peter over the head with a bottle of beer. Peter convalesces at the home of Lips-Peter; Luise nurses him and she falls in love. They marry, on the same day as Christian and Sulmire. The latter couple and guests celebrate lavishly; their relationship deteriorates, while the former strengthen their attachment without luxury; the narrator lavishes praise on their spirit of generosity and honest contentment, which qualifies as "Liebe rechter Art" or "fromme Liebe" (26; love of the right kind or devout love). Rotermund's pastoral narrator stands firmly on the side of Peter's faith and ethical behavior. Meanwhile, Christian declines.

The allegiances and alliances, calibrated by attraction and marriage, by greed and desire, ultimately heed a higher call. While common language remains important, the historical figure of the provincial president, Gaspar do Silveira Martins, has a more galvanizing effect on the group. The pronouncement is followed by a taxonomy of Germanness: Jakob and Peter hail from Birkenfeld, a small enclave in Oldenburg. We read that even the smallest region has rival groups as Rotermund describes a tribalism, the maintenance of which seems absurd in the *Urwald* colony. Onto the landscape of Brazilian nationhood, Rotermund maps formal and informal political and politicizing spaces. Readers encounter Idarbänner, Hanbukler, Hünsrücker, all of whom curse and compete with each other (21–22). The characters attribute this fractiousness to the death of the *Konsul*, Rot-Fritz from Wolfstal (22), who played an ad hoc leadership role in the colony. A select circle decides that Lips-Peter should serve as *Konsul* over the Pomeranians, Mecklenburger, and Hanoverians (22); this positions him as a moral and political center of gravity for the other characters, and for the reader. The story gathers momentum toward some type of unity. Brenner-Karl insists, "Wir sind keine Brasilianer, sondern Birkenfelder" (22; We are not Brasilianers, we are Birkenfelder). In his reassertion of regionalism and *Lokalpatriotismus*, the character resists identification with the nation; colonists seem stuck in feudal fiefdoms. This event opens the second part of the novella.

The visit of Silveira Martins brings the competitive tribalisms in dialogue with the politicization of slavery. Increasingly, scholarly attention to the archive of German-language engagement with theological justifications of enslavement, white-centric historiography, and the colonization of southern Brazil illuminates overlapping anxieties between European settlerism and African, American, and Indigenous peoples and spaces. The cameo appearance of Silveira Martins persuades an otherwise skeptical character, imbued with leadership charisma, to identify with the whitening of southern Brazil as part of a national project that transcends theological differences. Known for his defense of non-Catholics and support of the German colony communities, Silveira Martins is welcomed; he quotes Schiller and insists, "Wir müssen viel aus der deutschen Literatur lernen" (41; We must learn a lot from German literature). The Germans are described as "good Brazilians" (41) and the invocation of the German cultural heritage is accompanied by the insistence that the colonists not become white slaves to replace enslaved Blacks (41–42). Slavery remains a constant point of historical reference, a cautionary tale to leverage reconciliation, peace, and prosperity among the German speakers of the province, both among themselves and with their new world compatriots. With this, a young girl gives a prepared speech in Portuguese (44). The province of Rio Grande do Sul should be as one: "der klaffende Riß zwischen Deutschen und Brasiliane[n] war geheilt" (46; the gaping tear between Germans and Brazilians was healed). With this newly minted ethnic national identity, the novella works out the subplots of home life; the "Schlampe" Sulmira loses her no-good husband, whom Peter tries to save.[37] She marries Peter's brother Eduard, and the narrator assures the reader of a moral catharsis for the colonists. What survives is the cultivation of German identity—by eschewing a form of enslavement reserved for others—despite the wild environment. This entertainment literature, disseminated by the author and publisher to locals

---

37. For a sustained reading of Rotermund's Luise as a model of rural female evangelical identity, the counterpoint is the city dweller, Sulmire. See Irmgart Grützmann and Mateus Klumb, "Idendidade feminina modelar em Os Dois Vizinhos, de Wilhelm Rotermund," in *Mouseion, Revista Eletrônica do Museu e Arquivo Histórico La Salle*, no. 31 (dez. 2018): 9–26, esp. 23. Their illuminating analysis of the religious framing of the opposing characters of Luise and Sulmire contextualizes the late nineteenth-century European rubrics of the feminine. By contrast, I explore these identities as they unfold against the background of racial and political difference.

and readers in the homeland, relies on print media to recruit and reform any internecine rivalries directed at the new citizens of the wilderness. It encourages overcoming regional differences, or transposing them to the local conflict between the urban and rural, and superseding these through German territorializing of the new nation-state. Asserting political agency and learning the lessons of whiteness in Brazil provide the necessary leverage. The *Urwald* of Brazil invites German-speaking readers into a territorialized space in which Blackness and Indigeneity rival white masculinity. In the next section, the New World "wilderness within" of a young female protagonist in a coming-of-age story complicates the model of the German feminine ideal through her remigration to Germany during the Age of Empire. She brings the internalized uncultivated landscape with her.

From the Brazilian *Urwald* to Civilization

Directed at a younger reading audience, Maria Hellemeyer's prose appeared around 1900 in *Auerbach's Deutscher Kinderkalender auf das Jahr 1902*, for example, and in a fairy-tale series, and as a two-volume set, often assumed to be autobiographical. The story "Die kleine Urwälderin" (The little jungle girl) and its illustrations were published in the *Kinderkalender*, which was founded in 1833 by Dr. August Bertold Auerbach. First housed in Berlin, it moved after 1887 to the Fernau Verlag in Leipzig. Under the direction of its fourth editor, Georg Bötticher (1848–1918), the 1902 edition of the *Kalender* contains a six-page story by W. Helmar, Hellemeyer's pseudonym, accompanied by two of Max Loose's illustrations. It narrates a day in the life of a young German protagonist, Anita Villinger, who lives on a plantation in the jungle with her father and the domestic servant, Caschumka. Anita must earn the right to play with her beloved doll, Liesl, who is attacked by a monkey on a ride through the jungle. The tropes of a forest fairy tale are defamiliarized,[38] transformed into a colonial fantasy that elides historical contexts of latent and manifest colonialism. Bracketing harsh realities of history, from centuries of African slavery in the Americas to European exploitation of the Amazon and its resources, the story is a cautionary adventure about the consequences

---

38. Susanne Zantop, *Colonial Fantasies: Conquest, Family, and Nation in Precolonial Germany, 1770–1870* (Durham, NC: Duke University Press, 1997), 2.

suffered by a doll in the wild. A monkey attacks the doll, but Caschumka repairs her with bird skin and feathers. Liesl, the story concludes, thusly returns to Germany.[39]

In his study of literature from and about Brazil aimed at young readers and children, Franz Obermeier characterizes much of the work as an attempt to process "die soziale Realität des Landes" (the social reality of the country),[40] though he leaves a wide margin for the unspecific scenarios common to fairy tales and children's stories. We can speculate about authorial intention to make Brazil palatable for emigration around 1900; after 1888 and the abolition of slavery, a conscious effort to "whiten" the population prompted Brazilian politicians and diplomats to commit their efforts and resources to recruiting European families. The German settlements, however, thrived in the south (Rio Grande do Sul). After 1889 and the end of the monarchy, further changes took place within Brazil, but the work of Hellemeyer and others remains largely oblivious to external realities. Obermeier observes that travel literature was rewritten for younger readers and sometimes reworked as fiction.[41] He clarifies the composition of the target audience for Brazilian adventures: "Das gefährliche Abenteuer präsentierende Land bot sich einfach mehr für die Selbstbewährung Jugendlicher oder junger Erwachsener an, als für Reisen von Kindern" (The country and associated presentation of a dangerous adventure simply appealed more to the self-examination of adolescent or young adult readers than for children's travel).[42] The lengthier work targets a German-speaking audience, specifically thematizing the consequences of remigration. Though he treats W. Helmar's *Vom Urwald zur Kultur. Erlebnisse eines Mädchens* (From the jungle to civilization: Experiences of a young girl, 1898) elsewhere, he does so dismissively, attributing the inadequate understanding of cultural difference in Brazil to the shortcomings of the writer.[43] Speculating on her gender, he does not identify Maria Hellemeyer as the

---

39. For an in-depth reading of the story itself and "Die Giraffe," also published in a later edition of Auerbach's *Kinderkalender*, see Simpson, *The Play World*, 138–40.

40. Franz Obermeier, *Brasilien "für die Jugend und das Volk": Kinder- und Jugendliterator aus und über Brasilien vom 18. Jahrhundert bis in die Mitte des 20. Jahrhunderts*, Christian-Alberts-Universität zu Kiel, 2016, published online: https://macau.uni-kiel.de/servlets/MCRFileNodeServlet/macau_derivate_00000404/JugendliteraturBeide.pdf, 70.

41. Obermeier, *Brasilien "für die Jugend und das Volk,"* 70.

42. Obermeier, *Brasilien "für die Jugend und das Volk,"* 70.

43. Obermeier, *Brasilien "für die Jugend und das Volk,"* 132. Obermeier offers a brief analysis of the novel, 131-32.

author behind the pseudonym. Indeed, little is known about her life.[44] While she did not achieve critical acclaim or even notice, her work reproduces a paradigm about ethnographic play and practicing whiteness that has considerable purchase on the development of European notions of culture and civilization through competitive colonization, often independent of historical reality. Obermeier notes, for example, that Brazil functions for her as a "Versatzstück einer exotischen Prägung einer Normabweichung" (a set piece for the exotic impression of a deviation from the norm).[45] I do not disagree, but the nature of those impressions interests me. That her work appears in the *Kalender* for young readers suggests she reached the intended audience. That the "exotic" involves the protection and preservation of white skin and an amalgamation of African and American colonial tropes of the wilderness prefaces her sustained narrative about the metonymic relationship between the wild and the maturing woman.

Adventure stories about play around 1900 unfold with the nation as a recent phenomenon and German colonization of Africa a contemporary reality. Following the unification of the German states in 1871, Germany enhanced its national narrative with colonial ambitions. As historian David Ciarlo cogently observes, however, the majority of Germans evinced little interest in the colonies: "despite a brief surge of interest (buoyed largely by the press), the German public seemed, at least to the die-hard colonial 'enthusiasts,' to largely ignore Germany's colonies."[46] At the same time, Germans abroad in North and South America identified with the imperial desires of the homeland, self-defining as colonies and pioneers on selected frontiers.

---

44. She is listed as the author behind the pseudonym in Sophie Pataky, *Lexikon deutscher Frauen der Feder. Erster Band A-L* Eine Zusammenstellung der seit dem Jahre 1840 erschienenen Werke weiblicher Autoren, nebst Biographieen der lebenden und einem Verzeichnis der Pseudonyme *Erster Band A-L* (Berlin: Carl Pataky Verlag, 1898; Deutsches Textarchiv [DTA]. (Berlin 1898; Deutsches Textarchiv [DTA]), with only the *Märchenschatz* publication attributed under the cross-referenced pseudonym (332; DTA Bild 0350): https://www.deutschestextarchiv. de/book/view/pataky_lexikon01_1898/?hl=W.&p=350; and the address Düsseldorf, Karl-Anton Strasse 6 (329; DTA Bild 0347): https://www.deutschestextarchiv.de/book/view/pataky_lexikon01_1898/?hl=Hellemeyer&p=34. Proximate and subsequent publication dates account for the absence of Hellemeyer's works. Ancestry databases and some passenger lists suggest a female Hellemeyer (farmer) sailed to North America, but even contact with possible descendants has yielded few reliable details.

45. Obermeier, *Brasilien "für die Jugend und das Volk,"* 132.

46. David Ciarlo, *Advertising Empire: Race and Visual Culture in Imperial Germany* (Cambridge, MA: Harvard University Press, 2014), 4.

The subtitle of Hellemeyer's volumes, *Erlebnisse eines Mädchens* (Experiences of a girl), opens a view of specifically female traits, bred in the jungle and unlearned in "civilization." With frequent self-deprecation, the narrator gains perspective on competing versions of herself that align with the processes of colonization. How do these prepare her for or hinder remigration?

The protagonist learns survival through encounters with Black and Indigenous characters. The character Caschumka, illustrated as black in the story (published in black and white), described with "bronze skin," opens part 1 of Hellemeyer's *Bildungsroman* for European girls with a pronouncement about the Indians: "Es sind schlimme Leute, die Indianer; grausam, tückisch und undankbar. Sie rauben, morden und plündern." (They are bad people, the Indians; cruel, treacherous, and ungrateful. They steal, kill, and pillage).[47] In this narrative, Caschumka serves as a housekeeper and enforcer of local lore. During the rainy season, she tells "Schauergeschichten" (horror stories) focused on Indian raids (I:11). The protagonist and narrator, Juanita, resists the label "R*thaut" (I:13; r*dskin), and, suffering from cabin fever, she insists on riding her horse Pittie into the jungle. With her descriptions of the surrounding natural world, mentions of monkeys, and the size of lizards, Juanita uses European standards for comparison throughout, until she tries to convey her perception of the foliage. For this, she resorts to the thousand-and-one nights, familiar to readers but indicative of imaginative limits (I:23). The intent is to convey "Märchenpracht" (I:24; fairy-tale splendor) and the "Zauber des Urwaldes" (I:23; magic of the jungle). Chapter 1 grounds the reader in a fairy-tale world, but engages loosely with a realistic topography.

The story provides few topographical markers, but Juanita finds herself in view of the Llanos, a signpost that she has strayed from her path (I:27). On the ride home, a Tupi boy, about twelve years old (like herself), helps her get oriented. The Tupi may be familiar to the reader from Staden's elaborations on cannibalism, deeply embedded in the European imagination about the New World wilderness. Juanita, her initial fear overcome, learns from him in this contact zone: "Weiße Leute töten Indianer immer" (I:31; White people always kill Indians). Toros, the new friend and guide, tells of dead parents and unprincipled settlers and hunters. Juanita retorts, "So abscheuliche weiße Leute giebt es heute nicht mehr" (I:33; Such horrible white people do not

---

47. Hellemeyer, published under the pseudonym W. Helmar, *Vom Urwald zur Kultur: Erlebnisse eines Mädchens* (Berlin: Verlag von Otto Janke, 1898), I:3. Further references to this two-volume text will appear with volume and page numbers in parenthesis.

exist any more). The possibility of bonding and sympathy opens up; Juanita expresses her own loss and recalls the simple cross marking her own mother's grave. Toros refers to the "Blaßgesichter" (I:34; pale faces) who signify the enemy. Her attempts to maintain a friendship are thwarted, not least by the servant Mameluk (the word itself means "mulatto" in Portuguese), whose Indian grandmother implants self-hatred in him. At the end of the first chapter, racial hatred, from which the narrator seems immune, reasserts itself along with hierarchy, entrenched in a fairy-tale structure.

With racialized models in place, Juanita's narrative turns to details of competing European and *Urwald* behaviors. Years pass unnarrated, and, reminiscent of the youngest princess in the Grimms' tale "The Frog Prince," in which she progresses from child's play to marriageability within a paragraph, Juanita displays signs of maturity. She adopts riding side-saddle, though she wears her gloves out faster than a European would (I:47). Her father's horse and Pittie are the only ones groomed in a European manner, attending to insect bites, eyes, hooves, and mouth. The black groom rubs the horses down (I:49). Except for having to shoot a horse bitten by a bat, which damaged the gloves, the narrator herself develops in peace. She insists that their herds, coffee, and sugar fields stay safe: "Auch von Indianern hatten wir noch nie eine Beunruhigung erfahren" (I:51; We had not even experienced any unrest from the Indians). Her account of life on the jungle plantation includes stories of exchange with Indians, who share a set of beliefs: "Alle Indianer und N*ger glauben an Zauberei und wenden vielerlei Mittel als Gegenzauber an, der vielleicht nach ihrer Meinung die Wirkung verliert, wenn man ihn verrät" (I:56; All Indians and N*groes believe in magic and employ all types of countermagic, which perhaps they believe loses its effect if they reveal it). Señorita Villinger, as she is known, is poised between Indigenous knowledge and European imports.

The disruption occurs with a letter from Europe and the decision that she will return. Appropriate clothing for her European debut is ordered. The sense of European problems and politics approaching the outpost is heightened. In the "culture" section of Hellemeyer's book, national unity enters the discourse about a revived military masculinity. In the jungle, while some emigrants needed to affiliate themselves with the army, the protagonist singles out those who saw battle. News of German victory even penetrated the deepest jungle, she informs her reader. Caschumka, we learn, has to sew a tricolored flag. Juanita meets an officer and confesses: "Ich hatte eine grenzenlose Verehrung für das Heer und für jeden Soldaten, der mit im Krieg gewesen, im besondern" (II:86; I had a boundless admiration for the army and especially for those soldiers in particular who had been in the war). Military admiration morphs into desire for the professional German male. On a ride, the protagonist meets a young German engineer who works with the railway, arranging houses for the wives of other workers and himself. Her father meets them; he instantly notices her dirty attire and orders her to change clothes. Feeling herself, Juanita asks for her mother's dress, crinoline and all. Inexperience ruins her grand entrance; she tries to sit and the petticoat snaps up "wie ein empörtes Ungetüm" (I:87; like an outraged monster). The commentary indicates that little changed between her first donning of European fashion and her future narrative self: "Später—in der civilisierten Welt—habe ich erkennen gelernt, welch tyrannischen Einfluß die Mode dort auf die Menschen ausübt. Im Urwald hat man davon natürlich keine Ahnung, da heißt es: Nur praktisch und bequem!—weder chic noch hochmodern" (I:88; Later—in the civilized world—I learned to recognize what a tyrannical influence fashion has on the people there. In the jungle, one has no idea about that naturally, there the rule is: Just practical and comfortable!—neither chic nor highly modern). As the love story begins, the reader learns that you can take the girl out of the jungle, but not the jungle out of the girl.

Reader, she married him. Beyond the eighteenth-century novel of manners and the prospect of a love marriage and an enviable, fairy-tale outcome, the literature and social structures of German colonialism revolved around the dread of miscegenation. Lora Wildenthal has argued most effectively that the loss of rights, as much as racism, moral panics, and white fear, prompted German women to participate in the colonial project as cultural interlocutors. By contrast, in these volumes, the purported feminine influence of the protagonist falters by European standards. In one episode, again one which involves shame, Winkmann surprises her in the kitchen; she drops a basket and injures herself. His attentiveness moves her, and she explains that in the jungle, pain and injury meet with the admonishment to bite the bullet. Juanita shares that she read about European women's hands and shows him her uninjured, toughened one. He takes it; she notices his is "weich" (I:96; soft). Pushed to the limit of her understanding, she blurts out a question: "Warum sind Sie denn überhaupt aus Ihrem schönen Deutschland weggezogen, wo man ohne Moskitonetze schlafen kann, wo man nicht vor Schlangen, Jaguaren, Pumas und so weiter auf der Hut sein muß, in lichten Wäldern? Wo es Eisen, Heinzelmännchen und Nixen giebt und allerlei geheimnisvolle, zauberhafte Dinge?" (I:96; How could you have left your beautiful Germany, where you can sleep without mosquito nets, where you do not have to be on the lookout for snakes, jaguars, pumas and so forth, in light forests? Where there are iron, elves, and nixies, and all sorts of secretive, magical things). The character's knowledge of Brazil seems as culturally mediated as her knowledge of Germany: she exchanges one fairy-tale world for another, European forests and South American jungles. Eschewing the spirituality of the Indians and Africans, she opts for elves and nixies. His bitter reply, consonant with stories of opportunity elsewhere, reveals that he could not find meaningful work. Her naïve question, whether he means money, meets with his surprise. "Ich brauche nie Geld" (I:97; I never need money). Their moment of connection is marked by the first time she shows no shame for her intimacy with a jungle epistemology. Hellemeyer portrays her eschewing money as a positive gender trait. Winkmann offers his perspective: "In Europa, überhaupt außerhalb des Urwaldes brauchen die Damen alle viel Geld, oft viel mehr, als ein Mann herbeizuschaffen vermag" (I:97; In Europe, anywhere beyond the jungle in fact, women all need lots of money, often much more than a man is able to provide). Astonished, she asks what they could possibly need the money for—he laughs, clearly amused, and remarks that he has made an "Entdeckung" (I:97; discovery). Using the language of adventure, he discovers a woman who does not know what money can buy. Though she is sensitive about his response, she continues to contemplate women's need for money and asks her father for some to prove her Europeanization.

Leaving the jungle presents challenges. Juanita undergoes a series of trials, including the performance of a dance (I:129–30) Caschumka taught her to prove herself civilized when necessary, though he laughs at her, comparing her to a puppet on a string. When Winkmann's hut is ready, and he takes leave of her, she resists and complains. News of new raids and resistance to the railway work cause the anxiety. In despair, she seeks her mother's grave; she hears her mother's voice encouraging prayer, and Juanita's thoughts turn to Toros. She searches for him in the jungle, calling his name. The split in narrative awareness of fear comes into play: "Was Nerven sind, kannte ich damals noch nicht—die bekommt man erst in Europa—dennoch zitterte ich in diesem Augenblick am ganzen Körper" (I:145; At the time, I did not know what nerves are—you get those only in Europe—still I was shaking all over my body in this moment). This pivot in the narrator's perception of herself, from innocent self-sameness in the wild to European nerves, inscribes female perspective into the increasingly popular opposition between fin-de-siècle gender types popularized in psychoanalysis, philosophy, and contemporary literature. The modernist malaise featured in Joseph Breuer's and Sigmund Freud's case studies, Friedrich Nietzsche's herd mentalities, and Lou Andreas-Salomé's novellas inhabits the periphery of the still robust Juanita.

Beyond the literary references, the narrator demonstrates a growing awareness of other treacheries. Before her former friend shows himself, she believes herself to be in mortal danger. The language evokes the fear of rape. Toros appears and assures her of his continued friendship, and she asks him to protect the white man and his work. Fully aware of her betrayal of Toros's trust and the race implications, she insists the white man in question is her brother. Toros overcomes his reluctance, but she is the "white flower" (I:147); he helps, informing her that the raid was planned for that very night. The plot drives forward toward her transformation and acculturation. She dashes to Winkmann's hut and stays, though he tries repeatedly to send her home. Her father appears, hits Winkmann before she can explain, and she speaks her first "Abbitte" or apology without shame (I:156–57). She finds it emancipating. The reader understands that the unwritten conversation between Winkmann and Villinger seals Anni's fate; her father calls her that for the first time at this juncture (I:158), lamenting the loss of her mother.

In the moment she is promised, she returns to European genealogy, but not before brokering rapprochement between the railroad and the Tupi. The second volume continues the tale after the rupture of travel. Tensions compete for acceptance, between the superego-like pronouncements about those "aus einem civilisiertem Lande" (II:3; from a civilized country) and the narrator's id-like "[w]ir armen Waldmenschen" (II:3; we poor forest people). On the ship, now responding to the name "Anni," she abides by her husband's friendly but firm command, "Nicht kindlich," when other women aboard eye her and she buries her head in his shoulder (II:7; not so childish). Civilized behavior, she learns, is relative. The self-awareness of her own level of cultivation in the jungle shatters; she mutters about the other passengers with Caschumka, imagining the "wild gauchos" to be above them (II:10). While she helps a sailor who explains things to her, she overhears a male passenger say "Die Wilde ist dort" (II:10; The savage is over there); she leaps at him and she compresses his windpipe in fury. Her husband drags her away from the laughing audience; the man sends her an apology shawl of red silk and asks forgiveness for his inappropriate but well-intentioned jest (II:11). Once ashore, her robust father seems to fail, and her re-education continues.

The protagonist's encounters with *Kultur* revise perceptions of the *Urwald*. Upon arrival, Anni's father murmurs to her, "Hab's sie Dir ersparen wollen, die Civilisation. Nun leidest Du hier unter Deiner freien Entwicklung in der

Wildnis" (II:33; I wanted to spare you this, civilization. Now you will suffer from your free development in the wilderness). A couple of children ran alongside their conveyance, having observed Caschumka's skin color. Others join them, and Anni notices her husband's shamed, reddened face: "nichts war ihm so sehr verhaßt, als besprochen, belacht zu werden. Wohl niemals war es ihm passiert—jetzt bei der Heimkehr mit seiner Frau geschah es" (II:33; nothing was more hateful to him than being gossiped about, laughed at. It probably had never happened to him before—now it occurred at the homecoming with his wife). In her new role as wife in Germany, Anni continues to heap embarrassments on the family inadvertently. Racial difference, as in the children's gazes, also causes Anni's self-consciousness. Observing herself in a mirror, she thinks, "Nun war es mir immer schon ein Kummer gewesen, daß meine Hautfarbe gelb war. Heut, wo mich der elende Spiegel wie eine Mulattin erscheinen ließ, war ich geradezu unglücklich. Mein tiefbraunes, fast schwarzes Haar, die dunklen Augen und der gesamte Eindruck meiner Persönlichkeit, die so gar nichts Deutsches hatte, brachten mich rein zur Verzweifelung. Jetzt sah ich auch, daß ich gelbe Hände hatte, und wünschte mir sehnlichst ein Paar Handschuhe" (II:70; It had always grieved me that my skin color was yellow. Today, with the miserable mirror letting me appear like a mulatta, I was really unhappy. My dark-brown, nearly black hair, dark eyes, and the complete impression of my personality, which completely lacked anything German, brought me to despair. Now I saw as well that I had yellow hands and wished desperately for a pair of gloves). Desire for whiteness plagues Annita; she channels it into consumption, purchases a pair of white gloves, then insults her husband's potential client in her eagerness to show them off. Eventually, she understands her beauty, after a shopkeeper envies her "südländisches Gesicht" (II:106; southern face). Anni confirms her dark appearance in the mirror: "Ob ich erwartet hatte, daß ich plötzlich blendend weiß, blond und rosig geworden sei?" (II:106; Perhaps I had expected that I had suddenly become white, blonde, and rosy?). With so much emphasis on appearances, she embraces herself not as German but as "Brazilian" (II:111).

The superficiality at the core of *Kultur* enhances appreciation for the practical simplicity of the *Urwald*. Anni detects this appreciation in her father, but also recognizes her husband's need to work and earn money. She attributes the simplicity to Amerindians, who refer to gold as "deadly dust" (II:102). The narrator expands on the linguistic label, expanding on their knowledge of hidden gold stores, the metal "das die erste Ursache zu ihrer Vernichtung gewesen ist" (II:102; that was the first cause of their destruction). From her perspective, *Naturvölker* live simply, eschewing money and material goods; *Kulturvölker* live for money. Her story infuses nature into culture. The two major differences discussed during courtship in the jungle, money and nerves, are connected in the second volume. Aware of greater financial and social responsibilities, Anni comes to understand neuroses. She also learns harder lessons as a consequence of her unconventional behavior. On a short trip with her father and Caschumka, she goes to the circus, spellbound by the trick riders. After a series of bad decisions, she performs herself, only to be molested by a man backstage after the performance. During another adventure, she shares a ride with a duke who kisses her hand, declares his love, and makes sexual advances. All the while, household work is supposed to be her only responsibility; she leaves it to her mother-in-law, whose loving ministrations eventually instill acceptably feminine tendencies (II:147).

The pursuit of prosperity civilization underwrites has to be interrupted for the moral of the story about female remigration to emerge. Herr Villinger dies; Winkmann dedicates himself to work; Anni grows ill, and a doctor encourages travel. When she returns home, her mother-in-law is dying of pneumonia, her husband's uninsured building burned down, and the bank failed. In the face of these dire circumstances, she demands to know from her husband why he had not summoned her home: "Du warst doch krank gewesen, mußtest Dich erholen; die Sorgen sind für mich" (II:159; You had been ill, had to recover; the worries are for me). In that moment, she understands that real love must be selfless. The Indian wisdom about deadly gold finally hits home: "In den Sorgen der Hausfrau, vergaß ich meine Grillen, mein Aufbäumen gegen die Kultur, sah ich mit klarem Blick, wie schlichte Fürsorge beglückt, wenn man sie nur anerkennen will" (II:160; In the worries of a housewife, I forgot my minor complaints, my rebellion against culture; I saw with a clear view how simple caring can make you happy if you can just recognize it). In the birth of two children, her education is complete: "Bei ihrem Heranwachsen lerne ich ihn erst so recht schätzen, den Segen der Kultur im deutschen Vaterlande" (II:160; As they grow, I am really just learning to cherish it, the blessing of culture in the German fatherland).

In concluding the autobiographical trope of learning German love of family and fatherland through the acceptance of a conventional, non-Brazilian model of femininity, Hellemeyer expands the range of female ideals to include the masculinity of her protagonist's life in the Global South. The acquisition of nervous disorders in European culture alludes to the fin-de-siècle hysteric, the neurotic bourgeois housewife familiar from Freud's case study of Dora, in which he nods agreement with the crude judgment that if a woman lacks love and has an inattentive husband, she produces illness as a weapon: "the spoiled wife would forget all her sufferings if her child were to fall dangerously ill or if some catastrophe were to threaten the family circumstances."[48]

Missing from this remigration fiction is the femme fatale, though the reference to Anita's "southern" face posits a beauty that associates her appeal with the unfamiliar (in German towns and cities). Further, the spectacle of skin color and racial, "phenotypical" differences that attract the attention of curious children and shame Winkmann intersects with the popular ethnographic displays of the era, the *Völkerschau* and parks of Carl Hagenbeck. Eric Ames observes that Hagenbeck explicitly developed a "post-Buffalo Bill" ethos in a revision of the Wild West shows of William F. Cody. "At the same time," he writes, "going a step further than the Wild West shows of 1890, Hagenbeck's *Völkerschau* stakes a claim not only to history, but also to fantasy."[49] The history of German emigrants in Brazil intersects with the male fantasy of a wild woman from the jungle, tamed by heteronormative behaviors and desires that channel national and religious subordination. Ames quotes one Hagenbeck guidebook, in which fantasy and imaginative fiction are exposed and repurposed: "When people speak of Indians, nobody thinks of the numerous tribes in Brazil or in the rest of South American, in Central America or Mexico. They always mean the famous Prairie Indians of legend and history."[50] The culmination of jungle traits, the display of human beings, and the performance of German Brazilian gender in the *Bildungsroman* takes place in the crucial climax, Anni's circus performance. There, away from her husband, she displays her riding and shooting skills, which associates her with a realm of popular entertainment that announces the availability of female performers. The nameless worker who advises against Anni's participation warns the aspiring middle-class wife of dangers; the warning goes

---

48. Sigmund Freud, *Dora: An Analysis of a Case of Hysteria* (1905 [1901]), introduced by Philip Rieff (New York: Collier, 1963), 61–62. See also Jess Sully, "Challenging the Stereotype: The Femme Fatale in Fin-de-Siècle Art and Early Cinema," in *The Femme Fatale: Images, Histories, Contexts*, ed. H. Hanson and C. O'Rawe (London: Palgrave Macmillan, 2010), 46–60. Though Sully's primary interest is on the transition of the trope from academic art to screen, the argument highlights the sexual promiscuity of female "otherness" and cites the literature that associates this with the immigrant in dominant powers, 47.

49. Eric Ames, *Carl Hagenbeck's Empire of Entertainments* (Seattle: University of Washington Press, 2009), 130.

50. Quoted in Ames, *Empire of Entertainments*, 131.

unheeded. We learn that Anni gave the trick rider the horse she had trained, then she learns of death. Hellemeyer's cautionary tale participates in regulating the display of masculine traits in her protagonist, whose acceptance of German blessings is facilitated by the cultural appropriation of Amerindian epistemology and history. Ultimately exculpatory, the lesson learned effaces the history of imperialism and genocide in the competing colonialism narratives of European powers.

Germans as *Rassenvolk*

The marginalized Indigenous character Toros, left behind in the wilderness, recedes from Hellemeyer's story of female civilization in a postsettler existence in Germany. Toros has a fictional counterpart in the novella of rival neighbors: the Black servant, Mico, who plays a supporting role as Christian's contemporary and recipient of the *Wirt*'s verbal lashings. Not until the story approaches its end does Mico's fate gain significance, largely because it foreshadows the final demise of Christian. The reader first encounters him as Christian's helper, "der N*eger, Mico genannt" (3; The N*eger, called Mico), complete with exonym to designate his imposed identity. As they grow up, the casual construction of violent agency, handed down and across from generation to generation, men to women, neighbors to others, and all to the enslaved, suggests a similar bond between master and servant: "Mico wuchs mit ihm heran und teilte gewöhnlich seine körperlichen Uebungen. Wo die beiden sich umhertrieben, wußte man selten zu sagen" (4; Mico grew up alongside him and usually took part in his physical exercises. No one really ever could say where the two of them were hanging around). From the tone and the context, it is clear they were up to no good. Subsequently, Mico assists Christian in herding and moving the mules (8) and changing horses during the race (31), but he is also at the *Wirt*'s beck and call. In the fight scene, after the *Wirt* smashes a bottle over Peter's head, he yells for Mico to clean up the blood (23). The final three mentions of Mico's name occur when a neighbor reports to Sulmira that her husband is wanted for selling stolen mules in Campos da Sina do Serra in the northeastern part of Rio Grande do Sul. In dialogue with his mother, Christian informs her, that Mico will not be coming back. When Sulmire hears her mother-in-law muttering "Der kommt nicht wieder," she assumes the demonstrative pronoun "he" refers to Christian. The latter shouts "'Mico kommt nicht wieder!'" (51; "Mico will not be coming back!"). Sulmire wants to know why. Her mother-in-law urges the young woman to ask no further questions about the fate of Mico, indicating that in the *Campahna* and on the *Serra* things happen, but she stresses the loss of her son. The ambiguity requires context to understand the racial divide in the novella. Mico is expendable; the reader must infer either that he was killed or ran away. At the time Rotermund wrote the story, several antislavery laws were in place, some for appearance only. Historian Keila Grinberg works on the legal arguments used in freedom/re-enslavement lawsuits in the late nineteenth century to determine in part the reliance on legal protections: "It is clear that the Brazilian courts played an extremely important role in securing the emancipation of African slaves and their descendants. This importance is evidenced not only by the large number of freedom lawsuits, but also, primarily, by many rulings favorable to the effective liberation of slaves."[51]

Rotermund reserved certain types of commentary for the newspaper he founded, though he airs his opinions in the fiction examined earlier through projections of specific ethical and political positions onto his characters. German-language newspapers in the Southern Cone played a role in fostering a sense of community, in part by maintaining a level of commitment to the mother tongue, but also to keep individuals apprised of their civic duty and, in some cases, reinforcing the responsibility of racial identity. In a book about his life and work, Dr. Erich Fausel marks the centenary of Rotermund's death with a eulogizing account of the pastor's contributions to the German community in southern Brazil. Of particular interest, the section on the "Rassenfrage" historicizes Rotermund's articles about Brazilian racial politics and policies. Fausel opens this section with reference to Brazilian race researchers' surprising resistance to French influence, represented by the works of Arthur de Gobineau (1816–1882) on Luso-Brazilian race theory and racism. Noting differences between Brazilian and North American perceptions of race and immigration, Fausel elaborates on North America's European immigrants and defines the "melting pot" as the assimilation of white Europeans "zu einem amerikanischen Standardvolk" (to a standardized American folk): meanwhile, "die Gelben, Roten und Schwarzen werden zwar auch durch die Zivilizationsmaschine gejagt, aber nur um brave citizens zu werden und nicht

---

51. Keila Grinberg, "Re-enslavement, Rights and Justice in Nineteenth-Century Brazil," in *Translating the Americas, U-M Center for Latin American and Caribbean Studies*, vol. 1 (2013), no pagination. Translated by Mark Lambert from Grinberg, "Re-escravização, direitos e justiças no Brasil do século XIX," in *Direitos e justiças: ensaios de história social*, ed. Silvia Lara and Joseli Mendonça (Campinas: Editora da Unicamp, 2006): 101–28.

amerikanische Volks- und Vollbürger" (the yellow, red, and black people are indeed chased through the civilizing machine, but only to become brave citizens and not people and full American citizens).[52] Here, Fausel injects "brave citizens" in the German; the reader perhaps hears *brave* as in the adjectival plural meaning "well behaved," which makes sense in the context. According to his position, the North American excludes races, "die er nicht für vollwertig hält (183; he does not consider to be complete) from the process of civilizing to the extent that it would encompass legal rights. By contrast, Brazil looks toward a 100 percent assimilation, the result of mixing whites and other races. These "Nativisten" (184; Nativists) crafted a "kolonisatorisches und politisches Programm" (184; colonializing and political program) with the goal of preserving the best traits in the former and ameliorating the worst traits in the latter groups. The idea that drove this racial politics: immigration would lead to complete assimilation (184). In this context, he introduces a German professor and academic from Bahia, Dr. Egas Moniz Barreto de Aragão, who believed in the innate superiority of the German race. Enter Wilhelm Rotermund.

Noteworthy is the compunction Fausel feels to preface his summation of Rotermund's race theory with the assurance that Moniz Barreto, not the German-born Rotermund, insisted on the superiority of the German race. Moniz Barreto attributed the "sickness" in the Brazilian social order to the race mixing between Portuguese and African. The only way to cure this disease, Fausel reports on the gymnasium professor's writings, was an infusion of pure German blood (184). That a Brazilian broadcast this race theory elevating Germanness in this way emboldened Rotermund, so Fausel speculates. In his series of articles in the *Deutsche Post* (1896–1897), Rotermund took a stand against the assimilation theory of the Nativists and for the Germans as a *Rassenvolk*.[53] In his dissenting racial logic, the correlate of Germanness as a race is an argument against intermarriage with "romanischen Rassen" (Rotermund, quoted in Fausel, 186; Latin races). Self-preservation, for Rotermund, becomes a patriotic act. Against this race theory, the moral of Rotermund's transprovincialism in "Die zwei Nachbarn" is a plea for overcoming German divisions to preserve the best in the race. While he vehemently opposed a race

---

52. Erich Fausel, *D. Dr. Rotermund: Ein Kampf um Recht und Richtung des evangelischen Deutschtums in Südbrasilien* (São Leopoldo: Verlag der Riograndenser Synode, 1936), 183. Fausel uses "brave citizens" in the original, implying that they are nonetheless excluded from the rights of citizenship. Further references appear with page numbers in parenthesis

53. Fausel, *D. Dr. Rotermund: Ein Kampf*, 185–86.

war, he advocated for preserving racialized integrity, "daß jeder Stamm für seine eigene Ausbildung und Veredelung sorgt" (Rotermund, quoted in Fausel, 187; "that every ethnic people attends to its own education and edification). Rather than commit racial suicide, Germans would better serve the homeland and the fatherland through their dedication to work, language, and customs, rather than dissolving into the Luso-Brazilian population. The pedagogical projects he undertook, too, can be reimagined in the service of racial identity, with the recognition that racialization alters gendered identities as well.

The alignment between the stories of the German *Kolonien* in Brazil, the periodical articles about race, and the pedagogical project around 1900 is not always legible. The occasional literature delivers a moral about integrating German regionalists into a Brazilian-German cohesive province that is consonant with a migration and antiassimilation politics that posits an essential German race. The *Fibel für deutsche Schulen in Brasilien*, which began publishing in 1878,[54] disseminates an upbeat, instructional pedagogy directed at young German speakers born in Brazil. Its material transcends tales of hardship, sacrifice, and exploitation many did experience. This exercise book, geared toward early learners, looks forward to the preservation of German identity through language and custom in Brazil.

The *Fibel* invests deeply in the transmission of cultural patrimony in German-speaking colonies. Patricia Weiduschadt and Elias Kruger Albrecht, in their study of *Fibel* illustrations, observe that education at the time in Brazil was limited, designed to serve urban elites. Their work focuses on the representation of gendered labor and social roles imparted by the images in Rotermund's primer and the later *Mein Rechnenbuch*, first published in 1933.[55] The

---

54. The second edition appeared in 1896 (co-attributed to R. Heuer); in 1908, a ninth edition was published with H. Nack. The fifteenth edition, the only solely authored by Rotermund, appeared in 1922, under the auspices of his publishing house, according to World Cat. https://www.worldcat.org/title/fibel-fur-deutsche-schulen-in-brasilien/oclc/72069986/editions?referer=di&editionsView=true. 5. Auflage 1927 (4. Auflage, 1888–1902 as per Karl Georgs Schlagwortkatalog, google book) Wilhelm Rotermund / R. Heuer. Beyond the local references in this immigrant pedagogy, later series of young-adult fiction focused attention on the world beyond. See for example Walter Stölting, *Baumanns siedeln in Argentinien* (Leipzig: Franz Schneider Verlag, 1934). An exhibit at the Ibero-Amerikanisches Institut in Berlin featured literature for children and young adults, curated by Ulrike Mühlschlegel and Ricarda Musser, November 13–30, 2006.

55. Patricia Weiduschadt and Elias Kruger Albrecht, "German Primers from the Rotermund Publishing House (1927–1933); Gender Representations in Rural Work," *pro-posições* 32 (2021): 1–26, 3 and 2.

authors further note that the immigrants sought to educate their children in Lutheran schools associated with the synod, thus relying on religious institutions to foster learning. Dedicated to preserving the language, Rotermund's *Fibel* insists on the value of instruction, provides learning strategies to use images and repetition, and accounts for the use of German and Latin script. All, according to the preface, is provided to comply with requests from German teachers in Brazilian states.[56] The integral function of the pictures, in addition to their ability to appeal to multiple senses important for language acquisition, is that they offer the authors, teachers, and pupils an opportunity to integrate local environments with German identity.

In his work on the relationship between Brazil and Germany pre- and post-World War I, Stefan Rinke writes, "To sum up: until the First World War, German-Brazilian relations remained part of a hierarchical world order in which spaces were represented in terms of power politics. Yet, underneath the surface of power, lay dimensions of contact and of interactions, for example, amongst commercial houses, in expert cultures, and in the everyday life of migrants, which gave solidity to the relationship between the two distant countries."[57] Rinke examines the persistence of economic relationships between Germany and Brazil, the two nation-states, even after the "rupture" of the war.

Rotermund's story about the feuding neighbors includes the violation of maintaining fences. The signifier of community maintenance appears in the primer (figure 14).

The image on the lower right of the page depicts an intact fence, and a working ride for farmhand and child. The texts, strategically geared toward particular letters, include the tensions between the fauna and the farmer. In the illustration for the letter P, the parrot, the cornfield, and the father figure clash (figure 15): "Die Papagei ist ein schöner Vogel. Aber der Vater sieht die Papagei nicht gern" (65; The parrot is a lovely bird. But father does not like to see the parrot).

The primer conveys the plight of the farmer, whose children admire the birds, and delivers a message of survival in the prose, which attempts a certain lyricism in this scene of instruction.

---

56. Wilhelm Rotermund and Reinhardt Heuer, *Fibel für deutsche Schulen in Brasilien*, "Vorwort zur 3. Auflage," no page. Further references to this volume appear as page number(s) in parenthesis.

57. Stefan Rinke, "Germany and Brazil, 1870–1945, a Relationship between Spaces," *História, Ciências, Saúde—Manguinhos* 21, no. 1 (Jan.–March 2014): 1–16, 6, https://doi.org/10.1590/S0104-59702014005000007.

The New World Wilderness

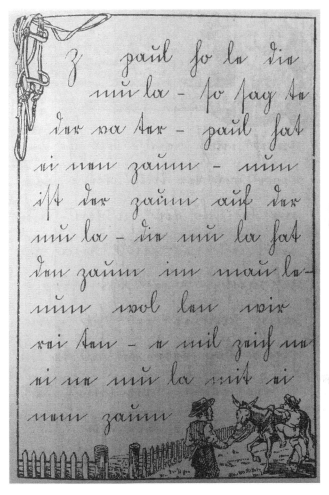

Figure 14. Rotermund-Heuer *Fibel für deutsche Schulen in Brasilien*, 3rd edition, "Zaun" (44; fence).

Finally, the primer invokes German history in language instruction. In the section, "Für fleißige Schüler" (44; For industrious pupils), the teaching of syllabification, though seemingly random, is quite purposeful:

was war da los—wa rum	what was wrong—why
wei nen bei de—war paul da bei	are both crying—was paul there
—nein—er war in der schu le	no—he was in school

Figure 15. Rotermund-Heuer *Fibel*, "Sie richten gern Schaden unter dem Mais an" (65; They like to do damage to the corn).

—pa pa—wo ist mein schaf—   papa—where is my sheep
es ist im gar ten—bit te ho le   it is in the garden—please fetch
es—e mil hat ei ne neu e gei ge   it—emil has a new violin
—pau line sag te—e mil gei ge   Pauline said—emil play
—am mon tag kam pa pa—er   on Monday papa came—he
war auf der ko lo nie ge we sen—   had been to the colony
er kauf te mir ein pferd—e mil   he bought me a horse—emil
be kam ei ne schach tel sol da ten—   got a package of soldiers
pa pa war deut scher sol dat—ich   papa was a German soldier—I
schrei be—um den gar ten ist ein   write—around the yard there is a

| zaun—der zaun ist aus ei sen– | fence—the fence is of iron |
| das ist ein ei ser ner zaun. (44) | that is an iron fence. |

The paragraph, which I take the liberty of dividing into nearly poetic lines, recapitulates the life of a German child living on a farm near a German-speaking enclave, such as São Leopoldo. There are musical instruments, trips to the *Venda* for toy soldiers, a horse, the sheep in the garden, and the iron fence. Finally, in the pedagogical poem to teach script, the father figure has a past as a German soldier. The seemingly random associations between letters and syllables connects history of conscription to immigration. The drive to assert German identities over non-German spaces involves learning the language of history.

The transmission of military paternity, conveyed intellectually to the present through language instruction and materially through the gift of toy soldiers, raises the question of which war was fought, for and against whom, and for what cause. It is crucial to re-evaluate nineteenth-century German-language texts to put them into dialogue with and decolonize national histories. In each case study for this book, decolonization encompasses colonialism and immigration, albeit asymmetrically. An important intervention into this effort, João Biehl and Miqueias Mugge's *Escritos Perdidos: Vida e obra de um imigrante insurgente* (Lost writings: Life and work of an insurgent immigrant) comprises the work of Johann Georg Klein (1822–1915), a German Lutheran who defended the Mucker, a sect in a district of São Leopoldo. The complexity of this theological conflict led to persecution and massacre, radical enough to warrant the violent deployment of the Brazilian army.[58]

Beyond religious conflict, the practical, economic struggle for southern Brazil echoes in the proclamation of the Riograndeser as hybrid citizens, not neither/nor but both. Here, history and political jockeying in the Southern Cone provide a subtext to the rejection of enslavement. In specifying his use of "Southern Cone," Quijano refers parenthetically to Argentina, Chile, and Uruguay; he does not include Paraguay or Brazil, which, despite language difference, often appears in German-ethnic immigration discussions given the recruitment and settlement history of its southernmost provinces, but possibly as well to respect the nation-states' individual histories. In parsing

---

58. João Biehl and Miqueias Mugge have published their new book *Escritos Perdidos: Vida e obra de um imigrante insurgente* (Lost writings: Life and work of an insurgent immigrant) (São Leopoldo: Oikos, 2012, 2022).

subsections of the exonym "Latin America," we find ourselves repeatedly in definitional quandaries. What is the most accountable way to examine the history of individual nations when the nation itself is a construct imposed by European colonization, which had elided or erased precolonial power stuctures that organized peoples and geographies into Indigenous empires? The stories of German-speaking immigrants complicate the histories of those spaces, already ruptured by other Europeans, even as colonies made up of post-*Heimat* communities come to identify with political elites, established in many cases through shared whiteness. The literature and print media they produced and consumed so often falls through disciplinary cracks, too minor or topical a literature, lacking in aesthetic sophistication, or too ambiguous an origin for studies organized by nation, rather than language. Academic disciplines increasingly benefit from embracing prepositions that signify movement through time and space: trans-, inter-, intra-. In the case of southern Brazil, the stories represent provincial loyalties and rivalries from the past, and they demonstrate how these transferred to a new province defined by ethnic Germanness. The tropes the reader encounters generated a German-speaking European image to superimpose on familiar models: the adventurer, the soldier, the pioneer, the farmer, the professional, doctor, engineer, the educator. In each artifact analyzed in this chapter, anxieties about whiteness become visible. Finally, German whiteness is reinforced. In retrospect, the direct line from Schäffer's recruitment tome to fellow German speakers' immigration becomes visible. Embedded in his discourse, exculpatory racism forms a cornerstone of settlerism and with it an entitlement to land and livelihood earned through military service. The soldier and farmer tropes entwine.

The 1835 Guerra dos Farrapos or Revolução Farroupilha was not that distant a memory; the "Ragamuffin" rebellion originated in São Leopoldo, opposed slavery, and fought for enhanced economic terms for the region, which suffered from Uruguayan and Argentine competition. German immigrants, too, fought this battle.[59] Moreover, the cause enlisted Black and Indigenous soldiers as well. The representation of the battle visually asserts racial identity in the *Riograndeser* army (figure 16). The painter Guiherme Litran (1840–1897) portrays the army riding into battle and carrying flags, the colors of which read ambiguously. They are dark green, red, and yellow, the emblematic colors of Rio Grande do Sur. Upon viewing

---

59. Witt, *Em busca de um lugar ao sol*, 310.

The New World Wilderness 147

Figure 16. Guiherme Litran (1840–1897), *Carga de cavalaria Farroupilha*, 1893. Acervo do Museu Júlio de Castilhos. (Photo by Ricardo André Frantz.) Public Domain from Wikimedia Commons.

the painting, the dark green of the horizontal stripes reads black, red, and gold, possibly a reference to the "schwarz-rot-gold" of the Lützower Jäger.[60] Against this political topography the story of feuding neighbors unfolds. Rotermund, as author and publisher to locals and readers in the homeland, relied on print media to recruit and reform any internecine rivalries directed at the new citizens of the wilderness. It encouraged overcoming regional differences, or transposing them to the local conflict between the urban and rural. Rotermund's publication circuit declined throughout the 1920s while facing financial difficulties.[61] Yet his work continued to exert pedagogical influence over the colony. The continued publication and cir-

---

60. My thanks to Doris Couto, director of the Museu Júlio de Castilhos in Porte Allegre for taking a close look at the painting for me.
61. Schulze, *Auswanderung als nationalistisches Projekt*, 326.

culation of his German-language textbooks for Brazilian Germans fostered linguistic and pedagogical connections to the mother tongue, if not a motherland. It encouraged overcoming regional differences, transcending them through a new transprovincial identity. In a German-language newspaper, Rotermund intervenes in the politics of race in Brazil. Fiction, however diaphanously veiled, delivers the moral and messages of racialized ethnic traits, which in turn affect models of gendered behavior and its accrual of "national" standards. The legacy of another war populates the associative logic of the poetic "war deutscher Soldat" above. Won wars, fought for settler rights, remain within the realm of reference.

Along with the acquisition of military history, the language primer carries forth subliminal and explicit cultural knowledge about the wild and tamed or trained forces of nature. Lessing's fable of the dancing bear, cultivated to imitate courtly behavior to the point of self- subjection and virtual enslavement, is echoed in the European entertainment practice of the *Tanzbär* (dancing bear). The primer purports to give instruction on a series of capital letters with a vignette about a child who sees a bear, which "war gar nicht wild; es war ein Tanz bär. Der Bär en füh rer schlug ei ne Trom mel, und der Bär tanz te"[62] (was not wild at all; it was a dancing bear. The bear's master beat a drum, and the bear danced). When the bear growled, the master threatened it with a club. In southern Brazil of the middle to late nineteenth century, there were traveling equestrian circuses.[63] European entertainment history of animals performing "contrary to their nature" extends back to the tenth century.[64] Rotermund's *Fibel* outlives the author in delivering the message that the farmers needed to be cultivated themselves; the references to fathers as soldiers, instilling masculine German values, and trained wild animals tamed to entertain with the language, inculcate the learner with the knowledge that there is a grammar of Germanness, especially "auf dem Lande." In cultivating any wilderness, the learner recognizes "primitive" energies of the conquered and harnesses them to build modernity. The farmer and soldier alike assume the attributes

---

62. Rotermund and Heuer, *Fibel*, 65.
63. Dominque Jando, *Short History of the Circus*, Circopedia: *The Free Encyclopedia of the International Circus*. http://www.circopedia.org/SHORT_HISTORY_OF_THE_CIRCUS.
64. Pelin Tünaydin, "Pawing through the History of Bear Dancing in Europe," *Frühneuzeit-Info* 24 (2013): 51–60, here 51. http://www.bearconservation.org.uk/Pawing_through_the_History_of_Bear_Danci.pdf.

of military masculinity cultivated to tame the next frontier. The rural, "wild" Juanita herself undergoes a civilizing process, one that involves conforming to the "rural female evangelical" model. Through the rejection of Black and Indigenous masculinity, both German migrants and remigrated Germans leverage gender to maintain a narrative of racial superiority while appropriating the raw strength and generative tribalism of the wilderness within.

CHAPTER FIVE

German Pioneers

The previous chapter told a story from the experience of the New World wilderness in anticipation of encountering the wilderness within, brought to light in stories of mobility as told in print media, entertainment literature, and the communicative network between North and South America. Imagined connections between the Global South and the German settlers of North America reinforce a heroic identity as pioneers, and the texts and objects under examination in this study lean into the tropes. This chapter leans into the construction of immigrant identity as pioneer, with emphasis on mid-to-late nineteenth-century Argentina. Often the point of reference is the North American pioneer, an image circulated strategically in serialized literature and print media. The popularization of "pioneer" literature appealed to Germans in Argentina—revolving around the better-known North American model of the European settler or homesteader on the "frontier"—but still in a contested space, with major differences in immigration and recruitment patterns from those seen in southern Brazil. Still, continuities exist: reference to the early modern lineage of a German explorer as a credential for ethnic emigrant entitlement; victories, however brutal or symbolic, over Indigenous peoples and their purported barbarity; and the supremacy of industriousness and reason imported with German-language education. These durable traits feature in this chapter's literary examples, which include poems about the prairie by Friedrich (Martin von) Bodenstedt (1819–1892) and, more poignantly, an 1879 novel by Friedrich Spielhagen (1829–1911) that bridges the (reading) experience between German settlers in the north and south of the transatlantic world by positing them as virile and vigorous underdogs who have overcome conditions comparable to enslavement. Spielhagen's novel, serialized at a time when his popularity waned in Germany, intersects with narratives about Europeans renegotiating gendered identities in immigration, crossing and drawing the borders of contact zones with Indigeneity and enslavement that encompass the epistemology of whiteness with the conditions of emigration through contact in the Atlantic world. The last short text considered is a colonial-era poem by Max Brewer, "Deutsche Diamanten" (German diamonds). As in each chapter, the network of tropes that model the experience of mobility and emplacement—settler, pioneer, farmer, provider, fighter—spans the Atlantic, arriving on African and American shores intact. German-specific national sacrifice for the acquisition and defense of land drives the narrative interweaving between the pioneer, attributes of savage masculinity—summoned to defend the hearth, home, and kin—and the sense of opportunity for extreme articulations of gendered identities in officially Germanized territories. Mobile, transferable masculinities, articulated as separate from that of other Europeans, successfully subsumed the "pioneer" into the attributes of global German identity.

German Pioneers: Argentina and America

German immigration to the Rio de la Plata extends back to 1835, with a colony of about seventeen thousand inhabitants by the late nineteenth century.[1] As Jennifer M. Valko and others have pointed out, recruitment began in midcentury.[2] The mutual reinforcement of European epistemologies, evident in the rhetoric of science, geography, and political power, is instantiated in the work and policies of Domingo Faustino Sarmiento (1811–1888). Among his achievements, he lived life as a writer, activist, national advocate, and journalist, and he served as president (1868–1874). His major work, *Facundo: Civilización y barbarie* (Argentina 1845), was written and partially serialized during one period of exile in Chile.[3] Aarti Madan argues convincingly that Sarmiento was in dialogue with Alexander von Humboldt and that he, along with other Argentine intellectuals who combined literary productivity and national interests, participate in creating what she calls "marketable geography."[4] One nuance she observes is

---

1. Bernd Wulffen, *Deutsche Spuren in Argentinien: zwei Jahrhunderte wechselvoller Beziehungen* (Berlin: Ch. Links Verlag, 2010), 93.
2. Jennifer M. Valko, "Transnational Mercenaries as Agents of Argentine National in Moritz Aleman's Immigration Propaganda (1874–1908)," *German Studies Review* 40, no. 1 (February 2017): 41–60, here 43.
3. Domingo F. Sarmiento, *Facundo: Or, Civilization and Barbarism*, intro. Ilan Stavans (London: Penguin Reprint Edition, 1998).
4. Aarti Madan, "Writing the Earth, Writing the Nation: Latin American Narrative and the Language of Geography" (PhD diss., University of Pittsburgh 2010), 37–38.

Sarmiento's claiming of a native landscape that eludes European models. She claims that "he literarily snatches Argentina's lands back from the grips of occidental geographers."[5] That insight opens an aperture into the settler/colonist mindscape: the challenge to overcome not only the natural world, but to experience the sublime danger of contact zones and prevail. Endangerment itself is the lure, the edge, recuperated in the Romantic aesthetic of survival and tranquility. For this reason, I believe, the print media models and moralizes—not uniformly—immigrant life as rugged pioneering.

In the same year Sarmiento published *Facundo*, the German painter Johann Moritz Rugendas (1802–1858), who had expressed the intent to be "the illustrator of life in the New World," painted *El rapto de la cautiva* (figure 17). His work exerted considerable influence over the self-image of the region, with collections in multiple museums.[6] With this painting, he visualizes an image of capture portrayed by the Argentine poet Esteban Echeverría (1805–1851). Rugendas (also Rugendaz) joins the ranks of German-born artists who embarked on lives in the New (or newer) World in which their experiences, from the sublime to the quotidian, are elevated and valorized by their foreign freshness. Here the artist and legal scholar Zacharias Wagener (1614–1668) comes immediately to mind for his portrayals of human beings, along with flora and fauna, from the spectrum of his travels. As Susan Broomhall and Jacqueline Van Gent have written, Wagener's illustrations "played their part in locating colonised populations in terms of contemporary European ethnographic interests rather than individuals with political rights."[7] Awnsham also published a translation of Wagener's travels the same year (1704). Known primarily for the five hundred lithographs of life in Brazil, sometimes described as ethnographic images, his focus there on human beings was on the lives of enslaved Africans. The interplay between artistic and scientific observation remained a legacy of early modern European epistemologies. That legacy continued to inform the representation of contact zones between white Europeans and those "natives" they encountered. In the age of Latin American Romanticism, the eruption of violence involved in the "opening" of territories dominates those representations and stakes victorious claims over lives; again, the collapse of fauna and enslaved peoples into one observable

---

5. Madan, "Writing the Earth," 39.
6. See under "Memoria chilena," https://www.memoriachilena.gob.cl/602/w3-article-668.html#imagenes.
7. Susan Broomhall and Jacqueline Van Gent, *Dynastic Colonialism: Gender, Materiality and the Early Modern House of Orange-Nassau* (London: Routledge, 2016), 154.

German Pioneers 153

Figure 17. Mauricio Rugendas, *El rapto de la cautiva*, 1845.

category forges strong transhistorical connections. In pursuit of knowledge, Rugendas himself spent years in Latin America; he accompanied a scientific expedition as an illustrator and traveled widely.[8] Dom Pedro II welcomed him and supported him with commissions. His work interacts in complex ways with the narratives about Argentine nation building, the role of cultural discourses, and the problematizing of land ownership as constitutive of immigration identity. Carlos Riobó analyzes the latter dynamic in his work on the trope of the captive in Argentine verbal and visual arts. He argues convincingly that Rugendas must be counted among those whose works "attempted to deny the possibility of transculturation in Argentina."[9] This image high-

8. Christopher Conway, "Gender Iconoclasm and Aesthetics: Echeverría's *La Cautiva* and the Captivity Paintings of Juan Manuel Blanes," *Decimónica* 12, no. 1 (2015): 116–33; this information is noted, 124.

9. Carlos Riobó, *Caught Between the Lines: Captives, Frontiers, and National Identity in Argentine Literature and Art* (Lincoln: University of Nebraska Press, 2019). See also Saúl Sos-

lights the scene of capture, which itself works within a kind of uncivil contract among the writer, the viewer, and history.

Rugendas composed three "captive" paintings, based on the incident of a white girl taken in a raid near a town in Chile; she was later rescued.[10] In the painting, the demonized Indian warrior has captured the victim; the artist takes the moment of flight on horseback to direct the gaze of the captor at the spectator, while the female captive looks up to the heavens in despair. Of this painting, Christopher Conway writes that it "achieves a nearly impressionist sense of unity, with the fleeing Indian and his female prisoner suspended in smooth, blended waves of tan, brown and yellow that represent the desert, the horizon, the brush and the sky itself."[11] Conway does acknowledge the passivity, passenger status of Rugendas's captive, though the original poem portrays María as fragile but violent when attacked. This constellation, and the interaction between the verbal and visual texts, recapitulate the psyche of white fragility, though here the portrait is complicated by gender. In Echeverría's epic poem, María assumes the bellicose traits of a woman warrior and avenging angel, in other words male traits and savagery,[12] only to succumb to death when she learns of the death of her children. The subtext between the epic poem and painting not only appeals to the pioneer imaginary, but rather it reifies it. Rugendas entitled the painting "el rapto," which connotes both "rape" and "rapture," in conjunction with abduction, a radical disjuncture that the poem resolves. In the former meaning, the threat of rape is overt, exacerbated by the representation of the perpetrator. In the latter connotation, the "rapture of the captive" is indicative of a hagiography with the reference to the canonical dialectic of agony and ecstasy. In this sense, the *cautiva* is always already hybrid. The gender lines bend and break along the vicissitudes of the frontier. In many ways, the coincidence of the entertainment with the

---

nowski, "Esteban Echeverría: el intelectual ante la formación del estado," *Revista Iberoamericana* 47, no. 114–15 (enero-junio 1981): 293–300.

10. Conway writes in "Gender Iconoclasm and Aesthetics": "These paintings were inspired by the true story of a sixteen-year-old white girl named Trinidad Salcedo, who was kidnapped by a band of Pincheyra Indians in 1826, near the Chilean town of Talca. During a chaotic skirmish between the Pincheyra and a military force led by Colonel Thomas Sutcliffe, a British officer serving the cause of Independence in Colombia, Peru and Chile, the young girl escaped and was rescued. [...] In Chile, this image became so iconic that other painters reproduced it in the 1830's, and Claudio Gay printed a lithograph of it in a historical atlas published in 1854" (124).

11. Conway, "Gender Iconoclasm and Aesthetics," 125.

12. Conway, "Gender Iconoclasm and Aesthetics," 117.

high literary genre involved in the popularizing of the pioneer identity locates these iconographic images in the genre of "humanitarian pornography."[13]

This pictorial gesture recapitulates a number of tropes relevant to the discussion of German coloniality and the nexus of immigration and settler colonialism. First, the contemporary German-language immigrants in Argentina consider themselves to be in a new country, especially those who were recruited from Switzerland. Some produced immigration propaganda.[14] The tensions among European immigrants, some of whom must acclimate to the national differences among Argentina, Chile, and other countries of the Southern Cone, nonetheless plays into the Sarmiento model of civilizing and barbaric influences. The German speakers consider themselves among the civilizers who must resist, especially for the sake of their families, the lure to become gauchos. Yet, as in the pictorial trope, in which the captive is inspired by a Chilean historical event and transposed onto an Argentine Romantic epic, the frontier dangers transform the helpless (white) female into an agent of barbarity. The immigrant, cast as a pioneer, must dare greatly to face the exigencies of climate, Indians, and the loss of language and cultural heritage. Etched onto this projection, print media in the 1870s foster the nobility of farming and intellectual development, emphasizing education and, tautologically, German-language newspapers. At midcentury, prior to the unification of Germany in 1871, the readers worked to differentiate themselves from other European groups; but also they generated entertainment literature that wrote them into pioneer narratives and cowboy stories to create their own settler identity separate from the gauchos and European proletariat populating Buenos Aires.

In the retrospective gesture of commemorating the centenary of German immigration to Argentina, the Deutscher Klub of Buenos Aires sponsored a volume to revisit ethnic history and justify an ancestral claim to the land. The authors mythologize the earth itself: "Die Erde wartet auf den Menschen, der sie erschließt. Jahrtausendelang hat sie nur die sanfte Gewalt der Sonne, des Regens und Windes erfahren. Unter den Händen des Menschen erwacht sie zu einem Leben, das zu leidenschaftlicher Unruhe erfüllt ist und alle ver-

---

13. Mario Klarer, "Humanitarian Pornography: John Gabriel Stedman's 'Narrative of a Five Years Expedition against the Revolted N*groes of Surinam' (1796)," *New Literary History* 36, no. 4 (2005).

14. Valko, "Transnational Mercenaries," 41.

borgenen Kräfte zur Reife bringt" (The earth waits for the human being who opens it up. For millennia, it has experienced only the gentle power of the sun, the rain, and the wind. Beneath the hands of the human being, she awakens to a life that is full of passionate unrest and brings hidden powers forth to maturity).[15] The authors vaguely allude to Genesis and the creation of the world, but with a dash of sexual awakening. Here, human hands stir the passions of a passive planet, touched hitherto by gentle *Gewalt*, both power and violence, of natural agency. The verb erschließen, too, echoes through the summation of later historical upheavals: the "Erschliessung" of the Chaco region, and he titles the section on the first diplomatic mission to Argentina in 1856 that included scientists "Deutsche Wissenschaftler helfen das Land erschliessen" (German scientists help open up the land).[16] The authors mention Hermann Burmeister (1807–1892) by name. The opening of the Chaco region is synonymous with the displacing of Indigenous peoples. Extracting value from the land inflicts damage that constituted progress, the scope of which posterity is just beginning to comprehend. The point is that the story has deep roots, some of which resemble other Europeans' explorations, some of which bear a peculiarly German stamp. The location of early ancestry in the exploration of the Americas is not specific to German-language cultures. In their volume of Jewish identity and Latin America, Amalia Ran and Jean Cahan note, for example: "The Jewish presence in Latin America may be traced to the arrival of the first Europeans to the continent, with Christopher Columbus and the conquest of America." Yet as they continue, they show that this migration was predicated on persecution and expulsion.[17] The former difference, with distinction, stands in contrast to other nationalized allegories, which can be implicated in a defense of entitlement. The "first German" explorer, Ulrich Schmiedel, a mercenary foot soldier in the service of the Welser economic powerhouse, qualifies for the title of conquistador (figure 18).[18] Besides Staden, Schmiedel (also Schmidl) recorded his travel experiences; both prove lasting sources of the "German" influence in the Global South. Subsequent forefathers include Hans Brunberger, a Fugger representative who is "der erste Deutsche, der sich in Argentinien angesiedelt und eine bodenständige Fam-

---

15. Wilhlem Lütge, Werner Hoffmann, and Karl Wilhelm Körner, *Geschichte des Deutschtums in Argentinien*, hrsg. vom Deutschen Klub in Buenos Aires zur Feier seines 100jährigen Bestehens, 18. Oktober 1955 (Buenos Aires: Deutscher Klub, 1955), 9.

16. Lütge et al. *Geschichte des Deutschtums*, 268 and 216.

17. Ran and Cahan, "Rethinking Jewish Identity," 3.

18. See Mark Häberlein, "Schmidl, Ulrich," in *Neue Deutsche Biographie* 23 (2007), 161–162 [Online-Version]; URL: https://www.deutsche-biographie.de/pnd118945882.html#ndbcontent.

German Pioneers

Figure 18. "wie Federmann in Venezuela und Staden in Brasilien, so hat am Silberstrom Ulrich Schmidel seine Erlebnisse aufgezeichnet," from Wilhlem Lütge, Werner Hoffmann, and Karl Wilhelm Körner, *Geschichte des Deutschtums in Argentinien*, hrsg. vom Deutschen Klub in Buenos Aires zur Feier seines 100jährigen Bestehens, 18. Oktober 1955 (Buenos Aires: Deutscher Klub, 1955), no page.

ilie gegründet hat" (the first German who settled in Argentina and founded an autochthonous family).[19] The telling adjective *bodenständig* encompasses

---

19. Lütge, Hoffmann, and Körner, *Geschichte des Deutschtums*, 19. For a reference to his travel diaries from South America and their attesting to the role of Nuremberg ironware in the slave trade, see Wendy Sutherland, *Staging Blackness and Performing Whiteness in Eighteenth-Century German Drama* (London: Routledge, 2019; New York: Ashgate, 2016), 47.

a range of meanings, including Indigenous and native. The rootedness to the land confers legitimacy. This legitimacy is almost audible in the image.[20]

Multiple German-language newspapers and periodicals spread across not only Argentina, but southern Brazil, Chile, and Uruguay as well. *Die "Heimath"* began publishing in Rio de la Plata in the mid 1870s, with the designation "Organ für die deutschredende Bevölkerung am Rio de la Plata" (*DH*, April 4, 1877). Contemporary competition emerged from the *Deutsche Zeitung*, with love of the fatherland the lightning rod for national identity and warring editorials. These periodicals served a commercial purpose alongside the ideological and political. Their pages contain sustained debates about which South American nations practice successful recruitment and sustainability; the plagues German colonists suffered, among them yellow fever, malaria, and smallpox; and spirited condemnation of Germans who dismiss the fatherland and their compatriots. Those who remigrate do so with horror stories about the harsh conditions and deaths. The press presents counterpoint to this melancholy melody.

The *Deutscher Pionier* am Rio de la Plata, edited by Hermann Tjarks, enjoyed wide circulation, enough to advance from a weekly publication to producing three issues a week. The front page of an edition from June 1, 1879, announces the justification proudly: the paper garnered praise, not all of it local, "ja von allen Enden der Welt sind uns die herzlichsten Beweise der Anerkennung und der Freundschaft zugesandt worden" (indeed, we have been sent, from every end of the earth, the most heartfelt proofs of recognition and friendship). Tjarks leans into the praise "Die vielseitigen Ansprüche und die vergrößerte Zahl unserer Abonnenten haben es uns nun nöthig erscheinen lassen, unser Blatt in vergrößerter Form dreimal wöchentlich herauszugeben" (Due to the multiple demands and the increase in subscriptions, it seemed to us necessary to publish our paper in a larger format three times a week). This paper would eventually transmute into the conservative counterpart to the *Argentinisches Tageblatt*, which, to put the conflict in reductive terms, represented a liberal, democratic, and cosmopolitan perspective from the German-language press; later, other papers with a more conservative leaning would enter into conflict with the moderate tone and politics of the *Tage-*

---

20. From the preface to the second edition, Robert Lehmann Nitsche, *Ulrich Schmidel. Der erste Geschichtsschreiber der La Plata Länder 1535–1555* (Munich: M. Müller & Sohn, 1912). Nitsche, professor of anthropology at the Universities of La Plata and Buenos Aires, notes the first edition (1909) only ran three hundred copies and sold out quickly. He suggests it would behoove the Germans "im Auslande" to be informed about Schmidel.

German Pioneers 159

blatt.[21] From the middle of the nineteenth century, European immigration to Argentina centered in the Río de la Plata, with Buenos Aires, also in the Río de la Plata, remaining the urban destination. Some historical demographers refer to the bucolic imaginary, the nostalgic pastoral involved in the European pursuit of acreage and flight from metropolitan poverty and squalor. Bjerg writes of the "elocuente titulo" or "eloquently entitled" "Ley de Inmigración y Colonización" that it invoked an image of the pampas "como un idílico jardin de agriculutores europeos" (as an idyllic garden of European farmers).[22] Several government offices, among them the Departmento Central de Inmigración and the Oficina de Tierras y Colonias[23] accompanied the "law of immigration and colonization" to oversee the parceling, protection, and profitability of the land. Between 1850 and the end of the 1870s, seventy colonies were established in the region. Growth increased between 1880 and 1890, during which time an additional three hundred colonies formed. In the first census, during the Sarmiento presidency, the province counted more than 89,000 inhabitants; by 1895, there were more than 400,000 inhabitants.[24] In Argentina, a single individual and civil servant could exert enormous influence over immigration, which is the case with Samuel Navarro.[25] Germans, while not among the larger immigrant groups, nonetheless contributed a specific character to the transatlantic demographics impacting Argentina at this time. Small businesses brought the taste of home to the table (figure 19).

Intrinsic to the nation-based political identity of the publication, despite the celebration of frontier experiences, the *Deutscher Pionier* in its early years included entertainment literature and reviews of cultural experiences. These tighten the network of German-speaking migrants and citizens of the New World; they propose a transatlantic temporality that forges bonds across borders. Perhaps due to Sarmiento's activism, German speakers in Argentina

---

21. Substantial scholarly works have addressed the politics of the South American German-language press, especially in Argentina. The contrasting politics between the conservative regional and the more liberal urban newspapers are also addressed. See especially Georg Ismar, *Der Pressekrieg: Argentinisches Tageblatt und Deutsche La Plata Zeitung 1933–1945* (Berlin: wfb, 2006), for the polarization of politics between the two newspapers in the interwar period through the end of World War II.

22. María Bjerg, *Historias de la inmigración en la Argentina* (Buenos Aires: Edhasa, 2009), 53.

23. Bjerg, *Historias de la inmigración*, 53.

24. Bjerg, *Historias de la inmigración*, 55–56.

25. Ernest von Bruyssel, *La République Argentine: ses ressources naturelles, ses colonies agricoles*, ed. Th. Falk (Brussels: Librairie Européene C. Muquardt, Libraire du Roi et du Comte de Flandre, 1889), 147.

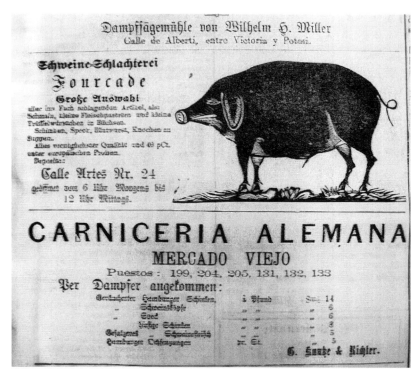

Figure 19. Butcher advertisement, including imported meats from Germany, *Deutscher Pionier am Río de la Plata*, Sonntag, den 10. August 1879. Ibero-Amerikanisches Institut, Berlin.

later search for early modern evidence of their entitlements; they do so to underscore the validity of their immigrant identity, predictably at significant anniversaries, such as the centenary. They lean into Argentina's nationhood, occasionally employing exculpatory arguments about a history unburdened by the institution of slavery. More nuanced narratives about national identity, immigration, and the epistemological labor of Eurocentrism emerge. For German readers in the Río de la Plata and beyond, these variations on the theme of immigration whetted an appetite for pioneer models. In the first year of publication, the newspaper featured poems and reports of Friedrich Bodenstedt, for example, who trained in Russia and Persia before a professional appointment in Germany and a trip to the United States (1879–1880).[26]

26. The edition of *Deutscher Pionier am Rio de la Plata*, January 21, 1880, reports on Bodenstedt in America.

Bodenstedt's volume, *Aus Morgenland und Abendland* (From the orient and occident; second edition 1884) is made up of a prologue, seven books, and an epilogue. His work furnishes such a model. Moreover, the newspaper instrumentalizes such literary language to integrate multiple Germans and their respective geographies in the Atlantic world.

Bodenstedt's poems and verse sayings span a range of topics, from odes to a candle and nature.[27] The newer pieces, notable more for their topicality than their literary quality, explore dualistic themes, such as "Weisheit und Thorheit" (18; wisdom and foolishness); and homages to the German landscape, indeed, even the German language ("An die deutsche Sprache; 39–41; To the German language). Of interest here is the seventh book, *Aus der Neuen Welt*. The exploration of New World tropes piqued the interest of the Argentine German editors and journalists, intrigued and inspired by Bodenstedt's poems to "Niagara" (207–9); "Milwaukee" (210); and a three-part poem "In den Prairien" (211–17; In the prairies). For the traveling German, the prairie becomes an "ungeschriebenes Blatt" (216; blank page); the plowshares of German farmers inscribe it. Moreover, he develops a longer poem, "Aus Indianerlanden," wandering into the genre of ethnographic verse that doubles as race reportage. His literary representations of the Americas, serialized to foster transnational community identities across German colonies on two continents, contrasts sharply with the benign travel literature of the German American spaces of Penny's unbound history.[28] Bodenstedt represents the New World in a verse prologue, contrasting it to the ancient former glory of the *Morgenland*. He writes,

> Ich sah in fernen Abendlanden,
> Aus alten Völkern buntgestellt,
> Ein neues Leben auferstanden,
> In einer neuentdeckten Welt. (IX)

> I saw in distant western lands,
> From old colorful peoples,
> A new life resurrected,
> In a newly discovered world.

---

27. Friedrich Bodenstedt, *Aus Morgenland und Abandland. Neue Gedichte und Sprüche*, 2nd ed., 5 and 8. Further references to this edition appear as page numbers in parenthesis. Leipzig: Brockhaus, 1884.

28. H. Glenn Penny, *German History Unbound: From 1750 to the Present* (New York: Cambridge University Press, 2022), 63–74.

Bodenstedt dates the prologue July 10, 1881; it takes on the patina of late nineteenth-century European ennui, underscoring the capacity for resurrection in the New World. The energizing renewal could remind the reader of the infusion of inspiration Goethe and Schiller found in borrowing from other cultures. The vitality Bodenstedt goes on to describe is inspired partially by the rush for gold and wealth, thus in a different ethical register; he opines that these do not constitute happiness. Instead, he celebrates more the process of rejuvenation:

> Wo alte Rassen sich verjüngen,
> Der Stamm- und Glaubenshader schweigt,
> Der Fortschritt sich in Riesensprüngen,
> Beim steten Wettkampf Aller zeigt,
> Und was der Zwangsmacht unserer Ahnen
> Nicht in Jahrtausenden gelang,
> Aus weiten, selbst geschaffnen Bahnen
> Ein freies Volk im Flug errang ... (IX)

> Where old races rejuvenate themselves,
> The tribal and religious struggle is silent,
> Progress shows itself all over
> In constant competition of all,
> And the coercive force of our ancestors,
> Could not achieve in millennia,
> On wide, self-forged paths,
> A free folk in flight accomplished ...

In this stanza, one of few with enjambment and ellipses to vary the structure, Bodenstedt identifies freedom as constitutive of success, and the need to emigrate. The reader will hear echoes of Goethe's Faust, here updated as national character traits without borders; these portable signifiers of identity radiate outward from language and regionally specific personality to include more encompassing attributes: work ethic, sociability, jovial and loyal natures, and stalwartness. The arrested development of German imperial identity sheds light on the particularities of provincialism embodied by Germans without German national borders. The cultivation of land, the colonialist trope par excellence, has deep roots in the German literary tradition, adjacent to the quest for youthful striving and material wealth. The literary segues into the agri-colonial and military in ways that expand the notion of Germanness that is translocal and provincial. We can embark with the delusional musings of the blind Faust, opining about his land reclamation project, envisioning a free people on "unencumbered soil":[29]

> If I can furnish space for many millions to live—not safe, I know, but free to work in green and fertile fields, with man and beast soon happy on the new-made soil and settled in beside the mighty hill a dauntless people's effort has erected, creating here inside a land of Eden—then there, without, the tide may bluster to its brim, but where it gnaws, attempting to rush in by force, communal effort will be quick to close the breach.[30]

Bodenstedt's indirect reference to "ein freies Volk" invokes this literary moment—posterity yields readers, however, who overlook the irony of Faust's delusionary vision. The destiny of self-optimization, touted by Bodenstedt and his depiction of the New World, prefigures the neoliberal ideology of late capitalism, here configured as triumphant colonization.

Strictly speaking, Germans in the Americas were not colonists, which did not prevent them from self-defining as pioneers. Further, the legacy of Goethe's work was preserved in Argentina, not only through schooling and print media but also through the stunning popularity of Gounod's opera. It is worth noting that a foundational work of Argentine Romanticism by Estanislao de Campo (1834–1880), is titled *Fausto* (1866). Upon his return from exile in France, Campo created a comic figure in the gaucho. His protagonist, El Pollo (the chicken), attends an opera performance—which he comically does not recognize as an opera—with the libretto based on Goethe's *Faust* I with its focus on the love story between Faust and Marguerite (Gretchen, Margarete), at the Teatro Colón, which had opened in 1857. Gerald Martin writes that de Campo "saw in the rural gaucho a somewhat comic symbol of Argentine nationhood."[31] In the year of serialization, the also published "Briefe eines Laien" (Letters of a layman), which treated the season of opera; among these

---

29. Johann Wolfgang von Goethe, *Faust* II, *Sämtliche Werke. Briefe, Tagebücher und Gespräche*, edited by Dieter Borchmeyer et al. 40 Vols. (Frankfurt a. M.: Deutscher Klassiker Verlag, 1985 ff.), l. 11,580.
30. Goethe, *Faust* II, 1994: ll. 11,563–11,572.
31. Gerald Martin, "Literature, music and the visual arts c. 1820–1870," in *A Cultural History of Latin America: Literature, Music, and the Visual Arts in the 19th and 20th Centuries*, edited by Leslie Bethell (Cambridge and New York: Cambridge University Press, 1998), 3–46, here 2.

is a long report on the relationship between aesthetics and material culture in Buenos Aires, using the example of a production of Gounod's *Faust*.[32] Any mention of the Faust material, even the oblique reference in Bodenstedt's prologue, would have resonated with the *Deutscher Pionier*'s reading public. The cultural capital circulating in the region relied more heavily on Argentine Indigeneity, the minimizing of slavery, and the European artistic tradition.

The literary influences shape the ontology of immigration and labor, even to the point that these attribute to nature a racist agency. With two examples from Bodenstedt's New World poems, I elaborate on this naturalization to preface the reading of Spielhagen's novel. "In den Prairien" (211–17) takes the reader on an imaginary tour of the regional expanse, replete with the signifiers of America's "wilderness," such as buffalo grass, bison, and antelope (211); also peopled by Indians, who cluster near springs in tipis, smoking their pipes with murky thoughts while the women roast meat (212). The newly discovered desert land, as Bodenstedt describes the prairie, awakens to history only with the arrival of the "Siedler" (216; settlers), indeed "Aus allen Ländern der Alten Welt" (216; From all countries of the Old World). The western desert is the location: "Wo seit ungezählten Jahrtausenden / Die Natur ihren Reichtum / Barg vor den Wilden" (216; Where for millennia / Nature hid her riches / From the savages). The second example, the two-part poem "Aus Indianerlanden" (221–24; from Indian country), condenses the history of Indigenous peoples' relationship to the land, the nation, westward expansion, and genocide; Bodenstedt cites the building of the railroad and white victors who "zwangen die Rothen zu dienen" (222); forced the "reds" to serve). Trained as a linguist, he turns to the language of the Dakota and his response to its euphonic sounds (*Wohllaut*). Bodenstedt recognizes the assertion of cultural superiority retained in the speaking of Dakota, an act of linguistic defiance, undercut by his rhyming it with Minnesota and Manitoba, thereby collapsing the identity of places and their settlement by the "conquerors." In the process of preserving the echoes of an apparently losing language in his poetry, Bodenstedt delivers a simile that encapsulates the garbling of a Germanic language (English or German, in this case) with an act of Indigenous resistance. When Indians attempt to speak other languages, he writes, "Doch sofort mit Zähnenfletschen, / Jedes fremde Wort zerquetschen, / Um den Wohllaut zu zerstören, / Der das Ohr entzückend traf— / Gleich als dürft' es nun als Sklav / Nicht sich selbst mehr angehören" (223; But at once, with

---

32. *Deutscher Pionier* Sunday, June 15, 1879.

gnashing teeth, / Every foreign word they crush, / To destroy the pleasant sound, / That met the ear so delightfully— / Just as though it, like a slave / Did not belong to itself anymore). This is a strange association. Bodenstedt praises the sounds of Dakota, a language he cannot understand nor speak. He reacts only to its euphony. The imposed language of the colonizer undergoes a de-euphonization, linguistic defiance. The word, in the mouth of a Native American, is subject to enslavement; it is dispossessed of itself. Bodenstedt offers praise while aestheticizing a language under erasure. Though the poet ends on a purportedly positive note, it romanticizes the beauty of the song, destined to survive even after the tribes disappear. The intertwining of language death, cultural death, genocide, and aestheticization, insisting on the joined fate of Indians, here rendered harmless and remaindered, the agency of resistance unrecognized, lays the groundwork for a longer examination of the Spielhagen novel.[33]

German Pioneers in Canada Creek

A communicative network among print media, popular novels, and the immigration experience undergirds the serialization of the novel *Deutsche Pioniere*, which began to appear in the July issues of the *Deutscher Pionier* during the year the newspaper expanded its production, distribution, and readership. Friedrich Spielhagen's prominence dwindled in his lifetime, but he reached a wide audience. His writing appeals to a persistent, transcultural German provincialism that receives sporadic scholarly attention.[34] The appearance of Spielhagen's *Deutsche Pioniere* in the Argentine newspaper of nearly the same name suggests an elective affinity between the editors in

---

33. Germans did write about the Argentine "wilderness" as well. See *Alemanas en la Patagonia: narraciones de Bertha Koessler-Ilg, Ella Brunswig y Christel Koerte*, ed. Regula Rohland-Langbein, *Cuadernos del Archivo DIHA* Año 1, nr. 2 (2017), See also Max Tepp, *Arboles y Arbustos de la Cordillera Patagónica* (Buenos Aires: Del Umbral Argentino, 1936). Considerations of this work go beyond the scope of my analysis, which focuses on the trope of the "pioneer" emerging from Argentina and medial identification with the better-known North American model. My thanks to Robert Kelz for making this connection.

34. Jeffrey Sammons, *Friedrich Spielhagen* (Tubingen: Niemeyer, 2004); Elstyn Griffith, "Provincialism, Private Life and the Marginal Hero: Germany after Unification in the Works of Gustav Freytag, Friedrich Spielhagen and Paul Heyse," in *Germany's Two Unifications: Anticipations, Experiences, Responses*, ed. Ronald Speirs and John Breuilly (New York: Palgrave Macmillan, 2005), 209–23.

Río de la Plata and the readership's identification with the pioneer enterprise. This correspondence strengthens the connection not only between Europe and the Americas, but also the conditions of German immigration and, by overreaching comparisons, to the conditions of slavery.

Most frequently treated in the context of realist fiction, Spielhagen reception and scholarship tends to concentrate on the impact of his work on German identity in the new nation, but the South American serialization of this particular work underwrites a different tactic. His work is an expression not only of a Karl May–related fascination with American Indians and the American West, but also of a pioneering German identity. Curiously, that pioneer impulse is often coterminous with identification with Native Americans themselves. Historian H. Glenn Penny has written extensively about the cross-identification and its consequences.[35] American studies scholar Franck Usbeck projects the one-sided elected affinity between Germans and Native Americans onto its instrumentalization by the Nazis, relying on the impulses that "interwove Romantic notions, cultural despair, and conservative nationalism during the late nineteenth century. These traditions helped construct national identity by asserting the image of Germans as an original indigenous people who were distinct from other Europeans."[36] These associations posit a naturalized affinity between German identification with nature and entitlement to the wilderness in addition to asserting the narcissism of minor differences over and above other European colonizers.

This strategy enables an exculpatory narrative about German expansionism as entertainment. The historical framework of the novel, which involves a complicated family love story in addition to the defense of a German homestead, locates it sufficiently in the past to absolve the reader from contemporary political judgment. Spielhagen sets his frontier story in 1758. The story begins with the docking of a three-mast ship flying the Dutch flag. Immediately, the reader identifies with an association between the Dutch as colonizers, New York as New Amsterdam, and the prerevolutionary pushes and pulls of European dominance. Of the ship, he writes, "aber die Waare war deutsch" (410; but the cargo was German). Apart from the later deployment of Hessian mercenaries, Germans had little direct involvement with the colo-

---

35. H. Glenn Penny, *Kindred by Choice: Germans and American Indians since 1800* (Chapel Hill: University of North Carolina Press, 2013).

36. Franck Usbeck, "Learning from 'Tribal Ancestors:' How the Nazis Used Indian Imagery to Promote a 'Holistic' Understanding of Nature among Germans," *ELOHI*, 4 (2013): 45–60, here 46.

nies. Spielhagen embeds the early history of immigration from the Palatinate to New York (412). As Philip Osterness has written, between June and August of 1710, nine ships carrying Germans arrived in New York; not uncommon in eighteenth-century voyages of two or three months, there was widespread disease and deaths.[37] In the novel, the implications of this resurrected history tie it into to a paradigm of reconnecting with early modern roots in the New World, supplied elsewhere by the fortress Groß-Friedrichburg, Bartolomé Flores's acquisition of land, and the landfall of Germans in the American colonies prior to the revolution. Immigration entitlements, culturally constructed, reach a German-speaking audience in Argentina of the late nineteenth century, not through religious discourse, but through an adventure novel in the local newspaper. In the novel, a Mr. Brown takes the side of the German immigrants, prompted by the ethnicity of human cargo. Spielhagen opens with ethnic pride.

As the story unfolds, we learn that the young German from Canada Creek rescues and falls in love with a lovely pastor's daughter, whom he meets at the dock. Alone in the world after the death of her father during the punishing voyage, Katharine Weise accompanies Lambert Sternberg to Canada Creek, a fictionalized version of a town located now in upstate New York. West Canada Creek, also known as Gayahora or Kuyahoora, is more of a river, the Indian name of which means "winding waters."[38] In the German colony, Lambert lives with his brother, Konrad, nicknamed "der Indianer" after spending three years with the Mohawk. Konrad encounters Katherine in the home and believes her to be the wife he asked his brother to arrange. The love triangle tests the racist phylogenic descriptions of the characters: the "Indian" has blue eyes, a preference for life among those presumed to be closer to nature, thus more in touch with their instincts and their contempt for cowardice. With shifting allegiances among European powers and Indian nations during this period in history, the German DNA rises above the rest.

In the opening chapter, several minor characters introduce the situation of Germans in the New York region, also supplying commentary on the status

---

37. See Philip Otterness, *Becoming German: The 1709 Palatine Migration to New York* (Ithaca, NY: Cornell University Press, 2004), 78–88. He writes about the historical circumstances of the Palatine migration; their struggle in London (51); the plan to resettle them (66); the difficult voyage to New York (78–83); and the settlement in the Hudson Valley along with relationships to Native Americans. Spielhagen's novel mobilizes less historically accurate material.

38. Janet Burt, "Introduction," in *Kuyahoora Towns* (Kuyahoora: Kuyahoora Valley Historical Society, 2003), 7–9, here 7.

of immigrants. The reader learns that the Lambert brothers have a home in Canada Creek; they are farmers and fur traders. His brother, Konrad, assumes Katharine is his. Konrad is the wilder of the two, and his strength and decidedly non-European behavior vis-à-vis women is attributed to his years living with the Mohawk. The conflict between ethical German masculinity and the brute force of the German colonist "gone native" functions as a performative, modeling the moral of migration stories to a German-speaking readership. The two brothers fall out in rivalry over Katharine. Once the colony comes under attack, however, Konrad heeds the call to defend the "Vaterhaus, unser Stammesgenossen . . . aus dem alten Heimath" (537; the paternal home, our compatriots . . . from the old homeland).

For my purposes, however, the rhetoric of enslavement is significant. Spielhagen identifies the emigrants in the syntax of slavery: The Germans are compared to freight; they arrive in New York starved and worked to death; they must be purchased with a "Kopfgeld" (411; bounty); one marginal German American character on the docks compares the new arrivals explicitly to enslaved Africans. When the French, having allied themselves with two Indian peoples, make one attempt to negotiate a surrender, a mealy-mouthed warrior-wannabe who calls himself Roger de Saint Croix appears at the door. The valiant Konrad declares, "So kehrt zu Euren Leuten zurück und sagt ihnen, daß wir hier vereinigten deutschen Männer, Einer wie Alle und Alle wie Einer entschlossen sind, das Haus zu halten." (553; Just go back to your people and tell them that here we are united German men, one for all and all for one and determined to hold this house). One of the men realizes Roger is in fact a former "Galeerensclave" (galley slave) who wanted to marry a neighbor's black servant, who deemed him unworthy, and her boyfriend Hans Kessel beat him and sent him on his way (554). The lot of the slave and the privilege of the lover cross racial boundaries, but German masculinity prevails. The foil thereof is presumed French, a traitor, and a rejected suitor.

The racialized metaphor extends to the frontier. Rather than identifying as white settlers or colonizers, the Germans ally themselves with the Indians against the French, who constitute the real enemy. Thick description elevates the appreciation of the wilderness landscape in a way that evokes the words of Standing Bear: that only the white man looks at nature and sees a wilderness. The function of this fiction performs past the page: German readers in Argentina see their lives reflected in the adventurous, pious, community-centered narratives of their northern neighbors. Exhorted to set aside personal and political differences to survive and thrive in the New World, the

German reader performs imperial citizenship abroad. And gets the girl. This "fait" is "accompli" through winning the moral competition with the Dutch and French and appropriating aspects of indigeneity and an ennobling of enslavement by claiming it figuratively as integral to the German immigration story.

At the same time in the United States, the cultivation of land and the rights of citizenship coincided. In the 1904 *Baltimorer Blumenspiel* (Germania Club der Stadt Baltimore), the nature of German American identities unfolds in the awareness of the agricultural imperative; this time, however, the farmers are pressed into military service to prevent the spread of Civil War. In a poem by Dr. Emil Schneider of Hoboken, NJ, "Die Deutschen von Boonville in Missouri,"[39] we read about the legacy of German Americans in the border state:

"Wir haben den Boden fleissig bebaut, / Wir haben dem Tod in das Auge geschaut,/ Nun will man vom Heim uns vertreiben. Rebellen befehlen: "The Dutchman must go!" Sag' Colonel Eppstein, heisst es nicht so?/ Und dürfen wir hier noch verbleiben?" (29)

We industriously cultivated the land. We looked death in the eye, Now they want to drive us from our home. Rebels command: "The Dutchman must go!" Say, Colonel Eppstein, is that not so? And are we permitted to remain here still?"

The poem celebrates the victory of the Boonville Home Guardsmen, under the leadership of Colonel Joseph A. Eppstein, in the second battle of Boonville on September 13, 1861. The guardsmen were made up chiefly of antislavery German immigrants, who, having proved themselves as farmers, garnered fame as soldiers: "Drum wo auch vom Kampfe man redet und singt, / Den Deutschen von Boonville man Ehre bringt / Sie haben sich wacker geschlagen" (30; Thus, wherever they sing and talk of battle, / They bring honor to the Germans of Boonville / They fought bravely).

In closing this brief survey of the motivated relationship between German landownership and historical imperial identity, I triangulate the evidence with reference to a colonial poem by Max Bewer, "Deutsche Diamanten" (German

---

39. Germania-Club der Stadt Baltimore, *Das Baltimorer Blumenspiel 1904*. Further references to this poem appear with page number in parenthesis.

diamonds), which appeared first in *Kolonie und Heimat* and was reprinted in Emil Sembritzki's 1911 compilation, *Kolonial- Gedicht- und Liederbuch.*[40] The poet contemplates and questions the origin of the precious stones "in Afrikas heißem Sand" (56; In African's hot sand). His answer is a skewed account of specifically German sacrifice in German Southwest Africa and praise of colonial white masculinity: "Das sind die Wassertropfen, Nach welchen manch armer Soldat In des Herzens Fieberklopfen / Den letzten Erdgriff tat!" (56; Those are the drops of water, After which many a poor soldier / In the fever beat of the heart / Gripped the last piece of earth).

Like his American compatriot and contemporary, Bewer's German soldier represents a warrior adjacent to the dedicated farmer who cultivates the otherwise unproductive land as a pioneer while the soldier defends the possessions; but here the sacrifice of German military identity creates a proprietary relationship between the agency of colonial masculinity and national entitlement. The Junkers and the Rhinelander are characterized as martyrs. In celestial sympathy for the fallen, God weeps diamonds into the land itself. The final stanza reads like an indictment of the potentates: "Nun tragt sie, Ihr deutschen Fürsten / In ihrer Krone Rand / Und denket derer, die dürsten, / Und sterben für's Vaterland!" (57; Now wear them, You German princes In the rim of your crown And remember those who thirst And die for the fatherland). The poet celebrates the sacrifice of rank-and-file soldiers who fell in what were broadcast as the "Herero Wars," 1904–1907; the Herero and Namaqua genocide.

Reclaiming German Roots

Historical scholarship of the mid-1930s reiterates the importance of German interventions into colonial expansion as integral to a sustained struggle for national legitimacy, if not supremacy. Schmiedel plays but a supporting role in the interwar colonial discourse at a time when Asia and Africa seemed more popularly urgent. Among those voices raised in favor of recuperating a German-specific early modern colonial legacy is Mathilde Auguste Hedwig

---

40. Max Bewer, "Deutsche Diamanten," in *Kolonial-Gedicht und–lieder*, ed. Emil Sembritzki (Berlin: Deutscher Kolonial-Verlag, 1911), 56–57; originally published in *Kolonie und Heimat*. I thank my colleague Dr. Adjaï Oloukpona-Yinnon for calling my attention to this collection. Further references to this poem appear with page number in parenthesis.

Fitzler (1896–1993), also Fitzler-Kömmerling after her marriage to the Pirmasens industrialist Karl Kömmerling in 1937. Her extensive writings about colonial history led to her appointment as the first female professor in Brazil (Rio de Janeiro, 1922). Based on archival research, her "Der Anteil der Deutschen an der Kolonialpolitik Philipps II. von Spanien in Asien" (The role of Germans in the Asian colonial politics of Spain's Philip II) encompasses a series of spirited economic enterprises and imperialist potential, thwarted by the inability of a strong leader to protect the entrepreneurs. Fitzler makes quick work of Schmiedel:

> Obgleich Deutschland eine der ältesten und reichsten kolonialen Traditionen besitzt und im Gang seiner Geschichte wieder und wieder bewiesen hat, da Kolonisation und die damit verbundene räumliche und wirtschaftliche Ausdehnung den innersten Notwendigkeiten deutschen Wesens entsprechen, so hat es doch sehr lange gesäumt, dieser großen Tradition in der Überseegeschichte genauer nachzugehen und ihre Träger im 15. und 16. Jhd. der Vergessenheit zu entreißen. Es ist heute mit eine der wichtigsten Aufgaben der deutschen Geschichtsforschung, die hier klaffenden Lücken zu schließen. Am besten sind wir noch über Südamerika unterrichtet, wiewohl auch hier außer der Tätigkeit der Welser und ihrer Beauftragten, außer Ulrich Schmiedel, Staden und einigen anderen Namen noch viel künftiger Forschung zu klären bleibt.[41]

> Although Germany has one of the oldest and richest colonial traditions and has proven itself again and again in the course of its history, since colonization and the associated spatial and economic expansion correspond to the innermost necessities of German nature, it has for a long time been lagging behind this great tradition to investigate the history of overseas and to wrench its bearers from oblivion in the 15th and 16th centuries. It is one of the most important tasks of German history research to close the gap here. We are best informed about South America, although here too, in addition to the work of the Welser and their agents, Ulrich Schmiedel, Staden and a few other names, much future research remains to be clarified.

---

41. M. A. Hedwig Fitzler, "Der Anteil der Deutschen an der Kolonialpolitik Philipps II. von Spanien in Asien," *Vierteljahrschrift für Sozial- und Wirtschaftsgeschichte*, 28. Bd., H. 3 (Franz Steiner Verlag, 1935), 243–81, here 243. Stable URL: https://www.jstor.org/stable/20726789.

She rehearses the history of economic imperialism as colonialism, participating in the interwar discourse not about the acquisition of land, but the right to economic prosperity through the *Kolonialwirtschaft*. Germany, she concludes, forfeited this right due to its lack of national unity:

> Das Deutsche Reich, das noch keine nationale Einheit besaß, machte seine Hoheit zur See niemals geltend. Während England, Frankreich und Spanien die Interessen ihrer Kaufleute förderten und alle Unternehmungen wagemutiger Landeskinder über See zu schützen bereit waren, erwog man im Reich wohl einige Male den Plan einer Reichsadmiralschaft, um die Hanse fahrten gegen Angriffe zu sichern, aber den Gedanken in die Tat umzusetzen, dazu vermochte sich der deutsche Kaiser nicht aufzuschwingen. So gingen der hervorragende deutsche Unternehmergeist, die unermüdliche Tatkraft und die große kaufmännische Opferwilligkeit der deutschen Handelshäuser dem Vaterlande verloren und brachten nur fremden Nationen Nutzen und Vorteile. Der koloniale Gedanke, den die Rot, die Fugger, Welser und Kron und mit ihnen andere oberdeutsche und hansische Kaufleute, aber auch deutsche Soldaten in Übersee in sich trugen, vermochte für Deutschland im 16. Jhd. nichts Fruchtbares zu wirken, weil ihm die einzige Grundlage zum Wachsen, der Rückhalt einer starken nationalen Staatsgewalt fehlte.[42]

The German Reich, which had no national unity, never asserted its sovereignty at sea. While England, France, and Spain promoted the interests of their merchants and were prepared to protect all undertakings of their daring children of the sea at sea, the plans of the Reich's admiralty to protect the Hanseatic League against attacks were considered several times, but the German emperor was never able to achieve this and put the idea into practice. The excellent German entrepreneurial spirit, the tireless energy, and the great willingness to make sacrifices of the German trading houses were lost to the fatherland and brought benefits and advantages only to foreign nations. The colonial idea that the Rot, the Fugger, Welser, and Kron and with them other Upper German and Hanseatic merchants, but also German soldiers overseas, yielded nothing fruitful for Germany in the sixteenth century, because it lacked the only one basis for growth, the backing of a strong national government.

---

42. Fitzler, "Der Anteil der Deutschen," 281. It is worth noting that Werner Hoffmann wrote a play about Schmidl, which presents a Nazified perspective on Schmidl's meaning for German immigrants in the 1940s. I thank Robert Kelz for this reference.

The complaint against colonial history stems from the lack of a national history. Fitzler-Kömmerling's training and ideology earned accolades. After her marriage, she continued to write colonial history and establish a women's circle; she had no formal position.[43] Her interests skimmed over Ulrich Schmiedel (figure 18 above), though the Deutscher Klub of Buenos Aires recultivates his German roots.

While careful reconsiderations of Schiller's metaphors of enslavement and Goethe's exclusionary universality may invite more rigorous critiques of the Enlightenment legacy, they nonetheless ascended in the ranks of German-language cultural patrimony. Despite their historical belonging primarily to a court, a city, a supportive patron, their work ensconced them in the German nation-state, or at least led to their iconic status as a contested site for nationalist politics and pushback. In twentieth-century Argentina, nationalist discourse gained volubility along with raised voices with competing politics about the ontology of immigration. The abnegation of imperialist militarism, underwritten by print media in German-speaking Argentina, counters the provincial entitlements of German identity and land acquisition claimed by M. A. Hedwig Fitzler. She mapped German rights onto an imperial project, one that asserts essentialized connections between farming and fighting, reinforcing the opposition between civilization and barbarism, and extending a colonial project to migration, in this case, to Argentina. That entitlement, though moderated in immigration narratives, still projects a myth of German Enlightenment and moral superiority onto the world, wherever it is, "upon the water."

---

43. See A. A. Bispo, "Mathilde Auguste Hedwig Fitzler Kömmerling (1896–1993) e o papel do Brasil no movimento feminino alemão. Da questão do 'pré-descobrimento português do Brasil," *Revista Brasil-Europa: Correspondência Euro-Brasileira* 130, no. 4 (2011:2). http://www.revista.brasil-europa.eu/130/Hedwig_Fitzler.html.

CHAPTER SIX

Upon the Water

Immigration as Destiny

Around 1900, the rhetoric of imperialist hegemony and the politics of empire intersect with immigration stories. In his address to the North German Regatta League in 1901, Kaiser Wilhelm declared that "our future lies upon the water. The more Germans go out upon the waters, whether it be in races or regattas, whether it be in journeys across the ocean, or in the service of the battle flag, so much the better it will be for us."[1] The kaiser connects the sport of rowing with naval ambitions, economic expansion, and any form of conquest, driven by the need to accomplish "what the Hanseatic League could not . . . because they lacked the vivifying and protecting power of the empire." Around 1900, the dialogue between the Reich and the German-speaking enclaves outside the nation reflected a recent history of emigration, alternatively viewed as a safety valve for demographic shifts and overcrowded cities, accompanied by agricultural decline and the additional "push" factor of political disappointment and dim professional prospects of the mid-nineteenth century. Kaiser Wilhelm's rhetorical recuperation of Germanness abroad into the protectorate of empire recodes the history of a mobile population, coerced or coached into departure. His proclamation elides immigration stories; at the same time, he subsumes immigrants as agents of history into a colonial narrative.

The narrative had political backing from Berlin. At the German Colonial Congress, convened in Berlin in 1902, the discussion of a surplus population and emigration made international headlines. For example, one speaker

---

1. Kaiser Wilhelm II of Germany, "Speech to the North German Regatta Association, 1901," quoted in C. Gauss, *The German Kaiser as Shown in His Public Utterances* (New York: Charles Scribner's Sons, 1915), 81–183. Quoted from: https://web.viu.ca/davies/H101/Kaiser.speech.imperialism.1901.htm/.

suggested Germans should go to the Southern Cone rather than to Australia.[2] The *Spectator* reported that a geographer, Dr. Jannasch, endorsed southern Brazil, rather than America or Australia, where German speakers were absorbed into the respective populations.[3] Presided over by Foreign Secretary von Richthofen, in the name of the kaiser and Chancellor von Bülow, many spoke to the need for increased trade, industry, and shipping. Another noted the impossibility of peacefully acquiring colonies. The *New York Times* reported Duke Johann Albrecht's caution against antagonistic rhetoric. Representing the Norddeutscher Bank of Hamburg, Max Schickel spoke directly to shared interests in overseas trade: friends of the Colonial Congress should leave antipathies aside and "seek to promote a good, honorable understanding with both our racially kindred competitors."[4] The *Times* article gave Dr. Prandl, a English chair at Berlin University, the last word. He proposed an annual budget to support schools abroad, to "strengthen the mysterious, powerful bond of language." This brief overview from the English-language press glimpses the issues key to my study, for the debate about the countries of the Southern Cone at the time was addressed in the German-language press, precisely around political discussions about making "unofficial" colonies official, alliances based on race, and the support of language as a "mysterious" vehicle of racial identity. Race, language, and German heritage became key to self-identification with Germans in Chile.

In the latter half of the nineteenth century, migration and immigration from German-speaking lands rewrote earlier accounts of colonial conquest in search of a destiny outside either a nation-state or an empire. A widespread assumption persists that the presence of Germans in South America was a product of World War II and mid-twentieth-century tragedy and exile. The histories of immigration and migration go back to the early modern period, and historiographic writing of later generations tends to focus on genealogies to legitimize that presence. One example features an account of the relationship between a German ancestor and an Amerindian. In Chile, late nineteenth-century historiography renames Don Bartolomé Flores (1506 or 1511–1585), dubbing him "Blumen" and asserting his German ancestry. On a

---

2. "German Colonial Congress. Emigration to Brazil Urged," *Sydney Morning Herald*, Oct. 14, 1902, 5.

3. "News of the Week," *The Spectator*, October 18, 1902, 2. http://archive.spectator.co.uk/page/18th-october-1902/2.

4. "GERMAN COLONIAL CONGRESS.; One Speaker Advocates the Co-operation of Germany with America and Great Britain," *New York Times*, Oct. 11, 1902, 8.

sixteenth-century voyage and expedition, he accompanied Pedro de Valdívia (1497–1553), the Spanish conquistador who became the first royal governor of Chile. The sense of vying for prominence and legitimacy among German Chileans varies with the exigencies of local, national, and international politics and events; this variation corresponds to the acquisition of citizenship, rights, and power. The discourse about origin and ownership, however, is further modulated by race. The hierarchy of colonial powers plays a role not only in the national imaginary about entitlement to noncontiguous geographies, but also in the narrative about immigration as destiny. This narrative leans into issues of racial difference; additionally, it complicates the story and raises the stakes about destinations: Africa, North America, and South America.

The story is under constant revision. During World War I, the German-Chilean historian Salvador Soto Rojas published a study titled *Los Alemanes en Chile 1541–1917* in the year before the conclusion of World War I.[5] He begins with a genealogical treatment of aristocratic families in the early modern period (3), with particular emphasis on the individuals of German heritage who played a foundational role in establishing Chile as a nation. His project attempts to look past the narrative of Spanish colonial domination, with a focus on "la raza jermánica" (4; the Germanic race). The essay, delivered as a conference paper, fast-forwards through German scientists, geologists, and engineers, all of whom left a legible impact on the development of the Chilean economy. Exculpatory in some ways, this focus on "la raza teutona" (the Teutonic race) does not overlook German cultural patrimony. He insists on the history of German influence on Chilean national identity. We have, he reminds his audience, been living in peace and harmony "con la patria de Bismarck, de Goethe, de Wagner, Eberling y von Moltke" (34; with the country of Bismarck, of Goethe, of Wagner, Eberling, and von Moltke). Rhetorically, he asks: Why distrust it now? Why disavow the science, the heritage that lifted Chile beyond barbarity? All these gains he prefaces with a German-Indigenous relationship between Bartolomé Blumen (also Blumenthal, also Flores) and Doña Elvira. Their illegitimate daughter, Agueda Flores, married a German, securing a merger of land and legacy (6–9). The historiographic purpose of the narrative legitimizing the German presence in Chile deflects hostility, local and global, directed at Germans abroad during World War I.

---

5. Salvador Soto Rojas, *Los Alemanes en Chile 1541–1917* (Valparaiso: Imprenta Victoria, 1917). Further references to this text in the upcoming section appear with page number(s) in parentheses.

His inaugural tale intertwines German and Chilean genealogies. This stabilizing allegory elides tensions that emerge in nineteenth-century life writing about the German immigration experience.

Rojas's recap of history valorizes the German influence by connecting Flores to the Inca empire. Though there are conflicting accounts of whether he and Elvira were in fact married, he legalized the legacy of land ownership through his bequest to their daughter. That period in history produced numerous contact and conflict zones that invoke colonial brutality during Spanish colonial rule. The legitimizing, compensatory narrative about the originary German from Nuremberg who acquired his land from the Inca empire through sexual relationships sanctioned by European inheritance laws bypasses the legacy of Spanish conquest and abuse. To return to Rojas's tome, the German or Teutonic race—which he is defending in a time of war—deserves honor for its civilizing impact on Chile.

The claims about "civilizing" German influence in South America invoke an Enlightenment discourse that pervades colonial tropes about the role of race and gender in national identity. Mobility, toward a new or temporary homeland, accrues ontological significance; that status ennobles daily life, elevating the everyday to the level of narrative. Travel writing and recruitment literature are supplemented by life writing that confirms existence through work. These perspectives are articulated in the stories of two German-Chileans whose lives and work make up the case studies on gender and "Germanness" of the *Deutschtum* beyond the nation-state. In the following, I examine several of the personal and professional medical letters of Karl Theodor Piderit (1826–1912), a doctor and psychologist who worked in Valparaiso (1851–1859). Himself disappointed politically by the failed revolutionary impulses of 1848, Piderit set off for Chile. He arrived in January 1850, prepared to embrace the "zweite Heimat" (second homeland) and to test his masculinity. As a medical professional, his work in the field inspired not only letters and reports, but also occasional poetry in which he documents the trials of life in emigration. At the same time, his medical prose reveals assumptions about racial and national identity as scientific. He finds certain observations reinforced by his immersion in environments of the global Global South. Additionally, gender relationships and essentialized traits occasionally infuse his writings. Motivated in part by his failure to find an appropriate wife, Piderit returns to Germany to start a family and continue his career with the experience of life *im Ausland* as a cosmopolitan credential.

By contrast, Frau Magdelene Barbara Hörz (geb. Aichele) left Swabia for

Chile in 1852. Admittedly, the single female immigrant sent ahead to reconnoiter for the family is exceptional. Aichele examines the conditions for farming, writes home, and marries in Chile, never to return to the nation-state. Unlike Piderit, she emigrates without preconceptions about the cultural superiority of Germanness. The contrast with what can best be described as provincial is mobile, professional, and cosmopolitan. The professional identity of Piderit, a male doctor, proves more exceptional than the provincial outlook of Aichele, who embodies the agricultural aspirations and successes familiar from recruitment pamphlets. Both Piderit and Aichele establish divergent senses of Germanness in Chile through critical observations of female contemporaries. The common ground claimed triangulates gendered and national identities that naturalize the German in South America. To make this argument, I consider excerpts of life writing, diaries, and letters, supplemented with images projected in German-language print media from South American German speakers ca. 1900, in an effort to contextualize the discourse emerging from and about contact zones with Indigenous people and other immigrants and a sense of belonging, either through language communities as ethnic epicenters or, eventually, citizenship. To different degrees, these writings extend a genealogy of German forefathers as accidental conquistadors, but without the brutalizing histories of dominant Spanish, British, and Portuguese powers, and intentional immigrants who forge connections between the German experience and geographies of the Global South.

In his defensive, commemorative mode, Rojas foregrounds the intricacies and validities of German influence on the southern provinces of Chile. He makes a clear effort to tell a countercolonial story; it challenges the hegemony of Spanish influence. His emphasis on the positive influence colors not only his rhetorical strategy, but also his selective recourse to genealogy. He writes, "Desde el descubrimiento de América, y en los primeros años de la dominacion española, era prohibido, aun a los peninsulares mismos, pasar a las Indías sin un permiso especial de la corona de Castilla" (5; Since the discovery of America, and in the first years of Spanish domination, passage to the Indies without special permission of the Castilian crown was prohibited, even for the *peninsulares* themselves), accenting the need for dispensation from Spain to enter the Indies. His next move takes the audience into the realm of national character:

> Como hombre de raza teutona, su conduct coñóse siempre a la más discreta prudencia, siendo mero espctador en todos los conatos de rebelion entre los

españoldes, y en cualquier acto de vioencia conta los indíjenas. Flores, más que guerrero, más que vasallo servil, manifestó ser siempre un eximio hombre de negocios, tan emprendedor como afortunado. El cargo de rejidor en el Cabíldo, hízole desplegar mucho iniciativa, ayudando y confícencia. A él cupo la honra de fundar uno de los primeros molinos, y cuyos cimientos se alzaron al pié del Santa Lucía (el Huelen indíjena) hácia la calle de la Merced. (6)

As a man of the Teutonic race, his conduct was always of the most discreet prudence, being a mere spectator to all the acts of rebellion between the Spanish and those acts of violence against the Indians. Flores, more than a warrior, more than a servile vassal, always proved himself to be a successful businessman, as enterprising as he was fortunate. The position of alderman in the Cabíldo made him display a lot of initiative, assistance, and confidence. He had the honor of establishing one of the first mills, the foundations of which were built at the foot of the Santa Lucía (the Indigenous Huelen) toward the street of Merced.

Flores then engages with "el cacique Talagante," more intimately with his niece, whom Rojas describes as "una hermosa jóven india de 18 primaveras" (6; a lovely young Indigenous woman of 18 springs), and the acquisition of her land. With a brief mention of Adalbert von Chamisso's voyage on the Rurick, Chamisso did not come ashore, Rojas fast-forwards to the importance of El General Don Pedro Lisperguer, a natural citizen of Worms, Leisperberg, who would marry doña Agueda Flores. Their son, Juan Rodulfo Lisperguer y Flores, served more than twenty years (9). The narrative shifts to science, geography, and geology, with a note about Adalberto von Chamisso's voyage on the Rurick (he did not come ashore, 10). Curiously, he makes no mention of the most notorious and controversial member of the family, the infamous "La Quintarella" (also La Quintarala). Even cursory searches yield information that identifies Flores as a Spanish conquistador. More recently, his granddaughter's alleged cruelty and dozens of crimes garnered attention from feminist scholars. The legacy further is claimed as German in origin, so the legitimation continues.[6] The crime that most riveted the attention of the

---

6. See Daniel Piedrabuena Ruíz-Tagle, *Los Lísperguer Wittemberg: una familia alemana en el corazón de la cultura chilena: Identidad y esplendor de la primera familia colonial de Chile. Los protegidos del César*, vol. 2 (Asturias: Booksideal, 2014).

Chilean public sphere involved her torturing an enslaved person to death and not burying him.[7]

The invitation extended to German emigrants originated, according to some sources, with Dom Pedro.[8] German scientists of the mid-nineteenth century, however, were enlisted to assist in recruitment, among them Bernhard E. Philippi (1811–1852) and J. E. Wappäus (1812–1879).[9] The 1846 volume *Süd-Chile in einer ersten Beschreibung* (South Chile in a preliminary description), published with Wappäus, documents the history of German emigration.[10] Philippi's relatives remained in Chile and exerted influence over the development of numerous scholarly fields. Wappäus, who traveled to Cape Verde and Brazil, became a professor in Göttingen and penned tomes about the economies, topographies, and statistics of the Americas. The recruitments interventions that met with significant success in attracting entire communities of skilled labor also extended to scholarly depictions of the Global South. In 1871, Wappäus published *Panama Neu-Granada Venezuela Guayana Ecuador Peru Bolivia und Chile geographisch und statistisch dargestellt* (Panama, New-Granada, Venezuela, Guayana, Ecuador, Peru, Bolivia, and Chile presented geographically and statistically).[11] The legacy that aligns German science with progress is celebrated by Rojas; it includes the German interaction with Amerindians. Rojas asks why disavow the science, the heritage that

> fueron arrancadas a la abarbarie, y entregadas a todos los goces y progresos de la civilizacion, gracias al empuje, la sobreidad, la intelijencia y la constancia en el trabajo de los hijos de Alamania de aquellos hombres esforzados que,

---

7. Contemporary portraits shy away from depicting her violent acts, whereas her legacy of beauty and cruelty influenced artists of the 1940s. See http://www.memoriachilena.gob.cl/602/w3-article-67627.html.

8. See Father M. Dedekind, *Die deutsch-evangelische Diaspora in Brasilien* (Leipzig: Verlag von Strauch & Krey GmbH, 1930).

9. According to Rojas, Philippi was commissioned by "our governor" to recruit immigrants in Germany in 1848 "con objeto de fomentar la emigracion jermánica a nuestro pais" (with the objective of encouraging Germanic immigration to our country").

10. Bernhard E. Philippi, *Süd-Chile in einer esten Beschreibung. in einer esten Beschreibung* (Göttingen: J. E. Wappäus). Mit einem Vorwort von Federico Saelzer Balde. Dokument zur Geschichte der deutschen Einwanderung, 1846; 1969. Further references to this volume appear as page numbers in parenthesis.

11. Wappäus, *Panama Neu-Granada Venezuela Guayana Ecuador Peru Bolivia und Chile geographisch und statistisch dargestellt* (Leipzig: J. C. Hinrichs'sche Buchhändlung, 1871).

despues de luchar titänicamente contra la naturaleza y los salvajes de la antigua Araucania, convirtieron aquellos valles y aquellas selvas en campas de los más variados cultivos, y en vastos emporios de riqueza, provenientes de la agricultura y la industria fabril. (78–79)

they were uprooted from barbarity, and delivered to all the joys and progress of civilization, thanks to the drive, the superiority, the intelligence, and the constancy of the work of the sons of Germany, of those hard-working men who, after the Titanic battle against nature and the savages of the ancient Araucania, converted those valleys and those jungles into fields of the most varied crops, and into vast emporiums of wealth, coming from agriculture and manufacturing.

Again, immigration success and the taming of their land, the ancient Araucania, took place through its cultivation. He concludes, "Por fin, que los cultures del arte, los poetas, los pintores, los novelistas; y, en suma, los hombres de pincel y pluma que conocen la historia patria, y estudian los probleas del porvenir; que observen y admiren a traves de aquellas rejiones el soberbio, esplendente cualdro de la Naturaleza, realzado por la mano y la intelijencia de hombre" (79; Finally, that the cultures of art, the poets, the painters, the novelists; in sum, the men of the brush and the pen and know the history of the country, and study the problems of the future; who observe and admire across those regions the superb, the splendid figure of Nature, realized by the hand and intelligence of man). The homology between transformation of people and lands, application of scientific knowledge, and overcoming the Indigenous becomes the calling card for the recruiter.

Philippi earlier provided the science for this elective affinity between the nation of Chile and the German, In "Ueber die Vortheile, welche das südliche Chile für deutsche Auswanderer darbiete," he touts Chile's political stability, the foundation for "die grössten Fortschritte in seiner geistigen wie in seiner materiellen Entwickelung" (13; On the advantages that southern Chile offers German emigrants; the greatest progress in its intellectual as well as in its material development). In advertising the south, its meadows and its primeval forests, he insists that even Andalusier "ihrem Vaterlande vorziehen" (13; prefer it to their fatherland). The hook he dangles is the sparse population and need for labor; he attributes the first to two factors. First, the colonization of Chile progressed from north to south, and the numerous wars the Spanish waged against the Araukana Indians "haben der Ausbreitung derselben in diesem Theile des Landes mächtige Hindernisse in den Weg gelegt" (13; have created many powerful deterrents for their expansion in this part of the country). Second, the *Bergwerke* (mines) of the north afforded more opportunity for rapid development than the agricultural south enjoyed: "Dagegen sind Ackerbau, Viehzucht und Holzhandel jedenfalls sichere und dauernde Quellen des Wohlstandes in diesen Gegenden" (13–14; In contrast, agriculture, cattle breeding, and lumber are in any case safer and more lasting sources of prosperity in these areas).

Much of the rhetoric elevating Germans is predicated on disparaging others. The competitive colonial attitudes discussed throughout this study extend to immigration cultures. As the recruitment pitch continues, "Wie gross die Unwissenheit und Indolenz der Creolen, welche hier leben, in allen Dingen ist, und wie gross die Vortheile sind, welche ein fleissiger Landbauer hier erwerben kann, wird im Folgenden auseinander gesetzt werden" (13–14; The following will address the issues of how great is the ignorance and indolence of the creoles who live here in all matters; and how great the advantages are that the industrious farmer can gain here). The description of German-cultivated land in Valdivia dominates the profile. In contrast to the indolent "Creolen," "ein fleissiger Landbauer" will thrive. In the denouement, he writes," "Auffallend mag es daher erscheinen, dass bisher bei uns Chile, wo auch die Einwanderung fleissiger Colonisten gerne gesehen wird, dennoch so wenig die Aufmerksamkeit derjenigen auf sich gesogen hat, welcher der deutschen Auswanderung sowohl im Interesse der Auswanderer selbst zum Vortheil ihres Mutterlandes eine neue Richtung geben möchten" (It may therefore seem striking that up until now, here among us in Chile, where the immigration of industrious colonists is welcomed, there is still so little attention paid by those who would like to give German emigration a new direction, in the interest of the emigrants themselves to the advantage of the motherland). The combination of circumstances, including a hospitable government and immigration provisions, culminated in a published *Einwanderungsgesetz*, "welches den Colonisten wie persönliche so auch religiöse Freiheit gewährte" (26; which granted the colonists personal and also religious freedom). Though there is acknowledgment of Indian conflicts and other wars, there is also discernible appreciation for Indigenous knowledge of the land. German-Chilean immigration in the nineteenth century, in the aftermath of slavery's abolition, followed a pattern: attract families with skills to work the acquired land, cultivate, and extract. In the latter half of the century, print media and educational institutions took on the task of tightening the communicative networks across the Atlantic. Active recruitment persisted into the early twentieth century; with the growth of German-speaking *Colonien* emerged a need for news media and schools. Prior to that, however, professionalization became synonymous with Germanification, and the rise of the female farmer brought gender into focus.

Theodor Piderit: Medical Practice and the Chilean *Wanderjahre*

Piderit places great stock in his experience; he maintains self-awareness in his personal and professional epistles, documenting and conveying life as a doctor and immigrant in southern Chile. His *Briefe aus Valparaiso (1851–1859)* were not published until this century.[12] But during his sojourn in Chile, he sent missives, which conveyed information about illnesses, patients, medical treatments, medication, and actual patient case studies to Germany; these appeared in the *Feuetillon* section of the journal *Deutsche Klinik. Zeitung für Beobachtung aus deutscher Kliniken und Krankenhäusern* (German clinic: Newspaper for observation from German clinics and hospitals). The doctor and psychologist Piderit, in response to the change in political climate, sought distant shores. His brother settled in New Orleans, and the tension between North and South is duly noted: "Von den Yankees habe er keine gut Meinung, aber er bewundere deren Kraft und unentwegten Einsatz bei der Entwicklung ihres Landes" (25; He does not think much of the Yankees, but he does admire their strength and persistent commitment to developing their land). Most of the forty-nine letters he addressed to his father, recounting the highs and lows of his practice. Compelling in this context, Piderit asserts his professional identity with his gendered, German identity. In so doing, he exposes the overstatements of recruitment narratives through an insistence on the material reality he faces. Piderit adjusts his frame of reference as he gathers experience as a doctor and member of a community. His gaze, evident in letters, reports through the lens of an immigration ontology that further determines his production of scientific, medical knowledge. In effect, he transcends the model of the nineteenth-century migrant worker; instead,

---

12. Piderit, *Briefe aus Valparaiso (1851–1859)*, edited and commentary by Ernst Christian Hengestenberg (Munich: self-published, 2007). Further references to this volume appear with page numbers in parenthesis.

he approaches his professional service in Chile as a stage in his training, the *Wanderjahre*, or journeyman years familiar from the guild system of apprenticeship through mastery.

Piderit details both major and minor events in the Chilean chapters of his life. Topics vary widely: They range from earthquake devastation (38), what women wear to Sunday services (42), reading about a brave doctor who assisted with the dead and wounded from Urida's regiment—himself (45), dismay about German politics and the failed revolution (63–65), and dealing with his own loneliness (66). On occasion, his musings grow more profound. In the act of writing, he edits his responses into moments of the sublime in the Kantian sense, the profound, and even the ridiculous. In the sixteenth letter, for example, written from Valparaiso on January 14, 1853, he marks the second anniversary of his departure as a rite of passage. Piderit acknowledges the day as the most important of his life, of his "subjektiven Wiedergeburt" (65; subjective rebirth). Sustaining the metaphor of reincarnation, he continues: "selbst schnitt ich mir die Nabelschnur anfänglicher Vorurteile, schnitt mir die Lebensquelle des mütterlichen Bodens ab, die mir so viel süße und so viel bittere Säfte ins Herz geführt hab. Am Tage meiner Geburt wurde ich ein Mensch, am 15. Januar wurde ich ein Mann!" (65; I cut my own umbilical cord of early prejudice, cut myself off from the life source of the maternal earth that funneled so many sweet and bitter juices into my heart. On the day of my birth, I became a human being, on the 15th of January I became a man!). The implicit midwifery of assisting a birth Piderit regenders as a doctor and man. By contrast, he would also publish a case study: the patient he described as a "Bauernmädchen" with a robust constitution who gave birth on her own and resumed work immediately. She developed a fistula, which he treated.[13] Figurative language facilitates the gender transformation that enables his rebirth, perhaps modeled on the amateur delivery of a farm girl. In masculinizing birth, Piderit sets the threshold for this rite: it is leaving the homeland, and he genders the destiny of German professional in a state of emigration.

Piderit's experience of nature is textbook Kantian sublime. Called to treat an ill patient during a season when travel poses hardship, Piderit and his companion, the painter Otto Grashof (also Graßhof) set out on horseback to attend the sick man, who is responsible for establishing a copper smelter and refinery deep in the mountains. Accompanied by Indian guides, they

---

13. Piderit, "Briefe aus Chile," in *Deutsche Klinik. Zeitung für Beobachtungen aus deutschen Kliniken und Krankenhäusern*, ed. Alexander Göschen. Vol 5 (Berlin: Georg Reimer Verlag, 1853), 531–32.

traverse a mountain range that inspires both. In a letter to his father, dated July 25, 1824, Piderit writes, "Ich habe in den Alpen nichts gesehen, was mit dieser fremdartigen und grandiosen Szenerie zu vergleichen wäre, und Grashof war ganz in Entzückung" (72; In the Alps I have not seen anything that could be compared to this strange and grandiose scenery, and Grashof was completely delighted). Along the way, they encounter severe weather and inhospitable conditions. At one point, he sits in the middle of a river for an hour to recover. Based on his report, they traveled through "el Cerro de las Bischaos," orthographically, el Cerro des las Vizcachas, a mining region in the Andes range with an altitude of slightly more than 2,000 meters (6,500 feet). Inspired to see the view, Piderit decides to summit: "Der Sieg musste vollkommen sein, ich wollte die höchste Spitze erklimmern,—doch die empörten Berggeister geboten dem aberwitzigen Menschenkinde Halt!" (72; The victory had to be perfect, I wanted to climb the highest peak,—but the outraged mountain spirits ordered the crazy human child to halt!)

When he is safe, he kisses the ground "mehrere Male höchst unsanft" (72; many times, highly ungently). The experience of heights, along with the associate challenge of conquering mountainous terrain, characterizes much of the German cultural experience. In their volume on this cultural legacy, Sean Ireton and Caroline Schaumann approach this topic "rooted in European— more specifically German—cultural history."[14] In the Anglo-American sphere, historian Michael Reidy has written on mountaineering, gender, and geographies of empire and empirical discovery.[15] Piderit, by contrast, tests his masculinity in a context culturally elevated but subjectively downcast. His attempts thwarted, he fires his pistol in frustration, only to hear it whimper: "der schwache Knall verhallte in der dünnen Luft" (72; the feeble bang faded in the thin air). Reborn in emigration, his pursuit of a transcendent epiphany in the mountains eluded him.

Among Kant's most influential theories is his assertion from the *Critique of Pure Reason* (1781) that the sublime is uncontainable. By contrast, the beautiful is limited. The human mind encountering the limitlessness of the sublime must engage the imagination to supplement the immensity it cannot otherwise comprehend. The attempt involves pleasure in the ambition, but pain in the inevitable failure. Piderit has a Kantian moment. Defeated

---

14. Sean Ireton and Caroline Schaumann, "Introduction," in *Heights of Reflection: Mountains and the German Imagination from the Middle Ages to the Twenty-first Century* (Rochester: Camden House, 2012).

15. Michael S. Reidy, "Mountaineering, Masculinity, and the Male Body in Mid-Victorian Britain," *Osiris* 30, no. 1 (2015). https://doi.org/10.1086/682975.

and disappointed, Piderit sublimates his moment of Romantic aesthetics in a mock-epic poem. He opens with an elevated description of the natural surroundings and their impact, then turns to his companion:

Trauernd tief saß Otto Graßhof;	Mourningly deep, Otto Grashof sat;
Otto Grashof steht am Fenster,	Otto Grashof at the window,
Stützt den Kopf in seine Rechte'	Head propped with his right hand
Und er schaut hinaus ins Freie,	And he looks out into the open,
Schaut hinaus zum grauen Himmel,	Looks out at the gray heavens,
Schaut auf die graue Erde,	Looks at the gray earth,
Seufzet dann—und saget gar nichts.-	Then sigh—and says nothing at all.-
Darauf rückwärts blickend spricht er	Looking backwards then he says
Zu dem Dokter Piderite:	To Doctor Piderite:
Zu dem Tal der Albarados,	to the Valle of Albarados,
An dem Fuße Biscacha	At the foot of the Biscacha
Sind im Winter festgveregnet (sic)	They are snowed in in winter
Don Quichott und Sancho Pansa.	Don Quixote and Sancho Panza.
Abenteuer gibt es eine;-	There is an adventure;-
Rülpse, Flöhe, Ratten, Zwiebeln,	Burps, fleas, rats, onions,
Schlechten Tee und schlechten Stuhlgang-	Bad tea and bad bowel movements-
Das ist alles was wir fanden	That is everything that we found
In dem Tal des Albarados!-	In the valley of Albarados!-
Ach, und nimmer find ich meine	Alas, and never will I find my
Dulcinea von Tobosa!- (73–74)¹⁶	Dulcinea of Tobosa!-

His brush with natural transcendence in the quest to fulfill his professional obligations despite inclement weather and a lunatic trek across the mountains transforms into a quixotic adventure, complete with bad beverages, rodents, and constipation, and absent adoring women.

Piderit nurtured personal, political, and professional hopes for his voyage to and residence in Chile. In addition to seeking growth, relief from oppres-

---

16. The first half of the poem reads, "Keiner war wohl je so traurig!- / In dem Tal der Albarados, / Auf der kahlen Bergeshöhe / Liegt ein Rancho still und einsam, / Rings umragt von Bergesgipfeln, / Die mit ihren Felsenzacken Ragen in den Wolkenhimmel. / Weiße Nebelschleier wallen / In dem tiefen dunkeln Tale, Und der Regen, unaufhörlich, Prasselt nieder auf die Hütte, / Auf das Dach von Palmenzweigen. / Ringsum aus den dunklen Schluchten / Stürzen gelbe Wasserbäche, / Donnernd reißen sie die Felsen / Mit sich in die Täler nieder, / Und die Höhen des Gebirges / Sind in tiefen Schnee begraben.-"

sion, and an opportunity to practice, he sought a wife. At each turn, different attributes of intersectionality enter into his decision-making process and serve his literary purposes. His letters, while rarely self-indulgent, do convey the disappointment of not finding anyone suitable for him; these segue into medical commentary on race, nationality, and gender.

Throughout, Piderit connects personal and professional ambitions. Persistent in his efforts to maintain scientific connections with Europe, he counted himself among the amateur collectors who stocked Berlin museums. Glenn Penny and Matti Bunzl, in *Worldly Provincialism*, interrogate the role of anthropology and ethnographic exploration in the Age of Empire; Penny's contribution on Bastian in this volume, and his later sustained examination of Franz Boas and the vast network of amateur collectors who helped amass Berlin's ethnographic collections, are salient.[17] On a much more modest scale, Piderit connects his local experience and environment with museumification. Two brief examples illuminate the erasure of Indigenous knowledge in his pursuits: "Zu Pferde und von einem alten Indianer begleitet, ritten wir die Vorberge hinauf mit Bäumen und hohen Gesträuch bewachsen, waren sie von einer ungeheuren Mass Vögel belebt, die an dem frühen, fröhlichen Morgen lustig durch einander zwitscherten und sangen" (71; On horseback and guided by an Indian, we rode up the foothills overgrown with trees and high bushes, that were animated by a huge number of birds; on that early and joyful morning, they were all twittering and singing happily). He erases the expert guidance of the old Indian, and dwells instead on the songbirds, noting "und ich werde die Bälge für das Detmolder Museum zu reservieren suchen" (72; and I will try to reserve the bellows for the Demold Museum). A similar moment occurs when he observes two Chilean swans with black necks, and he sees "eine Zierde des Detmolder Museums" (99; an ornament for the Detmold Museum). Chile and everything in and about it contributes to his subjectivity; everything he touches turns to material for his European German identity. Generating knowledge and his discoveries, revenants of the natural habitat, are embodied.

Professional, scientific credentials become constitutive elements of that

---

17. See H. Glenn Penny and Matti Bunzl, eds., *Worldly Provincialism: German Anthropology in the Age of Empire* (Ann Arbor: University of Michigan Press, 2010). In his contribution to the volume, Penny's focus is on "Bastian's Museum: On the Limits of Empiricism and the Transformation of German Ethnology," 86–126. Later, he examines the extensive collecting network Bastian generated in *In Humboldt's Shadow: A Tragic History of German Ethnology* (Princeton, NJ: Princeton University Press, 2021). Though Bastian's project aimed at inclusive universality, the impulse lent itself to politicization and racialization in the acts of "hypercollecting."

identity. Toward this end, Piderit's practice provides raw material for medical reports. Several contributions appear as installments in medical publications. The extent to which the information can be categorized as medical or scientific poses problems. In essence, he writes about human afflictions, their causes and treatment. To orient the German-speaking public, he sketches an overview of his patients: "Die Bevölkerung des Landes ist eine Mischlingsraçe von spanischen und indianischen Blute. Daher im Allgemeinen dunkle Gesichtsfarbe, schwarze üppige Haare, schöne Augen und platte indianische Nasen" (525; The population of the country is a mixed-race of Spanish and Indian blood. Therefore, in general dark facial coloring, black lush hair, beautiful eyes, and flat Indian noses). Beauty and subjectivity blend with his European medical gaze. Additionally, he observes, "Reine spanische Schönheiten sind sehr seltene Erscheinungen" (525; Pure Spanish beauties are extremely rare occurrences). Without drawing attention to his own preferences, he translates Indian influences on physiognomy into the realm of the unattractive, while Spanish features designate appeal.

Piderit continues with a description of gendered behavior, which he maps onto all Spanish-influenced countries in South America. Again, in an objective tone, he writes that the women are superior to the men in their talent and energy, and they get involved in the political turmoil of the day (525). The personal letters to his father, by contrast, paint a different picture: he seems fixated on the women wearing mantillas and their coquetry of the half-mask (42); the Chilean woman gets up around midday, barely gets dressed, and does not do her hair until the afternoon (49–50). Here, he lauds the German woman: "Unsre deutschen Hausfrauen würden sich wundern, wenn sie die Wirtschaft in einem chilenischen Haus sähen" (49–50: Our German housewives would be amazed if they could see the way a Chilean house is run). The disjuncture between his personal and professional transmissions raises questions about his intended audience and reveal his bias toward the industrious German wife, while titillated by the appearance and behavior of Chilean women, with their Spanish and Indian antecedents.

The power of observation, enhanced by instruments and augmented with medical training and practice, form the foundation of Piderit's professional skills. Both for his stamina and knowledge, he gains respect from some. On the way to el Cerro, he writes, "Der Indianer bezeugte mir einen außerordentlichen Respekt" (73; The Indian showed me extraordinary respect). Yet he complains that the patients lack a sense of appreciation for the modern medical professions, hence a doctor like himself, because they grew so accustomed to charlatans and barbers doing surgeries ("Briefe aus Chile," 525–26). Some even consider him a "Hexenmesiter" ("Briefe aus Chile," 526; master of witches). Though sincere in the conduct of his duties, he adopts a superior attitude when communicating with his German-speaking peers through the medical journal. Racialized and gendered thinking about patients begins to appropriate other elements. Piderit sketches twenty-three ailments and his treatment, along with two more sustained case studies (one male patient with cancer, the other a female patient with fistula, noted above). Interlaced with the professional argot, he hastens to add, "dass das eben geschilderte Publicum hauptsächlich nur den niederen Klassen angehört und vorzüglich den im Innern Lebenden" ("Briefe aus Chile," 527; that the population just depicted mainly belongs to the lower classes and mostly reside in the interior of the country). At pains to assure his educated audience, Piderit differentiates between those living inland and the city dwellers of Valparaiso. In a discussion of syphilis and the peculiar treatments people inflict upon themselves, he shifts rhetorical registers, commenting on "die verschiedensten Nationalitäten" (the most different nationalities) he encounters, all with different constitutions, such that he has to adapt treatments to nationality and ethnicity, even if the patients suffer the same symptoms ("Briefe aus Chile," 527).

Piderit's European epistemological framework structures his experience in emigration. He masculinizes the rebirth of himself as a professional, a liberal, and an immigrant. In the process of comparing and contrasting not only European colonialists, categorizing them according to race, ethnicity, and gender, he trains the same gaze on Germans in the colonial landscape. His brother, mentioned above, settled in New Orleans, and his preference for speaking English over German sustains his life in the United States, as Theodor writes their father. But Dr. Piderit asserts his professional identity as a German over the life of farming, with a hint of disdain for the sibling who complains about the Yankees and prefers their language: "Das kann nur ein Deutscher tun!" (Only a German can do that!) and he continues, "die Sucht sich zu amerikanisieren ist in den Vereinigten Staaten nicht selten unter den Deutschen und so lange dieses Haschen nach Fremden und diese Geringschätzung des Eigenen noch möglich ist, wird Deutschland stets der Bediente des Auslands bleiben" (94; The addiction to Americanize oneself is not infrequent among Germans in the United States and as long as this chasing the foreign and belittling of one's own is still possible Germany will always remain the servant of the foreign country).

"Bring blue thread": Magdelene Barbara Aichele Hörz

In her substantial monograph on national and gendered identity in the discourse of nineteenth-century immigration epistles, Alexandra Lübcke argues persuasively that work must be thought of in gendered registers.[18] She refers to post-Nazi historiography that (after 1945) attached the concepts of *Volkstum* and *Deutschtum*, along with genealogically grounded "science," with the Germans in Chile.[19] Her examination of national discourse and German immigration focuses on the letters of women who emigrated to Chile in the nineteenth century. According to her research, the highest number of Germans headed for the Americas between 1853 and 1855, with a surge again around 1880, but approximately 5 percent went to South America.[20] The inherited notion, developed by Wappäus and disseminated in the 1846 *Deutsche Auswanderung*, that Germans have an innate tendency to cultivate the land is a point of departure for Lübcke's analysis, though positing an ethnic connection between land and German national destiny predates the mid-nineteenth century. Lübcke also addresses the innate racism, seemingly congenital to immigration: "Aber diese Überführung eines Zeichens vollzieht sich auch auf einer anderen (Be)Deutungsebene. Der 'schmutzige', 'hässliche', 'tierisch-barbarische', aber unterworfene Indianer, exotischer Einwohner der 'Neuen Welt', eine Konstruktion des neuzeitlichen Amerikadiskurses, wird auch zu einem Element in der Herstellung von Differenzen"[21] (But this transfer of a sign takes place on another level of meaning/interpretation. The 'dirty,' 'ugly,' 'animalistic-barbaric,' but subordinate Indian, exotic inhabitant of the 'New World,' a construction of early modern American discourse, becomes an element in the production of differences). Her analysis rings true in so many ways it seems untoward to point out the exception, as demonstrated in my reading of Piderit, who remarks on the respect earned by an Indian guide and the beauty of some eyes, perhaps exculpatory. Briefly, the specifics vary the theme. Aichele and Piderit are on the same page about German industriousness and entitlement to land.

---

18. Alexandra Lübcke, *"Welch ein Unterschied aber zwischen Europa und hier." Diskurstheoretische Überlegungen zu Nation, Auswanderung und kulturelle Geschlechteridentität anhand von Briefen Chileauswanderinnen des 19. Jahrhunderts* (Frankfurt a/M: IKO Verlag für interkulturelle Kommunikation, 2003), 225.

19. Lübcke, *Welch ein Unterschied*, 12. She elaborates on the historiography and its impact on publications of the 1920s and 1930s.

20. Lübcke, *Welch ein Unterschied*, 37.

21. Lübcke, *Welch ein Unterschied*, 198.

Aichele, a woman who set out for Chile on her own, identifies as a working colonist; she is also a writer of letters, which, unlike Piderit, she does not claim as part of her identity.[22] Yet her letters appeared for German readers. Pfarrer Dr. Schünemann Frutillar published several in the evangelical *Gemeindeblatt* in Chile. She is not working to return, but to prepare for the arrival of her family.[23] Her parents, Johann Michael Aichele und Barbara, née Mauz, and her siblings planned to follow. Aichele sought out Swabian and Nellinger immigrants, always with the intention of accommodating her relatives: "Ihr schreibet mir, wie ich mein Land umtreibe und ich weiss noch nicht, wo ich es nehmen soll, (. . .) wo die anderen Deutschen sind, hat es noch so schöne Parzellen und gute Viehweide und so werde ich warten bis ihr kommt mit einer Parzelle zu nehmen" (quoted in Lübcke, 273–74; You wrote me about the search for some land and I still do not know where I should take it [. . .] where the other Germans are, there are still such lovely parcels and good cattle pastures and so I will wait until you come to take a parcel). Service work is available for her sisters, she assures her private readers. In her next missive, she reports her marriage: "Ich habe mich verheiratet mit David Hoerz von Ruith, den 16. Sept. 1854. Ich bin aber in meinem Dienst geblieben" (quoted in Lübcke, 274–275; I married David Hoerz of Ruith on September 16, 1854. But I remained in service). From this life story, Lübcke concludes:

> Zwar sind die Frauen in den Chile-Texten des kolonialen Auswanderungsdiskurses als Komplement zu den männlichen Protagonisten entworfen und ihre Tätigkeiten immer geschlechtsspezifisch konzipiert. In ihrer Naturalisierung als "fleißiger Gemeinschaft" von Eingewanderten treffen sich jedoch diese Entwürfe.[24]

The women in the Chile texts of the colonial emigration discourse are indeed seen as a complement to male protagonists and their activities are always conceived in sex-specific ways. In their naturalization as part of an "industrious community" of emigrants these images are however accurate.

Lübcke further contextualizes Aichele's reports in the typology of the lazy Chilean woman.[25] We recognize this stereotype from Piderit's description of

---

22. On her identity as a working colonist, see Lübcke, *Welch ein Unterschied*, 273.
23. I consulted documents in the Emil Winkler Archive in Santiago, Aichele PER 100 AIC.
24. Lübcke, *Welch ein Unterschied*, 276.
25. Lübcke, *Welch ein Unterschied*, 276.

the Chilean housewife who rises late and remains in a state of dishabille until midafternoon. The destiny of working the land for family—and for supporting the family still in the homeland—drives Aichele in a way that indicates her labor is more than supplementary.

In a third letter, documented in the archive, Aichele admits she cannot send the promised money yet. It is also clear that she is serving to ease the parental burden:

> Ich hätte Euch wohl können dringender schreiben, daß Ihr kommen soll, aber ich weiß wohl noch, was mir der Vater gesagt hat, daß er in Amerika nicht mehr so arbeiten wolle als in Deutschland, und hier sieht man in den ersten 2 Jahren nichts anderes vor sich, als viele Arbeit, wie Ihr Euch denken könnt, aber dann bekommt man es besser. Ich habe in Eurem Brief gelesen, daß Ihr es nicht alles so glaubt, wie ich Euch geschrieben habe, und es ist in der Tat besser, als Ihr glaubt.[26]

> I probably could have written with greater urgency that you should come, but I well know what my father said, that he does not want to work as hard in America as in Germany, and here, for the first two years you can only see how much work there is, as you can imagine, but then it gets better. I read in your letter that you do not believe that everything is as I have written, but it is in fact better than you think.

Aichele clearly strives to be a reliable narrator. She entreats her family to believe her eyewitness accounts of the Chilean experience. In contrast to perhaps more outlandish, gold-fever-driven narratives about the New World, hers remains modest and circumscribed, but reassuring nonetheless. To enhance her credibility, she estimates the amount of money they will need, informs them about the cost of cows, defends the quality of the soil, and mentions that a doctor (possibly Piderit) serves the community of colonists. Aichele writes with an urgency born not of loneliness, but of desire to demonstrate a degree of self-actualization. She scouts for the family and negotiates her family's immigration destiny. Again, the work ethic for which German-speakers are renowned, factors prominently in her appeal:

> Die Kolonisten befinden sich gut, natürlich ist es auch wieder ein Unterschied, wer nicht arbeiten will, soll nur draußen bleiben, die kommen hier zu

---

26. Otto Schuster to Aichele, 106–8.

nichts wie in Deutschland, es ist die Hauptsache, wenn man auf einer Parzelle ist, daß man recht Vieh hält, so kann man das Geld jetzt besser anwenden als wie wir hierher kamen, da hätte man nichts kaufen können. (1–2)

The colonists are doing well, naturally there is a difference, whoever does not want to work can just stay outside, they amount to nothing here just as in Germany, the main thing is, when you are on a parcel, you have to keep the cattle properly, so that you can use the money here better than we did where we came from, there you could not afford to buy anything.

The acquisition of land remains central, and is interwoven with family and religion. In reporting her marriage, she writes, "Mit der Religion steht es so, es kann ein jedes glauben was es will, die Eingeborenen sind zwar alle katholisch, aber man kann überall Gott dienen. Eine Kirche ist jetzt schön ausgebaut, weiß und blau angestrichen von der Regierung, und es wird aber noch nicht so gleich ein deutscher Pfarrer herkommen" (2; In terms of religion, anyone can believe what they want, the natives are all Catholic, but you can serve God everywhere. A church has been built, painted white and blue by the government, but a German pastor probably will not be arriving any time soon).

The ecumenical Christianity would be the best compromise for the parents, she implies, while acknowledging that the "natives" practice Catholicism. Finally, after assuring her private readers of the absence of snow, she exhorts them: "zögert nur nicht mehr lang und kommet so bald ihr könnet, wir wünschen euch von Herzen Glück zu eurer Reise. Gottes Engel geleite euch. Wir verbleiben eure Kinder bis in den Tod" (2; do not delay any longer and come as quickly as you can, we wish you a good trip from our hearts. May God's angel guide you). Her husband now in the family, they sign off as eternal children. The pastor who published the letters in the evangelical circular informs the congregation: "Die Eltern der Schreiberin sind dann wirklich 1855 bzw. 1856 nach Chile nachgekommen und mit ihnen die beiden jüngsten Brüder Christian Gottlieb und Friedrich Gottlob, während zwei der älteren Töchter, Marie Rosine und Anna Marie 1854 nach Nordamerika auswanderten, und von Neuyork aus, wo sie wohnten, bis an ihr Lebensende mit ihren Eltern und Geschwistern in Chile in Verbindung blieben" (2; The parents of the writer then really did come to Chile in 1855 and 1856 and with them the two youngest brothers Christian Gottlieb and Friedrich Gottlob, while the two older daughters, Marie Rosine and Anna Marie, emigrated to North America in 1854, and from New York, where they lived, they stayed in contact with their parents and siblings in Chile for the rest of their lives).

Aichele asks her family to bring blue thread when they come, and a few other small items that amount to trifles. In contrast to the vaulting hopes articulated in the Piderit oeuvre, rife with scientific knowledge, occasional self-deprecation, and epic ambitions, Aichele expands her world view to replicate the German farmer experience abroad. Her connection to the new homeland, not formalized by citizenship, is nonetheless predicated on the reliable agency of local agents and immigration officers. Her marriage, religion, and work ethic sustain an intergenerational transatlantic family that disperses between North and South America, though translocality dominates transatlantic epistemologies. In contrast to Piderit, who returned to Germany, married, and continued to develop his professional practice and reputation, immigration in Chile was not a chapter, but the rest of Aichele's life. The preservation of her letters, due in part to the pastor who saw the potential for recruitment narratives in them and published her words, leaves posterity with insight into the uncanny provincialism, born more of humility than arrogance, that also marks a contrast with Piderit's cosmopolitanism. The later decades of the nineteenth century effect media changes, with German-language publications that shift the focus to local political power structures and the jewel in the immigration crown: citizenship.

Citizenship as Destiny: *Culturpioniere*

In response to border conflicts and demographic shifts, German Chileans began to redefine their role in the new homeland. Moving forward from the case studies of Piderit and Aichele, who in their own ways became protagonists in their respective immigration narratives, the last two decades of the nineteenth century would bear witness to the establishing of reliable print media. Company newsletters and church circulars segued into newspapers, replete with the signifiers of recruitment and nationalization literature. A prominent example of this medium is the *Deutsche Zeitung*. In the September 21, 1887, issue of the *Deutsche Zeitung für Süd-Chile*, the political climate indicates naturalization is in order. The paper, self-defined as the "Organ für alle Deutschen in Chile," printed a front-page headline that reads, "Werdet chilenische Staatsbuerger!" (Become Chilean citizens!). The editor of this German-language publication, Johannes Frey, challenges his readership to initiate the naturalization process in order to become citizens of their new homeland. Based in the German stronghold of Valdivia, the founders of this newspaper strived to bring news from Europe and Chile to its audience, both for edification and entertainment. German speakers were recruited. In the early nineteenth century, southern Chile supported at best a languishing economy. With organized efforts under the leadership of Chilean diplomat Vincente Pérez Rosales (1807–1886), in the wake of others mentioned above, German-speaking Europeans were recruited to develop agriculture and expand industries, such as mining, especially through the employment of emerging technologies. An estimated thirty thousand German-speaking immigrants settled in this part of Chile between 1846 and 1914.

Chilean democracy was a contested mode of government from the time of independence forward. The recruitment efforts of the mid-nineteenth century extended to the protection of immigrant rights, or at least the promise thereof. German publicists in Chile rely on the 1862 German-Chilean "Freundschafts- und Handelsvertrag" (friendship and trade agreement) which pledged "den Schutz der deutschen Rechtsansprüche in Chile" (the protection of German rights in Chile)[27]; along with forty hectares of land, the German-speaking immigrants considered themselves fortunate. Albert Hörll, who had worked for the *Deutsche Post*, assumed leadership of the *Deutsche Zeitung* in 1904, in part as a survival strategy of the periodical.[28] The tone emphasizes that the German community of immigrants also considered itself to be an integral component of Chile's overall arc of progress and economic modernization. With its victory against Peru and Bolivia in the War of the Pacific (1879–1883), Chile expanded its sphere of influence northward to include the Peruvian territory of Tarapacá, the Bolivian department of Litoral, which cut Bolivia off from the sea, and temporary control over the Peruvian provinces of Tacna and Arica. President Balmaceda inaugurated a discourse about Chilean prosperity that resonated within the German-speaking immigrant communities, even though European immigration was not a prominent concern.[29] With the rise of this liberal government in Chile, the German-

---

27. Hoerll, *Deutsche Zeitung*, June 1904, 1.

28. See Patricio Bernedo Pinto, "Historia de las estrategias periodísticas del periódico Valdivia's Deutsche Zeitung: 1886–1912." *Historia* 33 (2000). Online ISSN 0717-7194, section 4.

29. After the war, Jose Manuel Balmaceda, an upper-class politician, was elected president, but not without piquing his enemies, Conservatives and dissenting Liberals alike. He threw his weight behind public works programs and defense, in effect committing Chile's prosperity to redistributing wealth during his term, which lasted from 1886 to 1891 and ended in civil war. His policies included improving life in the nation through social programs for the poor, education, land reform, and infrastructure. Congress thwarted his efforts, he left his post and committed suicide.

language discourse about identity shifted from a "universal," enlightened concept of the rights of man, rights to be exercised within a transportable "cultural" nation, to a more specific ontology of immigration, predicated on political rights and citizenship.

This shift is marked in the issue of the *Deutsche Zeitung* devoted to the integration of German colonists through the pursuit of citizenship rights in Valdivia. Frey writes, "So lange die Regierung liberal bleibt, wird sie stets in ihren deutschen Colonisten gute Unterthanen haben; es brauchte also keine Seite zu beklagen, wenn wir alle insgesamt uns mit dem Gedanken vertraut machen wollen, dass wir eigentlich doch Chilenen *sind*, und mit der Naturalisierung nur noch eine *blose Form* erfuellen, die aber zur Ausuebung staatsbuergerlicher Rechte nothwendig ist" (As long as the government stays liberal it will always have good subjects in their German colonists; neither side would need to complain if we are all acquainted with the idea that we *are* actually Chileans, and with naturalization we would just be filling out a *mere form*, which is however necessary for the exercising of citizenship rights). The type of "integration" that the German-speaking press advocated, however, is predicated less on a commitment to local contiguity; instead, the strategies of integration privilege not a metonymy, but rather a synecdoche of citizenship, through which the "microsociedad, como la de los alemanes de Valdivia"[30] established and asserted its identity, projecting its self-defined and consensual attributes onto the palimpsest of the new *Heimat*.

This call for naturalization of German-speaking immigrants marks the moment of transition in the ontology of immigration in South America during which the parameters of cultural, national, and linguistic identity become more locally and explicitly "Chilean" and at the same time more "hyphenated" in the embrace of new national realities and rights. In this and subsequent issues of the *Deutsche Zeitung*, the editor and reporters focus on the celebration of German economic and cultural success, the proud implementation of German technologies, and the attempts to gain political power through naturalization in order to enhance integration but also to advance the prosperity of the colonies. The German immigrants responsible for writing the copy and representing the colonies produced newspapers in which there is a subtext of German emergence as eager imperial subjects, a colonial presence in the world, and key players with the power to exert their influ-

---

30. Patricio Bernedo Pinto, "Historia de las estrategias periodísticas del periódico Valdivia's Deutsche Zeitung: 1886–1912." *Historia* 33 (2000). Online ISSN 0717–7194*Historia*, n.p.

ence over the migration ebb and flow in response to economic downturn in Europe and population surpluses. In part, they envisioned their roles as recruiters to attract the skeptical countrymen. One such voice belonged to Dr. A. Ried, who offered a diagnosis from Valparaiso in July 1847 about the thousands of emigrants who abandon their family in the homeland and take the risk of emigrating; they are possessed by "einem wandernden Dämon besessen" (a wandering demon).[31] Ried proceeds to extol some of Chile's virtues, among them the landscape and climate, but also the specific privilages for Germans: the law of November 18, 1845, Article 4 of which stipulated the remission of all the duties and taxes for colonists between Cape Horn and Concepcion. Article 5, in turn, made it possible to obtain citizenship and privileges.[32] Hoerll, too, refuted the popularized stereotypes of Chile among Germans in Europe: Chile was a land "donde se creía que los que emigran a Chile venían a la esclavitud, a un pais lleno peligros, con animales feroces y culabras venonosas"[33] (where they came into slavery, to a country full of dangers, with ferocious animals and poisonous snakes). There is kind of goading, daring the timid to join the pioneers in the Southern Cone.

These agents of immigration inscribed their experience as imperial citizens into their presence in South America as well, in part to facilitate a sense of community, but also to preserve a separate but equal identity. In these commentaries, the established colonial powers of Europe are critiqued for their reckless interventions. This narrative, however, unfolds alongside a labor and regional history that challenges the trope of modernization and economic

---

31. Aquino Ried, M.D. *Deutsche Auswanderung nach Chile* (Valparaiso: July, 1847); *Das Ausland. Ein Tageblatt für Kunde des geistigen und sittlichen Lebens der Völker*, issue 21 (Stuttgart and Tübingen: Cotta, January 1, 1848), 3–4, here 3. The conclusion follows in the next issue (January 3, 1848), 7–8. Quoted from the Googlebook: https://books.google.com/books?id=FYKNOA80r9IC&pg=PA3&lpg=PA3&dq=A.+Ried+Deutsche+Auswanderung+nach+Chile+einem+wandernden+D%C3%A4mon+besessen&source=bl&ots=-fL9GXW2gJn&sig=ACfU3U2OCOey8EDw5GfLY5kaYzts6av8qw&hl=en&sa=X-&ved=2ahUKEwjAleiD1s2AAxWPF1kFHTyrCs8Q6AF6BAgjEAM#v=onepage&q=A.%20Ried%20Deutsche%20Auswanderung%20nach%20Chile%20einem%20wandernden%20D%C3%A4mon%20besessen&f=false.

32. Ried, *Deutsche Auswanderung*, 4.

33. Alberto Hoerll, "La Colonización Alemana en Chile," in *La colonización alemana en Chile, in Los Alemanes in Chile. Homenaje de la Sociedad Científica Alemana de Santiago a la Nacion chilena en el centario de su independencia* (The Germans in Chile. Tribute from the German Scientific Society of Santiago to the Chilean nation on the centenary of its independence), vol.1 introduced by Dr. Ernesto Maier (Santiago: Imprenta Universitaria, 1910), 1–57, here 8.

progress through the integration of immigrants. As labor historians argue, "La explosion urbana vivida por Valdivia y Osorno, se debió exclusivamente a la generación de un Nuevo y pujante Mercado laboral—industrial como commercial—que incentivó la migración poblaciones sin calificaión hacia las villas"[34] (The explosion of urban life for Valdivia and Osorno was due exclusively to the generation of the new and vigorous labor marker—industrial as well as commercial—that incentivized the migration of unskilled labor populations into the towns). The contiguous relationship between local populations existed primarily in the economic sphere and intersects a colonizing discourse about German identity vis-à-vis citizenship and other European immigrant groups.

The German-speaking Chileans see their destinies as extensions of the early modern narratives of belonging and integrating—if not civilizing— free from the problematic histories of Spain in the Americas or England in India and South Africa. This self-awareness, I argue, contributes to a desire to achieve "German" identity, first through immigration, then through citizenship, while also expressing a desire to exert influence over Chilean political identity. That political imaginary comprises a colonializing relationship to local cultures; interconnections did exist in the late nineteenth century, but these were mediated through a growing labor market that casts the German landowner as employer. This partially fulfilled desire, however, was accompanied by a discourse about labor, culture, and modernity that informed local cultural interconnections in problematic ways.[35] Ethnic identity as South American Germans is discursively constructed in part through the historicization of early modern genealogies, the mapping and rerouting of identity itineraries through recruitment rhetoric, reports from those in country, and the rise of a German-language press. At each step along the way, Germans self-identify with the elite—not the local poor—of the nation. As Muñoz and Silva write, "La pobreza de los emigrados, la austeridad de la vivienda y los excesos al beber y comer, genararon en la percepción de los germanos una impression imborrable: en comparación con el trabajador germano, el chileno era inferior"[36] (The poverty of the emigrants, the austerity of the living circumstances, and the excesses of eating and drinking generated in the

---

34. Jorge Ernesto Muñoz Sougarret and Daniel Silva Jorquera, "La modernidad viste de capa española: la utilización de mano de obra infantil arrendada y presidiaria durante la conformación de los mercados laborales en Osorno en la segiunda mitad del siglo XIX," (2010): 87–105, here 91.
35. Muñoz Sougarret and Silva Jorquera, "La modernidad," 90.
36. Muñoz Sougarret and Silva Jorquera, "La modernidad," 92.

Germans' perspective an indelible impression: in comparison with the German worker, the Chilean worker was inferior). In this process of differentiation, the German-language press plays a key role by reinforcing a generalized colonial identity that aligns with the discourse of superiority through labor.

The purpose of the *Deutsche Zeitung* originated in a desire to maintain the integrity of the community. The first edition, which appeared on April 10, 1886, compares the newspaper to a plant, "die nur durch freundliche Pflege und liebvolles Interesse erstarken und gross werden kann"[37] (that can strengthen and mature only through friendly care and loving interest). Further, the publication insists on its responsibility to awaken interest in "allgemeinwichtige Angelegenheiten, damit durch die allseitige Theilnahme dieselben um desto mehr gefördert werden, denn 'Einigkeit macht stark'"[38] (issues of general importance, so that through the collective participation they can be furthered even more, for "unity makes us strong"). Apart from the shared experience of carrying the torch for the *Deutschtum* in Chile, the German-speaking press focused on such unifying issues as celebrating the kaiser, the growth of trade and industry, and acknowledging contributions from the arts and sciences.

The epistemology of migration is posited in the discourse about German identity in "diaspora"[39]—a problematic term applied to forced exile that has been expanded—as evidenced in print media produced in southern Chile (and elsewhere in South America), warranting a closer examination of the categorical aspects of Germanness. The affiliation with empire proves crucial in establishing a sense of Germanness as cosmopolitan agency. Reverence for the kaiser articulates a collective desire for political paternity that potentially unites all German emigrants. In a series of articles about German colonization, the authors strike a chiliastic pose in their portrayal of colonialism in order to assert moral and political superiority over the British and Spanish. In

---

37. Johannes Frey, *Deutsche Zeitung*, 1886, 1. For an overview of Johannes Frey's editorial career and work for the *Deutsche Zeitung für Süd-Chile* (1886–1887), see Pinto, *Historia* 33 (2000), III/1.

38. Pinto, "Historia," n.p.

39. See Krista O'Donnell, Renate Bridenthal, and Nancy Reagin, "Introduction," *The Heimat Abroad: The Boundaries of Germanness* (Ann Arbor: University of Michigan Press, 2005), 1–16, here 5. See also Howard Sargent, "Diasporic Citizens: Germans Abroad in the Framing of German Citizenship Law," in O'Donnell, Bridenthal, and Reagin, *The Heimat Abroad*, 17–39. Sargent's research demonstrates the concern that the exclusion of non-Germans from citizenship around 1913 was complicated by the need to keep the loyalty of Germans abroad (28).

the press, a subtext becomes legible in a narrative of German emergence as a colonial presence in the world, also in South America, but the author claims superiority because Germany is unburdened by the problematic histories of Spain in the Americas or England in India and South Africa. The ostensibly neutral "observations," however, depart significantly from the prevailing and exculpatory European narrative that praised French and British colonial—and as a corollary, exhibition—practices because these countered then pedagogically displayed the "violent brutality of indigenous Africa."[40]

The tone continues in this edition that locates current immigration issues in a sweeping historical perspective. The author begins with the history of Columbus in America but incorporates historical German greatness into the perspective: "Als die deutsche Hansa niederging, bestand in London der sogenante Stahlhof. . . . Die Hansa verfiel, und deutsche Kaufleute traten in englische Dienste"[41] (When the German Hansa fell, the so-called Stahlhof came into existence in London. . . . The Hansa fell, and German businessmen entered into English service). This sweeping sense of bourgeois manifest destiny echoes contemporary responses to the spectacles of world fairs and exhibitions. Corbey writes, "In high euphoria, the bourgeoisie celebrated progress, the attainment of world power, and the creation of Western middle-class culture by its own efforts—which, in its own eyes, was the purpose to which world history (and indeed cosmic evolution) had been directed from its earliest beginnings."[42] The inscription of German colonial identity into this model of dominance is evident in the narratives of print media as well. The article continues with the collapse of the Hanseatic League, which signaled the centuries-long dominance of the British, but the author stakes a claim to the moral high ground: "Naturvölkern Kultur bringen, das heisst auf englisch: Plündere das Volk aus, nehme ihm was es hat, und morde und brenne was sich hindernd in den Weg stellt"[43] (To bring culture to natural peoples, in English that means: plunder the people, take away whatever they have, and murder and burn anything that stands in the way). In leveling this judgment, the author exposes the civilizing rhetoric of colonial Britain and inverts the discourse about the moral imperative to civilize "natural peoples," in a gesture that overturns the power hierarchy between "Naturvolk" and "Kulturvolk."[44]

---

40. Raymond Corbey, "Ethnographic Showcases, 1870–1930," *Cultural Anthropology* 8, no. 3 (1993): 342.
41. *Deutsche Zeitung*, 2.
42. Corbey, "Ethnographic Showcases," 338–69, 341.
43. *Deutsche Zeitung*, 2.
44. Sara Friedrichsmeyer, Sara Lennox, and Susanne Zantop, "Introduction," in *The Imperial-*

In the conclusion, the German-language critique of the British colonial conquest of India, for example, measures accomplishments not by economic prowess, but by the relationship to the conquered peoples. The author hastens to point out that the Indians (in India) under the [British] "Kaiserreich" suffer enormously: 70 percent are illiterate, most live on the street under conditions that are worse than those of animals. "Wie viele dieser englisch-indischen Kaiserreich-Unterthanen würden sich wie ein König fühlen,— wenn sie so leben könnten wie die Haustiere auf dem englischen Eiland, das der europäische Kontigent wie einen Aussätzigen von sich weg ins Meer hinausgeschoben hat?!" The ungenerous prediction: "Die Zukunft wird die Rächerin sein"[45] (How many of these English-Indian imperial subjects would feel like a king—if only they could live like the house pets on the British Isles, that expelled the European contingent like pushing a leper into the sea?! The future will take revenge).

Identification, however theoretical, with a German imperial imaginary serves as a template for the mapping of citizenship within the community in southern Chile. Identificatory paradigms shift to accommodate sometimes competing, if not mutually exclusive, desire to essentialize Germanness, mobilize its signifiers, and assert entitlements to local power. The German-language press from the mid-1880s to circa 1910 undergirds these transformations. With imperial citizenship inculcated into the readership *im Ausland*, the history of migration takes center stage. For one feature article, the headline reads "Zur Auswanderung nach Chile"[46] (On emigration to Chile). The history of immigration suggests a teleological relationship between the conquest of Indigenous peoples and other European ethnicities that results in the presence of German-speaking communities as a constitutive element in the Chilean national imaginary. The article recounts the Chilean government's 1883 defeat of the "Araukaner," which enabled the immigration of four thousand French, Spanish, Swiss Germans, and other Europeans between 1883 and 1887, followed by a few hundred from England and Scandinavia. After a brief flourishing of villages, small cities, and industry "in der bisherigen Wildniss," the German-speaking immigrant groups became discontent: "Der Zufluss der Kolonisten, besonders der Schweizer und Deutschen, wurde infolge der ungünstigen Berichte der ersten Ansiedler geringer und

---

ist Imagination: German Colonialism and Its Legacy, ed. Sara Friedrichsmeyer, Sara Lennox, and Susanne Zantop (Ann Arbor: University of Michigan Press, 1998), 22.
  45. *Deutsche Zeitung*, 2.
  46. *Deutsche Post* XVI. Jahrgang 18. Mai 1901, No. 19: 1.

die Regierung liess bald nur eine beschränkte Anzahl sogenannter freier Einwanderer, Industriearbeiter, in Europa anwerben"[47] (The influx of colonists, especially the Swiss and Germans, decreased due to the unfavorable reports of the first settlers and soon the government allowed only a limited number of so-called free immigrants, industrial workers, to be recruited in Europe). The author openly disparages subsequent immigration flow from France, Spain, and Italy, totaling eighty thousand between 1887 and 1889: "Aber die Mehrheit der durch Agenten angeworbenen bestand aus Abenteurern, die arbeitsunfähig oder arbeitscheuen waren und der Regierung nur Aerger und grosse Kosten einbrachten"[48] (But the majority of those recruited by agents were adventurers who were unable to work or were shy about work and who brought only anger and great costs to the government). Many returned to Europe or swelled the ranks of the proletariat in Buenos Aires and Montevideo. The author counts the following factors among the reasons for failure: each colony had immigrants from three or four different nationalities, but all civil servants were Chilean. The groups could not understand each other; there were no doctors, apothecaries, churches, or schools worthy of the name: the classes were empty or the pupils did not understand the teachers who spoke Spanish or a bit of French because they had "wie Halbwilde herangewachsen"[49] (grown up like half savages). It should be noted that much of the newspaper copy is devoted to German schools and their administrators. The critical tone is directed at the "adventurers" and unindustrious Europeans and lax Chilean regulators. The article surveys this history to advocate improvements, for the Chilean government, the author maintains, demands a lot of immigrants who must pay their own passage. On the other hand, Chile's accommodation of German immigrants is duly noted: "Die Vortheile, welche Chile andrerseits dem europäischen und speziell deutschen Auswanderer bietet, sind gross. Staatslaendereien in den Sued-Provinzen" (The advantages Chile offers to European and especially German emigrants are great. State lands in the southern provinces).

Valdivia, in particular, is praised for its climate, the cultivation of grain and potatoes, the transportation infrastructure, and the relatively corruption-free local governance. Not least, "Das Beste aber, was Chile dem fremden Ackerbauer bietet, ist, dass es ihm ein kleines Landgut schenkt. Der Wunsch nach

---

47. *Deutsche Post* XVI. Jahrgang 18. Mai 1901, No. 19: 1.
48. *Deutsche Post* XVI. Jahrgang 18. Mai 1901, No. 19: 1.
49. *Deutsche Post* XVI. Jahrgang 18. Mai 1901, No. 19: 1.

eigenem Besitze, nach eigener Scholle ist es, der den deutschen Tagelöhner auf Auswanderung bestimmt. In Nordamerika und in Argentinien hat die Regierung kein für den europäischen Ackerbauer geeignetes Land mehr zur freien Verfügung der Einwanderer muss das Geld mitbringen oder sich erst im Lande verdienen, um dann später ein kleines Besitzthum zu pachten oder zu kaufen" (But the best thing Chile has to offer the farmer is that he gives him a small estate. The desire for personal possessions, to own property, that qualifies the German day laborer for emigration. In North America and Argentina, the government no longer has the arable land suitable for European farmers. Immigrants have to bring the money with them or have to earn some money in the country to later lease or purchase a small place). The forty hectares thus tip the scales in favor of Chile. The article concludes, "Die Zukunft Chile's hängt in erster Linie von der europäischen Einwanderung ab"[50] (Chile's future primarily depends on European immigration).

As Chile's future is predicated on European immigration, immigrants in Chile construct their national identity through mediation. By the mid-1880s, the model of the world's fair or exposition had become popularized, with London Crystal Palace (1851), the Philadelphia Centennial Expo (1876), and the Chicago World's Columbian Expo just ahead (1893). Benedict Anderson writes of the colonial imaginary in *Imagined Communities*, analyzing the ways "the colonial state imagined its dominion—the nature of the human beings it ruled, the geography of its domain, and the legitimacy of its ancestors."[51] Expositions became an integral part of colonial optics: spectacle, technology, and power displayed in a built yet naturalized environment. Colonial possessions and imperial fantasies intersected in Wilhelmine Germany with the new fervor as elsewhere in Europe after the Berlin Congress. In the same year the Colonial and Indian Exhibition took place in London, a similar venue provided Berlin with an opportunity to display its empire.[52] In other words, the fair materialized Berlin as a capital of European hegemony with a German accent. The fervor with which Chilean Germans welcomed and supported the opportunity to represent their accomplishments at the exposition in Berlin may seem astonishing, given the presumptive power hierarchy between motherland and colony. Ethnographic research illuminates

---

50. *Deutsche Post* XVI. Jahrgang 18. Mai 1901, No. 19: 1.
51. Benedict Anderson, *Imagined Communities: Reflections on the Origin and Spread of Nationalism* (London: Verso, 1983), 164.
52. Corbey, "Ethnographic Showcases," 339.

the impulses of such spectacles as world fairs and colonial exhibits. Corbey writes, "The world fair can also be read as a microcosm, created by the Promethean Western middle classes, with their unlimited trust in Enlightenment ideas and the rational constructability of the world—a world made after their own image, to European standards."[53] Corbey also differentiates between the exhibitions of colonial subjects in European venues and the self-colonizing agency of those Europeans who, like the Chilean Germans, want to put their accomplishments on display.

In the *Deutsche Post* of July 3, 1886, the lead article is devoted to the South American exhibition in Berlin, permeated by a tone of injury: "Deutsche Patrioten haben seit Jahrzehnten mit Schmerz wahrgenommen, dass die Auswanderung für Deutschland in mehrfacher [Weise] einen schweren Verlust bedeutet, viel schwerer als für die meisten anderen Nationen" (German patriots have for decades painfully realized that emigration for Germany means in many [ways] a heavy loss, much heavier than for most other nations).[54] Laments and critical comments about North America and the complete integration of Germans into American culture and politics serve as a refrain in many articles about South America. Slighted, the author mentions representation of the German communities in Santiago and Valparaiso, noting, "Es wäre nun wirklich traurig, wenn der *Mittelpunkt deutschen Lebens* in Chile, Valdivia, unvertreten bliebe" (It would be really sad if the *center of German life* in Chile, Valdivia, were not represented) and exhorting the readers to send in objects: "Mögen also die Landsleute in Valdivia bei dieser Gelegenheit, bei welcher die deutschen Pflanzstädte in Südamerika sich gewissermassen dem Publikum im alten Mutterlande vorstellen, nicht zurückbleiben, sondern wie immer in erster Linie sich auszeichnen!" **M**. (So on this occasion, when the German transplant cities in South America in a way introduce themselves to the public in the old mother country, let the compatriots in Valdivia not be left behind, but rather as always primarily distinguish themselves! M.).[55] The paper has an insert with the program, emphasizing trade relations and the generous support of the "Centralverein für Handelsgeographie" (Central Association for Trade) and the Kosmos-Linie (Dampferschiff/ Hamburg), which offered to help ship any objects collected. The Kosmos-Linie was a frequent advertiser in the newspaper.

---

53. Corbey, "Ethnographic Showcases," 340
54. Corbey, "Ethnographic Showcases," 340.
55. Corbey, "Ethnographic Showcases," 340.

The pride in German identity *im Auslande* transported to Berlin for the 1886 South American Exhibition continues to thrive in the representation of the German Chilean communities throughout a series of anniversaries. Both positive and negative positions, however, are maintained regarding naturalization. The exigencies of national and geopolitical change did not prevent the Valdivia German-speaking immigrants from self-identifying as accomplished and worthy subjects. To commemorate the fiftieth anniversary of the Deutsche Schule in Osorno, the February 1, 1904, edition of the *Deutsche Zeitung* printed on the front page a poetic tribute by Herr Gustav Schmidt, which concludes with praise of the nation:

> Und wie die stolzen Gipfel deiner Berge
> Mit ihrem Fuss in dir gewurzelt stehen
> Und doch mit ihrem Haupt die Wolken küssen,
> So wach's in deinem Boden auch der Deutsche,
> Dein Sohn, dein Bürger und dein Eigenthum.

> And like the proud peaks of your mountains
> With their base standing rooted in you
> And yet kissing the clouds with their head
> So the German also grows in your land
> Your son, your citizen, and your property.

The sentiment expressed in this verse echoes an amplified discourse about the relationship between the German son, citizen, and possession and the Chilean state. In the same year, the *Deutsche Zeitung* ran a series about the presence of German immigrants, and the tenor and content both suggest more a proprietary relationship, one predicated on the Germanizing of the Chilean South, than an interrelationship with the local culture. The laudatory narrative covers the period between 1840 and 1904, and the editor Hörll pays tribute to his forefathers: "Wäre ihre freiwillig gesuchte Mission fehlgeschlagen, wir hätten heute kaum einen deutschen Süden, überhaupt ware das Verhältnis zwischen Deutschland und Chile kein so intimes geworden, wie es fast ein halbes Jahrhundert war"[56] (If their voluntarily sought mission had failed, we would hardly have a German south today, and the relationship between Germany and Chile would not have become as intimate as it was

---

56. *Deutsche Zeitung*, December 17, 1904, 1.

almost half a century ago). The editor stresses the German investment in cultivating and making profitable what was "alles bis dato herrenlose Land" (ibid.; all up to now unowned land). The construction of German immigrant identity is built on a foundation of presumed vacancy: the now uncontested geography of Valdivia, Osorno, and Llanquihue, the historical homeland of the Mapuche (pejoratively known by the exonym the Araucana), is discursively transformed into a topography of postcolonial conquest, a rhetorical gesture that wipes the slate and state clean of Indigenous inhabitants. The poem to celebrate the fiftieth anniversary of the Osorno Schule makes a similar rhetorical claim that the German youth in Chile aspires to be worthy of his forefathers: "Und damit auch ein gern gesehener Bürger / Der neuen Heimath an der pacif'scher Küste"[57] (And with that also a welcomed citizen / Of the new homeland on the Pacific coast). In a subsequent edition (February 25, 1904), the editor turns to the role of German emigration and the responsibility of the *Colonien* to attract others to the Southern Cone with the argument that the Argentina Brazil Chile (ABC) states remain more attractive than the Union-Staaten (USA), which continue to tempt compatriots: "Denn die deutschen Colonien müssen um ihrer selbst willen Nachschub aus dem Stammlande erhalten, junges deutsches Blut, das noch die kräftig pulsierende deutsche Art in sich trägt und anregend und belebend wirkt"[58] (For the German colonies must recruit others from the homeland, young German blood, that carries within it the ever powerfully pulsating German way and has an exciting and energizing effect). Yet this assertion of better blood is not necessarily predicated on racial superiority. In the very next issue, for example, the editor objects to antisemitism in Germany and maintains that the "Semite" "ist doch ein würdiges Glied der civilizierten Menschheit"[59] (is still a worthy member of civilized humanity). The stance is a principled response to the larger debate about exclusionary politics originating in the German Empire, which accounts at least in part for the defense of plural citizenship. A 1904 treatise purported to change laws governing citizenship of Germans abroad[60] at the same time the kaiser announced that the future "liegt auf dem Wasser"[61] (rests on the water). While the imperial impulse intersected with

---

57. *Deutsche Zeitung*, February 6, 1904, 1.
58. *Deutsche* Zeitung, February 25, 1904, 1.
59. *Deutsche Zeitung*, February 28, 1904, 1.
60. For a sustained study of citizenship and German abroad, see Eli Nathans, *The Politics of Citizenship in Germany: Ethnicity, Utility, and Nationalism* (New York: Berg, 2004).
61. *Deutsche Zeitung*, October 22, 1904, 1.

the Chilean Germans self-definition, the threat to original citizenship of the Reich destabilized a discourse about belonging to the new homeland. The editor writes. "Zweifelsohne liegt die deutsche Zukunft auf, resp. über den Ozeanen, wo deutsche Söhne die Pflugschar führen und die Kraft und der Geist für den Erhalt und die Ausbreitung des Deutschtums tätig sind, also am Bau des grossen Gebäudes der deutschen Weltherrschaft wirken" (There is no doubt that the German future lies ahead, and across the oceans, where German sons wield the plowshare and the strength and spirit work for the preservation and expansion of German life, i.e. on the construction of the large edifice of German world rule).[62]

In contrast to my opening quotation, the drive to naturalization has segued into an imperial claim to the *Stammlande*. In the third continuation, Hörll writes about other European immigrants, singling out Italians and Spaniards, and describes in pejorative terms their "colonial" mentality vis-à-vis Indigenous peoples: "Letzterer Haupterfolg liegt nach dem Bericht des Protectors de Indíjenas der Frontera an die Regierung in der Ausbeute der Inder"[63] (The main success of the latter, according the report of the Protectors de Indíjenas der Frontera to the government lies in the exploiting of the Indians). While other sources corroborate German exploitation of Indigenous groups, the press maintains a colonial model, but one that remains superior to contiguous immigrant groups, such as the Italians and Spaniards. The German desire for integration in late nineteenth and early twentieth-century media epistemologies is founded on a discursively constructed imperial identity that ultimately resists seamless assimilation and establishes ethnic emigrant supremacy.

Hörll emphasizes that the German community of immigrants considered itself to be an integral component of Chile's overall progress and economic modernization. The articles and editorials put forth an epistemology of migration that exploits the role of the German pioneer. In an editorial about the citizenship status of Germans "*im Auslande*," Hörll writes about German-specific recruitment of "*Culturmenschen*" and "*Culturpioniere*" (cultural people and cultural pioneers).[64] The author finds ways to accommodate national loyalties between the adoptive homeland and the fatherland. The tone shifts again in dealing with colonial fantasies.

---

62. *Deutsche Zeitung*, October 22, 1904, 1.
63. Hörll, *Deutsche Zeitung*, December 24, 1904, 1.
64. *Deutsche Zeitung*, June 11, 1904, 1.

The affiliation with empire proves crucial in establishing a sense of Germanness as cosmopolitan agency. In a series of articles about German colonization, the authors strike a chiliastic pose in their portrayal of colonialism in order to assert moral and political superiority over the British and Spanish. For example, the *Deutsche Post* published a front-page article in 1902 with the headline: "Friedensnachklänge. Betrachtungen über England und Süd-Afrika" (Echoes of peace. Observations about England and South Africa). A subtext becomes legible in a narrative of German emergence as a colonial presence in the world, also in South America, but the author claims superiority because Germany is unburdened by the problematic histories of Spain in the Americas or England in India and South Africa.

After the Herero and Namaqua genocide, then referred to as the Herero Wars (1904–1908), Chilean German media sought common cause with, rather than a moral high ground above, competing colonial powers. German colonial discourse up until this time tended to direct antipathy not at the Indigenous and subjugated, but rather at the competing European power. The ethnic epistemology and accompanying narrative of naturalized German dominance pivots to achieve racial allegiance. In his editorial from January 10, 1907, Hörll comments on the war in German Southwest Africa from the perspective of imperial citizenship. First criticizing the colony for its violence and cost to Germany, he proceeds to indict the British, who foster conflict in their own interests until they encounter the "schwarze Gefahr" (black danger). He writes, "England wird sich nun, hoffentlich endgültig, von seiner verkehrten Eingeborenenpolitik abgewendet haben und für die Folge die Interessengemeinschaft der Weissen in Afrika wahren" (From now on, and hopefully once and for all, England will have turned away from its Indigenous politics and intervene for the collective interests of whites in Africa). The attributes of identity, German nationality and Chilean citizenship are distilled into the elixir of racial allegiance that purportedly must transcend political borders. From the *Kolonien* of south Chile, the German press proclaims ties with the colonial enterprise in Africa, occluding borders and transcending geographical divisions—even in competition with other colonial powers—to claim allies in the war for epistemological and material supremacy.

Decades later, the history of lost colonies features prominently in pedagogy. The demise of the Hanseatic League in the fifteenth century that occurred with the major shift of Europe's economic epicenter to the New World was invoked by Kaiser Wilhelm, whom I quoted at the beginning of this chapter. In lamenting the later defeat after the catastrophic world war,

Grand Admiral Alfred von Tirpitz (1849–1930) reflected, "the German people do not understand the sea."[65] The loss of empire was felt within and beyond the border of the German nation-state; their recovery stoked the politics of recolonial fantasies. The bitter tone of one example from 1935 can be found in the thirty-eighth edition of a school book, the *Geschichtsbuch für die deutsche Jugend*, used in German-language schools in Chile as well. The rancor over lost territory is broadcast without ambiguity. In the dedication, the author exhorts German youth "zur Vertiefung der Liebe zu Volk und Vaterland" (to the deepening of love for the people and the fatherland). [66] It is hard to miss the overt attack on victorious allies of World War I in the discussion of the Versailles treaty. The schoolmasterly tone turns taunting at the loss of the colonies to the "Völkerbund," allegedly the "more advanced nations."[67] Each segment of ostensibly objective summation of historical events is followed by a discussion question: What does it mean? In this case, "badly disguised robbery"; in fact, the authors argue, Germany performed the "wertvolle Kolonisationsarbeit geleistet" (valuable work of colonization).[68] In the text's conclusion, laments about the loss of German land in Europe serve to amplify the call to nationalism, because "much more appalling than the loss of land, money, and valuables that brought us peace [is] the loss of German blood. The *Volksbund* does an important job for *Deutschtum* abroad." The lesson to German Chilean youth forges blood bonds between immigrants and fallen soldiers, positing a symmetry between loss of homeland and sacrifice of life. The experiences of immigration and colonization racialize ethnicity. German identity becomes the answer to an either/or question. German (and white European) or Black, Indigenous; and enslavement or indenture. Increasingly, this revised binary opposition accommodates other differences, such as gender, toward solidifying identification across oceans and frontiers.

---

65. Alfred von Tirpitz, *Erinnerungen* (Leipzig: Koehler, 1919), 387. Quoted in Keith W. Bird, "The Origins and Role of German Naval History in the Inter-War Period of 1918–1939," *Naval War College Review* 32, no. 2 (March-April 1979), 42–58, here 42.

66. Dr. Ulrich Haacke and Dr. Benno Schneider, *Geschichtsbuch für die deutsche Jugend*. With Dr. Bernhard Kunmsteller. Leipzig: Verlag von Quelle & Meyer, 1935. *Geschichtsbuch*, dedication page.

67. Haacke and Schneider, *Geschichtsbuch*, 372.

68. Haacke and Schneider, *Geschichtsbuch*, 372.

PART III

Global Imaginaries

CHAPTER SEVEN

Global German Frontiers

Sebastian Conrad poses a question: What is global history. One effect of that interrogative is a decentering of the "methodological nationalism" intrinsic to any Eurocentric approach.[1] This logic derives from eighteenth-century European enthusiasms for the "genre of world and universal history."[2] Asking such sweeping questions puts pressure on the metanarratives of the "nation" as an epistemic category, but it also implicitly demands a closer look at the incremental installments of constructing that national identity in the spaces defined by other than the "unbound" of Penny's German history. The Valdivian newspaper imagined German immigrants in Chile as cultural pioneers[3] (as discussed in the previous chapter). While adopting a settler mentality, these communities negotiate identity differently, depending on circumstances. As demonstrated in the previous chapter, the narratives tack from empathy with the Indigenous peoples and contempt for abusive colonial powers to contempt for Indigeneity and empathy with the British. Some aspects of this discourse, which informs performative immigrant identities—seen in converting legitimacy into naturalization and enfranchisement—pertain to Germans across the Southern Cone. Variations occur along national boundaries. In Chile, the story of Bartolomé Blumen-Flores's legitimizing German-Indigenous land ownership and the familiarity of a mountain landscape confer rights on the nineteenth-century transplants from German-speaking Europe.

Concurrently, German advocates of colonization enhanced a national narrative with colonial ambitions. Constant attention to the cultivation of German attributes alternately emphasized gender, class, race, religion, and

---

1. Sebastian Conrad, *What Is Global History?* (Princeton, NJ: Princeton University Press, 2016), 3.
2. Conrad, *What Is Global History?*, 28.
3. Uche Onyedi Okafor uses this term with regard to Carl Peters and Friedo von Bülow in the context of colonial writing from Germany in "Mapping German Colonial Discourse Fantasy: Reality and Dilemma" (PhD diss., University of Maryland, 2013), 168–98.

choice of geographical relocation. Masculine and feminine attributes varied in response to the relative density of dominant and subordinate populations: southern Europeans, colonially superior French and English, Black and Indigenous interlocutors. But the importance of language cannot be overlooked in the network of communication between and about Africa and the Americas.

The German-language press in southern Chile positioned itself in a global political network connected by language, which fueled the construction of a colonial ethnic identity if not within, at least with reference to, the nation-state. As demonstrated by the commentary on colonial wars and advocacy of global white alliances, despite turf wars and competition with England, France, or Spain, the "Organ für das Deutschtum in Chile" encoded Germanness with innate entitlements, accentuated by racial superiority. The editorial intervention into the preservation of a "pure" register of German showcases the degrees to which Germans outside the homeland cultivated pride in their origin stories. With the amplification of a race discourse (the "Teutontic" race; the "Chilean" race) around 1900, some German-language institutions, among them schools and the press, took a closer look at the way the mother tongue fared locally.

In 1902, the *Deutsche Post* published a series of articles about the centrality of language to identity. Its editorial eye roams the globe for topics of immediate interest to immigrants, emphasizing the role they are playing as cultural pioneers. Crucial to the emigration enterprise is the language of the Motherland. After examining the enclaves of German speakers in Europe (September 2, 1902), Hoerll extends the horizon to the corruption of German in the one settler colony. A front-page headline reads, "Sprachverwilderung in Deutsch-Südwestafrika" (September 4, 1902). The article, a combined editorial and news piece on a lecture in Windhoek, exclaims over the impact of the event; it even influenced the Reichskanzler: "Das Kauderwelsch, eine grauliche Vermengung von Holländisch, Englisch, Herero und Nama, wächst, sobald sich der Ankömmling ins Innere des Landes begiebt" (The gibberish, an outrageous mixture of Dutch, English, Herero, and Nama, grows as soon as the newcomer moves into the interior). The preacher, Prediger Anz, condemns the linguistic *Missbildungen*, (deformities) Germans use, such as *vuur* (*Feuer* or fire) and *revier* (*Fluss* or river). These foreign borrowings, Anz argued, had the natives laughing at Germans: the Nama and Herero,

> lachen über uns, wenn wir mit beharrlicher Ausdauer ihre Sprache so fehlerhaft wie nur möglich zu ihnen sprechen. Sollte uns nicht die Scham darüber

zu dem Entschlusse treiben: Von jetzt an zwischen Deutschen und von dem Deutschen zu seinem eingeborenen Diener kein anderes als deutsches Wort mehr zu sprechen.

laugh at us when we speak their language to them as incorrectly as possible with persistent perseverance. Should not the shame of it drive us to the decision: from now on between Germans and by the German to his native servant no other word but a German one will be spoken.

The speech was delivered in Windhoek, written about in southern Chile, and drew attention from the Allgemeiner Deutscher Sprachverein (1885–ca. 1944). Reichskanzler Grafen von Bülow received a copy of it, which inspired a further budget for German-language education.[4] Hoerll accentuates the power hierarchies that shape language politics outside the Motherland, applying colonial logic. In America (the United States), Germans defer to dominance. In contrast to America, in German Southwest Africa, "Hier herrscht der Deutsche" (Here the German is in charge), and only insufficient German self-awareness could be the cause of the weak will that allows the mother tongue to deteriorate, and with it are lost "deutsche Bildung, deutsche Erziehung und deutscher Geist" (German education, German upbringing, and German spirit).

As Ciarlo cogently observes, however, the majority of Germans at home evinced little interest in the colonies: "despite a brief surge of interest (buoyed largely by the press), the German public seemed, at least to the die-hard colonial 'enthusiasts,' to largely ignore Germany's colonies."[5] At the same time, Germans abroad in North and South America identified with the imperial desires of the homeland, self-defining as colonies and pioneers on selected frontiers. This era still generates narratives about racial, national, and gendered identities that capture an alignment between provincialism, posited in opposition to cosmopolitanism, and Germanness. At their nexus, such nar-

---

4. Von Bülow thanks the Sprachverein and designates new funding in the 1902 budget (Haushaltsgesetz) "zur Unterstützung deutscher Schulen und zur Verbreitung der deutschen Sprache in unseren Schutzgebieten ... und hofft, dass die Bestrebungen der Kolonialverwaltung, durch eine planmässige deutsche Besiedelung des Schutzbebietes dem gerügten Uebelstande abzuhelfen, in weiten Kreisen unseres Volkes volles Verständnis und die erforderliche Unterstützung finden werden."

5. David Ciarlo, *Advertising Empire: Race and Visual Culture in Imperial Germany* (Cambridge, MA: Harvard University Press, 2011), 4.

ratives recast the relationship between German identity and imperial temporality, the exigencies of which inspire tropes appropriated by the German colonist circa 1900. The force of early modern tropes, including the evangelizing missionary savior, the scientist, explorer, and enterprising adventurer, animates the experiences of German colonists of the nineteenth century, self-identifying as enlightened redeemer, German world citizen, and ennobled yeoman. The performativity of these tropes calls for a reframing of German colonialism as a blip in the historical continuum. Rather, the interaction between narration and migration in German-speaking Europe inscribes a complex story predicated on centuries of engagement with coloniality, with the German farmer-settler—der Farmer—as protagonist.

In his work on resistance and hegemony, James Scott elaborated the "hidden transcript" of the disempowered: the "*ideological* insubordination" found in "rumors, gossip, folktales, songs," analogous to the resistance practices of peasants and the enslaved, such as "poaching, foot-dragging, pilfering, dissimulation, flight."[6] He contrasts this with the "public transcript," the "*self*-portrait of dominant elites as they would have themselves seen."[7] Scott's model, both persuasive and illuminating, has powerful but not complete explanatory force for the public transcript of the German farmer at the frontier. To begin this chapter, I turn to a conversion story, "Christian Afrikaner," which appeared anonymously in a volume published by the German-language press of the Missouri-Ohio Synod in the late nineteenth century.[8] This text, directed at a young-adult, Lutheran, German-speaking audience on the American "frontier," reasserts religious identity, displaces racial struggle to the African continent, and extols a fictionalized, revisionist history of the German colonial enterprise by invoking moral superiority over the Dutch. This territory overlaps with the real existing colony, German Southwest Africa; the historical veracity of the material of African resistance, figured

---

6. James C. Scott, *Domination and the Arts of Resistance: Hidden Transcripts* (New Haven, CT: Yale University Press, 1990), xii.
7. Scott, *Domination and the Arts of Resistance*, 18.
8. Frederik Schulze, *Auswanderung als nationalistisches Projekt. "Deutschtum" und Kolonialdiskkurse im südlichen Brasilien (1824–1941)* (Cologne: Böhlau, 2016), writes about the outreach of the synod, perceived as competition, to southern Brazil, beginning around 1900: "Die von deutschen Auswanderern in den USA gegründete Synode wurde als Konkurrenz wahrgenommen, da sie zwar in deutscher Sprache arbeitete, Deutschtumsarbeit aber nicht betrieb. Ihre Gemeinden hatten keinen Kontakt zu detuschen Organisationen, 1937 waren 77 Missouri-Pfarrer aktiv" (76–77).

first by Jager ("Christian") Afrikaner, then his descendent, Hendrik Witbooi, is tampered with both in the religious literature and the memoir of a German woman, a farmer's wife, who writes to vindicate her violent husband and absolve him of racism. Under the conditions of colonialism, the frontiers host the actual struggles, active and passive, that portray African decolonial agency, either as subsumed into deracinated Protestantism or indentured under colonial rule.

The trope of the "Farmersfrau" emerged around 1900 from encounters between German and Anglophone colonizers. These adjacencies inscribe female identity into ancillary roles, but historical exigencies of social mobility through immigration and ideological services rendered by colonizing for the German nation-state reinscribe them into political allegories, accessing specific myths of empowerment. The "Farmersfrau" encompasses the South American immigrant woman as pioneer; the North American as fighting frontierswoman; and the German of colonial Südwestafrika as the self-sacrificing, hard-working, and gender-fluid caregiver. The word itself garners attention. In Ada Cramer's 1913 *Weiß oder Schwarz. Lehr- und Leidensjahre eines Farmers im Südwest im Lichte Rassenhasses* (White or black: Years of apprenticeship and suffering in Southwest in light of racial hatred), her "public transcript" serves as racialized allegory of a Farmersfrau in battle for survival against the *Eingeborenen*. She recounts the story of her husband's constant battle against the Black workers who resist German colonists. Lamenting the seeming alliance between German administrators and African workers, Cramer insists Black racism—their hatred of whites—lies at the root of all evil. Their son, Ernst Ludwig Cramer, later published a Nazi-era memoir, narrated in part as a work of mourning for the loss of their son Helmut, *Die Kinderfarm* (1941); it purports to commemorate the stories his deceased son Helmut would have told his German peers about life in German Southwest Africa. The memoir not only perpetuates a myth of German colonial maternalism, but also advocates an imperial agenda, made legitimate, even imperative, by their own intergenerational, interwar trauma that aligns the reclaiming of lost colonies with the politics of National Socialist family values. At an important historical juncture, the discourses of immigration and colonization began to circulate on the same register. Around 1900, key colonial administrators and activists also take and switch sides to map the world as German-centric around a common story. The works I analyze in this chapter portray the historical and fictional German frontiersmen and women as they position their identity in relation to the religious community, German-speaking neighbors, and enslaved or Indigenous people. These agents of German identity revise images of European masculinity and femininity ca. 1900 to subsume gender difference into a single defense of German frontiers. Curiously, all frontiers lead to German Southwest Africa.

Frontier Morality and the Allegorical Afrikaner

A mediated political position toward African slavery, written in German and published in what is now referred to as the Midwest of the United States, continues and varies the theme in this section. A state since 1821, Missouri's history—leading to the Missouri Compromise that legislated the geography of slavery—is pivotal in the racial wars fought on American soil in the nineteenth century. American history notes that Missouri joined the union as a "slave state"; the Kansas-Nebraska Act and the repeal of the Missouri Compromise contributed to the heightened tensions between the Union and Confederacy, culminating in the Civil War. Missouri's role during that time period remains fractured. German immigrants tended to oppose slavery as an institution, while occupying a settler mentality. Lutheran activism is evident in one particular story, though the discrepancies between history and fiction undermine that position on a moral high ground. Published for a young adult readership, the story "Christian Afrikaner" relies on a rebellious literary precursor to narrate a historical tale of religious conversion in early nineteenth-century Namibia. Jager Afrikaner (1769–1823), a historical figure who opposed colonial abuses and ultimately converted to eponymous Christianity is the focus. The edition of *Kinder-Lust* in which the historical fiction "Christian Afrikaner" appears brims over with stories of young adults who confront trauma—economic privation, downward mobility, noble victimization—with stalwart Christian values and behave according to the Ten Commandments, some of which are invoked as a moral gloss at each story's end. The protagonists populate the middle class, for the most part; without exception, the young protagonists of this reverent fiction prevail in the end. "Christian Afrikaner," however, belongs to the series of historical fictions in the second half of the volume; these are meant as exempla.

The *Kinder-Lust* series itself, published by the Missouri-Ohio Synod, is a product of conservative immigrant politics and isolationist practices. According to theological historian Frederick C. Luebke, the Missouri Germans especially insisted on separatist views of their lives in emigration. Motivated by religious rather than economic reasons, most of those from Saxon Germany arrived in Missouri via New Orleans in 1839.[9] The preservation of German language and culture frequently drove theological matters. Luebke writes, "The Lutheran leaders believed, therefore, that every effort had to be made to preserve doctrinal purity in the alien and hostile American environment."[10] This position differs markedly from the experiences and aspirations of German speakers in Buenos Aires, as Benjamin Bryce argues. Between 1880 and 1930, with the influx of German immigrants to the city, their ideas about the future "drove German-speaking immigrants to carve out a place for ethnicity and pluralism within the cultural and linguistic landscape of Buenos Aires."[11] Part of the belonging involved persistent affiliations with religious communities, Protestant and Catholic. By contrast, Luebke's interpretation of Missouri Germans tells a story that encapsulates the insistence on moral exempla, revived from an early modern historical colonial context, in order to advance an immigrant German ethos in and hostile to an American environment. In other words, the contested relationships between enclaves of German immigrants and the dominant culture creates tensions among attributes of intersectional identity itself dominated by whiteness. Kathleen Canning and Sonya Rose advanced alternatives for a model of citizenship predicated primarily on voting rights, instead recognizing a broader set of relationships between peoples and states.[12]

The synod was established in 1847 to serve German-speaking Lutherans in the region. By the 1880s, many in the denomination were fully bilingual in English and German. Issue No. 13 is presumed to date roughly from the late 1880s through the early 1890s. As the allegorical nature of the eponymous protagonist indicates, Christian becomes a model of the "good" African. In so doing, this historical antihero turned protagonist eschews his rebelliousness against colonial powers. This leaves us with persistent, stubborn, yet achievable whiteness. The prose reflects a (mid)western German American conscientious objection to slavery and posits religious conversion as a means of racial redemption. The story of an African rebel leader who finds content-

---

9. Frederick C. Luebke, "The Immigrant Condition as Factor," in *Germans in the New World: Essays in the History of Immigration* (Urbana: University of Illinois Press, 1999), 1–13, 5.

10. Luebke, "The Immigrant Condition as Factor," 6.

11. Benjamin Bryce, *To Belong in Buenos Aires: Germans, Argentines, and the Rise of a Pluralist Society* (Palo Alto, CA: Stanford University Press, 2018), 1.

12. See Kathleen Canning and Sonya O. Rose, "Gender, Citizenship and Subjectivity: Some Historical and Theoretical Considerations," *Gender and History* 13, no. 3 (2002): 427–43.

ment in conversion, written in German for a Lutheran audience, asserts the dominance of religious, ethnic identity over the surrounding political environment. It overrides citizenship in favor of tropes of the pioneer, the settler, the missionary, the tamed revolutionary who sets aside race for religion. For this, the narrative resorts to colonial competitions between the Dutch and English, retold in German to achieve a sanctioned pioneer identity.

The scope of "Christian Afrikaner" dates back to the seventeenth century, alluding to the Dutch farmers' activity in what is now Namibia. Its protagonist is loosely based on Heinrich von Kleist's celebrated and infamously violent and somehow simultaneously ethical Michael Kohlhaas. The former—at least in his fictional incarnation—ultimately regrets and repents his violent acts, implemented to combat the subjugation of his people; his realization is leveraged by conversion to Christianity. The missionary accounts, provided by German and British missionaries sent by the London Missionary Society, provide a source of written accounts, which were mandatory, of the precolonial (1884) activity of Europeans in the area.[13] In German-language publications from Habsburg, Austria, to the American plains, tensions mounted between Catholic and various Protestant missionary interventions across Africa (and elsewhere), some of which worked their way into the literature of the time. In one example, the plays of Catholic nun Maria Theresa Ledóchowska[14] have received some scholarly attention. (It is not surprising that these missions also opposed the spread of Islam or any animistic beliefs as well.) In the Lutheran synods of the midwestern US states, Missouri, Ohio, and Iowa, for example, church periodicals included updates on the "heathen" missions along with some disparaging responses to Catholic criticism. The competitive colonial narratives between the German and British voices are subsumed in the story at hand, with mutual resentment leveled at the Dutch.

---

13. Khokhoi replaces "H*ttent*t"; San replaces "Bushmen." Ursula Trüper, *The Invisible Woman: Zara Schmelen, African Mission Assistant at the Cape and in Namaland*, trans. Loretta Carter and Bettina Duwe (Basel: Basler Afrika Bibliographien, 2006), 4.

14. See for example Cindy Brewer, "Fantasies of African Conversion: The Construction of Missionary Colonial Desire in the Dramas of a Catholic Nun, Maria Theresa Ledóchowska (1863–1922)," *German Studies Review* 30, no. 3 (2007): 557–78. See also Esaie Djomo and Dorine Mbeudom, "Maria Theresia Ledóchowska as an Activist in the Religious Colonization of Africa," in *Gender and German Colonialism: Intimacies, Accountabilities, Intersections*, ed. Elisabeth Krimmer and Chunjie Zhang (New York: Routledge, 2024), 245–59; and my "From Miracles to Miscegenation: Enlightening Skin," in *Colonialism and Enlightenment: The Legacies of German Race Theory*, ed. Daniel Leonhard Purdy and Bettina Brandt (London: Oxford University Press, forthcoming).

Briefly, the LMS was established in 1795 as a coalition of mostly Congregationalist missionaries, committed to the work of evangelizing. The far-flung missionaries were obligated to write and submit regular reports; these have provided historians and scholars with a trove of knowledge about the "contact zones" or encounters between Europeans and their respective target audiences. The missionary work extended to the east and midwestern German immigrant communities in the United States. What does this fictional account of Christian Afrikaner's broadcast to German American readers?

The story opens with discursive description of the Capland and nearby vineyards, with reference to the dry and arid climate, alleviated only by the monsoon-like rains. The narrator introduces the Khokhoi (he uses the offensive term) into this landscape; through contact with Europeans, they assumed the "family name" Afrikaner. The Dutch colonists are describes as a "wildes und rohes Geschlecht"; the Khokhoi are portrayed as innocent victims of this "rohe Gewalt" (raw violence).[15] In a German-language critique of the Dutch colonists, the conventional associations of the "African" with the barbarian is inverted, applied instead to the allegedly "civilized" Europeans, who, indeed, run amok. As the Dutch imposed nearly slave-like working conditions on the Khokhoi, the chief turned over power to his son, the story's protagonist and hero, Jager Afrikaner. In the service of a historical persona, the character Piemaar, the younger Afrikaner acquits his duties admirably: "Er bewies in diesem Dienste Mut und Treue" (In this service, he proved to be courageous and loyal),[16] defending his master's livestock against theft by neighboring peoples. The brutal Dutchman, however, gives European Christians a bad name: "Der Christ behandelte den armen braunen Heiden mit Grausamkeit und Härte" (The Christian treated the poor brown heathen with cruelty and harshness).[17] The inhumane treatment led to "bad blood" between them, which rekindles in the mind of the chief the anger of his progenitors.

---

15. "Christian Afrikaner," *Kinderlust. Eine Sammlung kurzer Erzaehlungen fuer die christliche Jugend*, No. 13, hrsg. von der Verlagshandlung der Ev. Luth. Synode von Ohio und anderen Staaten (Columbus, OH: no date, ca. 1890), 165–76, 162. My gratitude to Bettina Hess at the Joseph P. Horner Memorial Library and Shannon Kupfer-Trausch, State Library of Ohio, for assistance in approximating the date of publication. Additionally, I found reference to this series, possibly the first volume, in the *Kirchliche Zeitschrift*, Jahrgang XV, no. 5, published under the auspices of the Theological Seminary in Dubuque, Iowa (Dubuque, Iowa: Wartburg Publishing House, 1891). Under the rubric "Literarisches" (literary matters) with the praise: "Und zwar eine recht feine Sammlung" (And indeed a truly fine collection), 160.

16. "Christian Afrikaner," 163.

17. "Christian Afrikaner," 163.

Again, in this story, baptizing—the act of naming—is critical: the Christian behaves barbarically, and the "barbarian" learns violence and firearms in the service of the "civilized," whom he overthrows. In the American frontier—at the time—in the aftermath of the Civil War, the moral of the story is a scene of racial instruction.

The narrator locates Afrikaner on a moral compass, familiar to a Lutheran readership. The characterization of Afrikaner's rebellious spirit provides a psychological, spiritual, and ethical justification for his subsequent action. Sustained mistreatment and privation, at the hands of a Christian, erect a framework in which the reader can comprehend the escalation of violence that ensues. The German-American narrator, flying in the face of history, sides with the oppressed Afrikaner instead of the reckless Christian Dutch farmer. It is Afrikaner who intends to use reason to plead for better treatment.[18] His brother, Titus Afrikaner, accompanies him. The lord of the manor greets them with violent welcome, shoving Jager down the steps; brother Titus uses his flint and kills their oppressor. The "H*ttent*ts" take over the territory and are feared by the British and Dutch alike. They band together with the so-called "Bastardh*ttent*tten" from neighboring lands along the river, uniting against a common enemy: "Jager Afrikaner wurde nun der Schrecken des Caplands" (Now Jager Afrikaner became the scourge / terror of Capland).[19] This development extends to his entire people: "So wurden sie der Schrecken der weissen und der farbigen Leute in einem grossen Teile des Caplandes" (Thus they became the scourge of the white and colored people in a large part of the Capland).[20]

The arrival of two historical missionaries in 1806, Christian Albrecht and Johann Seidenfaden, marks a turning point. They established a mission at Warmbad, near the Afrikaner stronghold, to evangelize. Surprisingly, Jager Afrikaner appears and accepts them initially because the English, not his oppressors the Dutch, sent them. At this point, the narrative shifts gears: the missionaries make a deep impression on the "wilden Häuptling" (wild / savage chief).[21] For the first time, after the encounter with the missionaries, the

---

18. "Da entschloss sich Jager Afrikaner, die Klagen und Beschwerden seines Volkes persönlich vor die Ohren ihres grausamen Dienstherrn zu bringen" (164; Jager Afrikaner then decided that he would personally bring the complaints and grievances of his people to the attention [literally "ears"] of their cruel employer).
19. "Christian Afrikaner," 165.
20. "Christian Afrikaner," 166.
21. "Christian Afrikaner," 167.

author ascribes the modifier "wild" to the protagonist, Jager Afrikaner. The narrator provides material for the rich archive of scholarship on the designation "wild."[22] For a time, peaceful relations prevail, with Afrikaner sending his children to the mission school to hear the word of God.

The narrative reaches another breaking point when a landowner named Hans Drayer enters into a dispute with Afrikaner; the latter kills the former. The violence of this incident escalates and spreads to all of Warmbad: "Der wilde Häuptling zog heran" (The savage chief drew closer [to the mission]).[23] Afrikaner, now semantically ensconced among the "Wilden," burns the town and the mission along with it. The attribute "wild" appears twice in this paragraph, whereas in the previous description, Afrikaner was "Unser Häuptling" (our chief).[24] Time passes; in 1813, the missionary Campbell travels to South Africa, making his way to the Orange River. He makes peaceful overtures to Afrikaner, who responds favorably at the gesture of forgiveness and reconciliation and allows his people and himself to be baptized, hence "Christian." In 1817, Moffat arrives, and despite the desperate predictions of his early death, he enters Christian Afrikaner's village. The chief learns to read, carries a New Testament with him everywhere, and begins a new life in advanced middle age: "Er wurde ein Mann des Friedens, ein Freund der Armen und Betrübten, ein Vater und Wohlthäter seines Volkes" (He became a man of peace, a friend of the poor and downtrodden, a father and benefactor to his people).[25] He laments his past deeds, claiming that all that remains of the violent deeds is "Scham und Reue" (shame and regret).[26]

After this true conversion, not in name only, Afrikaner's reputation for gruesome and unbridled acts changes to reflect the new life. Moffat is called to Capstadt and brings Afrikaner with him. His reputation precedes him, but all marvel at the kind-eyed man, whose narrative redemption is complete. He becomes the shepherd of his people, preaching to them until his death in 1823: "Mein vergangenes Leben ist mit Blut befleckt, aber Jesus Christus hat mir vergeben, und ich gehe jetzt in den Himmel" (My past life is stained with blood, but Jesus Christ has forgiven me, and now I am going to Heaven).[27]

---

22. Urs Bitterli, *Cultures in Conflict: Encounters Between European and Non-European Cultures, 1492–1800*, trans. Ritchie Robertson (Stanford, CA: Stanford University Press, 1986).
23. "Christian Afrikaner," 168.
24. "Christian Afrikaner," 166.
25. "Christian Afrikaner," 170.
26. "Christian Afrikaner," 171.
27. "Christian Afrikaner," 176.

The narrative concludes with a quotation from Isaiah 53:12: "Therefore will I divide him a portion with the great, and he shall divide the spoil with the strong; because he poured out his soul unto death, and was numbered with the transgressors: yet he bare the sin of many, and made intercession for the transgressors."[28]

The complex intertextuality of this story interweaves a range of references in this concluding citationality. The inaugural diaspora of the Israelites, driven from their homeland and later enduring the suffering of Babylonian captivity, are inscribed into the biblical reference. The fictional Christian Afrikaner dies a devout Christian and African, one whose life bears the imprimatur of sinner and saved alike. In the African context, the historical figure of Christian Afrikaner, whose life and actions figure prominently in the missionary reports, was far shrewder a player than his mild-eyed fictional counterpart. He gained status, credibility, and power by associating with the missionaries. The contrast to the myth of missionary benevolence is pronounced.

According to historical documents, the white settler, Petrus Pienaar (1755–1796) employed the Afrikaner to herd, hunt, and serve as auxiliary troops in the conflict with the San Titus, and Christian Afrikaner reported to the missionary Robert Moffat (1795–1883)[29] that they shot Pienaar for having laid hands on their wives, not because Jager was seeking justice for his people. Not least, to defend Pienaar's property, they were given guns and ammunition. Theirs was also an economic project: to build up and to maintain legal commercial relations with the Cape colony. The murder of a white settler and the bounty of 1,000 Rixdollars complicated matters further. Yet through contact with the mission, the Afrikaner learned the commercial languages of Dutch and English. According to Trüper, "During this time, the Orlam were still of the opinion that their status in the racist society of southern Africa could be raised if they became Christians."[30] Jager Afrikaner, for example, was involved in a dispute with the chief of the Bondelswarts, and the latter also courted missionary presence in order to gain access to munitions. John Campbell (1766–1840)[31] did offer reconciliation. Ebner was the instrument of baptism; he also gave arms only to those who had been baptized. The drought in the region followed the Scotsman Moffat's 1818 arrival. Moffat did succeed

---

28. American Standard Version translation.
29. Trüper, *The Invisible Woman*, 20–21, note 22.
30. Trüper, *The Invisible Woman*, 21.
31. Trüper, *The Invisible Woman*, 35.

in reconciling and "rehabilitating" the chief through a trip to Cape Town: "The appearance of the most dreaded robber, chief Jager Afrikaner, in Cape Town at the side of his missionary proved to be a great success for Jager and the mission. . . . Jager, on the other hand, finally got a pass, which allowed him to move freely in the Cape Colony at all times. In addition, the relieved governor gave him an ox wagon, maybe as a replacement for the wagon his employee Drayer should have bought."[32] With this gesture of restitution, justice is restored, finally, and according to historical documents, Christian Afrikaner's New Testament was known for being thumbed and worn from constant use. Finally, Jager, or Christian, and his two baptized brothers David and Jakobus, did continue to hold worship services, and after bequeathing duties to his son Jonker, Jager died at Afrikaner's Kraal.

Christian Afrikaner is a rogue with a thirst for justice, an ethical terrorist. But rather than serve as a model of the righteous revolutionary, in this story he capitulates into the role of Christian ally. The racial category of intersectional identity is whitened by conversion, aligning Protestant antislavery politics with anticolonial racial politics for a Lutheran American readership. The ethics of early modern colonial competition, with German inserted into the economic and religious discourses, find a new center in North American political interventions. These texts and artifacts tighten a triangular relationship among Europe, Africa, and the Americas, with a bolder border drawn between North and South. These narratives extend to warmer climates as well.

Tropical Frontiers

The larger context of immigration and colonialism widens the lens through which German colonialities of power can be examined. In this, the intermedial roles of key colonial administrators and proponents demonstrate the importance of transatlantic networks and their performative force in consolidating German imperial identities. The intricacy of these networks illustrates further the power of tropes to transcend regional borders, establishing the German cultural pioneer as a common denominator. The entitlements of the pioneer/settler rely on the cultivation of a persecuted heroism in the face of nature, climate, and racialized antagonists. The Cramer case thematizes

---

32. Trüper, *The Invisible Woman*, 36–37.

gendered roles reversing and transferring in the colony; the feminine gains strength required to prevail in supporting the family and a colony outside the homeland. Decolonizing these narratives demands first examining their construction, which, I contend, relies on the gendered division of labor as constitutive of the German beyond Germany, informed by tropicalized identities from the Americas to Africa. Germans did not necessarily self-identify as agents in the transatlantic slave trade, and making these networks legible contributes to the process of decolonizing German studies.

Reference to a relatively obscure colonial activist and publisher, Gustav Hermann Meinecke (1854–1903), helps frame the analyses of overlapping imaginaries between settler colonialism and immigration, as these mobilities revolve more tautly around the late nineteenth-century polycentrism of an imperial German-speaking European male. Author, editor, and colonial politician, Meinecke thematized migration, remigration, and racial differences in his fiction and nonfiction. Historian David Ciarlo counts him among a group of "professional colonists," German nationalists who promoted the colonial project around the turn of the century. Prior to Meinecke's explicit interventions into colonialization for Germany and its economic investors, he engaged with the Americas in fiction to relocate and recuperate German-specific stories. In 1888, he published a collection, *Aus dem Creolenlande* (From the land of the Creoles), made up of a preface and four narratives that focus on German-speaking actors and agents and their intersections with American borderland histories. The stories take place in the Mississippi Delta, New Orleans, San Antonio, and Berlin. "Im Mississippisumpf" (In the Mississippi swamp), a Creole son is on a mission to reclaim his father's lost plantation. Against this personal conflict, a racialized power struggle among Baptists, Catholics, and indentured, formerly enslaved, practitioners of African religion (voodoo) plays out against the political maneuvering between Democrats, who oppose emancipation, and a German "Baron" who fought against the South; he invokes the name of General Grant when needed and identifies as a member of a secret National Republican Executive Committee of the State of Louisiana. The "Baron" allies himself with a German-speaking Jewish merchant (Beruch) and the formerly enslaved Blacks to join forces against a plantation owner and other white elites. His aim is to win an election for sheriff by securing the support of the newly enfranchised (the "N*gervotum," 57–58). "Der Fall des Alamo" (The fall of the Alamo) takes the narrator to the site fifty years after the memorable defeat (1836). The heroism of Eugen Weigand, champion of the oppressed and disillusioned revolutionary, drives the plot toward the triumphalism of the besieged, but also a love story between the gallant Weigand and a young Mexican woman he helps raise and educate, then marries. The narrator learns that she joined him in the fort and in death. In the shortest story, "In der letzten Stunde" (In the final hour), a German bartender, occupying a minor role, witnesses the story of Creole Marion, who has vowed to run away from his wife; he believes she is having an affair, but a storm brews, and he abandons his plans, returns to their threatened home, and ensures her safety. The man he believed to be her lover turns out to be a "desperado," her brother, who intervenes to repair the damage before he flees from the law. The final story, "Gumbo" (Gumbo), recounts the transatlantic networking between Americans and Germans; in Wilhelmine Berlin, the superficiality and false polish of the southerner, the "hot-blooded" Creole Cäsar Dujardin of New Orleans, are exposed. Son of a slave trader, Cäsar pursues a wealthy young woman, following her to Berlin, where they plan to marry. His fiancée, Miss Florence Giles, resides in a respectable establishment run by Frau Holkmann. Initially duped by Dujardin's surface charms, meanwhile, she permits him to stay in close proximity to his alleged beloved, who is under her care. The protagonist, John Valter, connects the love story through his erstwhile friendship and former business associate, Giles's father, and an acquaintance with the widowed Frau Holkmann, whose daughter, Amalie, his son courts apparently without success or her mother's approval. Or so it seems. These intrigues are complicated by Dujardin's love for another (a Creole woman whose racial lineage is thematized), but he needs money, so his motives for marrying Florence in Berlin, without her father's consent or approval, prove sinister and self-serving at best. And Amalie's apparent indifference to Alfred's overtures disguises her true affection for Valter's son, which she eventually confides in Valter senior. Meanwhile, Valter is characterized as suffering from hypochondria, which weakens his stalwartness and connects the various dots of the complex plot. To resolve the protagonist's problems with his own diminished masculinity and his loss of agency within his family and friend circle, Meinecke invokes emigrant entrepreneurship, Indigenous knowledge of botanicals, and the condemnation of slavery. These attributes accrue to "German" gendered identities and their transferability to those in proximity and open to formative Enlightenment influences.

Valter, a German remigrated from America, resides in the vicinity of Berlin's botanical gardens; he often sits near its "America" section, and experiments with cuttings he takes from various plants. He does so to develop his own treatment for a chronic liver ailment, dismissed by Berlin doctors as imagined. To regain a sense of health and purpose for his male protagonist of waning capacity, Meinecke takes recourse to a past life as an immigrant in America. Additionally, the collections of flora, fauna, and objects from all over the world, gathered and displayed in Berlin, the imperial capital, form the nexus of conflict between civilization and barbarism, the metropole and the "wilderness." This nexus also hosts the conflict between Eurocentric and Black and Indigenous epistemologies. The ailing Valter remembers the formerly enslaved old "Dave" telling him about the mysterious "gumbo" (*Laurus Benzoin*), a plant with marvelous medicinal properties found in the gulf. This knowledge, shared with trepidation, is summarized by racial side effects: "'Gumbo macht gesund und krank'—hat der alte N*ger geheimnißvoll geflüstert—'macht Weiße gesund und N*ger krank'—hinzugefügt und ihm damit ein werthvolles Heilmittel empfohlen, welches seine Schmerzen stets gelindert hatte" (139; "Gumbo can make you well and sick"—the old N*gro whispered secretively—"whites well and N*groes sick"—he added and with that recommended a valuable remedy that always had relieved his pain). The American experience can only make sense intellectually in Berlin.

Valter only learns the scientific names of the plant in the Berlin botanical garden, and to cure himself, he stealthily takes cuttings from various "Laurus" plants to prepare teas, but the process of elimination goes poorly. One day, he overhears an English-speaking couple on a stroll discuss a plant they know from home in Louisiana: "Gumbo." Dujardin names it with disgust and reluctance when prompted by Florence, who questions only from curiosity. Their reported reaction to the plant gives the reader insight into their respective characters. As Dujardin's unease among the upright Germans grows, Florence feels ever more at home. Amalie discourages her from going against her father's will and allowing an "Entführung" (abduction) in Berlin, a custom that had fallen out of favor even in the South. Instead, she convinces the American to write to her father and clear up the murky details of his role in Dujardin's downward mobility. We learn that Florence lost her mother at a young age; her naivete and apparent flightiness recede in Berlin. When she arrived, she claims, she was "unwissend wie ein Kind" (148; ignorant as a child), but she admires the forthrightness of the Berliners, becomes uncomfortable with the ambiguity of the engagement, and pursues a life of the mind. When Dujardin storms home after encountering the Berlin bureaucracy— the need for documents in order to marry—she defends the local customs. While he wants to decamp to Paris, she wants to stay to continue her education, until she gained everything she may "aus dieser Wissenschaftlichkeit, welche alle Verhältnisse durchdringt" (148; "from this scientific thinking that permeates everything"). A German narrator's perspective shifts the image of Florence from flightiness to gravitas, while Cäsar's ulterior motives come to light and his stock goes down.

In this novella, the relationships between parents and children unfold under the influence of colonial settlement. Valter contemplates his son Alfred's fate and recalls his youthful sense of adventure, a "Sehnen nach Glück" (154; a longing for happiness): "Es hatte ihn als Jüngling übers Meer—in die Wildniß getrieben" (154; As a young man it had driven him across the sea—into the wilderness). Valter attributes his physical ailments to the time spent in the wild; with regret, he observes his son pursuing the same path to seek fulfillment unavailable to him at home. Instead of studying medicine, Alfred did not take his father's advice and studied agriculture. He will seek his fortune "in Afrika" (155; in Africa). The urge to move beyond the limited bourgeois horizons of Berlin appear to have affected Amalie; her mother mistakes her interventions with the young Cäsar for love and a plan to run away. In conversation with Valter, Frau Holkmann confides her awareness of this plan: "Doch nicht nach Afrika?' 'Nein. Wohl nach Amerika?" (160; "Indeed, not to Africa?" "No. Probably to America?"). Meinecke's fiction and nonfiction provide a larger framework in which to understand the intersection of migration and colonial theory and practice.

The persistence of Indigenous knowledge acquired in bayous of Louisiana carries medicinal benefits and magical thinking the remigrated Valter must condemn. The selective cultural appropriation is informed by race. In conversation with Frau Holkmann, he laments the barbarity of Black and Indigenous ways of knowing. With their adult children seeming to go astray before their eyes, the two convene and end up talking about superstition in the late nineteenth century. Frau Holkmann insists she is not superstitious, then mentions that Amalie joked with her friends about cutting the butter as a single person. According to contemporary ethnography: "Wenn bei Tische ein Unverheiratheter die Butter anschneidet, so muss er noch 7 Jahr ledig bleiben" (If a single person at the table cuts the butter first, so he must remain single for seven years).[33] This lighthearted anecdote elicits a lament from Valter: "Oh Afrika, Afrika! Welche Barbarei verbreitest du in alle Welt! Ich

---

33. E. Krause, "Abergläubische Kuren und sonstiger Aberglaube in Berlin und nächster Umgebung. Gesammelt in den Jahren 1862–1882," *Zeitschrift für Ethnologie*, vol. 15 (1883): 78–94, here 91.

sehe sie auch uns näher rücken; sie wird in Europa wieder festen Fuß fassen. Davon bin ich überzeugt" (162; "Oh Africa, Africa! What barbarism you are spreading throughout the world! I see it coming ever closer to us; it will gain firm footing in Europe again. I am convinced of it). In his immediate circle, Africa comes to Europe by way of the slave trade, his exploits in the bayou, and racialized gender categories that defend Berlin bureaucracy, customs, and cosmopolitan aspirations to defeat Creole Indigeneity and Blackness, Southernness, and superstition.

Valter's disparaging of African belief systems ties together plots lines Meinecke pursues throughout the collection. Meinecke posits a homology between the American north and Berlin in the process. In "Mississippi-sumpf," the Black Baptist preacher threatens, "Wenn der Weiße seine Rolle ausgespielt hat, tritt der N*ger in sein Recht, und wenn unsere Zeit kommt, dann wehe! wehe! Dem Antichrist, der weißen Race!'" (30; "When the white man has played out his part, then the Black man will come into his own, and when our time comes, then woe betide, woe to the anti-Christ, the white race!"). Meanwhile, the old man who clings to African religion deals in the power of fetishes and curses the white race: "Verflucht sei die weiße Brut, die uns stahl, und verflucht—'" (35; Cursed be the white brood who stole us and cursed). A white man, the German "Baron," interrupts the "Voudou-Zauber" (35; voodoo magic) with the political proclamation of emancipation by shouting General Grant. The barbarism implicit—according to Meinecke—in Creole epistemologies meets its match in the socialization of Miss Giles. While the Creole woman must be avoided (she is Black), Florence gets in touch with her northern self: "Aber ich bin die Tochter der Purintaner" (148; But I am the daughter of Puritans). The discourses of race and gender intersect in the condemnation of Dujardin, the son of a slave trader: "welcher das Weib zur Sklavin erniederigen wollte" (177; who wanted to humiliate the woman by reducing her to a slave). In sum, colonial knowledge had to be applied to immigration itineraries: the trajectory of civilizing Germanness must remain a one-way street.

Woher?

During the 1890s, Meinecke served as editor of the *Deutscher Kolonialzeitung* as well as director of the *Deutsches Kolonialmuseum*. In addition, he published the *Koloniales Jahrbuch*[34] and endorsed a range of publications from the mainstream media to loftier print venues. Meinecke was a key organizer of the 1896 Colonial Exhibition in Berlin, for which he produced the accompanying catalogue and for which he is best known. In 1899, Meinecke founded a publishing house and printed his own work, such as the *Deutsche Kolonien in Wort und Bild*. Meinecke's earlier work from the early to mid-1890s exposes a more encompassing mental map of the German world and the place of Germanness in it. He elaborates on research and investment in his *Deutsche Kultivation in Ostafrika und der Kaffeebau*.[35] Ciarlo notes that he sat on the board of the Pangani-Gesellschaft, an East African sugar company.[36] Meinecke's personal and professional interests overlap considerably in his 1895 *Zuckeruntersuchungen am Pangani*.[37] Beyond the imperial and ideological investments in Africa, Meinecke cast a worldwide net.

One example of this expansiveness is Meinecke's *Katechismus der Auswanderung*, which provides a wide readership with a hands-on, how-to guide for Germans who were weighting the pros and cons of migration. This work, unlike any other, forges strong connections between German migration, colonization, and a cosmopolitan worldview. By 1896, the "catechism" had gone into its seventh edition. Perhaps for good reason, Meinecke's literary prose works have garnered little scholarly attention. In the *Katechismus*, Meinecke presumes the luxury of agency for the German emigrant. After he describe the factors driving emigration in the late nineteenth century, that is, population growth and demographic changes more generally, in addition to industrialization and diminished agricultural production, he praises the Germanic character's resolve in making the decision to leave. To reduce any cognitive dissonance that might ensue from the dilemma just described—choosing an exit strategy to express nationalism—emigration becomes patriotic. Crucial is the question: "Wohin," and here, he speaks to the global distribution of Germans and the imperative to form communities in order to attain a critical

---

34. Christian S. Davis, *Colonialism, Anti-Semitism, and Germans of Jewish Descent in Imperial Germany* (Ann Arbor: University of Michigan Press, 2012), 165.

35. Gustav Meinecke, *Deutsche Kultivation in Ostafrika und der Kaffeebau* (Berlin: Carl Heymanns Verlag, 1892). The title page informs us that this is a "Vermehrter Sonderdruck aus der Deutschen Kolonialzeitung mit einer kolorirten Karte."

36. Ciarlo, *Advertising Empire*, 145.

37. Gustav Meinecke, *Zuckeruntersuchungen am Pangani*. Vegatationsbilder von Dr. Otto Warburg, 2nd ed. (Berlin: Deutscher Kolonial-Verlag, 1909).

mass of Germanness and preserve the investment of labor and education: "Damit hängt nicht nur das Wohl der Auswanderer selbst, sondern auch das Interesse des Mutterlandes zusammen"[38] (On that depend not only the well-being of the emigrant himself, but also the interests of the Motherland). Meinecke imputes a national, nearly genealogical teleology to migration, which I turn to in the next chapter. In this rhetorical register, the answer to the practical question *wohin* is ultimately the existential *woher*? When he turns his attention to the official German colonies, he shifts into a political register.

On the African continent more generally, he questions why any German would want to live under French colonial rule in Algeria. He foregrounds business connections in South Africa. The German colonies, however, must be considered carefully for reasons of climate, for they are "Tropenkolonien," and as such,

> eine deutsche Auswanderung nach dorthin so gut wie ausgeschlossen, solange nicht nachgewiesen ist, daß der Auswanderer in einer bedeutenden Höhenlage, welche vorläufig für Besiedelung allein in Betracht kommt, gedeihen kann und solange nicht die notwendigen Verbindungen zwischen diesen Gegenden und den ungesunden Küsten geschaffen werden sind.[39]

> German immigration there is virtually impossible as long as it remains unproven that the emigrant can thrive at a significant altitude, which for the time being alone is suitable for settlement, and as long as the necessary connections between these regions and the unhealthy coasts have not been established.

Without a critical mass of Germans and development, the only realistic possibility remains German Southwest Africa, "obwohl man sich auch hier vor Illusionen bewahren muß"[40] (although here, too, one must be wary of illusions). To dispel those illusions, Meinecke investigates the climate first, then the racial composition of the population.

---

38. Gustav Meinecke, *Katechismus der Auswanderung. Kompaß für Auswanderer nach europäischen Ländern, Asien, Afrika, den deutschen Kolonien, Australien, Süd- und Zentralamerika, Mexiko, den Vereinigten Staaten von Amerika und Kanada*. 7th ed. Vollständig und neu bearbeitet. Mit 4 in den Text gedruckten Karten (Leipzig: J. J. Weber, 1896), 8. Emphasis in the original through letter spacing.
39. Meinecke, *Katechismus*, 45.
40. Meinecke, *Katechismus*, 45.

Die Bevölkerung im nördlichen Teil besteht vorwiegend aus Schwarzen, den Ovaherero, die ausschließlich Viehzüchter sind und sich mit dem Landbau nur dann beschäftigen, wenn sie auf den Stationen von den Missionaren dazu besonders angehalten werden. Sie sind geizig, bettelhaft, hochmütig, halten an dem Hergebrachten fest, aber gute Viehzüchter.[41]

The northern population consists mostly of Blacks, the Ovaherero, who are exclusively cattle breeders and only engage in farming when they are urged to do so by the missionaries at their stations. They are miserly, beggarly, arrogant, cling to traditions, but they are good cattle ranchers.

The redeeming quality of the Ovaherero, their animal husbandry skills, is countered by their character. Meinecke's judgment recalls the rebellious nature of Christian Afrikaner from the previous chapter, who rose up against oppression—at least in religious fiction—yet lived to repent his violent ways and convert, whereas the historical analogue proved to be a shrewd entrepreneur and calculating polyglot.

The racialized discourse about African peoples during the late nineteenth century has roots in Enlightenment theories of natural correspondence between geography and genealogy. Meinecke's characterization of the Ovaherero locates them in their habitus; he shifts, however, into an evaluation of their abilities, providing evidence of a rationalization of their labor. In the conversion and redemption story, published by the German-language, midwestern American synod, the political subtext, though consistent with an antislavery stance, ultimately reproduced the trope of the Black man radically abused by other Europeans, but brought back to the good side by the right Christians. Contemporaneously, Meinecke charts the racial territory of the German protectorates with a keen eye toward color, traits, and work potential. Moving to the south, he adds religion to the intersectional identities of the colonized:

Die gelben H*ttent*tten im südlichen Teil des Schutzgebietes sind etwas mehr civilisiert, zum größten Teil wohl Christen, sind beweglicher, kriegerisch, geistig entwickelter, arbeiten aber nicht gern und haben auch manche unangenehme Charakterzüge, welche den Deutschen viel zu schaffen gemacht haben.[42]

---
41. Meinecke, *Katechismus*, 46–47.
42. Meinecke, *Katechismus*, 47.

The yellow [Khokhoi][43] in the southern part of the protectorate are a bit more civilized, for the most part probably Christians, they are more mobile, warlike, intellectually more developed, but they do not like to work and also have some unpleasant character traits that have caused the German a lot of trouble.

First published a decade before the Herero-Nama genocide, the latter a Khokhoi people, Meinecke's description of the troublesome character attributes an inborn bellicosity to them, rather than acknowledge the colonial politics that forged alliances between the British and local tribal leaders or between the Germans and their allies. In this edition, Meinecke does allude to the war, which he celebrates as a German victory, and returns immediately to the model of investment most suited to German Southwest Africa:

Zwischen beiden Nationen tobte bis vor wenigen Jahren ein erbitteter Kampf, bis endlich durch die Besiegung des Hottentottenhäuptlings Hendrik Witboi durch die deutsche Schutztruppe der Friede wiederhergestellt worden ist. Das Land eignet sich im nördlichen Teile zur Viehzucht, im Süden zur Wollschafzucht.[44]

Up until a few short years ago, a bitter struggle raged between the two nations, until finally, through the defeat of the [Khokhoi] chief Hendrik Witboi by German troops, peace was restored. The land is suitable in the north for cattle breeding, in the south for wool sheep breeding.

Postcolonial scholars have overturned the rhetoric of peaceful restoration thanks to German military intervention that Meinecke employs here, taking aim at Hendrik Witbooi (1830?–1905), a descendent of Jager Afrikaner and anticolonial leader. More generally and differently destructive, the sidelining, converting, taming, and conquering stories reproduces a pernicious erasure of Black radicalism and resistance. Cedric Robinson formulates the effects of racist revisionist whitewashing, both in Africa and diasporic societies. By isolating uprisings against oppression and tucking massacres away into justifiable responses to attack from those being colonized, enslaved, or dispossessed, Eurocentric history telling interrupts a legacy of Black resis-

---

43. Throughout, I quote the original, which uses the derogatory term for the Khokhoi.
44. Meinecke, *Katechismus*, 47.

tance. The erasures contribute to a reliance on Marxist theories, themselves embedded in dialectical materialism that derives its considerable force from class conflict in turn specific to feudal, mercantile, industrializing, and capitalist Europe. Robinson writes, "Black radicalism is a negation of Western civilization, but not in the direct sense of a simple dialectical negation."[45] The German colonial experience in Southwest Africa occludes the biographies of two historical individuals who wrote radical history.

An ongoing research project investigates Witbooi's writings from perspectives beyond the polarized interpretations of his life and legacy; he was killed during a battle with the German forces and buried in an unmarked grave. He has since become a heroic African activist, and his image appears on Namibian bank notes. According to Hendrik Bosman, Witbooi's papers provide evidence of his Christianity, with an independent, African-specific identification with the biblical theme of Exodus. Inspired by the divine, he led his people north into conflict with the colonial powers, accepted a period of nonviolence with the signature of a *Schutzvertrag*, and obeyed the command of providence to rise up against the colonizers.[46]

Social historians of the Ovaherero bring a different perspective to the position of Witbooi, beyond the polarity of colonial oblivion and heroic rebel. Jan-Bart Gewald, for example, details the overlooked struggle for Herero succession in the late nineteenth century. Once again, consolidation of territory in Europe took precedence over colonial ambitions, as I demonstrate above during the reign of Frederick II. The missionaries present in the region from the 1840s forward requested protection, forthcoming from the British as Berlin prepared for the Franco-Prussian War.[47] At a time when Witbooi was raiding the cattle posts of the Okahanja, the chief succumbed to pressure to sign a protection treaty with the Germans. According to Gewald, "Unfortunately for the Herero, the Germans saw the treaty solely as a further substantiation of its claims to German Southwest Africa."[48] The internecine hostilities among the Herero entangled the colonial powers, only to support the narrative of Germans as the restorers of peace. Primary was the access to trade

---

45. Cedric J. Robinson, *Black Marxism: The Making of the Black Radical Tradition* (London: Zed Press, 1983), 96.
46. Hendrik Bosman, "A Nama 'Exodus'? A Postcolonial Reading of the Diaries of Hendrik Witbooi," *Scriptura* 108 (2011): 329–41, 331.
47. Jan-Bart Gewald, *Herero Heroes: A Socio-Political History of the Herero of Namibia, 1890–1923* (Athens: Ohio University Press, 1999), 30–31.
48. Gewald, *Herero Heroes*, 31.

routes, which Witbooi fought for with the zeal of a prophet. After years of conflict, Hendrik Witbooi and Samuel Maharero joined forces again the German military forces, though the vicissitudes of colonization drove a wedge between them again. But ultimately they united against a common enemy. The complex power struggle among the Herero that prefaced the war plays no role in the all-encompassing goal of securing peace for profit.

The colonial logic Meinecke follows dispels concerns about violence, while occluding radical African history, and proffers practical advice about German emigration to the protectorate in West Africa. He distinguishes between colonization and emigration economically, but unites them in a teleology of national German identity. In a comparison, he observes that the country is larger than Germany, though "wenig bevölkert." Before he closes with the high cost of the emigration and the difficulties of making the trip, Meinecke turns to infrastructure, speculating that maybe there will be more development once a railroad is built. Finally, he dissuades emigration unless under specific sponsorship of a *Siedlungsgesellschaft* or settlement company; "und ein gewisser Grundstock von deutscher Bevölkerung vorhanden ist und gedeiht" (and a basic stock of German population is present and thriving).[49] Meinecke's catechism, while differentiating among the African tribes whose histories and positioning for power prove troublesome, remains driven by racial entitlements and European prosperity. With sheep breeding dominant in the west, Meinecke explores other crops, products, and genres based on his investments on the other coast of the continent. His prose maps the continuing conflicts not only among colonizers, but the colonized.

Settlers

Enter the farmer and the Farmersfrau. The hidden and public transcripts from German Southwest Africa document the shift in perspective and purpose: from a war with the elements to a race war. In 1913, Meineke published Ada Cramer's *Weiß oder Schwarz. Lehr- und Leidensjahre eines Farmers in Südwest im Lichte des Rassenhasses* (White or Black, A farmer's apprenticeship and years of suffering in the southwest in light of racial hatred).[50] As bor-

---

49. Meinecke, *Katechismus*, 47
50. Ada Cramer, *Weiß oder Schwarz? Lehr- und Leidensjahre eines Farmers im Südwest im Lichte des Rassenhasses* (Berlin: Kolonial-Verlag, 1913).

der conflicts erupted and national lines were drawn firmly, the figurative wilderness of the New World, the unwritten pages of the prairie, the untamed, unowned jungles ready for cultivation, the empty pampas, the arable land of East and West Africa, all entered discursive, transnationally sanctioned German territory and geographic imaginary. The acquisition of land by settlers in the American West, enabled by the Homestead Act in 1862, sets the stage for conflict and more in the United States; in settler narratives, it legitimizes entitlements and homogenizes whiteness and national identity. The nations of Latin America share only sections of this trajectory. Citizenship rights, land ownership, and cultural autonomy in the South follow diverse itineraries that intersect with international law and policy. Scholars have examined, in particular, the German emigrant communities of southern Brazil as a colonial space; specifically, the ethos of industry and labor as constitutive of German civilization and cultural superiority feed into this discourse. As Cassidy writes, "Slavery was at the heart of the alleged Brazilian incapacity to work; the institution made work dishonorable. German nationalists in Europe and Brazil claimed that settlers would remedy this and remake the country and its people."[51] Closer examinations of cultural and literary history, however, pose challenges to the hegemony of economic and diplomatic history; the pioneer, farmer, or professional settler as German citizen and colonist assumes agency for the first time in history. Ultimately, gender issues disrupt the hegemonic model of German identity.

The public history of colonial politics implicates gender difference in sordid ways. On January 4, 1907, editor A. Herfurth titled his front-page opinion piece for the *Koloniale Zeitschrift* (colonial newspaper) "Warum müssen wir Kolonialpolitik treiben?"[52] (Why must we pursue colonial politics?). He enumerates reasons, but lays blame for diminished masculinity at the feet of a long period of peace, accompanied by a moral decline. With urgency, Herfurth unleashes a tirade against sexual degeneration on the home front, railing against the "Verhimmelung des Sexuellen" (glorification of the sexual), ubiquity of sexual imagery, and the "Wollustdelirium, das die Hetäre und Prostituierte auf den Altar des Glaubens erheben möchte" (1; the delirium of lust that would elevate the hetaera and prostitute to the altar of faith).

---

51. Eugene S. Cassidy, "Germanness, Civilization, and Slavery: Southern Brazil as German Colonial Space (1819–1888)" (PhD diss., University of Michigan, 2015), 2.

52. A. Herfurth, "Warum müssen wir Kolonialpolitik treiben?," *Koloniale Zeitung* 1, no. 8 (January 4, 1907): 1–2. Subsequent references to this editorial appear in parentheses. Unless otherwise noted, translations are my own.

On every available public surface, from bookstores to house facades and monuments, "macht sich Frau Venus vulgivaga in Stellungen breit, die auf den Lustkitzel berechnet sind" (1; Miss Venus vulgivaga spreads herself into positions designed to arouse lust). To drain this swamp, regain lost German manhood (*Männerwürde*), and honor "tausende blühender Menschenleben" (1; thousands of blossoming human lives), he calls for a readiness to sacrifice even more; for men to colonize to enhance their own self-worth and that of their people. The path to male salvation lies in battle and/or the colonies. In the colonial context, the toxic femininity of Herfurth's disapproving optics is recoded in the trope of the Farmersfrau.

The publication of Ada Cramer's exculpatory memoir of her family's colonial experiences in German Southwest Africa was truly a family affair. Her brother-in-law, husband Ludwig's younger brother[53] and Doctor of Law Otto Cramer, wrote a foreword (March 1, 1913): "Das vorliegende Buch ist von einer Farmersfrau geschrieben"[54]; and an introduction (March 21, 1913), in which he argues that the German administrators sided with the Blacks against the farmer, his brother. The case: poisoning. It is widely known that German soldiers, after the initial battles against the Herero-Nama, brutally massacred the enemy; they raped women, experimented on survivors, committed thousands to death in concentration camps, and provided German scientists with the remains of the dead for study. Not least, they poisoned wells and livestock to ensure death by starvation. The San, also victims in the genocide, traditionally used poison (from beetles) to ensure the lethal effect of their arrows. As she narrates their story, she includes their dire illnesses and the loss of livestock; they insist they were poisoned. The economic backstory and dedication to German family and colony drives his ambition to succeed as a farmer and his determination to provide for her and their children, according to her testimonial.

In the introduction, Dr. Otto Cramer turns away from the Farmersfrau to his brother's *Werdegang*. His brother turned to farming as he approached forty, with a career as an entrepreneur behind him. At the age of twenty-six, he cofounded the Hamburg trading company Wiskott & Cramer, "das er, als eine auf das Brasilianische Valorizationsgesetz gegründete Spekulation

---

53. For further biographical details, see Barbara Frey, "Der Fall Cramer," *Ravensberger Blätter*, Organ des Historischen Vereins für die Grafschaft Ravensberg e.V., Heft 2 (2011): 40–53, here 41.
54. Dr. Cramer, "Vorwort," iii–iv, here iii.

fehlschlug, so liquidierte, daß alle Gläubigen voll befriedigt wurden."[55] Frey recounts that Cramer married his cousin Adelheid, eight years his junior, in 1891.[56] She provides more context: though he lost a fortune, Ludwig Cramer had enough money left to start over with his wife as a farmer in the German colonies; they had no previous agricultural experience. They saw this as private destiny, independent of external forces. Like that of so many immigrants and colonists, their daily existence accrued epic significance beyond German borders. But these do not take place outside history. Without drilling down into too many details, after the abolition of slavery in 1888, Brazil made a concerted effort to "whiten" the population; this involved recruiting European families to work the land previously made profitable by enslaved African labor. The emergence of cash crops signified an economic shift from extraction to industrialization, with improved infrastructure (British engineers built railroads) and the move of the national capital south. Between 1909 and 1910, coffee prices dropped, and the valorization law kept production low in Brazil to avoid a collapse in prices.[57] In this midst, Cramer turned to colonial farming in German Southwest Africa. From her life writing, court documents, missionary witness, and the British use of this case as a cautionary tale about German imperial incompetence, legal proceedings began against her husband, Ludwig Cramer; on April 4, 1913, he was charged with inflicting "dangerous physical harm in combination with coercion,"[58] a prosecution that encompassed a history of violent, vengeful attacks primarily against Black women. Krista O'Donnell cites historical sources about the proceedings that document Cramer's brutality and unbridled rage directed at victims he considered "poisonous women."[59] Yet, even against this backdrop,

---

55. Dr. jur. Otto Cramer, "Einleitung," 1.
56. Frey, "Der Fall Cramer," 42.
57. Werner Baer, *The Brazilian Economy: Growth and Development* (London: Lynne Rienner Publishers, 2008).
58. Frey, "Der Fall Cramer," 40.
59. Krista O'Donnell, "Poisonous Women: Sexual Danger, Illicit Violence, and Domestic Work in German Southern Africa, 1904–1915," *Journal of Women's History* 11, no. 3 (1999): 32–54, here 32. O'Donnell also published this material in her book. See K. Molly O'Donnell, *The Servants of Empire: Sponsored German Women's Colonization in Southwest Africa, 1896–1945* (Oxford: Berghahn, 2023), especially chap. 4, "The Malice of Native Women," 124–47. O'Donnell's discussion of Cramer's memoir and the crimes committed by her husband is based also on trial transcripts in colonial newspapers, which refer to Lupatine as "Rupertine" and "Rupertina" (136–37). In an email exchange with the author (August 24, 2023), she noted the inconsistent use of German call names.

Cramer's violence stood out. The British, who assumed authority over German South West after World War I, cited this case as an example and proof of German imperial failure.[60] Exculpatory in intent, Ada Cramer's life writing illustrates a racialized allegory of a Farmersfrau in battle for survival against the *Eingeborenen* (natives) in ways that call attention to the shifting gender roles in colonial epistemics. Though her narrative proffers several vignettes of feminizing outreach and ameliorating solidarity with women, Cramer recuperates moral and racial superiority through recourse to her identity as a colonial wife and reluctant white caregiver.

Ada Cramer opens her narrative with exclamatory remarks about survival of the ordeal. She recounts the departure, leaving their four children in safe hands until they could settle, and the verve with which the couple embarked on the "Pionierarbeit fürs Vaterland" (17). "Daß diese fünf Jahre mich nicht zerbrochen haben, daß ich nach dem, was hinter mir liegt, noch hoffe, die geistige Spannkraft zu haben, die Fülle der Bilder und Erlebnisse, welche an meinem geistigen Auge vorüberziehen, niederschreiben zu können, scheint mir fast ein Wunder" (15; That these five years have not broken me, that I still hope, after everything I have been through, to have the spiritual strength to write down the abundance of images and experiences that pass before my mind's eye, seems like almost a miracle to me). Cramer next insists with self-deprecation: "Ich bin eine schlichte Frau und habe noch niemals die Feder zur Hand genommen" (15; I am a simple woman and I have never before taken up the pen). Cramer's subtext of religiosity and sacrifice lends a tone of martyrdom to the act of colonization; it drives her to assume agency in the act of writing. For many German emigrants, the fact of leaving ennobles the everyday, reframes the mundane matters of existence with the gild of a hero's journey.

Throughout the memoir, Cramer contrasts the profundity of her feelings with the sense of betrayal of that sincerity. From her point of view, the reader absorbs stories of unfair treatment, the failed purchase of a promised farm, acquiring half the amount of land (ten thousand hectares) farther afield from Windhoek than planned, along with numerous encounters with Herero and Khokhoi laborers. The emphasis on nurturing manifests on the journey to the farm, which unfortunately is farther away from the city than the colonial couple hoped. At one point, their small party camps near a military precinct. Ada Cramer adds fuel to the fire in the hopes that the soldiers will join them; this

---

60. See Frey, "Der Fall Cramer," 40 note 2.

transpires, and she offers them tea with rum, describing them admiringly: "alles junge, frische Gesellen mit frohen, erwartungsvollen Augen, frisch von Deutschland gelandet" (28; all young, fresh fellows with happy, expectant eyes, freshly landed from Germany). Their enthusiasm for battle impresses her, for they came "um den Erlag mit Simon Kopper klarzumachen" (28; to clarify the defeat with Simon Kopper). Kopper or Kooper, the exonym used to render the click consonants of Gomxab, (*–1913), was a captain of the Frans-Nama, allied with the Ovaherero and Germans in the Mbandero uprising of 1896, though his alliance was strategic; his band arrived after the battle to loot. Later allied with Witbooi against the Germans in 1904, he was taken prisoner and interred at the Shark Island concentration camp. The youthful military spirit of the German soldiers around the Cramers' bivouac fire gives a glimpse into the hidden transcript of Nama resistance, under the watchful and appreciative eye and writing hand of the Farmersfrau. On the facing page—they are approximately sixty kilometers from Gobadis, the locale of their twenty thousand hectares farm Oljifororini—she admires the land itself: "Das Land ist über Erwarten schön und fruchtbar, zum Teil schwerer Weizenboden, üppige Weide und viel Baumwuchs" (29; The land is beautiful and fertile beyond expectation, partly heavy wheat oil, lush pasture, and lots of trees). Her next observation captures the essence of the colonizing gaze: "Doch davon, daß nur vor wenigen Jahren ein zahlreiches Volk das Land bewohnt hatte, war nicht mehr das geringste zu spüren. Nichts, gar nichts zeigte davon, daß dieses Volk je in seinem Leben einen Finger zur Arbeit gerührt hatte, es war über dieses Land dahingegangen wie das Wild über die Weide" (29; But still there was not the slightest trace of the fact that just a few years ago, a large number of people had inhabited this land. Nothing, absolutely nothing showed that this people had ever in their lives lifted a finger to work, it had passed over this land like wild animals over a pasture). Her farming eye overtly erases its people and history from what was their land, now hers.

The Farmersfrau has maternal moments in the absence of her own children. At times she seems to be seeking common cause with other mothers, only to be shocked at their indifference, which enables her to regain moral high ground; she is staffing the farthest outpost, confirmed by the soldiers who report a nearby uprising. Unwilling to let themselves fret about the violence, the Cramers pick up workers from the district, not without complaint about their shabbiness and smell. The women help build the sleeping "Pontok," completed just before the rain. During a stormy night, some of the livestock break their confinement and escape. The "Kaffer" Jakob is sent after them, but the rain washes away any traces. The same night, three Herero women workers disappear; they leave four small children behind. Ada Cramer describes their plight: "Da saßen wir nun mitten in der Wildnis ganz allein und hatten noch für vier schwarze Kinder zu sorgen" (31; There we sat in the middle of the wilderness, completely alone, and had to care for four Black children). Her resentment does not deter her caregiving instincts: "Der kleinste Affe von 9 Monaten konnte unheimlich schreien, er bekam allmählich meinen ganzen Vorrat an kondensierter Milch, und wir tranken dem kleinen Schreihals zuliebe unseren Kaffee schwarz" (31; The youngest ape, nine months old, could scream unbelievably; eventually he got my entire supply of condensed milk, and for the sake of the little screamer we drank our coffee black). The almost affectionate, maternal tone suggests a term of endearment in the racial slur (*Affe*). Cramer tends the home fires, complaining about the mouths to feed: "Um unser Feuer saßen die vier schwarze Würmer, für die ich dreimal am Tag Suppe kochen mußte" (31; Around our fire sat the four Black worms for whom I had to prepare soup three times daily). The emphasis lies on the sacrifices they make and the extra work and food the abandoned children require. The district office assigned workers to farmers, a practice that naturalizes the master-servant hierarchy in which the Cramers participate with a sense of seigneurial privilege. The power structure does not factor in gender roles, and Ada Cramer finds herself practicing maternality with ambivalence, attributed to the race of her wards. Such sacrifices make the betrayals harder to bear, from her perspective.

As a Farmersfrau, Cramer casts herself in redemptive female roles as part of her new identity. On a difficult trip to Kehorro, sixty kilometers distance from Gobabis, the Cramers meet with multiple challenges while trying to move eight cows and purchase necessities for the farm. The cows get away (due to negligent oversight); a mule dies of colic. Additionally, Ada Cramer notes the death of a young Herero woman from pneumonia. She writes, "Ich habe sie vier Tage gepflegt und war empört über die Hartherzigkeit ihrer Stammesgenossen. Diese glaubten von Anfang an, daß die Frau sterben würde, und so war sie ihnen keinen Schlug Wasser mehr wert" (30, I nursed her for four days and was appalled at the callousness of her fellow tribesmen. From the beginning they believed that the woman would die, and so to them she was no longer worth even a sip of water). Cramer assimilates gender fluidity into the performative role of the Farmersfrau.

While the roles of the Farmersfrau include crossing gender boundaries, she poses the racial question as an either/or. Suspicious from the beginning of the district authorities and of Blacks, whom she purports to give the benefit of the doubt, she ultimately sees them allied against the hard-working, well-meaning community of colonists. Ada Cramer harbors deep resentment toward the colonial authorities for enforcing German laws against abusing African workers; she sees this as betrayal. Her loyalties thus disrupted, her narrative account corroborates the situational need to move nimbly between masculine and feminine signifiers. Having established a household, she notes with amazement in retrospect that she donned "Männerkleidung" to work beside an open flame (31). She still celebrates the satisfaction of domestic work, but her passive observance of fellow settlers is racially activated: Mit welcher Freude say ich den Weißen bei der Arbeit zu" (34; I felt such joy when I watched the Whites at work). When her husband is away, she dedicates herself to passing the time through "fleissige Arbeit" (50; industrious labor). In other words, Ada Cramer resolves any dissonance in her multiple subject positions as wife, mother, woman, caregiver, mistress, boss, and worker, through imperial whiteness.

In due course, she makes the reader aware of a growing estrangement between the colonial administrators and the farmers (52); the former she accuses of siding with the dissembling and duplicitous "natives":

Diesem Volke, dem jede Kultur, jeder sittliche Untergrund fehlt, bei dem man vergeblich ein Gewissen sucht, hat unsre Regierung die Gleichen Rechte mit unserem weißen deutschen Arbeiter gegeben. Was unser Volk sich durch Jahrhunderte mit Blut erkanft hat,—vor nicht viel mehr als 100 Jahren herrschte in Preußen noch die Leibeigenschaft—das bekommt dies rebellische Volk als Lockspeise hingeworfen. (52)

Our government has given this people, who lack any culture or civilization, any moral foundation, where one searches in vain for a conscience, the same rights as our white German workers. What our people acquired only through centuries with its blood—not even 100 years ago, serfdom was dominant in Prussia—has been tossed to this rebellious people as a sugar plum.

Here, Ada Cramer rehearses a familiar refrain in the discourse of German exceptionalism: she equates European serfdom with slavery, sidestepping any issue of racial difference, on which her own logic is predicated. The German farmer, "treuer deutscher Pionier" (53) does the heavy patriotic lifting of teaching "dieses arbeitsscheue Volk" (53) the meaning of work.

Cramer describes her illness (62) and her husband's grievous near-death experience (67). According to her report, they were poisoned, as were the salt blocks for their livestock or prize animals directly. One case comes before the authorities: a domestic servant, Lupatine, confesses to poisoning the "Missiß" (107) at the behest of Kadwakonda, her husband, and that she defended the Baas and the Missiß on the basis of their goodness, to no avail. The workers call the Cramers by their roles, the "boss" and the "misses." Their use of exonyms to define the Black domestic servants and works in this and other contexts exemplifies the performative power of language to erase identity and reduce the human subject to subservience. Their objectification continues. Driven to get proof of the truth, Cramer goes on a mission: he interrogates Maria, July's wife, who confesses further, through a Herero interpreter, to the crimes and their planning. In the fog of fear and self-righteous indignation, Ada Cramer addresses her reader directly: "Was hättest du, Leser, getan?" Is it a crime—which her husband was charged with— she continues: "daß er außer sich geriet, wenn er an seine Frau dachte, die monatelang durch die Schuld jenes Schurken wie tot auf dem Feldbett lag, daß ihn Entsetzen packet, wenn er an jene Nacht dachte, in welcher er sich in dumpfer Verzweiflung fast selbst verstümmelt hätte, um Frau und Kindern wenigstens seine Arbeitskraft zu erhalten" (111; that he was beside himself with rage when he thought of his wife, who for months through the fault of this scoundrel lay like dead on the camp bed, that horror gripped him when he thought of that night when in dull despair he nearly mutilated himself, so that his wife and children at least would still have his labor). These tendentious questions preface the ruthless beating. Ludwig Cramer finds and beats July, the alleged culprit. And he goes after the women in search of the poison. Ada Cramer ties the women's hands and facilitates a search, the complexity of which Marcia Klotz has analyzed with reference to Klaus Theweleit's "rifle" or phallic woman.[61] Ada Cramer envisions herself at war on the side of justice against the insidious poison and homicidal agency of the Black women. While Klotz foregrounds Ada Cramer's participation in sadistic and erotic fantasies, and observes that the latter

---

61. Marcia Klotz, "Memoirs from a German Colony: What Do White Women Want?" *Genders* 19 (1994): 154–73, here 162–63.

are not exclusively male,[62] I emphasize instead the expansion of female identity construction predicated on the explicit inclusion of white settler agency, the toxic feminine. Ada Cramer pulls herself back from the precipice of guilt by reverting to caregiver roles she cannot seem to shed. The following day, for example, insisting on the essential differences between women and men, Ada cares for July's wounds, because men and women must behave "ihrer Natur nach" (112; according to her nature).

Frey reports testimonies from the victims. In the frenzied search for poison, Ludwig Cramer whipped several female workers; he offered the opportunity to beat another (pregnant) woman to a colonist, also from Bielefeld. Ultimately, two women died as a result of the beatings; his floggings of pregnant woman twice caused miscarriages.[63] A missionary documented the crimes, and they were brought forth at the trial.[64] Ada Cramer alternately abetted her husband's crimes and sought mercy for his victims. Klotz's argument highlights a sexual component in Cramer's cruelty and violence and his wife's complicity in his apparent arousal. Ada Cramer indulges in violent fantasies of vengeance; and in one search, she knifes open a blouse. Her husband's excitement prompts his departure, and she continues the search under the woman's skirts. Of Ada Cramer's self-definition as woman, Klotz writes, "Her gender seems to slide back and forth from one sentence to the next."[65] Much of Klotz's analysis is persuasive; she sees in Ada Cramer's narrative an inconsistency, but I argue that the trope of the Farmersfrau determines this feminine behavior in the settler colony across gendered attributes. Not only does Cramer attribute warrior-like, masculine traits to the Black women, she also recounts the numerous failed attempts she herself undertook to play caregiver, nurse, and comforter to them. Ada Cramer occupies multiple subject positions simultaneously: she is humanitarian caregiver, ostensibly race-agnostic, yet she vilifies the administrators who grant humanity and human

---

62. Klotz, "Memoirs," 163.
63. Klotz, "Memoirs," 161.
64. Frey, "Der Fall Cramer," 50. See also O'Donnell, "Poisonous Women," 36; she recounts that he also sought out and beat Konturu, the wife of Katoakonda, whom Lupertine identifies as the ringleader. Konturu had two stillbirths "caused in this manner" (36). O'Donnell concludes, "Cramer's attacks on his female personnel reveal a brutal antagonism rooted in displaced sexual desire" (36). There is truth in this interpretation, but I would add that the context of German masculinity in the colonies allows for the displacement of the presumptive "civilizing" obligation; in the colonies, white men are uninhibited, freed to access selectively the savagery of tribal rivalries Freud describes in *Totem and Taboo*.
65. Klotz, "Memoirs," 163.

rights to Black Africans. Her discourse dehumanizes Blackness while canonizing German whiteness. To farm is to assert racial superiority. There is more to the story, but let me move to her closing arguments, an appeal to the reader for reason. She implores her readers to think of the

> weißen Kindern, die nicht zur Schule gehen können, weil sie das Vieh hüten müssen, welches der Schwarze im Stich läßt, von weißen Frauen, die sich die Hände wund und den Leib krank arbeiten, während Hunderte von schwarzen Weibern rauchend in der Sonne sitzen. Von den Farmern, deren Existenz durch die Tücke der Schwarzen bedroht ist, denen sie das Vieh morden und das gesegnete Erntefeld in Brand stecken. (131).

> white children who cannot go to school because they have to watch the cattle that the Black man abandons; of white women, who work their hands sore and their bodies sick, while hundreds of Black women sit smoking in the sun. Of the farmers whose existence is threatened by the treachery of the Blacks, who poison their cattle and set fire to their blessed fields of harvest.

After serving his sentence, Ludwig returned to the farm, where he died in 1917 while dynamiting (some say not an accident); Ada Cramer was deported to Germany after the League of Nations assumed the mandate in 1919; she died in 1962.[66] Daughter Hildegard remained on the family farm; her brother, Ernst Ludwig, acquired neighboring land, the setting for his commemorative work, *Die Kinderfarm*, to which I return in subsequent chapters. The trope of the ennobled farmer persisted in the ideology of the interwar period, beyond the loss of colonies at the end of World War I. In both his mother's memoir and Ernst Ludwig's representation of the contact between Blacks and German settlers, anxiety escalates into a hypervigilant fear of victimization.

---

66. Frey, "Der Fall Cramer," 52, 53.

CHAPTER EIGHT

Wohin? The Ungovernable

The Enlightenment project of knowing the world absolutely with a German center of gravity culminates in the production of knowledge, crops, and media during the Age of Empire. The rational definition of humanity, selectively universal, further naturalized by climate, then projected onto the skin and vectored onto maps of the globe, form the foundation of the German colonial project around 1900. With recourse to the centuries-old resentment of stronger European powers and early modern tropes of persecuted yet superior German essentialism, medicalized and epistemological narratives about racial and ethnic identity reconfigure in a different register, one that explicitly entangles the economics of colonial markets and desirable resources, crops, and Indigenous labor with the project of emigration. Around 1900, key colonial administrators and activists take and switch sides to reconfigure the world as German-centric. From west to east Africa, colonial agents during the Age of Empire forged associations between products and people, the acquisition and domination of which drove both settler colonialism, albeit in limited ways, but also emigration epistemologies. Answering the question *wohin* tended to overshadow the question of *warum*; replies to both emerge from the nexus of ideological and material conditions of belonging and belonging to. When Arjun Appadurai writes about the "unruliness of the world of things," he articulates a "tension between the rule of the commodity and the unruliness of thing itself."[1] In sending the "German" as export, not exile, the qualifier has to be quantified, its value converted into exchangeable currency. In this process, the "German" self confronts both the unruliness of things and contains the resistance of the ungovernable. Here, I invoke Luis Othoniel Rosa's theoretical framework for understanding anarcho-feminism as resistance, a reappropriation of knowledge through a "pedagogy of unrul-

---

1. Arjun Appadurai, "The Thing Itself," *Public Culture* 18, no. 1 (2006): 15–21, here 21.

iness,"[2] whereby "unruliness" as a "form of knowledge" cannot be explicated but can be "modeled and transmitted through examples."[3] In each of the imperial texts pertinent to my reading of colonial-era nonfiction and fiction, the writer inscribes these uncontainable moments; the inventories attempt to govern them through a process of performative repetition of enumeration, all in the effort to measure, regulate, and appropriate Indigenous forms through force. The allegorical "Germans" and their interrelated existence from Africa to the Americas encompasses an entire spectrum of colonial subjects and objects, from desired raw materials, inhospitable climates, scientific research, and strategies of discipline and punish to subjugate the ungovernable, the resisters who cannot (or will not) regulate themselves nor conform to the labor ethic exacted/extracted from them. The ungovernable become part of the picture beyond contemporary ethnographic curiosity and collection; they are commodified. Commodification in keeping imperial inventories devolved along dividing lines of race and gender.

Gustav Hermann Meinecke (1854–1903), whom I introduced above with reference to his interest in German Southwest Africa, establishes a totalizing logic that subsumes immigration and colonization into nationalized DNA. In contrast to Paul Rohrbach (1869–1956), whom George Steinmetz characterizes as a "cultural missionary,"[4] Meinecke wrote before the Age of Empire's demise and Germany's loss of two world wars. Unlike later colonial settler "heroes" celebrated by National Socialist politics, Meinecke's nationalism passed constantly through an optimistic prism; it ideologically aligned colonialism with emigration. His *Katechismus* elaborates on this homology, which encompasses the colonial connections across the African continent. Perhaps for good reason, Meinecke's literary prose works have garnered little scholarly attention. In novellas like *Der arme Sidi Abderrachman. Eine ostafrikanische Geschichte*,[5] originally published in 1897, Meinecke supplements the promoting and propagandizing mission of his nonfiction research publications with

---

2. Luis Othoniel Rosa, "Luisa Capetillo and the Pedagogy of Unruliness," *S/X* 69 (2022): 84–97. Rosa's focus is on the work of Luisa Capetillo, a "loud-reader" and activist whose practices of walking and writing and reading aloud in factories defies capitalist creations and circulations of knowledge and power.

3. Rosa, "Pedagogy of Unruliness," 85.

4. George Steinmetz, *The Devil's Handwriting: Precoloniality and the German Colonial State in Qingdao, Samoa, and South Africa* (Chicago: University of Chicago Press, 2007), xiii.

5. Gustav Meinecke, *Der arme Sidi Abderrachman. Eine ostafrikanische Geschichte* (Berlin: Deutscher Kolonial-Verlag, 6. Auflage).

embellishments and intrigue for entertaining reading, though even these are exposed within the fiction as colonial fantasies. Yet he ultimately replaces one kind of fantasy with another. Like several of his contemporaries, Meinecke left a mark on a range of genres and publications about the German colonial enterprise. His research, travel letters, reports, and editorial endeavors toggle in illuminating ways with his fiction. Meanwhile, the fictional *Sidi Abderrachman* reinscribes from his nonfiction much he had to say about economic tension, along with political descriptors and sociocultural markers. Meinecke updates similar themes from his earlier story cycle, *Aus dem Creolenlande* (From the land of the Creoles, 1888), such as racial difference and love across social, economic, and ethnic difference, but the stalwartness of Germanness as the decisive attribute of masculinity and femininity remains. His 1897 novella devoted to the East African story appeared in the series of "exotic" novels set in the German colonies. Four editions were published between 1897 and 1900. Sidi Abderrachman's tale is mapped onto the same territory in which the research and reports are devoted to coffee and sugar production. In this novella, Meinecke gazes at the hierarchy of color and gender; wealth, race, and rank, while Germans and English colonial rulers play off and are played off each other to enhance their respective power base with the different groups. While slavery as an institution had been limited, emancipation did not occur. In addition to depicting the enslavement of Blacks and Arabs, with some Indian influence on the power structures also in play, Meinecke adds gendered relationships in order to recode German masculinity, adapting it to the colonial imperative. For his purpose, harems serve as the institution of utmost cultural difference to the European male. Ultimately, however, the ethical dilemma of respecting or ignoring local custom is resolved for one administrator by his superiors. That process recapitulates the arguments about climate, race, and gender that had persisted since the Enlightenment. Together they recode a notion of universality that is predicated on the national, and map a German global imaginary onto colonial realities.

Crucial to the ontology of migration for the potential global German is the question: *Wohin?* The *Katechismus* lays out an ideology of national identity along with the practicalities to keep in mind while making a choice. In the *Katechismus*, Meinecke presumes the luxury of agency for the German emigrant. After he describe the factors driving emigration in the late nineteenth century, that is, population growth and demographic changes more generally, in addition to industrialization and diminished agricultural production, he praises the Germanic character for making the decision to leave:

Während nun andere Völker durch Arbeitslosigkeit und drohende Hungergefahr zu Unruhen und Aufständen getrieben werden, rafft der überlegende Germane sich kräftig auf und greift zum Wanderstabe, indem er den Weg über das Weltmeer nicht scheut, um mehr Ellbogenraum zur freien Bewegung und Ausbreitung zu gewinnen und womöglich ein eigenes Stück Grund und Boden zu erwerben, wie es im Vaterland für den Besitzlosen nur schwierig zu Erlangen ist.[6]

While other peoples are driven to unrest and uprisings by unemployment and the threatening danger of starvation, the superior German vigorously pulls himself together and seizes his walking stick, not shying away from the path across the ocean in order to gain more elbow room for free movement and expansion and possibly to acquire his own piece of ground and land, as it is difficult for those without means to obtain it in the fatherland.

The courage he attributes to the German who refuses to stay home and suffer the indignities of poverty and hunger, who seizes his walking stick and sets off across the sea is constitutive of the noble wanderer. The trope is reinforced in colonial cultures of the everyday, as in the board game pieces for Deutschland's Kolonien-Spiel (1890; figure 20).

Not only does he evoke the trope of the colonial explorer and adventurer, he conjures the moralizing tone of Kant's answer to the question "Was ist Aufkärung?" The condition of the unenlightened is self-imposed; the inertia of the comfortably compliant keeps them in a state of tutelage. Meinecke seeks common cause with an extended European family, elevating the English, Scandinavians, and Germans as examples "unter den Völkern des germanischen Stammes" (among the Germanic tribes) attributable to not only their skill and work ethic, but also their independence and individual autonomy. This, he claims, has only recently emerged "bei den romanischen Völkern, besonders den Italienern, eine bemerkenswerte Auswanderungslust" (among the Latin peoples, especially the Italians, a remarkable desire for emigration) often to the same regions, such as South America, also preferred by the Germans.[7] The pull factors of climate, lineage, and adventure I explored in previous chapters echoes in Meinecke's nonfiction; he thus augments the German-centric pres-

---

6. Gustav Meinecke, *Katechismus der Auswanderung. Kompaß für Auswanderer nach europäischen Ländern, Asien, Afrika, den deutschen Kolonien, Australien, Süd- und Zentralamerika, Mexiko, den Vereinigten Staaten von Amerika und Kanada*, 7th ed. Vollständig und neu bearbeitet. Mit 4 in den Text gedruckten Karten (Leipzig: J. J. Weber, 1896), 6.

7. Meinecke, *Katechismus*, 6.

Wohin? The Ungovernable 251

Figure 20. Playing pieces 2. Deutschland's Kolonien-Spiel (Germany's colonial game). Getty Research Institute Digital Collection, https://rosettaapp.getty.edu/delivery/DeliveryManagerServlet?dps_pid=IE1540602.

ence in extra-European spaces. Throughout the guide, Meinecke erects ideological and economic constructs to foster a sense of moral patriotism and allegiance to the nation the reader is poised to leave.

To resolve the cognitive dissonance that might ensure from the dilemma just described, Meinecke adds consideration for the Motherland to the list of priorities for emigration, inscribing an act of patriotism into departure for far-flung shores. Central to the sacrificial act of emigration is informed selection through which allegiance can be maintained in answer to the question of the "Wohin":

> Damit hängt nicht nur das Wohl der Auswanderer selbst, sondern auch das Interesse des Mutterlandes zusammen, denn nur wenn die Deutschen sich in hinreichender Anzahl in gesunden, fruchtbaren und wohlgelegenen Gegenden ansiedeln, erhalten sie ihre Nationalbildung vielleicht während einiger Generationen aufrecht.[8]

> On that depend not only the well-being of the emigrant himself, but also the interests of the Motherland, for only if Germans settle themselves in sufficient numbers in healthy, arable, and well-situated regions will they maintain their national character perhaps for a few generations.

---

8. Meinecke, *Katechismus*, 8. Emphasis in the original through letter spacing.

Meinecke imputes a national, nearly genealogical destiny to migration. Germans must gravitate toward other Germans in order to attain the critical mass that would preserve the investment in national education. Underlining this advice, he paints a dire picture, elaborating the consequences of spreading German selves too thinly: Germans lose their language, customs, and connections to the homeland, "so daß in ihnen wirklich ein Kapital an Geld und Bildung für Deutschland verloren geht, daß sie nur 'Völkerdünger' bilden[9] (so that a fortune invested in them of money and education is lost with them, that they serve merely as the fertilizer for other peoples). Widely used circa 1900, "Völkerdünger" accrues negative connotations perhaps unintended by German nationalists. Meinecke inflects the sense of racial squandering with economic waste, literally "manure," and preserves the sense of rivalry with other immigrants and natives who reap the benefits. Thus emigrating in isolation constitutes emigrating without purpose, a misspent investment of money and education that only serves to "fertilize" other nations and populations. Among a sufficiently German population, production implicitly flourishes and Germans reap the harvest.

With the world within reach, Meinecke broaches the topic of the tropics; climate is everything. In the *Katechismus*, he connects climate among Argentina, Brazil, South American countries, Southwest Africa, Central America, Australia: "daß die Jahreszeiten in jenen Gegenden ganz anders fallen, als bei uns oder in den unseren Klima mehr entsprechenden gemäßigten Teilen der Vereingten Staaten"[10] (that the seasons in those regions fall completely differently than at home or in the more temperate parts of the United States that correspond more to our own climate). In the section about the Near East, Africa, the German colonies, Australia, Central America, and Mexico—he considers the latter to be outside the region—he begins to answer the question of where Germans, in fact, can be found. Here he blurs any borders between displacement, migration, and colonization:

---

9. Meinecke, *Katechismus*, 8. He sketches the sad life of Germans scattered among other people: "wo sie vereinzelt, wie verlorene Posten, unter anderen Völkerelementen verstreut sind... ihre Bildung, ihre zum Teil unschätzbaren nationalen Eigentümlichkeiten nicht bloß zu erhalten, sondern auch nutz- und segenbringend fortzupflanzen und zu verbreiten. Nur zu oft geht ihnen aller Reiz, alle Freude des Lebens verloren, wenn sie so unter lauter Fremden wohnen, denen in ihrer Sprache sogar das Wort für 'Gemüt' fehlt, weil sie von der Sache selbst keinen Begriff haben" (36–37).

10. Meinecke, *Katechismus*, 32.

Wohin? The Ungovernable

Besser könnte man wohl fragen: Wo haben sich Deutsche **nicht** niedergelassen? Denn man mag die Welt umsegeln und sie durchziehen vom Ausgang bis zum Niedergang der Sonne—in allen Weltteilen, in den verstecktesten Erdenwinkeln, in den fernsten Urwäldern Nord-Amerikas, in der Tropenwelt Südamerikas, unter Afrikas und Indiens Glutsonne, in den weiten Reichen von Siam, China und Japan, im fernen Australien und auf Neuseeland, auf den lachenden Inseln der blauen Südsee und im hohen Norden an der Grenze des ewigen Eises—überall findet man Deutsche, die durch musterhaften Landbau, emsigen Gewerbfleiß, strebsamen Handelsgeist, durch die Macht der Wissenschaft, Kunst und Intelligenz zum materiellen Gedeihen wie zum geistigen und sittlichen Aufschwung des Landes beitragen, wo sie sich angesiedelt haben.[11]

One could more simply ask: Where have German **not** settled? For one may sail around the world and traverse it from the rising to the setting of the sun—in all parts of the world, in all the most hidden corners, in the farthest jungles of North America, in the tropics of South America, under Africa's and India's fiery sun, in the vast realms of Siam, China, and Japan, in distant Australia and on New Zealand, on the laughing islands of the blue South Sea and in the high North of the border of eternal ice—everywhere they have settled one finds Germans, who, through exemplary agriculture, industry, ambitious entrepreneurial spirit, through the power of science, art, and intelligence, contribute to the material prosperity and intellectual and moral upswing of the land.

Invoking the tropes of German industry and ingenuity, Meinecke makes them citizens of the world, implicitly unraveling any narrative about the provincial or belated nation. But he privileges North America and South America, in comparison to the position of Germans in Central America, due to an inhospitable climate. Important to his pitch is the possibility of attaining citizenship, thus he reprises the immigration laws for the respective destinations.

The East of Africa

The catechism of emigration charts the routes of global German imaginaries sustained throughout centuries without official nationhood or colonies, but

---

11. Meinecke, *Katechismus*, 35.

with a commitment to the practical during the Age of Empire. Meinecke's personal investment in sugar production, mentioned above, extends to the cultivation of other crops in the region. That publication aimed to persuade Germans to invest in the secure prospects of sugar cultivation in Pangani. His strategy: assure them of "ein fruchtbares und zukunftssicheres Alluvialgebiet haben, welches nur der Erschließung durch europäisches Kapital und europäische Technik bedarf, um die reichsten Erträge abzuwerfen" (having a fertile alluvial region, secure for the future, which needs only to be developed by European capital and European technology in order to yield the richest returns).[12] Included in this volume, travel letters describe the land, the ethnic groups, and also details on the punishment of infractions; the mode of punishment will occupy Meinecke's fiction as well, and I return to this point below. During a trip to the Island of the Dead, Meinecke notes visiting a Portuguese fort; this triggers thoughts about the morality model of colonizers. Referring to "Wilde aus Europa" (savages from Europe), he condemns those who douse their life of colonial monotony and boredom with excessive drinking; he concludes they should be sent home as soon as possible.[13] In doing so, Meinecke overturns, or at least destabilizes, the trope of the savage and civilized with the ideals of colonization, claiming that it is impossible to have a colony made up entirely of moderate people, "welche dem N*ger zum Muster dienen" (who serve as a model for the n*groes), but he insists the gap between the ideal and the real is excessively wide.[14] Consistently, the colonial investor and traveler reverts to the theme of morality, always comparing the hope of German retrospection and stalwartness with the vagaries of their predecessors: "Ich will auf diesen Gegenstand nicht weiter eingehen; eine fortschreitende Verrohung der Sitten würde uns zu Verhältnissen führen, welche von den holländisch-indischen des vorigen Jahrhunderts nicht allzuweit entfernt sein würden"[15] (I do not wish to engage with this object any further; a progressing deterioration of customs would lead us to relationships that are not all that distant from the Dutch-Indian ones of the previous century).

Repeatedly, Meinecke makes reference to the Dutch exploitation of Indigenous labor, which he cites as a negative example. In his *Deutsche Kultiva-*

---

12. Gustav Meinecke, *Zuckeruntersuchungen am Pangani* (Vegatationsbilder von Dr. Otto Warburg, 2nd edition; first edition 1895 (Berlin: Deutscher Kolonial-Verlag, 1909), Vorwort.
13. Meinecke, *Zuckeruntersuchungen*, 24.
14. Meinecke, *Zuckeruntersuchungen*, 24.
15. Meinecke, *Zuckeruntersuchungen*, 24–25.

tion in Ostafrika und der Kaffeebau, he delineates the cultural politics in East Africa with the aim of putting German trade in a prominent position; the inevitable byproduct of this achievement, he argues, elevates the natives to a higher level of culture ("die Eingeborenen auf eine höhere Stufe der Kultur zu bringen").[16] His target audience is made up of the German colonial societies, whom he baits with criticism of the Dutch and switches with translational research. As the region is not yet fit for German settlement, he focuses on the ability to work with the locals. The argument arcs away from the usual though unrealistic colonial script. Meinecke opposes slavery and advocates for a closer relationship between the German administration and Blacks. In part, he is leveraging the comparatively benign impression made by the German newcomers against the alignment between the British and the Muslims of East Africa. The Dutch he deems complicit:

> Auf ein staatlich organisiertes Arbeitssystem für die Eingeborenen nach holländlischem Muster, ein "Kultursystem," welches die Produktion der Eingeborenen in ungeahnter Weise erhöhen müßte, werden wir aber wohl in der nächsten Zeit verzichten müssen, da weder staatlicher noch privater Unternehmungsgeist sich vorerst an die besonders schwierigen ostafrikanischen Verhältnisse wird wagen wollen; aber wir sehen nicht ein, warum man jetzt noch zögert, mit der Anlage von privaten Pflanzungen vorzugehen, um gute Kapitalanlagen zu schaffen dadurch, daß man wenigstens einen Teil unserer aus andern Ländern einzuführenden Kolonialprodukte deckt.[17]

For the foreseeable future, however, we will probably have to avoid the state-organized labor system based on the Dutch model, a "cultural system" that would increase the productivity of native labor in unexpected ways, since neither state nor private entrepreneurship will venture into the especially difficult East African conditions for now; but we do not understand why there is still hesitation about starting private plantations in order to create good capital investments through covering at least a part of our colonial products to be imported from other countries.

---

16. Gustav Meinecke, *Deutsche Kultivation in Ostafrika und der Kaffeebau*, Berlin: Carl Heymanns Verlag, 1892), unpaginated. The title page identifies this publication as a "Sonderdruck aus der Deutschen Kolonialzeitung mit einer kolorirten Karte."
17. Meinecke, *Deutsche Kultivation in Ostafrika*, unpaginated.

The ability of the Germans to regulate the labor supply intertwines with Meinecke's racialized logic and a rejection of a "Dutch model" implemented in the West Indies to train administrators in the local culture in order to achieve better results.[18] In dealing with labor issues, potential alliances, animosities, or common interests with the English and Dutch need not always prevail. Elsewhere, for example, in the sugar book, he holds up the centuries-long history of Portugal and Spain as colonizers and recommends the German administrators learn from them without just shrugging their shoulders and turning to the British for models.[19] With relation to coffee, again, the Dutch should not be imitated. Florian Wagner elucidates the strategy that drove the Dutch model, which replaced Indigenous experts and administrators with ostensibly well-trained, knowledgeable, and climate-resistant Europeans: "According to the Dutch model, administrators should be specialists in native culture, resistant to the tropical climate, and rule independently of the 'unprofessional' bureaucracy in the mother country."[20]

In East Africa, Germans need to learn from the mistakes of other countries, and he cites the example of Holland's tobacco investments in Sumatra.[21] All endeavors should earn a profit for the *Mutterland* and the colonies. The moral of this story cuts across all crops and all colonizers.

The discourse about sugar pulls away from the fanciful and draws the audience to the research-based science of colonization. In a moment that recalls the letter, if not the spirit, of Lessing's insistence on the creation of knowledge in charting the world, Meinecke takes aim at the adventurers and thrill seekers, triggered by the need to realize the importance of the river. Disparaging the extant "Afrikaliteratur" that fails to provide any useful economic details, he lambastes the hunters:

> Es lag in der Natur der Sache, daß sich die Herren, welche nach Ostafrika gekommen waren, um Löwen zu schießen, ein Abenteuer zu erleben, oder sich den Ruhm als Helden, woran von vornherein Niemand zweifelte, attes-

---

18. See Florian Wagner, "The Dutch Model and the Reform of Colonial Training Schools," in *Colonial Internationalism and the Governmentality of Empire, 1893–1982* (Cambridge: Cambridge University Press, 2022).
19. Meinecke, *Zuckeruntersuchungen*, 82.
20. Wagner, "The Dutch Model," 110. https://www.cambridge.org/core/books/abs/colonial-internationalism-and-the-governmentality-of-empire-18931982/politics-of-comparison/78961A9801394335AD0321C251D6F737.
21. Meinecke, *Deutsche Kultivation in Ostafrika*, 8.

Wohin? The Ungovernable

tiren zu lassen, um wirtschalftliche Sachen wenig kümmerten. Neuerdings ist man aber auch auf dieser Seite zu der Ueberzeugung gekommen, daß der Kolonialbesitz ohne wirklich gesunde wirthschaftliche Entwickelung ein für das deutsche Volk recht theures Vergnügen ist, und bemüht sich, das nothwendige Verständniß zu Erlangen.[22]

It was in the nature of things that the gentlemen who had come to East Africa to shoot lions, to have an adventure, or to claim glory as a hero, which from the beginning no one doubted, did not concern themselves with economic matters. Lately, however, on this side one has come to the conviction that colonial possessions, without sound economic development, are an extremely expensive pleasure for the German people; and is concerned with achieving the necessary understanding.

Thus Meinecke disparages the lion-hunting compatriots whose desire for confirming their heroism outweighs the development of a German colonial economy. Trophies for big-game hunters do not count in the imperial inventories. Unproductive protectorates cost the German people, and the adventurers who view Africa as a proving ground or photo op do so at the expense of their fellow citizens. Arguing from the position of someone on the ground in East Africa, Meinecke advocates for an economic learning curve, as both a personal and political investor.

As in other works, the homogenization of local history serves Meinecke's rhetorical goal, not of attracting settlers from Germany, but financial support. He conserves a modicum of sensitivity to the unbalance of power relationships in the region for the hierarchy the Germans inherit: the European colonizers, Arabs, Africans, and the enslaved. In a description of the reluctant hospitality he received from Arab hosts, he casts the tension in political terms of beneficial alliances: "aber ich bin der Ansicht, daß der Araber—in diesem Landestheile wenigstens—bald zu der Ueberzeugung kommen wird, daß der Deutsche im Grunde sein Freund ist"[23] (but I believe that the Arab, at least in this part of the country, will soon come to the conclusion that the German is basically his friend). That affinity has in part to do with racial hierarchy, and I turn to this below. Meinecke's ultimate concern is the survival of the white race in the future of East Africa. Finally, he asks the question:

22. Meinecke, *Zuckeruntersuchungen*, 56.
23. Meinecke, *Zuckeruntersuchungen*, 62.

"Wird die weiße Rasse sich unvermischt erhalten und fortpflanzen können, oder wird sie in eine Mischlingsbevölkerung untergehen?"[24] (Will the white race be able to survive and reproduce itself unmixed, or will it perish in a mixed-breed population?). Because of the climate and the insufficient state of research into the questions, he cannot pass further judgment (*Urtheil*) on the future. He does, however, turn to fiction and colonial ethnography to find answers. While he blurs some borders, others need enforcement, because in the end, accounts must be settled.

Palmkerne . . . Elfenbein . . . Kakao

Under the rubric of trade, Meinecke introduces the economy of crime and punishment in taking inventory of products and their profitability. He takes stock of key products: palm kernels, used to produce oil, ivory, and cocoa. The Deutsch-Afrikanische Handelsgesellscht (alongside the English) was primarily responsible for driving trade. As he notes, "Im Kamerun selbst liegt der Handel zum größten Teil in den Händen der mit Weißen besetzten Faktoreien, wohin die Eingeborenen Produkte zum Verkauf gegen Erzeugnisse der heimischen Industrie bringen"[25] (In Cameroon itself, trade is largely in the hands of white-owned factories; the natives bring products to be sold in exchange for products from local industry). Local labor and the people who perform it become part of the overhead. They factor into Meinecke's inventory only in their need to be disciplined and punished.

In captioning the figures of Africans in chains on the same page, Meinecke repeats an assumption about racialized punishment for Black men and women alike. The image displays a thief in chains (figure 21), with the added and oddly exculpatory note: "Da der N*ger die Einsperrung als Strafe nicht empfindet, vielmehr al seine Art Pension mit freier Verpflegung ansieht, so läßt man die verurteilten N*ger im Freien an Ketten arbeiten, um Fluchtversuche zu verhinern" (Because the Black does not perceive imprisonment as punishment, but much more as a kind of hotel with free service, for this reason the condemned Blacks are allowed to work outside in chains, to hin-

---

24. Meinecke, *Zuckeruntersuchungen*, 82.
25. Gustav Meinecke, *Deutschen Kolonien in Wort und Bild: Geschichte, Länder- und Völkerkunde, Tier- und Pflanzenwelt, Handels- und Wirtschaftsverhältnisse der Schutzgebiete des Deutschen Reiches* 2n exp. ed. (Leipzig: Verlag von J. J. Weber, 1901), 29.

Wohin? The Ungovernable

Figure 21. "A thief in chains," from Gustav Meinecke, *Deutsche Kolonien in Wort und Bild*, "Kamerun" 29.

der escape attempts).[26] The workflow relies on the *"Eingeborenen"* to provide raw materials processed and sold by the white-owned factories. Meinecke's colonial gaze fixes on men and women who, he reasons, exist in a racialized space in which incarceration equals leisure. Meinecke posits a carceral ontology, theorized by Saskia Sassen in *Expulsions*, to account for the trope of the recalcitrant worker whose labor cannot be optimized. Sassen, whose earlier work defined the global city, looks at the trajectories of neoliberal capitalism's "expulsions,"[27] the forced and brutal displacement of economically "remaindered" (my term) human beings, destined for migration or incarceration. The projection of the lazy savage, familiar from Kant, reinforces the relationship between characteristics, appropriate climate, labor, and skin color.

Meinecke replicates the Enlightenment model of moral complexion as well as Schiller's chiasmus of somehow choosing the experience of freedom in absolute confinement. Meinecke further extends the alleged perception of confinement not as punishment, but as a "closed society," from Cameroon to German East Africa. In the caption in this image, also from *Deutsche Kolonien in Wort und Bild*, in the section on "Deutsch-Ostafrika,"[28] he attributes the same attitude to the woman in chains, this time with an Arab overseer who does use the whip (figure 22). "Von Mineralien sind Eisen und besonders Gold zu erwähnen" (Among minerals, iron and especially gold must be mentioned), he writes. In enchaining, iron is put to use. Though Meinecke acknowledges this brutality, he explains that it is also present in English territories. The Swahili word *mnioror* (*minyororo*) means chains. It is a metonym for the women themselves; their punishment is normalized as the means to force their labor. The plurals of this hierarchy evoke the inventory of races beyond the four Kant could imagine. Here I quote from a purportedly reliable narrator in Meinecke's novella, for his protagonist, on the ground in German East Africa, must come to terms with the new order: "Wir werden die Araber nie echt begreifen, denn eine Welt trennt uns von ihnen, wir können sie nur beherrschen"[29] (We will never really comprehend the Arabs, for a world separates them from us, we can only control them). Meinecke, who turns to fiction to explore the implications of this administrative logic, dis-

---

26. Meinecke, *Deutschen Kolonien in Wort und Bild*, "Kamerun" 29.
27. Saskia Sassen, *Expulsions: Brutality and Complexity in the Global Economy* (Cambridge, MA: Harvard University Press, 2014).
28. Meinecke, *Deutschen Kolonien in Wort und Bild*, "Deutsch-Ostafrika," 60.
29. Gustav Meinecke, *Der arme Sidi Abderrachman. Eine ostafrikanische Geschichte*. 6. Auflage (Berlin: Deutscher Kolonial-Verlag, 1897), 88.

Wohin? The Ungovernable 261

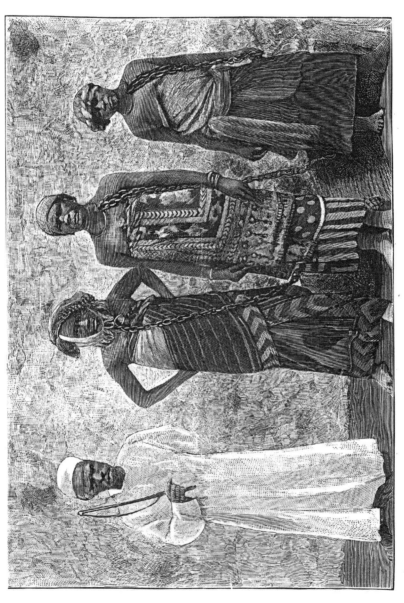

Figure 22. "Chained women prisoners with their overseer," "Deutsch-Ostafrika," 60.

plays the punishments employed across the continent by local customs to justify racial hierarchies.

Meinecke overlooks, or leaves unremarked, the agency of *their* gaze and their postures; it is possible to read defiance in the position of the hands and arms and the intensity of the direct look at the spectator. Scholar and activist bell hooks writes about the "oppositional gaze" of the Black female spectator, opening with her recollection of childhood punishment for staring. She recounts her surprise when learning that "white slaveowners punished enslaved black people for looking."[30] Reading Michel Foucault and Stuart Hall and her experiences, hooks sees the gaze in a global political context: "Even in the worst circumstances of domination," she writes, "the ability to manipulate one's gaze in the face of structures of domination that would contain it, opens up the possibility of agency."[31] Meinecke sees the containment, not the indictment, in the Black female gaze. Instead, he sticks to the script of honoring local customs, the employment of Arabs to oversee Africans, and the practices adopted by the colonizers, to punish harshly. Meinecke's fiction of the time also explores the colonial optics of German-centric masculinity in East Africa. His entertainment writing casts characters who cannot contain themselves or others, and some who are capable of understanding the literal and figural chains of sexual desire across cultural and racial boundaries.

From the Library of Exotic Novellas

Meinecke locates several works of fiction that engage themes of racial difference, emigration and migration, and family intrigue in the United States. In the preface to *Aus dem Creolenlande Erzählungen*, summarized in the previous chapter, he opens with mobility: he observes from an amused distance a "prairie" ship heading to "Arkansaw." Three editions appeared between 1888 and 1896. The only other work designated fiction in his oeuvre, Meinecke's East African story appeared in four editions published between 1897 and 1900. Sidi Abderrachman's unfolds in an official colony. The protagonist, an Arab in a position of precarity, despite his money and influence, experiences adversity because of a woman's desire. Considerations of gender among the

---

30. bell hooks, "The Oppositional Gaze: Black Female Spectators," in *Black Looks: Race and Representation* (Boston: South End Press, 1992), 115–31, here 115.

31. hooks, "The Oppositional Gaze," 116.

colonized and their interaction with the administration appear nowhere else in Meinecke's work, save the occasional observation about local domestic custom. Several scholarly works have highlighted the gendered discourses in the Age of Empire, foremost among them Lora Wildenthal's *German Women for Empire*. Literary studies of German women writers contribute significantly to the emancipatory and imperial desires of German women involved in colonial enterprises, both in the colonies and in the Motherland.

One figure in particular, Frieda von Bülow, is important in the context of my analysis of Meinecke's novella for several reasons. First, she writes from the same locales at the same time, and her perspective aligns and varies from Meinecke's in illuminating ways. Her ennobled envy of the British colonizers has received attention.[32] In East Africa, she describes the streetscape through a German gaze of mimetic desire. She recounts the view:

> Mit dieser Biegung verwandelte sich die Scene vor uns wie durch Zauber. Mitten in der N*ger-Armseligkeit, indischen von Unsauberkeit strotzenden Kramläden und arabischen Schutthaufen sieht man auf einmal ein Stück Englands vor sich mit seiner blanken in voll entfalteter Blüte stehender Kultur. Erstaunen, Bewunderung und nationale Eifersucht erfüllten mich bei dem überraschenden Anblick. "Wenn *wir* doch erst so weit wären!" rief ich. "Das wird wohl noch einige Jahrzehnte dauern," meinte lächelnd mein Führer, "hier steckt viel englisches Geld darin und jahrelange Arbeit."[33]

> Rounding this bend, the scene before us transformed as if by magic. In the midst of N*gro poverty, Indian general stores full of junk and Arab piles of rubble, you suddenly see a piece of England in front of you with its pure culture in full bloom. Astonishment, admiration, and national jealousy filled me at the surprising sight. "If only *we* had come this far!" I cried. "That will probably take a few more decades," my guide said with a smile, "there is a lot of English money invested here and decades of work."

The envy she articulates presents itself to the prospective colonizers as a challenge to achieve the level of British imperial presences across the continent.

---

32. Frieda Freiin von Bülow, *Reisescizzen und Tagebuchblätter aus Deutsch-Ostafrica*. First published by Walther & Apolant, Berlin 1889, edited and with an introduction, notes, and bibliography by Katharina von Hammerstein (Berlin: trafo, 2012). Von Hammerstein opens her introduction with the last sentence of the above quotation.

33. Bülow, *Reisescizzen und Tagebuchblätter*, 81.

The presence of German women in supporting roles was a focus of zealous colonial advocates, particularly after the banning of *"Mischehen"* (mixed marriages). In the fictional realm, Meinecke ultimately advocates for the presence of married German men in his interpretation of East Africa.

The narrative features the exigencies of Sidi Abderrachman, a Muslim slave trader in East Africa whose erstwhile wife, the beautiful, mercurial, and impetuous Fatme, seeks German colonial justice to obtain a divorce from the jealous and abusive Khamis, Sidi's friend. Despite the title and the narrative perspective, the fiction thematizes a moral message to German men about local laws and those they govern. The love-hate triangle story intersects with the lives of enslaved Blacks, British and German officers, public institutions, and private spaces. In the narrative present, the law preventing slavery disrupted more than the economic exploits of the East African locale: there was increasing difficulty with slave trading.[34] The reader learns that Germans do not speak Arabic; at best, they learn some Swahili, badly. German administrators are in the process of assuming governance of the protectorate. Meinecke incorporates political and economic topics, such as the local preference for German over English rule, trade in ivory across borders, efforts at manumission, and Arab elites recapturing those they had enslaved. Conversation topics among the colonizers range from the dangers of excessive drinking, the heat, availability of edible food, cooling wine, the unknowability of Arabs, the need to encourage Black labor and alliances with them, and the eccentricities of local customs. Throughout, Meinecke uses the Swahili words for concepts and social regulatory practices. The *Bezirksamtsmann* presides over the court or *Shauri*, for example. Khamis takes a second wife, a *Suari*, and Fatme insists she acknowledges his right to do so, even though it ostensibly contributed to her desire for a divorce. The moral of the story emerges from transgressing local and colonial logics that govern sexual relationships.

The harem features prominently in the tale of Sidi Abderrachman. The characters first tease their host about his marital status. Early in the story, the *Bezirksamtsmann* and the *Bezirksschreiber*, characters defined by their roles, approach Kharmis to hunt wild boar. He recommends they do so on Sidi's land; boars qualified as unclean. At the table, the conversation quickly turns to manly ridicule. The *Bezirksamtmann* teases Sidi: "He, Sidi,' rief jetzt der Bezirksamtmann herüber, 'zeige uns doch einmal Deinen Harem!'"[35]

---

34. Meinecke, *Der arme Sidi Abderrachman*, 36.
35. Meinecke, *Der arme Sidi Abderrachman*, 39.

(Hey, Sidi, the district officer called over, come on, show us your harem!). Sidi is embarrassed, and the district officer continues with what he perceives as a humorous story about harems. In responding to a fire in Pangani "im N*gerviertel," he encountered an example of how challenging it could be to respect local customs. One can, he insists, always tease an Arab about the harem: "denn das ist ein wunder Punkt" (for it is a sore point). He recounts his experience of trying to prevent the fire in the Makutihütten. The owner, "ein kleiner Schwarzer Kerl" (a little Black guy), would not allow the Germans into his place because of his harem. The district officer tells the owner a story that makes him laugh and drop the sword he threatens them with. The German prevailed, and found:

"Drei alte, verunzelte N*gerinnen.... Es gehe mir einer weg mit diesen Haremgeschichten, es ist alles eitel Humbug.... wie so vieles im Orient"[36] (Three old, unkempt Black women—It is just too much for me with harem stories, it is all vain humbug... like so much in the Orient). Then he pulls the story from his pocket and reads from "Unter Palmen," a tale involving erotic displacement to Egypt,[37] to prove his point. The listeners doze off. In addition to rounding up numbers for imperial statistics, the story embeds the meagerness of the "harem" to a realistic three women.

This episode prepares the central conflict between the district officer and local custom. Throughout, there are references to sexual encounters among Germans and others. In lamenting the behavior of some fellow officers and their search for diversion, he claims, "Andere unternahmen Expeditionen in das Innere, um Ruhm und Ehre zu gewinnen, und Manche vegnügten sich schließlich mit den schwarzen oder braunen Töchtern des Landes"[38] (Others undertook expeditions into the interior to gain fame and honor, and many finally amused themselves with the black or brown daughters of the land). Dalliances with the daughters is seen as something of a last resort. While this

---

36. Meinecke, *Der arme Sidi Abderrachman*, 39–40.

37. Meinecke, *Der arme Sidi Abderrachman*, 40–41. Scholarship on abusive and criminal acts and German-male/African-female relationships has received interest (see Lora Wildenthal, *German Women for Empire, 1884–1945*. Durham, NC: Duke University Press, 2011). For a more focused look at abuses in the German Southwest Africa colony, prostitution, predatory soldiers, interventionist missionaries, and specific cases, see Wolfram Hartmann, "Urges in the Colony. Men and Women in Colonial Windhoek, 1890–1905," *Journal of Namibian Studies* 1 (2007): 39–71. See also Daniel J. Walther, "Sex, Race, and Empire: White Male Sexuality and the 'Other' in Germany's Colonies, 1894–1914," *German Studies Review* 33, no. 1 (February 2010): 45–71.

38. Meinecke, *Der arme Sidi Abderrachman*, 83.

behavior is tolerated, fulfilling many a colonial fantasy, the breach of gendered justice has more serious consequences.

During an otherwise routine *Shauri*, a Swahili word for a public debate about rights and wrongs, with the district officer present and in charge, Fatme appears before the assembled men along with the Swahili women enslaved by her husband. She seeks European justice.

> Während die Araberin durch die Feinheit ihrer Form, um nicht zu sagen Zierlichkeit auffiel, repräsentierte dagegen das Suahelimädchen den fleischigen, mehr sinnlichen Typus der Negerrasse. Ihr ganzes Auftreten, ihre Blicke hatten etwas freies, gefallsüchtiges, aber dabei auch naives, wie es bei harmlosen Naturkindern noch gesunden werden soll. . . . [39]

> While the Arab woman was striking through the delicacy of her shape, not to say daintiness, the Swahili girl by contrast represented that fleshy, more sensual type of the n*gro race. Her entire comportment, her glances had something free, coquettish, but also at the same time naïve, as harmless children of nature should still be healthy.

Fatme is instructed to return in two weeks for a verdict. Khamis attempts to dissuade her, trying to provoke her temper with his references to the new wife, but Fatme feigns indifference, according him his Suria, the practice of enslaving a wife or concubine. As it turns out, Khamis realizes he actually loves her and refuses to let her go. This admission of emotional attachment suggest Khamis is a possible exception to the local rules governing male-female relationships. The heteronormative social practices, in which women's worth is measured by the male gaze, draws closer some aspects of German, Arab, and Black African male agency. Acts of violence and seduction put the Europeanness of the district officer's ingrained masculinity on trial.

In the interval between Fatme's original and second appearance at the *Shauri*, she becomes something of a celebrity; she receives visits from other women, for example, an indication of precarious female agency under conditions that raise questions about the similarities between enslavement and the harem, questions Meinecke does not resolve. Reports of Khamis's mistreatment of Fatme spread: "welche wie die Sage ging, von ihrem Ehemanne gefoltert wurde—man sprach sogar vom Brenneisen, mit dem der Elende

---

39. Meinecke, *Der arme Sidi Abderrachman*, 60.

sie zu quälen begann"[40] (who, as the legend went, had been tortured by her husband—one even spoke of a branding iron with which the wretched man began to torture her). Khamis endeavors to prevent his wife from seeking further assistance outside the realm of local custom. Meinecke makes clear his motive, which exceeds love, for Khamis contemplates, "wie Fatme dem Machtbereich der Europäer entzogen werden könnte"[41] (how Fatme could be removed from the European sphere of influence [or power]). Although the *Shauri* as an institution prevails, the district officer presides over it. During the proceedings, Fatme commits an unthinkable act: She unveils herself; the narrator describes her beauty at length before she asks for protection. The local men decry her brazen behavior; though she is debased, she is still a member of their community, and one man insists he will take her home. For the district officer, this is a bridge too far. He pulls a knife and defends her, playing the role of indignant hero: "Ich kümmere mich den Teufel um Eure Sitten, um Euer Desturi, mit dem Ihr alles zudeckt, was faul ist."[42] (I do not give a damn about your customs, your *desturi* [Swahili word for customs], which you use to cover up everything that is rotten). Meinecke's narrative voice editorializes: not the knife itself, but the man's personality-inspired fear: "Der eigenthümliche stählerne Glanz in den Augen des Bezirkamtmanns nahm sie alle gefangen. . . . sie kannten den Ausdruck."[43] (They were captivated by the peculiar steely glow in the magistrate's eyes. . . . they knew the expression). The district officer sees to her accommodation and seeks to untangle the complexities of his dilemma. Ultimately, Sidi takes her back, but higher-level administrators deliver the moral of the story on their official visit.

Meinecke invokes two colonial tropes to help the district officer see reason. During an official visit from the *Verwaltungsbeamter* and *Geheimrath*, the administrators mobilize the imperative to colonize and protect German investments in good and bad times, for the greater good of the empire; they also mobilize the importance of German women. After official meetings and duties, there is a celebration. The *Verwaltungsbeamter* toasts the kaiser:

> Es gilt, die große Idee der Entwickelung des Deutschtums in seinen so vielfachen Verzweigungen über den Erdtheil mit aller Macht zu verfolgen, unsere Stellung nicht nur wirthschaftlich und kommerziell, sondern auch politisch

---

40. Meinecke, *Der arme Sidi Abderrachman*, 79.
41. Meinecke, *Der arme Sidi Abderrachman*, 81.
42. Meinecke, *Der arme Sidi Abderrachman*, 97.
43. Meinecke, *Der arme Sidi Abderrachman*, 97.

zu stärken, und den weltumfassenden universalen Geist des Deutschthums nach den modernen Begriffen national zu vertiefen.[44]

It is a matter of this: to pursue with all our power the great idea of developing Germanness in its so many manifestations across the continent; to strengthen our position not only economically and commercially, but also politically; and to deepen nationally the world-encompassing spirit of Germanness in accordance with modern concepts.

The glasses are raised and the sentiment toasted harmoniously. This official articulates the trope of German universality as constitutive to the colonial project. German modernity itself takes center stage in the universal. This vision is the global German imaginary.

In conversation with the district officer, the same official, "der hohe Beamte," chastises him for not giving the woman to the Arabs, even if they were to kill her; it is their decision. The higher-level administrator bats aways all the district officer's objections and counterarguments. Ultimately, he says, we Germans can exert some influence over them, but Germans in East Africa are not in a position to force the issues. Waxing philosophical, he concedes that change may occur eventually, but the German presence is temporary because the climate is unsuitable. This official retires, and Meinecke offers another solution, issued from the mouth of the *Postbeamter*.

The presence of supportive German women forms the core of this official's message. Quite succinctly, he declares, "Meine Herren! Man kolonisirt mit der Frau, nicht mit dem Gewehr. . . ."[45] (Gentlemen! One colonizes with the woman, not with the gun). The celebration aboard the steamship provides the occasion for a debate about German men. The postmaster has brought his wife, who awaits him at home. The men know her; she enables his long-term service, and there is much winking about regular sex in the statements. Throughout, the success of the English in colonizing forms the subtext. The *Postbeamter* then challenges their masculinity: "Ihr seid alle so tief gesunken, daß Ihr keine große Mühe aufwenden wollt, Eure Bräute und Liebsten hierher zu bringen, daß Ihr mit einem Wort bei den deutschen Mädchen die Lust, Euch zu folgen, nicht rege machen wollt." (You have all sunk so low that you will not make the great effort of bringing your brides and loves ones

---

44. Meinecke, *Der arme Sidi Abderrachman*, 104–5.
45. Meinecke, *Der arme Sidi Abderrachman*, 111.

here, that you do not want to awaken in German girls with a single word the desire to follow you.); the response: "Ein allgemeines Oho! war darauf die Antwort"[46] (A general oho! was the answer). This alternative model to success of whiteness in Africa does not so much decommission colonization as weaponize gender. The implied culprit is the ungovernable within white masculinity. Only those who can govern themselves should wield power over others. In the novella, well-placed political officials disparage the Arabs, who, as quoted above, can only be subordinated; the Germans must ally themselves with the freed Blacks against the former enslavers and German rivals.[47] Meinecke's narrative incorporates manumission; Sidi shows gratitude toward the servant Saud, a minor character in the novella, by giving him his freedom for helping get Fatme back. Ultimately, Meinecke delivers a moral message of self-governance, temperance, and ethnocentrism, especially in sexual exploits. Triumph and tribalism resonate in this revisionist fiction, which whitewashes any form of resistance.

Recovering Resistance

In José Arturo Saavedra Casco's work on Utenzi, a literary genre "which traditionally depicted epic themes relating to the prophet Mohammed and the heroes and martyrs of the Muslim faith,"[48] the author takes a critical retrospective look at the literary resistance in Swahili narrative poetry of the late nineteenth and early twentieth century, inclusive of the wars fought between 1888 and 1910. Through his reading of this genre, he confronts a whitewashed legacy of allied African peoples and their opposition to German colonial forces. His decolonial practice further indicts a tradition of scholarship on the study of Swahili poetry by Western scholars, with a focus on missionary evangelizing activity and on German and British. This, Casco concludes, is a "result of the concerns of the colonial government about having a language for administrative and bureaucratic purposes."[49] Scholarly efforts to acknowledge Black or Indigenous agency as decolonial practices lag behind most his-

---

46. Meinecke, *Der arme Sidi Abderrachman*, 111.
47. Meinecke, *Der arme Sidi Abderrachman*, 104–5.
48. José Arturo Saavedra Casco, *Utenzi, War Poems, and the German Conquest of East Africa: Swahili Poetry as Historical Source* (Trenton, NJ: Africa World Press, 2007), 1.
49. Casco, *Utenzi*, 85.

toriography.[50] The Swahili of Meinecke's novella was "the most suitable language for proselytizing the Christian faith," and also "a tool for administrative control and political domination."[51] Of the Maji Maji war (1905–1907), the focus of much German colonial study, Casco writes,

> The ideological framework immersed in African religious practices through the use of a powerful protective water, the simultaneous involvement of more than twenty ethnic groups against the Germans, the violence that was generated and the terrible economic and demographic catastrophe that its aftermath left in the region of the war—all these elements have aroused the interest and fascination of scholars, colonial administrators, politicians, and artists since the suppression of the uprising.[52]

Casco additionally argues that some interpret this war from another perspective, as the first Tanzanian "resistance movement against colonialism."[53]

My intent, in concluding, gathers attributes from the geographical and temporal dispersion of German identities across cultural and familial landscapes, only to be refocused by the rising threat of National Socialism. The legacies of colonialism recuperate the histories of local German-speaking "colonies." These illustrate the hegemony of colonial subjectivity, forged in the crucible of competition with European rivals, with and without colonial subjects. Meinecke took the *a prioris* of Kant's argument, all that had been excluded or naturalized by climate: the attribution of laziness and savagery to the Black Africans, and turned it into an aporia. He subtracts the African history of resistance and rebellion embodied by Hendrik Witbooi—whose group was not alone in challenging German colonialism in German Southwest Africa[54]—and renders it less than a footnote in the progress of German expansion and climatically correct settlement. The colonial projects, with

---

50. For a substantive reading of Witbooi's role, see Adam A. Blackler, "From Boondoggle to Settlement Colony: Hendrik Witbooi and the Evolution of Germany's Imperial Project in Southwest Africa, 1884–1894," *Central European History* 50 (2017): 449–70. Blackler understands Witbooi's activism as "indigenous agency," 452. His book deals extensively with "colonial encounters" in Germany's only settler colony. See Blackler, *An Imperial Homeland: Forging German Identity in Southwest Africa* (University Park, PA: Penn State University Press, 2022).
51. Casco, *Utenzi*, 85.
52. Casco, *Utenzi*, 239.
53. Casco, *Utenzi*, 239.
54. Blackler, "From Boondoggle to Settlement Colony," 453.

guns and women as weapons, is decolonialized by Casco's treatment of the Maji Maji war as an anticolonial resistance movement. Meinecke ultimately instrumentalizes the role of German administration and mastery in the tropics through tropes of freedom and enslavement, with a cynical jocularity that posits the absurdity of confining Blacks with enslaved souls and bodies; then, in a further exculpatory mapping of the punishment by labor in chains to German East Africa, attributes the practice to the racial hierarchy that places male Arabs in charge of disciplining and punishing Black women, under German oversight. Ultimately, around 1900, we see the projection of "magical" thinking about racial transformation, made miraculous around 1700 by the iconography of conversion, into the images of commercialization.

The elision or erasure of resistance provides German-speaking colonial agents and settlers, the farmer, the businessman, the postmaster—and their wives and families—with a sustaining narrative of entitlement that stems from a naturalized superiority, founded in a faith that they are agents of cultivation, of civilization, with an imperative to translate the national epic into an imperial story. A continuum becomes legible, from the 1492 Nuremberg-centric worlding represented in Behaim's *Erdapfel*, through the hesitant steps into shipping and the transatlantic slave trade, to America and Africa, through the totalizing and polarizing event of World War I. The last chapter examines the "first" footprints and last words spoken and written and monumentalized to map German-centric morals onto the world.

CHAPTER NINE

First Footprints and Recolonial Fantasies

While Ada Cramer's Farmersfrau memoir posed the urgent question: white or black, her son, Ernst Ludwig Cramer, continued the family tradition of writing about the colonial experience in Southwest Africa from the settler perspective. From the Brandenburg fortress to the Farmersfrau and Kinderfarm, German speakers follow and forge the paths along which internecine European rivalries across continents and oceans sustained racist hierarchies that underwrote a global identity. E. L. Cramer's autobiographical writings serve as an occasion for him to imagine himself, as a German colonial settler in political exile in the homeland, in the same genealogical pool as Behaim. Centuries of European colonization, exploitation, and imperialism dissipate in E. L. Cramer's texts and paratexts about entitlements. In *Die Kinderfarm*, published in Potsdam in 1941, the Cramer son recounts and exemplifies an intergenerational colonial pathology of anti-Black racism. At a time when the country was no longer a German colony, but a British one, Cramer refers to the land as German Southwest Africa. Directing his prose at a young German audience of "Jungens and Mädels" (boys and girls), he regales them with stories of struggle and self-reliance: of his five children; of Helmut, nicknamed "Goebbels," whose death prompts the act of writing as an act of mourning; of encounters with poisonous snakes, wild boars, and shifty natives. In one excerpt, the descent of locusts invokes Old Testament plagues; drought and flooding interweave with domestic servants' thieving and insubordination. Cramer's memoir strikes a chord of hardship, adventure, and colonial pedagogy.

In the *Kinderfarm*, the author advances a nationalist politics linked to the colonial enterprise. This shift plays a major role in Cramer's sequel, *Kinderfarm-Briefe* (1942). His vigorous correspondence with Germans in wartime Germany overlays Nazi ideology with colonial-era racism, all subsumed into a recolonial fantasy to recover what was unjustifiably lost. In hard times, the Führer sent food; he supported German schools and held out the promise of a return to German hegemony in Africa. With this ideological subtext, E. L. Cramer writes the early modern history of Cape Cross (Kreuzkap), explored in 1484 by the Portuguese seafarer Diogo Cão: "Mit ihm zusammen betrat als erster Deutscher Nürnberger Forscher Martin Beheim die südwestafrikanische Küste. Vorher hatte noch kein Weißer seinen Fuß auf dieses Gebiet gesetzt"[1] (Together with him, the first German, the Nuremberg researcher Martin Beheim set foot on the southwest African coast. No white man had ever set foot on this area before). For the author, Beheim embodies the courageous German who paved the way for his future *Volk*, the revisionist footprint of a whiteness on the African coast.

E. L. Cramer employs early modern narratives to stake a white territorial claim on the African continent. Following in Beheim's tracks, the settler colonist lays the foundation for a story about German belonging in German Southwest Africa and its belonging to the German nation. Curiously, the textbooks about that history that E. L. Cramer would have read render the story differently, despite shared ideological goals. The need for local histories in German schools around 1900 became a matter of governance. Pedagogical materials, according to Daniel Walther, needed "to provide students and future generations with a sense of their past and thus create an affinity to the region."[2] Walther elaborates on the work of imperial school inspector Bernhard Voigt (1878–1945), who transferred to Windhoek in 1908 and quickly rose through the ranks. Commissioned to write such a local history, Voigt compiled a German Southwest *Land und Leute*.[3] Additionally, he wrote several popular works of fiction about colonial life in the new homeland. Voigt's version of European maritime milestones is not free from Western imperialist pride. The work alternates between original contributions and short essays, longer quotations, and extracts from other sources. Voigt follows an opening poem with an excerpt from the second volume of Hans Meyer's *Das deutsche Kolonialreich*: "'Nicht von Osten, sondern von Western aus glückte das Wagnis, Asien mit Europa zu verbinden" (2; The venture to connect Asia to Europe succeeded not from East but rather from the West). From the depths of history, the seafarer Diogo Cão is dropped—and there is no trace of Beheim and his alleged first footprint.

---

1. Ernst Ludwig Cramer, *Die Kinderfarm* (Potsdam: Rütten und Loening, 1941), 274.

2. Daniel Walther, "Creating Germans Abroad: White Education in German Southwest Africa, 1894–1914," *German Studies Review* 24, no. 2 (May 2001): 325–51, here 336.

3. Bernhard Voigt et al. *Deutsch-Südwestafrika. Land und LeuteEine Heimatkunde für Deutschlands Jugend und Volk*, ed. Kaiserliches Gouvernement von Deutsch-Südwestafrika (Stuttgart: Strecker und Schröder, 1913).

The trope of early modern German masculinity, adventurous, entrepreneurial, white, and first, is the genealogical forebear of this son of a farmer and Farmersfrau. After returning to Germany, Cramer experiences an epiphany: love of the land, the people, and Nazi ideology provide a lever to balance his personal and professional personae. With thanks to Hitler for sending food during droughts, Cramer the Younger stakes his identity on the reclamation of today's Namibia as the German colony of his youth. In broadcasting this legacy, the author and mourning father follows his mother's footsteps of defining Germans in opposition to Blackness. Ada Cramer appropriated serfdom in Prussia as a past enslavement from which the people emancipated themselves—and she identifies with this self-liberating agency—without political assistance. The unproven corollary in toxically feminine racial logic is Black victimization of German whiteness. On the historical stage of the interwar period, the once-desirable alliance between white colonial powers and the German nation, predicated on shared interests and enemies, is transformed.

E. L. Cramer's legacy bears witness to the ideological alignment between recapturing lost colonies, Nazi imperialism, and anti-Black racism. Between his memoir and its sequel, made up of his experiences and correspondence from within and beyond Nazi Germany in the late 1930s and during World War II, World War I dramatically shifted the narrative. Prior to the Versailles Treaty, images of an early modern colonial power served as prefaces to the successful attempt of the young German Empire to gain the remainders in Africa and the Pacific and make them profitable through benevolence, intelligence, and hard work. Colonial nostalgia for expansion constituted the emotionological foundation for imperialist politics throughout the 1930s. Ostensibly jealous, other colonial powers resented Germany's ability to make do with their dregs and still triumph. The loss of the colonies thus became a narrative of failure. Cramer's personal journey aligns him with recolonial fantasies, redirected to politicize the emotions of lost land, honor, and masculinity. Cramer's personal "homecoming" resonates with the urgent need to reconcile historical accounts for those losses.

The emergence of what I am calling recolonial fantasies requires some context for the public reception of Cramer's memoirs. Striking is the narrative pivot from the centuries-long colonial enterprise to the acceptance of its failure. Demonizing the allied forces who claimed victory and imposed punishing conditions became a team effort, from the writing of textbooks for German-language instruction abroad to the advertising of history in from the Cigaretten-Bilderdienst Dresden. Ciarlo has written eloquently about the literal and optical consumption of colonial logics during the Age of Empire, including his attention to visual imagery and its impact. Less attention has been paid to the use of cigarette packages and collectible cards in the propagation of recolonial fantasies.[4] The collectability of these postcards from the distant to recent past represents in images the visual grammar of a cyclical colonial logic. Such a card from the mid-1930s showcases a colonial pantheon, with a significant gap between Friedrich Wilhelm at the top (1620–1688), Bismarck to his right (1815–1898), and Carl Peters to his left (1856–1918). (See figure 23.)

Heffter recapitulates the major contributions of each in his brief origin of the colonial empire, but he attributes the failures to compete with European powers such as England and France to the absence of a strong national state.[5] Curiously, he decouples the pseudocolonial discourses about German immigration from the rhetoric of *Auslandsdeutsche*. Rather, they are marked losses to the nation-state: "auch Südbrasilien und Südchile sind zum guten Teil Kulturgebiete deutschen Fleißes und deutscher Tüchtigkeit" (southern Brazil and southern Chile are also to a great extent cultural areas of German efficiency and German diligence).[6] Emigration represents a loss of "valuable" people to the German nation. It is noteworthy that the historian leaves out Argentina. The respective positions of the German-language press in the aftermath of World War I differ politically; further, they reveal subsequent political dispositions toward the Third Reich and its recolonial fantasies. According to Fredrik Schulze, approximately two hundred thousand German-speaking immigrants landed in Brazilian ports up to the 1930s. German-speaking elites in Brazil allied themselves with Germany, and "The German-speaking press condemned the Treaty of Versailles and discussed the fate of the Germans abroad (*Auslandsdeutsche*)."[7] In Chile, proponents

---

4. See Hiram Kümper, "*Nichts als blauer Dunst?* Zigarettensammelbilder als Medien historischer Sinnbildung—quellenkundliche Skizzen zu einem bislang ungehobenen Schatz," in *Geschichte in Wissenschaft und Unterricht* 59 (2008): 492–507. In H-Soz-Kult, 08.09.2008, <www.hsozkult.de/journal/id/z6ann-103142>. Kümper calls attention to the collectible cards as an important and underutilized teaching source.

5. Heinrich Heffter, "Die Entstehung des deutschen Kolonialreiches," in his *Deutsche Kolonien* (Dresden: Cigaretten-Bilderdienst, 1936), 4. He repeatedly directs the reader parenthetically to the "Ehrentafel," which is not included in my copy but must have been on the dust jacket.

6. Heffter, "Die Entstehung des deutschen Kolonialreiches," 4.

7. Frederik Schulze, "German Immigrants (Brazil)," *1914–1918-online. International Encyclopedia of the First World War*, ed. Ute Daniel, Peter Gatrell, Oliver Janz, Heather Jones, Jennifer

Figure 23. Kolonial-Ehrentafel, cigarette cards ca. 1936.

of fascist ideology adapted the universal dictates to the national needs of the country, advocating for a strong state and against civilizational decline that inevitably attends democracy. Marcus Klein acknowledges the need for further study in his work on Chilean Nacismo and German Nazism; he writes off the assumption that the group "acted as the 'fifth column' of the Third Reich, preparing the way for its purportedly imperialist aspirations in Chile."[8] The local chapter of the party, along with a youth organization and popular support, shared admiration for Hitler's destruction of the Weimar Republic, a weak democracy blamed for the "humiliation" of the Versailles Treaty.[9] The number of German-speaking immigrants to southern Chile is estimated to be around eleven thousand before the First World War. Argentina, by contrast, was home to an estimated three hundred thousand German speakers by the late 1930s.[10] This snapshot of numbers and political leanings from the ABC countries of the Southern Cone raises the question of why Heffter omits Argentina? He argues for land entitlement with demographics: he includes a chart of European powers, with England at the top and Germany at the bottom. The former has the lowest population numbers, the most colonies and colonial subjects; the latter the largest population, no colonies. Argentina's German-language print media in the 1930s occupied a range of positions on the political spectrum, but the *Argentinisches Tageblatt* took a firm stance against Nazism while supporting German-speaking immigrants. Omission warrants closer scrutiny. Below, I examine two case studies from the early 1930s that demonstrate the influential newspaper's staunch solidarity with economic emigration and the right to cultivate the land outside the nation, and the open opposition to the imperialism of National Socialism with its recolonial rhetoric.

Keene, Alan Kramer, and Bill Nasson, issued by Freie Universität Berlin, Berlin 2014-10-08. DOI: 10.15463/ie1418.10456.

8. Marcus Klein, "The Chilean Movimiento Nacional Socialista, the German-Chilean Community, and the Third Reich, 1932–1939: Myth and Reality," *The Americas* 60, no. 4 (April 2004): 589–616.

9. Klein, "The Chilean Movimiento Nacional Socialista," 599.

10. Germán C. Friedmann, "The German Speakers of Argentina in the 1930s and 1940s," in *Transatlantic Battles: European Immigrant Communities in South America and the World Wars*, ed. María Inés Tato (Leiden: Brill, 2023), 144–63, here 144.

Warum nicht nach Argentinian?

I build the first case from an example of support and immigration recruitment strategy in the *Argentinisches Tageblatt*. First, I provide a bit of backstory. The *Argentinisches Tageblatt*, established in 1889 by the progressive publicist and Swiss emigrant Johann Allemann, is a German-language newspaper that published through 2022. Johann and his son Moritz journeyed to Argentina, at the invitation of President Sarmiento, as noted in the introduction, with a sense of European zeal combined with private enterprise and a commitment to liberal political values.[11] Included in this effort is education. Apart from establishing a newspaper, the Swiss emigrants were involved in founding a Pestalozzi Schule in Buenos Aires. The Allemann (spelling changed to Alemann to facilitate pronunciation) family newspaper assumed the noble burden of enlightenment. They are summoned to "represent" in contemporary terms the "other," better German nation, one that German-speaking immigrants in South America sustained with pedagogical theory and homage to literary classicism.[12]

In the April 17, 1931, edition, the editors begin a series of articles about Tirolian emigrants who were trying to secure a future in Paraguay: "Warum nicht nach Argentinien?" (why not to Argentina).[13] Austria's agricultural minister, Andreas Thaler, traveled to South America for negotiations with Paraguay. The first-person plural pronoun intervenes with sympathy and support for the two hundred Tirolian farmers; the editors stress the superior farming conditions in the Andes valleys. In a follow up from April 30, the editors supply further information about the conditions pushing immigration: three

---

11. Johann Allemann's politics are described as socialist: "In der Schweiz hatte der frühe Sozialdemokrat, sein Urenkel Peter Alemann nennt ihn in einer umfangreichen Biografie zum 100. Gründungstag des Argentinischen Boten gar einen Sozialisten, die Auswanderung eng mit der sozialen Frage verbunden. Johann war, obwohl er auch mit Sozialisten in Verbindung stand, mehr ein Radikaldemokrat, der sozialistische oder staatskapitalistische Wirtschaftsmodelle ablehnte und auf die Freiheit des Individuums setzte. Er war auch Genossenschaftler im Sinne der Idee von Schultze-Delitzsch oder Raiffeisen, glaubte an die Wirksamkeit von Konsumvereinen, an deren Gründung er sich in der Schweiz aktiv beteiligt hatte. Vor allem aber war er Realist. Dazu mögen auch seine gescheiterten Wirtschaftsunternehmen beigetragen haben" (Stefan Kuhn, "Von Bern über Santa Fe nach Buenos Aires. Die Vorgeschichte der Gründung des Argentinischen Tageblatts," *Argentinisches Tageblatt*. April 29, 2009. Nr. 31.716. 1–4," 3).

12. Erin Auf der Heide, "Representations of German-Speaking Exiles and Immigrants in Argentina" (MA thesis, Bowling Green State University, 2006), 13.

13. *Argentinisches Tageblatt*, April 17, 1931, 3.

hundred thousand unemployed in Austria; many farmers forced from the land into office work. An imperative emerges to ensure the dignity of their profession: "Bauersöhnen Gelegenheit geben, ihrem Beruf treu zu bleiben" (to give the sons of farmers the chance to stay true to their profession).[14] The two hundred farmers would end up in southern Chile, with the well wishes of the newspaper. Their advocacy placed the needs of the farmers themselves at the forefront, stressing the ennobling qualities of their mission: "Reichstum siuchen sie nicht, sondern Arbeit, freien Grund und Boden und Zufriedenheit" (they are not seeking wealth, rather work, free land and earth and contentment).[15]

The second case study involves a direct attack on the Nazi Party. Allemann editorializes against the absurdity of the plan to retake lost colonial possessions. The tenor of the paper generally stands firmly against discrimination and reactionary politics. They are against antisemitism, referring to it as an unfortunate European import (August 20 and 22, 1932, 3). In the edition of the newspaper from September 2, 1932, the editor writes about colonization and cruelty: "Afrika, der schwarze Erdteil, ist eine eingize Anklage gegen die brutale Unterdrückung des Schwarzen durch den Wiessen" (Africa, the black continent, is a single indictment of the brutal suppression of Black by white people). The editorial continues with near sarcasm when broaching the Versailles Treaty, with scare quotes around "'seine' Kolonien" ("its" colonies) to indicate derision. Apart from small settler colonies in German Southwest Africa, he continues, Germany had no significant shifts to offload citizens to the colonies. "Lüge und Heuchelei" (lies and hypocrisy) characterized all of European colonial policies in Africa, and the German Kaiserreich was not the exception: "Das neue Reich sollte sich lieber die Kolonialpsychose erwehren, als in die Fussstapfen eines Systems zu treten, das Deutschland in Niederlage und Elend geführet hat" (The new Reich should rather fight off the colonial psychosis rather than follow in the footsteps of a system that led Germany to defeat and misery).

With this countermodel to recolonial fantasies elucidated, I return to the visual and verbal grammar of their underwriting National Socialist ideology of land acquisition and cultivation throughout the 1930s. The Cigaretten-Bilderdienst Dresden that produced these and other cards edited a volume, *Deutsche Kolonien*, also published in 1936. Dr. Heinrich Heffter (1903–1975),

---

14. *Argentinisches Tageblatt*, April 30, 1931, 3.
15. *Argentinisches Tageblatt*, April 30, 1931, 3.

the historian quoted above, was engaged by Brockhaus and assembled the seventy-two-page volume, with embossed cover on high-stock paper, twenty-six pages of introduction to the colonies and forty-six pages of color cigarette card images overlaid on photographic backgrounds of landscapes and habitats. Heffter's preface opens with a lament: "Die deutsche Geschichte ist reich an jähen und schmerzlichen Wendungen, und so auch die Geschichte der deutschen Kolonien"[16] (German history is rich with sudden and painful turns, and so, too, the history of the German colonies). Eschewing triumphalism, Heffter proceeds to characterize the new German nation as the underdog of colonial powers who had "Das Beste" (the best) already firmly under their control; they left what appeared to them "nicht mehr wertvoll genug" (no longer sufficiently valuable). Heffter lists what he holds to be the great accomplishments of the brief German colonial empire, including driving out Arab slave traders from East Africa; putting down the bellicose Herero and H*ttent*ts; building infrastructure and schools in West Africa; taking the lead in treating disease in tropical climates, such as sleeping sickness (there is a shout-out to Robert Koch). Behind his extolling Germany's colonial history is an agenda: to refute the accusations of incompetence, mismanagement, and abuse leveled by the jealous "Feindbundmächte" (alliance of enemy powers), and here Heffter's ire at the "theft" of territories intersects with Cramer's family history. "Dem Raub," he writes, "wurde noch die schimpfliche Behauptung angeblicher kolonialer Mißwirtschaft und Unfähighkeit hinzugefügt" (To the robbery [of the colonies] was added the further ignominious allegation of supposed colonial mismanagement and incompetence).[17] While Heffter cites the participation of colonized soldiers as evidence of the "natives'" love for and loyalty to their German leaders, the British cited the "Fall Cramer" as evidence of brutality and misrule.

In search of nineteenth-century German-language migration stories, I sat in an archive in Santiago de Chile. On a browse through the stacks while awaiting documents, I found a copy of *Volk ohne Raum* (1926) on the shelves. The networking argument I had been drafting for this book occasionally struck me as random, but the interweaving of emigration and settler colonial narratives makes legible the imperial logic of hegemony. I opened the book to this passage, in which Grimm brandishes metaphors of prostitution, slavery, and thievery to cast the contemporary German people as victims:

16. Heffter, "Vorwort," *Deutsche Kolonien*, 2.
17. Heffter, "Vorwort," 2.

First Footprints and Recolonial Fantasies 281

> Es lebt der Sieche und lebt der Dieb und lebt die Hure und lebt das Gewürm, das einander frißt, aber der deutsche Mensch braucht Raum um sich und Sonne über sich und Freiheit in sich, um gut und schön zu werden. Soll er bald zwei Jahrtausende umsonst darauf gehofft haben? Und wenn du gerade und adlig zu sein vermagst von Körper und Sinn, und wenn deine Kinder noch nicht kranke Krüppel und verstohlene Diebe und arme Huren geworden sind, ist das dein Verdienst? Schau um dich, schau vor dich und bedenke die Enkel und Neugeborenen! Es gibt eine Sklavennot der Enge, daraus unverzwungene Leiber und Seelen nie mehr wachsen können. Ich aber, mein Freund, ich weiß, daß meine Kinder und mein Geschlecht und das deutsche Volk ein und dasselbe sind und ein Schicksal tragen müssen.[18]

> They live—the sick, the thief, the whore, and the worms that devour each other, but the German needs space around him and the sun above and freedom within in order to become good and beautiful. Should he have hoped in vain for two millennia? And if you can be upright and noble in body and mind, and if your children have not yet become sick cripples, stealthy thieves, and poor whores, is that your accomplishment? Look around you, look before you, and think of the grandchildren and newborns! There is an anguished enslavement from which unconstrained bodies and souls can never emerge. But I, my friend, know that my children and my people and the Germans are one and the same, and must bear the same fate.

Grimm's dire warnings about division deterritorialize and deracialize slavery, echoing the rhetoric of loftier Enlightenment philosophies, projected across time and place onto the experience of migration. The demographic shifts that drove emigration coincide with the gain and loss of a last-minute empire, mixing a toxic politics. With demographic shifts and economic pressures driving farmers off the land, the early 1930s witnessed an exodus, which had an impact on emigration stories, colonial mourning, and the formation of Nazi imperialist ideology. In the Global South, not all migration stories shared the frankly grim ideology of white supremacy.

In the postwar (World War I) nationalist epistemology, the Great Powers reduced the German people to poverty and destitution, reflected in the physical and moral degeneration of the race. Deprived of their colonies, the encumbered German people had to succumb to the conditions of enslave-

---

18. Grimm, *Volk ohne Raum*, 10–11.

ment, again. Grimm rewrites the narrative of racial subjection for the 1920s; the politicization of that slogan throughout the 1930s makes the argument that regeneration lies in the acquisition of land, somewhere to go.

In the preface to his *Deutsche Kolonien*, Heffter lavishes praise on Grimm's work, mapping a single German geography that spans the likeminded enclaves in southern Brazil and Chile, the colonial enterprise and its loss, and the literature that underwrites Nazism. Heffter argues metonymically for a land claim through bloodlines and literature. Referring to Grimm as "der deutsche Südafrikaner"[19] (the German South African)—Grimm spent fourteen years in the Cape Colony—Heffter transitions across borders and histories to lay claim: "In unseren Kolonien sind Siedlungemöglichkeiten für viele Tausende von Deutschen, zum Teil noch in Deutsch-Südwestafrika und vor allem in den fruchtbaren und klimatische für Europäer geeigneten Hochlandgebieten Deutsch-Ostafrikas. Wie viele in der Enge der Heimat gehemmte Menschen könnten da ihre Kräfte entfalten!"[20] (There are settlement opportunities for many thousands of Germans in our colonies, still to a certain extent in German-Southwest Africa and above all in the fertile highlands of German-East Africa, where the climate is suitable for Europeans. How many human beings, crowded into the narrow confines of the homeland, could develop their strengths there!). Heffter entangles recolonial fantasies, expansionist politics, and revisionist history—they are no longer "unsere Kolonien"—with nationalist fiction in the form of a self-help manual. While he cannot plant a flag in the earth, he stakes a claim to pages of history.

Footprints

The facsimile edition of the Behaim globe judiciously weighs the truth content of contemporary Behaim legend. Ravenstein attributes much of the distortion to a Hebraist, also a senator, professor at the University of Altenburg, and benefactor of the university at Nuremberg, Johann Christoph Wagenseil (1633–1705), who claimed Martin Behaim as, among other things, "a divine hero, whose accomplishments have hitherto been ignored."[21] The "unprinci-

---

19. Heffter, "Vorwort," 2.
20. Heffter, "Vorwort," 2.
21. Ravenstein, *Behaim*, 89.

First Footprints and Recolonial Fantasies 283

pled historian" further asserted that Behaim discovered the Azores, established a Flemish colony, and "subsequently roving the Atlantic, he examined (*pervestigavit*) the islands of America" and "that he did all this before Columbus and Magellan, whose fame was proclaimed by every mouth, while Martin Behaim, the real discoverer, was ignored."[22] Ravenstein cautiously debunks many a Behaim myth, or concedes the lack of sufficient extant sources to corroborate or disavow them. In such cases, he determines the source of the distortions, as in the exaggerated claims of Wagenseill, no doubt eager to fuel the self-importance of a Nuremberg audience. Despite such scholarly efforts to tell the story straight(er), Behaim leaves a huge footprint on German colonial history and recolonial fantasies. Ravenstein follows the trail of the Cape Cross monument in his history of the navigator, always in pursuit of auditable evidence. As he recounts, Cão reached the Congo during his 1485 expedition; near the Yelala Falls, there was found a rock with a coat of arms and an inscription marking the voyage. Ravenstein notes names could have been added subsequently. Cão erected two *padrãos*, one at Monte Negro, one at Cape Cross; the latter was taken and placed in the Museum of the Institut für Meereskunde in Berlin. "The German Emperor," Ravenstein writes, "has since caused an exact replica of it to be erected on the spot."[23] Ravenstein moves on from the monument.

The only monograph to follow Ravenstein, Peter Bräunlein's work on the man, his work, and the legend, attributes much to the 1908 facsimile edition, but draws attention to the national slant in motivation, though the research as such was impeccable for the time. Ravenstein's model was based on inaccurate facsimiles from the nineteenth century. Ravenstein himself was the son of an Augsburg publisher, an Englander by choice who served in the Royal Cartography Office and won the Queen Victoria medal for his work. Blackbourn's notice to Behaim references Bräunlein, specifically, the essential Nazification of science, German "firstness," and assertions of proprietary rights unjustly ripped from the nation. Bräunlein follows through with background on the woman who began the rally around the globe, which Hitler bought back for the Nürnberg museum. Cramer rejects any hybridity, any coexistence of "German" and African: the former exist rather to contain the latter.

---

22. Ravenstein, *Behaim*, 89.
23. Ravenstein, *Behaim*, 89.

Ungovernables

Throughout the third part of E. L. Cramer's book, the "ungovernables" keep appearing, intruding from the periphery and taking center stage. For his mother Ada, Indigenous toxicity and German administrators joined forces against German colonial farmers. For E. L. Cramer, under British rule and among like-minded German-speaking farmers, educators, and doctors, he and his fellow settlers staged their own acts of resistance. For example, when the British forbade German schools, the farmers paid for their own until German instruction was provided. When his daughter got upset because she did not get a penny to celebrate King George, Cramer consoled her with the blunt directive not to care, he had nothing to do with her (218). The motto for survival in Africa: "Alles macht man in Afrika selbst" (114; In Africa, you have to do everything yourself). The self-reliance cultivated on the "frontier" of civilization, through his colonialist lens, encompasses essentialist, ethnic, German self-control, a familiar refrain from Meinecke's prose and fiction. With this core strength naturalized and nationalized, Cramer (and others) apply this settler mentality consistently to assert superiority over Black workers and their children, but also to other whites.

The Boers fall into the latter category. Cramer cites the example of a fever outbreak to profile the superiority of German chemistry and medicine. In alignment with the claims of Heffter, who names the development of Germanin (Suranin) by Bayer in the 1920s as a major national achievement and jewel in Germany's colonial crown, Cramer recounts an incident he witnessed. Always careful to identify his characters by skin color, language, and ethnicity, he writes, "Auch unter den Buren, den nicht-deutschen Weißen in Südafrika, herrschte das Fieber. Die gebrauchen nicht die guten deutschen Mittel, sondern das gewöhnliche englische Chinin, und es starben sehr viele von ihnen" (94; Fever also prevailed among the Boers, the non-German whites in South Africa. They do not use the good German medicine, rather the usual English quinine, and thus many of their own died). He continues with a sad tale of a twelve-year-old girl whom the fever had orphaned. She, too, was afflicted, and she lay on an ox cart with her eyes wide open, staring into the sun. As a result, she was blinded for life. The German, by contrast, had a supply of Atebrin and Plasmochin, produced by Bayer in Germany (95).

With an avuncular, even paternal narrative tone, Cramer regales his young readership with stories of Black workers, though much less sympathetic toward the latter. The children of Gustav, one of the farm workers, also make appearances in the workforce and the narrative. Domestic theft, unrepentent bullying, and disrespect interlace the Kinderfarm. To amuse his readers, he gives the example of Magdalena, "ein schwarzes Hereromädchen" who "stahl wie ein Rabe" (148). He and his wife set a trap for her. While drinking the coffee she served, he catches her in the act: "Damit nahm ich ihr die Schüssel weg. Ich sagte sehr freunclih zu ihr—sie aber war statt schwarz grau vor Schrecken im Gesicht" (With that I took the bowl away from her. I said to her in a very friendly manner—she, however, was not black in the face but gray with horror). Cramer, in a practiced passive-aggressive manner, tells her how much the sugar cost and reports he deducted the two shillings from her monthly wages. "Helfen tat das aber gar nichts Das einzige, was half, war alles wegstellen und abschließen" (149; But it helped not at all. The only thing that helped was put everything away and lock it up). Magdalena stole "like a raven"; and Gustav's daughter, "Zarautis, die immer noch wie eine Elster stahl" (255; Zarautis, who still stole like a magpie), replaced her. The raven and the magpie, black-feathered birds metaphorically associated with neglect and theft, characterize the girls or young women as morally less-than and unteachable, incorrigible, ungovernable; that they could be hungry does not factor into the story. Perhaps more irritating, is Povian, her brother, who does not cower.

Cramer's children, the reader learns, were forbidden to play with Povian, though the boys defied their father's rule. At some point, during nap time, Cramer and his wife are alarmed by the sound of broken glass coming from the boys' room. They lay in their beds, covered to the chins and eyes shut tight. They tell on Povian, who had colluded with his sister to steal an entire cake. Later, after Zaratuis informed on the informant, Povian pushes one son down a lime kiln while he paused for a drink of water. The child fell two meters and sustained a serious head wound. With Gustav's help, Cramer spanks the boy, but during the punishment, with Cramer restraining him by holding onto the clothing, Povian tears himself away: "wie ein nackter Affe sprang er davon" (235; he leapt away like a naked ape). Cramer's narrative persona is enraged: "In sicherer Entfernung blieb er stehen. Er heulte gar nicht mehr, frech und wütend schrie er: Mister muß neue Hemd geben, Mister muß neue Hose geben'. 'Du Kröte!' rief ich ich warf ihm seine Lumpen nach. Er hob sie aber nicht auf, und rannte weg" (235: At a safe distance, he stood still. He had stopped crying, cheekily and furiously he screamed: "Mister must give new shirt. Mister must give new pants." "You toad!" I shouted and threw his rags at him. But he did not pick them up and he ran away). With a good dose of disbelief, Cramer recounts Povian's affrontery. He gets the Cramer children in trouble, eludes corporal punishment, expresses no gratitude for the "rags" he has received as hand-me-downs, and taunts "Mister" with all he is owed. So much of the narrator's fury derives from the conviction that he as a settler is owed everything, and he is left with unleashed fury, holding the hand-me-down-rags in his hand.

The Cape Cross and the legend of Behaim fuel Cramer's narrative of German belonging in Südwestafrika and its belonging rightfully to the German Reich. His life writing is a work of mourning subsumed into a political moment that captures the palpable belief in a recolonial Africa. He addresses the (young) readers directly, sharing stories of raising the swastika flag of a *Parteiappell* (160), of meetings punctuated with "Sieg Heil" and the "Horst-Wessel-Lied" (161). Cramer shares his firm belief that "einmal der Tag kommen wird, an dem der Führer unser Deutsch-Südwestafrika in Großdeutsche Reich zurückholt" (160; that the day will come when the Führer will reclaim our German Southwest Africa for the Empire). When he falls seriously ill (*Maltafieber*), Cramer convalesces at a hospital in Swakopmund. From there, he accompanies other German speakers on an expedition to Cape Cross. We approach the closing of the referential circle.

With the publication of *Kinderfarm-Briefe*, E. L. Cramer closes the colonial circle. The respective book covers align seamlessly, the 1942 version serving as a palimpsest of imperial nationalism. (Figures 24 and 25) According to some sources, Cramer fell ill and left the English colony he called home for treatment in Germany. Under the solicitous care of National Socialist clinics and politics, Cramer found himself back in the bosom of the Fatherland. Though bereft without his wife and children and devastated by the death of his son, he persevered with the support of his dedicated readers. Cramer stressed the active role his young audience played in his recovery. They sent letters, cards, and packages during the holiday season. His letters stoked their hopes and dreams of someday farming and working in their rightful African colony. This composite work abounds with signature lines of "Heil Hitler" and political commitment to a shared German homeland. In Nazi Germany, Cramer becomes something of a colonial celebrity. An emissary from the former colony, he appears on radio broadcasts in order to communicate somehow with his distant family. He gives lectures and readings and he engages in self-promotion that simultaneously endorses the prevailing politics.

E. L. Cramer's return to Germany is transformed through his activism into politically and racially motivated remigration. In the 1942 collection of letters, interwoven with his recollections, he reverses the direction of his distant pre-

Figure 24. Book cover, Ernst Ludwig Cramer *Die Kinderfarm* (1941).

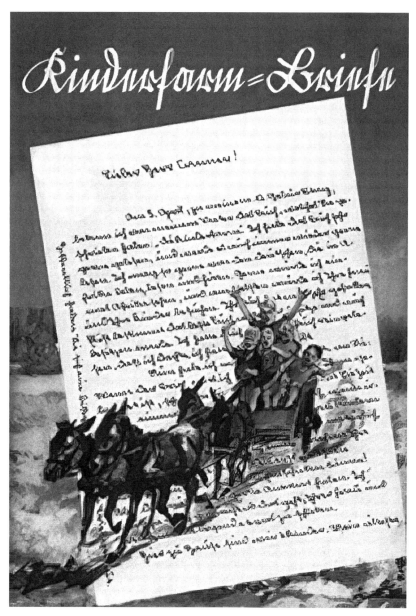

Figure 25. Book cover, Ernst Ludwig Cramer *Kinderfarm-Briefe* (1942).

decessor, Behaim. Behaim's *Erdapfel* miniaturized a half-imagined world prior to globalizing impact of European landfall in the Americas. Knowledge of the "globe" as an imaginable and realistic space connects to acts of taking imperial inventories. The Ur-German spherical model of the late fifteenth-century world is recast in the twentieth century through the lens of imperial entitlements. Two moments in the text stand out. Describing his arrival in Hamburg after a sea voyage, Cramer's own first footfall receives special attention: *"da trat ich mehrmals fest mit dem Fuß auf,* weil ich niemehr vergessen wollte, wie es gewesen war, als ich nach so langer Zeit diesen deutschen Boden wieder unter den Füßen spürte" (*I firmly stomped my foot several times* because I never wanted to forget what it was like to feel this German soil beneath my feet after so long a time (emphasis in the original)).[24]

In the second moment of interest here, Cramer recounts a memory of his German childhood, marked by an interracial encounter that needs retroactive attention. While he was ill as a young teenager, before his departure for German Southwest Africa to follow his parents, he was sent to Mecklenburg, to the country, to convalesce. His prose describes a respectable pension, run by a pastor; other children attended, including the son of a German war minister. The memory of another child, though, jogs Cramer's true racist politics: "Und ein schwarzer N*gerjunge aus Zentralafrika, der hieß Domingo Teixera de Matos" (and a young Black from Central Africa, he was called Domingo Teixera de Matos). Cramer recalls that Domingo had a sister, though he does not recall not her name. He continues with more information about the family. The father married a real Black African woman; and now, in the narrative past, those parents wanted the children to be German. The parents of the white children apparently thought nothing of the arrangement, which Cramer labels as learning with "mit Kafferkindern" (with Black children). Reading race retroactively and projecting racism: "Heute weiß jedes *Kind* in Deutschland, daß so etwas unmöglich ist!" (Today every single *child* in Germany knows that something like this is impossible).[25] Cramer recuperates a naturalized insistence on all forms of racial separation, stunned at the memory that it could ever have been otherwise. Cramer forges a bond with his young German readers through an appeal to common whiteness, united in a recolonial fantasy of lost land reclaimed.

---

24. Ernst Ludwig Cramer, *Kinderfarm-Briefe* (Potsdam: Rütten & Loening, 1941), 13.
25. Cramer, *Kinderfarm-Briefe*, 139.

Conclusion

Decolonial Fantasies

"no hay a dónde irse"
—ANÍBAL QUIJANO[1]

E. L. Cramer pens a hasty afterword to his first volume, in which he expresses thanks to those who helped shepherd the work into print, and he gives the readership a glimpse into the scene of writing. As an author and father, Cramer poses the question: What would Helmut, his son who died while he was in Germany, tell you about Africa if he had lived to tell you the stories himself. Channeling that voice, Cramer combines the work of mourning the death of his child with the loss of the colony where he grew up, where his father died, and where his family still lived, to the British. The enormous success of the volume with a young audience and their political mentors—parents, teachers, admired adults, national leaders—resonates with the National Socialist platform to reclaim that which was unjustly taken away. Cramer as colonist reinscribes his African story into the metanarrative of German empires and his own recolonial fantasies to recuperate the loss of history. His final words about his workplace embrace the layers of history that animate the scene of writing:

> Dann während ich an dem Arbeitsplatz dies schreibe und das Buch damit schließe, klingt vom Turm der Potsdamer Garisonkirche, der Grabstätte Friedrichs des Großen, das wunderbare Glockenspiel herüber: "Üb immer Treu und Redlichkeit."[2]

---

1. There is nowhere to go, my translation. Aníbal Quijano, Keynote, III Congreso Latinoamericano y Caribeño de Ciencias Sociales, August 25, 2015, Quito. FLASCO Ecuador. https://www.youtube.com/watch?v=OxL5KwZGvdY.strikes.

2. Ernst Ludwig Cramer, *Die Kinderfarm* (Potsdam: Rütten und Loening, 1941), 297.

Conclusion

For as I write this at my workplace and with it conclude the book, the wonderful chimes sound from the tower of the Potsdam Garrison Church, the burial site of Frederick the Great: "Always practice loyalty and honesty."

It has been the task of this book to decolonize Cramer's experience; the reader can almost hear the bells. His reference to this particular narrative moment in time and particular place first casts work, labor, as an act of patriotism; unable to farm as a settler, he works for the war effort. Next, he invokes a claim to the nation's illustrious past, played forward into the present. His writing is a performative act to generate interaction between the text and its context; between him as a German author and the readers as loyal Germans. In writing the work, Cramer strikes a tone of intimacy with the readership through his public act of mourning. The *Kinderfarm-Briefe* inscribe a sequel to the African-German settler story. With his fans, his radio broadcasts, and many public and pedagogical appearances, Cramer crafts a political persona who serves as a spokesman for the German farmer, a settler without a colony.

In another register, the cultural references that make this closure so sublime unravel before a decolonial gaze. Ludwig Hölty, poet of "Der befreite Sklave" (see chapter 3) wrote the poem that "Üb immer Treu und Redlichkeit" inspired. Published in 1776, it became a favorite folk song once set to music by Mozart (1791). According to some, it was so popular that Queen Luise ordered the garrison bell tower to play it every half hour. Queen Luise, known for her patriotic stance against Napoleonic occupation, predates the unification of a nation-state by about seventy years. According to another source, Joseph Goebbels claimed the virtues of loyalty and honestly as uniquely Prussian; he was the one who ordered the music played in intervals. In Hölty's twenty-stanza poem, "Der alte Landmann an seinen Sohn" (The old farmer to his son), a farmer commands his son to practice loyalty and honesty, eschewing the pursuit of worldly wealth, which some interpret as antisemitic. E. L. Cramer's first footprints and last words claim, reclaim, and proclaim a moral high ground that proves to be precarious. Decolonizing Cramer's last paragraph demands reading backwards through the multiple layers of misreading and rewriting ambiguity into a single story of supremacy.

This study began with a fifteenth-century globe. The Behaim *Erdapfel* of 1492 left a pedagogical legacy and manufactured venerable proof of global authority for the coloniality of power in German-speaking Europe. Blackbourn writes of the Behaim-produced artifact: "The likely purpose of the globe was demonstrative—to show Nuremberg's merchants the commercial opportunities that existed in an expanding world, from the gold of the West African coast to the spices of the east." I have taken this artifact—a World Heritage object—back to its origins and followed its impact on colonial projects, fantasies, and brutalities that enable at least in part an understanding of the National Socialist project as recolonial catastrophe with tremors felt worldwide. The preceding chapters have attempted to reframe German-speaking Europe's engagement with the Atlantic world through the critical lens of decoloniality, the practice of reading outside cultural constructions of national and imperial identity. The project of modernity, mapping the unrepresented Americas in the Behaim world view, persistently indexes the shifting contact zones that served to showcase the agency of monarchs, emperors, masters, and monsters, all of whom impact the dominant model of European whiteness.

Globes and maps function as ideological and material visuals of political vectors; inventories reflect different records. German empires obsessively exercise the agency of counting. Their epistemologies prove intransigently transhistorical; not bound by the logic of presence, they can function performatively. The red thread through the board game of Germany's colonies— without the Americas, an update of the Behaim globe—traces German conquests, connecting the representative red dots and splotches outward and away from the nation, down the African coast, around the Cape, and into the Pacific to China. (figure 26). The imperial eagle presides over the two-dimensional world. Voyagers place their start-up money in a till; they embark on the adventure from Hamburg, rolling the dice to advance across the channel to Kamarun, Damaraland, Gross-Nama, the British Cape of Good Hope, Sansibar in German East Africa, Neu-Guinea/Kaiser-Wilhelm-Land, from the Salomon to Samoa, to the Marshall Islands, Samoa, the Caroline Islands. He who reaches Khiantschou first wins and takes all. The fictional adventure, intended to stoke colonial fervor in young imperial citizens, is monodirectional, game over. Though skewed by Eurocentric fantasies of the entire globe, since approximately 1492, in a world of comprehensive colonization, "no hay a dónde irse" (there is nowhere to go).

That game drew a line across the world from Germany to China[3]; the competition for colonized spaces enacted the semantic performance of a game, between individuals and beyond imagined and curated communities of the

---

3. See Sarah Zabrodski's blog entry: https://primo.getty.edu/primo-explore/fulldisplay?vid=GRI&docid=GETTY_ ROSETTAIE1540602&context=L.

nation-state. Adam Blackler notes the importance of board games, played at home by the young, in establishing the "normalcy of empire."[4] The strategy of naturalizing German-specific possessions across the Atlantic and Pacific is manifest in other games and toys as well, but also in curricula. Blackler's focus remains on German Southwest Africa, noting the dangers and adventures involved in settling or passing through West Africa. Enforced by the *Völkerschauen*, geography texts, and colonial advertising, popular and material cultures underwrite the imperial project. Specific to German Southwest Africa, Blackler quotes the prevailing narrative of colonial conquest: "Where once only dry sand greeted the first German landings."[5] With Cramer reclaiming Behaim, those first footprints predate official settlement by four centuries.

Throughout my argument, I have included the critical voices, the marginalized writers, the lesser-known colonial administrators, the women immigrants, without necessarily raising the question: Who have been the villains, the antagonists? Chapter 1 casts the successful Danish and Dutch as the victors, hence once and future enemies. The unenlightened, including Frederick the Great, step into the role of villain in chapter 2, which takes aim against all tyranny. These are followed by the lazy enslaved, the cannibal who cannot be ennobled, non-German immigrants who would populate the world. In counternarratives, Frederick casts Montezuma as more human than the Spanish conquistadors. Seume's Huron embodies the same humanity and innate commitment to hospitality the French settler lacks. Goethe's Brazilian cannibal is relegated to the margins of canonical literature; the snakeskin belt, however, takes its place among the artifacts of world literature. Enlightened souls may choose to remain enslaved, while a century later, a colonial administrator and storyteller jests about Black workers enjoying confinement as if were a vacation. Things get complicated as the stories unfold. Resistance is relegated to historical footnotes. We encounter Indians who disagree about the goodness of the white man, other German men who are lazy or unable to control the ungovernable urges within. The inventory goes on: French colonists in the Americas; violent Hama rebels; the unconverted. Female figures from a range of ethnicities can be educated, domesticated, re-Christianized, re-Indigenized as Ur-Germanic, married, redeemed, depending on their race. Arab women can seduce; enslaved African women, with Arab overseers, can

---

4. Adam A. Blackler, *An Imperial Homeland: Forging German Identity in Southwest Africa* (University Park: Penn State University Press, 2022), 105.

5. Blackler, *An Imperial Homeland*, 108.

Figure 26. Deutschland's Kolonien-Spiel (Germany's Colonial Game, ca. 1890). Prints collection, Getty Research Institute, Los Angeles, 2004. PR.67*.

work in chains and be captured in a photograph, giving the oppositional gaze. Indentured domestic servants, women, men, and children, can poison, plot, and refuse to express gratitude. These are the villains and/or heroes in the stories of multiple empires and de-/re-colonial fantasies.

Quijano describes the persistent relations of social inequality that do not end with emancipation or independence; he concedes, there is nowhere to go. Recall Meinecke's catechism of emigration, how starkly his multiple answers to the question *wohin* contrast with Quijano's simple admission. Activism in the twenty-first century engages the colonial past of multiple nations as part of an urgent attempt to understand and dismantle systemic, institutional, and everyday racism. In the German-language cultural context, conversations about monuments, renaming streets and sites, and reparations have at least begun. Increasingly, scholars and activists whose aim is to dissuade Indian hobbyists, for example, from appropriative acts and join the efforts to educate have turned their attention to the repatriation of remains from German museums.[6] Museum curators make concerted efforts to decolonize their collections. The return of the Benin Bronzes, whether to be displayed or preserved in their places of origin, underscores the importance of recognizing meaning beyond a European epistemological bias that puts human remains and sacred objects on display.

Contemporary social justice movements unite in sending a message that racism takes multiple forms; anti-Black, anti-Asian, Islamophobic, antisemitic, gender-specific, in some cases, anti-Slavic; the list grows depressingly long, occluding the centrality of white supremacy at the core of each inflection. Racial differences factor into the humanitarian crisis that culminated in the so-called "refugee crisis" in 2015. The return of objects stolen or purchased, the controversies surrounding the opening of the Humboldt Forum, political positioning around the monolith of "German" identity that supersedes citizenship, all continually enter into discourse, the sides of which are articulated in a colonial logic of binarism that constantly repositions otherness at the far end of where whiteness is: not on a spectrum, but from the middle of a circle to far points on its circumference.

Archives of memory still tell decolonial stories, even those that were overlooked at the time. I found such a story in the dusty and damp news-

---

6. Glenn Penny has written extensively on German affinity with Native American cultures and peoples. See his *Kindred by Choice: Germans and American Indians since 1800* (Chapel Hill, NC: University of North Carolina Press, 2013).

Conclusion

paper archive in the basement of the Biblioteca Nacional in Buenos Aires. It was news to me. In the late 1930s, a group of German speakers in the Southern Cone pushed back against European barbarism. At the time, geopolitics and local elites debated German identity in ways that entered into a larger educational and political project.[7] In an appeal that was published in the *Argentinisches Tageblatt* (April 29, 1939), the editor, Ernesto F. Alemann (1893–1982), wrote:

> Menschenrechte und Menschenwürde, Gerechtigkeit und Freiheit, deren Verwirklichung Sinn der menschlichen Entwicklung ist, sind heute bedroht. Unter der Führung der Hitler, Goebbels und Goering marschiert Deutschland an der Spitze des neuen Barbarentums, das alle Kulturfortschritte der Menschheit mit Vernichtung bedroht. Deutschland, das Land Goethes und Schillers, wird heute geschändet durch Rassenfanatismus und Konzentrationaslager, durch Gestapo und Polizeiterror, durch Kriegshetze und Religionsverfolgerung. [. . .][8]

> Human rights and human dignity, justice, and freedom, the realization of which is the point of human development, are being threatened today. Under the leadership of Hitler, Goebbels, and Goering, Germany is marching to the height of a new barbarism that threatens the cultural advances of humanity with destruction. Germany, the land of Goethe and Schiller, is being violated today through racial fanaticism and concentration camps, through the Gestapo and police terror, through war mongering and religious persecution.

Alemann was also the lead author and first signatory of the above appeal on behalf of the group "Das Andere Deutschland" (the other Germany).[9] A democratic, antifascist German imaginary was, in essence, nurtured in Buenos Aires and later projected onto the ruins of postfascist Europe.[10]

---

7. Penny notes the recruitment of Swiss German speakers in the nineteenth century and their contribution to the establishing of print media and other institutions. *German History Unbound From 1750 to the Present* (New York: Cambridge University Press, 2022), 40; also Nazi ideology in Argentina in the 1930s, 250–53.

8. Friedmann, *Alemanes antinazis en la Argentina*, 32–33.

9. Penny elaborates on the work of the organization DAD as a relief committee, see *German History Unbound* (New York and Cambridge: Cambridge University Press, 2022), 253.

10. In *The Real Odessa* (London: Granta, 2002), Uki Goñi's monumental study of the complex, clandestine network that enabled Nazi war criminals to seek and receive safe haven in

In the excerpt cited above, the authors agitate against the notion that fascism and Germany are synonymous. On the contrary, the stewardship of cultural nationalism, supported by the transferable ideals of classical German-language literature, trump geographical location and citizenship.[11] This "portable" German identity, shaped by immigration in Argentina, also shapes the editor's South America as a continent to assume the leadership role once held by Europe. There, the "other" Germany espoused in the 1930s, characterized as a cultural nation, home of Goethe and Schiller, was barbarized by National Socialism.[12] In the Americas, missing from the 1492 globe and largely from the topography of Germany's colonial game, the possibility of a different, other narrative refused to cede its decolonized space of resistance. Recovering those voices is part of a larger project to acknowledge that there is no single alternative to metanarrative, and no totality can be known. Dismantling the construction of hegemonic racism and colonial logic, articulated in the German-speaking cultural worlds, has been the driving force behind this book. The turn and return of the Behaim globe and the stories that orbit around it has provided a frame of reference. It has since become a UNESCO World Heritage Treasure of Mankind. It is housed in the Germanisches Nationalmuseum in Nuremberg, and I close with it as a teachable moment. According to the website:

South America, especially Argentina, after the end of World War II, the journalist makes mention of the newspaper I rely on as a source. In his discussion of Reinhard Kops, a Nazi spy who worked for Perón's Nazi rescue office in Genoa (xiii), Goñi describes the *Argentinisches Tageblatt* in 1948 as "moderate" (239). In context, he is contrasting it to the openly Nazi-leaning *Freie Presse* and the monthly magazine *Der Weg*, where Kops, aka Juan Maler, found employment in Buenos Aires. Kops's career, while not my focus, nonetheless raises questions about the nature of "moderate" press coverage in the late 1940s.

11. Germán Friedmann, *Alemanes antinazis en la Argentina* (Buenos Aires: Siglo XXI, 2010), 166–67.

12. Immigration studies figure prominently in the reframing of colonial Germanness in Argentina. Among them, religion, language, and political affiliation have an impact on the formation of identity outside the nation. Benjamin Bryce (*To Belong to Buenos Aires: Germans, Argentines, and the Rise of a Pluralist Society* (Palo Alto, CA: Stanford University Press, 2018) has engaged with a range of historical sources to explore the history of disciplines, visual cultures, and specifics of immigration in and beyond colonial spaces. Robert Kelz, with a focus on German stages in Argentina in *Competing Germanies: Nazi, Antifascist, and Jewish Theater in German Argentina, 1933–1965* (Ithaca, NY: Cornell University Press, 2019), draws attention to the inflections across live performances of German-language dramas themselves and the interactions between individuals and institutions on two continents. He inscribes a history of the theater as a microcosm for the politics of identity formation in the twentieth century.

Conclusion

Now in hindsight, the globe makes clear how much the emergence of our modern world was based on the violent appropriation of raw materials, on the slave trade and the plantation economy. The Behaim Globe dates from and shows the first stage of the subjugation and division of the world by Europeans.[13]

---

13. See https://www.gnm.de/your-museum-in-nuremberg/collections/behaim-globe.

WORKS CITED

Alemann, Ernesto F. et al. "Das 'andere' Deutschland." *Argentinisches Tageblatt*, April 29, 1929.
Alemann, Ernesto F. "Vortrag." *Argentinisches Tageblatt*, August 11, 1947. 6. Continued on August 13, 1947.
Alemann, Johann. *Bilder aus der argentinischen Republik*. Buenos Aires: Dampf-Buchdruckerei des "Courrier de lat Plata," 1877. British Library Historical Print Edition.
Allison, Henry E. *Lessing and the Enlightenment: His Philosophy of Religion and Its Relation to Eighteenth-Century Thought*. Albany: State University of New York Press, 2018.
Altamirano, Carlos, and Breatriz Sarlo. *Ensayos argentinos. De Sarmiento a la vanguardia*. Buenos Aires: Ariel/Espasa-Calpe, 1997.
Althusser, Louis. *Essays on Ideology*. London: Verso, 1984.
Amerika, dargestellt durch sich selbst. Monat Juno 1818. No. 1–8. Nebst einer Beilage. Leipzig: Georg Joachim Göschen, 1818.
Ames, Eric. *Carl Hagenbeck's Empire of Entertainments*. Seattle: University of Washington Press, 2009.
Ames, Eric, Marcia Klotz, and Lora Wildenthal, eds. *Germany's Colonial Pasts*. Lincoln: University of Nebraska Press, 2007.
Amo, Anton Wilhelm. *Anton Wilhelm Amo's Philosophical Dissertations on Mind and Body*. Edited and introduced by Stephen Menn and Justin E. H. Smith. New York: Oxford University Press, 2020.
Anderson, Benedict. *Imagined Communities: Reflections on the Origin and Spread of Nationalism*. London: Verso, 1983.
Anonymous. "Neueste Erlebnisse aus Ost-Afrika." In *Koloniale Zeitschrift*, edited by A. Herfurth. Berlin: Verlag der Kolonialen Zeitschrift, 1907. February 28, 1907, Nr. 3: 8. Jahrgang, 86.
Appadurai, Arjun. "The Thing Itself." *Public Culture* 18, no. 1 (2006): 15–21.
Auf der Heide, Erin. "Representations of German-Speaking Exiles and Immigrants in Argentina." MA thesis, Bowling Green State University, 2006.
Auslander, Leora. "Beyond Words." *American Historical Review* 110, iss. 4 (October 2005): 1015–45. https://doi.org/10.1086/ahr.110.4.1015.
Avineri, Shlomo. *Hegel's Theory of the Modern State*. Cambridge: Cambridge University Press, 1972.
Baer, Werner. *The Brazilian Economy: Growth and Development*. London: Lynne Rienner Publishers, 2008.

Baetge, Dietmar. *Globalisierung des Wettbewerbrechts. Eine internationale Wettbewerbsordnung zwischen Kartell- und Welthandelsrecht*. Tübingen: Mohr Siebeck, 2009.
Barth, Emmy. *No Lasting Home: A Year in the Paraguayan Wilderness*. With a foreword by Alfred Neufeld. New York: Plough Publishing, 2011.
Bekers, Elisabeth, Sissy Helff, and Daniela Merolla, eds. *Transcultural Modernities: Narrating Africa in Europe*. Amsterdam: Rodopi, 2009.
Benjamin, Thomas. *The Atlantic World: Europeans, Africans, Indians and Their Shared History, 1400–1900*. Cambridge, UK: Cambridge University Press, 2009.
Berman, Nina. *Germans on the Kenyan Coast: Land, Charity, and Romance*. Bloomington: Indiana University Press, 2017.
Berman, Russell A. *Enlightenment or Empire: Colonial Discourse in German Culture*. Lincoln: University of Nebraska Press, 1998.
Bernasconi, Robert, ed. *Race and Racism in Continental Philosophy*. Bloomington: Indiana University Press, 2003.
Bersier, Gabrielle, Nancy Boerner, and Peter Boerner. *Goethe: Journeys of the Mind*. London: Haus Publishing, 2019.
Bewer, Max. "Deutsche Diamanten." *Kolonial-Gedicht und–lieder*. Edited by Emil Sembritzki. Berlin: Deutscher Kolonial-Verlag, 1911, 56–57.
Biehl, João, and Miqueias Mugge. *Escritos Perdidos: Vida e obra de um imigrante insurgente* (Lost writings: Life and work of an insurgent immigrant). São Leopoldo: Oikos, 2012, 2022.
Bird, Keith W. "The Origins and Role of German Naval History in the Inter-War Period of 1918–1939," *Naval War College Review* 32, no. 2 (March-April 1979), 42–58.
Bispo, A. A. "Mathilde Auguste Hedwig Fitzler Kömmerling (1896–1993) e o papel do Brasil no movimento feminino alemão. Da questão do 'pré-descobrimento português do Brasil.'" *Revista Brasil-Europa: Correspondência Euro-Brasileira* 130, no. 4 (2011), 2. http://www.revista.brasil-europa.eu/130/Hedwig_Fitzler.html.
Bitterli, Urs. *Alte Welt—neue Welt. Formen des europäisch-überseeischen Kulturkontakts vom 15. bis zum 18. Jahrhundert*. Munich: Beck, 1986.
Bitterli, Urs. *Cultures in Conflict: Encounters Between European and Non-European Cultures, 1492–1800*. Translated by Ritchie Robertson. Stanford, CA: Stanford University Press, 1986.
Bjerg, María. *Historias de la inmigración en la Argentina*. Buenos Aires: Edhasa, 2009.
Blackbourn, David. *Germany in the World: A Global History 1500–2000*. New York: Liveright Publishing, 2023.
Blackler, Adam A. "From Boondoggle to Settlement Colony: Hendrik Witbooi and the Evolution of Germany's Imperial Project in Southwest Africa, 1884–1894." *Central European History* 50 (2017): 449–70.
Blancpain, Jean-Pierre. *Immigration et nationalism au Chili 1810–1925. Un pays à l'écoute de l'Europe*. Paris: L'Harmattan, 2005.
Blancpain, Jean-Pierre. *Migrations et mémoire germaniques en Amérique Latine à l'époque contemporaine*. Strasbourg: Presses Universitaires, 1994.
Bodenstedt, Friedrich. *Aus Morgenland und Abandland. Neue Gedichte und Sprüche*. 2nd edition. Leipzig: Brockhaus, 1884.

Bosman, Hendrik. "A Nama 'Exodus'? A Postcolonial Reading of the Diaries of Hendrik Witbooi." *Scriptura* 108 (2011): 329–41.
Bowersox, Jeff. "Founding a Slave-Trading Company in West Africa." Black Central Europe. https://blackcentraleurope.com/sources/1500-1750/founding-a-slave-trading-colony-in-west-africa-1682-1683/.
Bräunlein, Peter J. *Martin Behaim: Legende und Wirklichkeit eines berühmten Nürnbergers*. Bamberg: Bayerische Verlagsanstalt, 1992.
Brewer, Cindy. "Fantasies of African Conversion: The Construction of Missionary Colonial Desire in the Dramas of a Catholic Nun, Maria Theresa Ledóchowska (1863–1922)." *German Studies Review* 30, no. 3 (2007): 557–78.
Broder, Henryk M. *Kritik der reinen Toleranz*. Berlin: WJS Verlag, 2008.
Broomhall, Susan, and Jacqueline Van Gent, *Dynastic Colonialism: Gender, Materiality and the Early Modern House of Orange-Nassau*. London: Routledge, 2016.
Brunner, Bernd. *Nach Amerika: Die Geschichte der deutschen Auswanderung*. 2nd edition. Munich: C. H. Beck, 2017.
Bruyssel, Ernest von. *La République Argentine: ses ressources naturelles, ses colonies agricoles*, ed. Th. Falk. Brussels: Librairie Européene C. Muquardt, Libraire du Roi et du Comte de Flandre, 1889.
Bryce, Benjamin. *To Belong to Buenos Aires: Germans, Argentines, and the Rise of a Pluralist Society*. Palo Alto, CA: Stanford University Press, 2018.
Buck-Morss, Susan. *Hegel, Haiti, and University History*. Pittsburgh: University of Pittsburgh Press, 2009.
Bülow, Frieda Freiin von. *Reisescizzen und Tagebuchblätter aus Deutsch-Ostafrica*. First published by Walther & Apolant, Berlin 1889. Edited and with an introduction, notes, and bibliography by Katharina von Hammerstein (Berlin: trafo, 2012).
Burt, Janet Burt, *Kuyahoora Towns*. Kuyahoora: Kuyahoora Valley Historical Society, 2003.
Canning, Kathleen, and Sonya O. Rose. "Gender, Citizenship and Subjectivity: Some Historical and Theoretical Considerations." *Gender and History* 13, no. 3 (2002): 427–43.
Carreras, Sandra, et al. *Auf dem Weg in eine neue Heimat. Deutsche Auswanderung nach Argentinien, Brasilien und Chile 1824–1914*. Berlin: Ibero-Amerikanisches Institut Preußischer Kulturbesitz.
Casco, José Arturo Saavedra. *Utenzi, War Poems, and the German Conquest of East Africa: Swahili Poetry as Historical Source*. Trenton, NJ: Africa World Press, 2007.
Cassidy, Eugene S. "Germanness, Civilization, and Slavery: Southern Brazil as German Colonial Space (1819–1888)." PhD dissertation, University of Michigan, 2015.
"Chaco War." Encyclopædia Britannica. http://www.britannica.com/EBchecked/topic/104130/Chaco-War. Accessed August 30, 2014.
"Christian Afrikaner." *Kinderlust. Eine Sammlung kurzer Erzaehlungen fuer die christliche Jugend*, No. 13. Hrsg. von der Verlagshandlung der Ev. Luth. Colombus, Ohio: Synode von Ohio und anderen Staaten. No date, ca. 1890, 165–76.
Ciarlo, David. *Advertising Empire: Race and Visual Culture in Imperial Germany*. Cambridge, MA: Harvard University Press, 2011.
Coffmann, D'Maris, Adrian Leonard, and William O'Reilly. *The Atlantic World*. London: Routledge, 2015.

Colin, Susi. "The Wild Man and the Indian in Early 16th Century Book Illustration." In *Indians and Europe: An Interdisciplinary Collection of Essays.* Edited by Christian F. Feest, 5–36. Lincoln: University of Nebraska Press, 1989.

Conrad, Sebastian. *What Is Global History?* Princeton, NJ: Princeton University Press, 2016.

Conway, Christopher. "Gender Iconoclasm and Aesthetics: Echeverría's *La Cautiva* and the Captivity Paintings of Juan Manuel Blanes." *Decimónica* 12, no. 1 (2015): 116–33.

Corbey, Raymond. "Ethnographic Showcases, 1870–1930." *Cultural Anthropology* 8, no. 3 (1993): 338–69.

Cramer, Ada. *Weiß oder Schwarz? Lehr- und Leidensjahre eines Farmers im Südwest im Lichte des Rassenhasses.* Berlin: Kolonial-Verlag, 1913.

Cramer, Ernst Ludwig. *Die Kinderfarm.* Potsdam: Rütten und Loening, 1941.

Cramer, Otto. "Einleitung." Ada Cramer. *Weiß oder Schwarz? Lehr- und Leidensjahre eines Farmers im Südwest im Lichte des Rassenhasses.* Berlin: Kolonial-Verlag, 1913, 1–13.

Cramer, Otto. "Vorwort." Ada Cramer. *Weiß oder Schwarz? Lehr- und Leidensjahre eines Farmers im Südwest im Lichte des Rassenhasses.* Berlin: Kolonial-Verlag, 1913, iii–iv.

Curran, Andrew S. *The Anatomy of Blackness: Science and Slavery in an Age of Enlightenment.* Baltimore: Johns Hopkins University Press, 2011.

Dal Lago, Enrico, and Constantina Katsari, eds. *Slave Systems: Ancient and Modern.* Cambridge: Cambridge University Press, 2008.

Da Silva, Denise. *Toward a Global History of Race.* Minneapolis: University of Minnesota Press, 2007.

Davis, Christian S. *Colonialism, Anti-Semitism, and Germans of Jewish Descent in Imperial Germany.* Ann Arbor: University of Michigan Press, 2012.

De Bivar Marquese, Rafael, and Fábio Duarte Joly. "Panis, disciplina, et opus servo: The Jesuit Ideology in Portuguese America and Greco-Roman Ideas of Slavery." In *Slave Systems: Ancient and Modern*, edited by Enrico Dal Lago and Constantina Katsari, 214–359. Cambridge: Cambridge University Press, 2008.

Dedekind, Father M., *Die deutsch-evangelische Diaspora in Brasilien.* Leipzig: Verlag von Strauch & Krey GmbH, 1930.

De las Casas, Bartolomé. *Brief Account of the Destruction of the Indies Or, a faithful NARRATIVE OF THE Horrid and Unexampled Massacres, Butcheries, and all manner of Cruelties, that Hell and Malice could invent, committed by the Popish Spanish Party on the inhabitants of West-India, TOGETHER With the Devastations of several Kingdoms in America by Fire and Sword, for the space of Forty and Two Years, from the time of its first Discovery by them.* From the English translation: "Composed first in Spanish by Bartholomew de las Casas, a Bishop there, and Eye-Witness of most of these Barbarous Cruelties; afterward Translated by him into Latin, then by other hands, into High-Dutch, Low-Dutch, French, and now Taught to Speak Modern English." *Brevisima relacion de la destruccíon de las Indias*, by Bartolome de las Casas. Seville, 1552. London: Printed for R. Hewson at the Crown in Corn, 1689. Projekt Gutenberg ebook.

De las Casas, Bartolomé. *The Devastation of the Indies: A Brief Account.* Translated by Herma Briffault, introduction by Bill M. Donavan. Baltimore: Johns Hopkins University Press, 1992.

Works Cited

Derrida, Jacques. "Archive Fever: A Freudian Impression." Translated by Eric Prenowitz. *Diacritics* 25, no. 2 (Summer 1995): 9–63.
Deutsche La Plata Zeitung. 6 Jahrgang: Nr. 2 (5. Januar 1876).
Deutsche Post. Organ des Deutschtums in Chile. Druck & Verlag: Luis Kober. Ed. Albert Hoerll. Jahrgang 31 Nr. 1 (August 1902).
Deutsche Post. Nr. 2 (September 2, 1902).
Deutsche Post. Nr. 3 (September 4, 1902).
Deutsche Post. Nr. 4 (September 6, 1902).
Deutsche Post. Nr. 5 (September 10, 1902).
Deutsche Post. Nr. 7 (September 17, 1902).
Deutsche Post. Nr. 8 (September 23, 1902).
Deutsche Post. Nr. 9 (September 15, 1902).
Deutsche Post. Nr. 11 (September 30, 1902).
Deutsche Post. Nr. 20 (October 21, 1902).
Deutsche Post. Nr. 23 (October 21, 1902).
Deutsche Post. Nr. 26 (November 6, 1902).
Deutsche Post. Nr. 28 (November 11, 1902).
Deutsche Post. Nr. 32 (November 20, 1902).
Deutsche Post. Nr. 33 (November 22, 1902).
Deutsche Post. Nr. 34 (November 25, 1902).
Deutsche Post. Nr. 35 (November 27, 1902).
Deutsche Zeitung für Süd-Chile. Jahrgang 1. Nr. 1 (April 10, 1886).
Deutsche Zeitung für Süd-Chile. Jahrgang II. Nr. 24. (September 21, 1887).
Deutsche Zeitung für Süd-Chile. Jahrgang VIII. Nr. 3 (January 21, 1893).
Deutsche Zeitung für Süd-Chile. Jahrgang IX. Nr. 18 (May 5, 1894).
Deutsche Zeitung für Süd-Chile. Jahrgang XVI. Nr. 19 (May 18, 1901).
Deutsche Zeitung für Süd-Chile. Jahrgang XIX: Nr. 1 (January 2, 1904).
Deutsche Zeitung für Süd-Chile. Jahrgang XIX. Nr. 66 (June 11, 1904).
Deutsche Zeitung für Süd-Chile. Jahrgang XXI. Nr. 4 (January 1907).
Deutsche Zeitung für Süd-Chile. Nr. 2 (April 17, 1886).
Deutsche Zeitung für Süd-Chile. Nr. 7 (February 18, 1893).
Deutsche Zeitung für Süd-Chile. Nr. 9 (January 21, 1904).
Deutsche Zeitung für Süd-Chile. Nr. 11 (January 26, 1904).
Deutsche Zeitung für Süd-Chile. Nr. 13 July 3, 1886).
Deutsche Zeitung für Süd-Chile. Nr. 19 (February 16, 1904).
Deutsche Zeitung für Süd-Chile. Nr. 21 (February 20, 1904).
Deutsche Zeitung für Süd-Chile. Nr. 29 (October 23, 1886).
Deutsche Zeitung für Süd-Chile. Nr. 36 (December 11, 1886).
Deutsche Zeitung für Süd-Chile Nr. 42 (April 12, 1904).
Deutsche Zeitung für Süd-Chile. Nr. 44 (April 16, 1904).
Deutsche Zeitung für Süd-Chile. Nr. 49 (April 28, 1904).
Deutsche Zeitung für Süd-Chile. Nr. 50 (December 15, 1894).
Deutsche Zeitung für Süd-Chile. Nr. 67 (June 14,1904).
Deutsche Zeitung für Süd-Chile. Nr. 77 (July 7, 1904).

Deutsche Zeitung für Süd-Chile. Nr. 79 (July 12, 1904).
Deutsche Zeitung für Süd-Chile. Nr. 141 (December 13, 1904).
Deutsche Zeitung für Süd-Chile Nr. 142 (December 17, 1904).
Dias, Camila Loureira. "Jesuit Maps and Political Discourse: The Amazon River of Father Samuel Fritz." *The Americas* 69, no. 1 (July 2012): 95–116.
Die Heimath. Buenos Aires. April 4, 1877.
Die Heimath. April 6, 1877.
Die Heimath. April 13, 1877.
Die Heimath. April 15, 1877.
Die Heimath. April 18, 1877.
Die Heimath. April 20, 1877.
Die Heimath. April 22, 1877.
Dill, Hans-Otto. *Die lateinamerikanische Literatur in Deutschland. Bausteine zur Geschichte ihrer Rezeption*. Vol. 11, Sprachen, Gesellchaften und Kulturen In Lateinamerika, edited by Kerstin Störl and Germán de Granda. Frankfurt/M and Bern: Peter Lang, 2009.
Djomo, Esaie, and Dorine Mbeudom. "Maria Theresia Ledóchowska as an Activist in the Religious Colonization of Africa." *Gender and German Colonialism: Intimacies, Accountabilities, Intersections*, ed. Elisabeth Krimmer and Chunjie Zhang/ New York: Routledge, 2024, 245–59.
Dreher, Martin M. *Wilhelm Rotermund: Seu Tempo—Suas Obras*. São Leopoldo: Editora Oikos, 2014.
Eicher, John P. R. *Exiled Among Nations: German and Mennonite Mythologies in a Transnational Age*. New York: Cambridge University Press, 2019.
Elmir, Claudio Pereira, and Marcos Antônio Witt, eds. *Imigração na América Latina: Histórias de fracassos*. São Leopoldo: Editora Oikos, 2014.
El-Tayeb, Fatima. *European Others: Queering Ethnicity in Postnational Europe*. Minneapolis: University of Minnesota Press, 2011.
Engelberg, Stefan et al., eds. *Koloniale und Postkoloniale Linguistik. Colonial and Postcolonial Linguistics*. Berlin: De Gruyter, 2015. Vol. 5. *Colonialism and Missionary Linguistics*. Edited by Klaus Zimmermann and Birte Kellermeier-Rehbein. Berlin: De Gruyter, 2015.
Eschwege, Wilhelm Ludwig von. *Geognostisches Gemälde von Brasilien und wahrscheinliches Muttergestein der Diamanten mit einem Kupfer*. Weimar, im Verlage des Gr. H. S. priv. Landes-Industrie-Comptoirs, 1822.
Eze, Emmanuel Chukwudi. "The Color of Reason: The Idea of 'Race' in Kant's Anthropology." *Postcolonial African Philosophy: A Critical Reader*. Edited by Emmanuel Chukwudi Eze Cambridge: Blackwell, 1997, 103–40.
Fabri, M. J. E. "Vorrede." Johann Jakob Hartsink, *Johann Jakob Hartsink's Beschreibung von Guiana oder der wilden Küste in Süamerika. Aus dem Holländischen übersetzt. Erster Theil. Mit einer Vorrede und Zusa4tzen von M. J. E. Fabri*, no translator named. Berlin: Johann Friedrich Unger, 1784, iii–vix.
Fausel, Erich. *D. Dr. Rotermund: Ein Kampf u Recht und Richtung des evangelischen Deutschtums in Südbrasilien*. São Leopoldo: Verlag der Tiograndenser Synode, 1936.

Feder, Ernst. *Goethes Liebe zu Brasilien. Mit vier Bildern und einem Vorwort von Professor Roquette Pinto*. Ijuí: Ulrich Löw, 1950.
Feder, Ernst. "Lessing entdeckt Brasilien." *Sonderdruck aus dem Serra-Post Kalender*. Rio de Janeiro, 1952.
Feder, Gottfried. *Programm der N.S.D.A.P. und seine weltanschaulichen Grundgedanken*. Munich: Nationalsozialistische Bibliothek, 1. Auflage 1927. Auflage, 251–75. Tausend, 1930.
Festenburg, Herman von. "Groß-Friedrichsburg." In *Kolonial- Gedicht- und Liederbuch*, edited by Emil Sembritzki, 9–13. Berlin: Deutscher-Kolonial Verlag, 1911.
Figel, Sara Eigen. "The Point of Recognition: Enemy, Neighbor, and Next of Kin in the Era of Frederick the Great." In *Enlightened War: German Theories and Cultures of Warfare from Frederick the Great to Clausewitz*, edited by Elisabeth Krimmer and Patricia Anne Simpson, 21–40. Rochester, NY: Camden House, 2010.
Fitzler, M. A. Hedwig. "Der Anteil der Deutschen an der Kolonialpolitik Philipps II. von Spanien in Asien." *Vierteljahrschrift für Sozial- und Wirtschaftsgeschichte*, 28. Bd., H. 3. Franz Steiner Verlag, 1935, 243–81. Stable URL: https://www.jstor.org/stable/20726789.
Foucault, Michel. *The Order of Things: An Archaeology of the Human Sciences*. Translated by Alan Sheridan. New York: Random House, 1994.
Frederick, Bonnie. "Reading the Warning: The Reader and the Image of the Captive Woman." *Chasqui* 18, no. 2 (November 1989): 3–11.
Freud, Sigmund. *Civilization and Its Discontents*. Translated by James Strachey. New York: Norton, 1962.
Freud, Sigmund. *Dora: An Analysis of a Case of Hysteria* (1905 [1901]). Edited and introduced by Philip Rieff. New York: Collier, 1963.
Frey, Barbara. "Der Fall Cramer." *Ravensberger Blätter*. Organ des Historischen Vereins für die Grafschaft Ravensberg e.V., Heft 2 (2011): 40–53.
Frey, J. *Deutsche Zeitung für Süd-Chile*. No. 24/II. Jahrgang (September 21, 1887).
Friedman, Max Paul. *Nazis and Good Neighbors: The United States Campaign Against the Germans of Latin America in WW II*. Cambridge: Cambridge University Press, 2003.
Friedmann, Germán C. *Alemanes antinazis en la Argentina*. Buenos Aires: Siglo XXI, 2010.
Friedmann, Germán C. "The German Speakers of Argentina in the 1930s and 1940s." *Transatlantic Battles: European Immigrant Communities in South America and the World Wars*, ed. María Inés Tato. Leiden: Brill, 2023, 144–63.
Friedrich II. *The Refutation of Machiavelli's Prince or, Anti-Machiavel*. 1740. https://archive.org/details/AntiMachiavelFriederricktheGreat/page/n1/mode/2up.
Gaede, William R. "Wie dachte Lessing über Friedrich II.?" In *Journal of English and German Philology* 35, no. 4 (October 1936): 546–65.
Gallero, María Cecilia. *Con la patria a cuestas: La inmigración alemana-brasileña en la Colonia Puerto Rico, Misiones*. Buenos Aires: Araucaria editora, 2009.
Gerbner, Katherine. "Protestant Supremacy: The Story of a Neologism." *Church History* 88, no. 3 (September 2019): 773–80.
Gewald, Jan-Bart. *Herero Heroes: A Socio-Political History of the Herero of Namibia, 1890–1923*. Athens: Ohio University Press, 1999.

Goethe, Johann Wolfgang von. *Faust* II. *Sämtliche Werke. Briefe, Tagebücher und Gespräche*. Edited by Dieter Borchmeyer et al. 40 Vols. Frankfurt a. M.: Deutscher Klassiker Verlag, 1985 ff.
Goethe, Johann Wolfgang von. "Todeslied eines Gefangenen." In Mathias Mayer, "Johann Wolfgang Goethe: 'Todeslied eines Gefangenen.'" "Frankfurter Anthologie" section of the *Frankfurter Allgemeine Zeitung*. June 12, 2015. https://www.faz.net/aktuell/feuilleton/buecher/frankfurter-anthologie/frankfurter-anthologie-johann-wolfgang-goethe-todeslied-eines-gefangenen-13644033.html.
Goñi, Uki. *The Real Odessa*. London: Granta, 2002.
Goossen, Benjamin W. "Mennonites in Latin America: A Review of the Literature." *Conrad Grebel Review* 34, no. 3 (Fall 2016): 236–65.
Griffity, Elstyn. "Provincialism, Private Life and the Marginal Hero: Germany after Unification in the Works of Gustav Freytag, Friedrich Spielhagen and Paul Heyse." *Germany's Two Unifications: Anticipations, Experiences, Responses*. Edited by Ronald Speirs and John Breuilly. New York: Palgrave Macmillan, 2005, 209–23.
Grimm, Hans. *Volk ohne Raum*. Munich: Albert Langen, 1926/1929.
Grimm, Jakob, and Wilhelm Grimm. *Deutsches Wörterbuch* online, 16 Bde. in 32 Teilbänden. Leipzig 1854–1961. Quellenverzeichnis Leipzig 1971. Online-Version vom 17.06.2020. Bd. 13, Sp. 22 bis 25.
Grimm, Reinhold, and Jost Hermand, eds. *Blacks in German Culture*. Madison, WI: Monatshefte Occasional Papers, 1986.
Grinberg, Keila. "Re-enslavement, Rights and Justice in Nineteenth-Century Brazil." *Translating the Americas, U-M Center for Latin American and Caribbean Studies*, vol. 1 (2013), no pagination. Translated by Mark Lambert from Grinberg, "Re-escravização, direitos e justiças no Brasil do século XIX," in *Direitos e justiças: ensaios de história social*. Edited by Silvia Lara and Joseli Mendonça (Campinas: Editora da Unicamp, 2006): 101–28.
Groesen, Michiel van, ed. *The Legacy of Dutch Brazil*. New York: Cambridge University Press, 2014.
Gruesz, Kirsten Silva. "Facing the Nation: The Organic Life of 'La cautiva.'" *Revista de Estudios Hispánicos* [Washington University in St. Louis] 30, no. 1 (January 1996): 3–22.
Grützmann, Irmgart, and Mateus Klumb. "Idendidade feminina modelar em Os Dois Vizinhos, de Wilhelm Rotermund." *Mouseion, Revista Eletrônica do Museu e Arquivo Histórico La Salle*, no. 31 (dez. 2018): 9–26.
Guthke, Karl S. *Goethes Reise nach Spanisch-Amerika. Weltbewohnen in Weimar*. Göttingen: Wallstein Verlag, 2016.
Haacke, Ulrich, and Benno Schneider. *Geschichtsbuch für die deutsche Jugend*. With Bernhard Kunmsteller. Leipzig: Verlag von Quelle & Meyer, 1935.
Habermas, Jürgen. *Theory of Communicative Action*. Vol. I: *Reason and the Rationalization of Society*. Boston: Beacon Press, 1984. https://teddykw2.files.wordpress.com/2012/07/jurgen-habermas-theory-of-communicative-action-volume-1.pdf. Accessed December 10, 2020.
Hartmann, Wolfram. "Urges in the Colony. Men and Women in Colonial Windhoek, 1890–1905." *Journal of Namibian Studies* 1 (2007): 39–71.

Hartsink, Johann Jakob. *Johann Jakob Hartsink's Beschreibung von Guiana oder der wilden Küste in Süamerika. Aus dem Holländischen übersetzt. Erster Theil. Mit einer Vorrede und Zusa4tzen von M. J. E. Fabri*. Berlin: Johann Friedrich Unger, 1784.
Heffter, Heinrich.*Deutsche Kolonien*. Dresden: Cigaretten-Bilderdienst, 1936.
Hegel, G. W. F. *The Philosophy of History*. Translated by J. Sibree. Kitchener: Batoche Books, 2001.
Helmar, W. (Hellemeyer, Maria). *Vom Urwald zur Kultur: Erlebnisse eines Mädchens*. Berlin: Verlag von Otto Janke, 1898.
Henao-Castro, Andrés. "Nietzsche and Haiti: The Post-Colonial Rebirth of Tragedy." *Theory & Event* 21, no. 2 (April 2018): 358–81.
Herfurth, A. "Warum müssen wir Kolonialpolitik treiben?" *Koloniale Zeitung* 1, no. 8 (January 4, 1907): 1–2.
Hesse, Volker. "'Ich habe [. . .] selbst eine Landschaft phantasiert'—Goethes Interesse an der wissenschaftlichen Entdeckung Südamerikas." In *Weltbürger Goethe: Schriften der Berliner Goethegesellschaft*, edited by Monika Estermann and Uwe Hentschel, 113–40. Berlin: Berliner Wissenschaftsverlag, 2019.
Hinterkeuser, Guido. "Visions of power: Andreas Schlüter's monuments to the Great Elector and Friedrich III and I." *Sculpture Journal* 22, no. 1 (2013): 21–35.
Hock, Beate. *In zwei Welten. Frauenbiografien zwischen Europa und Argentinien. Deutschsprachige Emigration und Exil im 20. Jahrhundert*. Berlin: edition tranvía Verlag Walter Frey, 2016.
Hoerll, Albert. "Chile und seine Kolonisation." *Deutsche Zeitung*, December 22 and 24, 1904.
Hoerll, Albert. *Die Deutsche Kolonisation in Chile*. Valdivia: Imprenta Comercio, Alberto Hoerll, 1925.
Hoerll, Albert, ed. *Deutsche Post*. Organ des Deutschtums in Chile. Administration, Druck & Verlag: Luis Kober Verantwortl. August 30, 1902.
Hoerll, Alberto. "La colonización alemana en Chile." In *Los Alemanes in Chile*. Homenaje de la Sociedad Científica Alemana de Santiago a la Nacion chilena en el centario de su independencia (The Germans in Chile. Tribute from the German Scientific Society of Santiago to the Chilean nation on the centenary of its independence). Volume 1. Introduced by Dr. Ernesto Maier. Santiago: Imprenta Universitaria, 1910. 1–57.
Hölty, Ludwig Christoph Heinrich. "Der befreite Sklave." In *Gedichte*. Hamburg: Bohm, 1783, 168. DTA. https://www.deutschestextarchiv.de/book/view/hoelty_gedichte_1783?p=208.
Holub, Robert. "Nietzsche's Colonialist Imagination: Nueva Germania, Good Europeanism, and Great Politics." In *The Imperialist Imagination: German Colonialism and Its Legacy*, edited by Sara Friedrichsmeyer, Sara Lennox, and Susanne Zantop, 33–49. Ann Arbor: University of Michigan Press, 1998.
hooks, bell. *Black Looks: Race and Representation*. Boston: South End Press, 1992.
Horkheimer, Max. *Critical Theory: Selected Essays*. Translated by Matthew J. O'Connell et al. New York: Continuum, 2002.
Hörz, Magdelene Barbara Aichele. Briefe. Aichele PER 100 AIC. Biblioteca y Archivo Histórica Emilio Held Winkler. Santiago, Chile.

Ilg, Karl. *Pioniere in Argentinien, Chile, Paraguay und Venezuela. Durch Bergwelt, Urwald und Steppe erwanderte Volkskunde der deutschsprachigen Siedler*. Mit 47 Farbbildern, 19 Zeichnungen und 5 Karten. Innsbruck: Tyrolia-Verlag, 1976.

Ireton, Sean, and Caroline Schaumann, eds. *Heights of Reflection: Mountains and the German Imagination from the Middle Ages to the Twenty-first Century*. Rochester, NY: Camden House, 2012.

Ismar, Georg. *Der Pressekrieg: Argentinisches Tageblatt und Deutsche La Plata Zeitung 1933–1945*. Berlin: wfb, 2006.

Jando, Dominque. *Short History of the Circus*. http://www.circopedia.org/SHORT_HISTORY_OF_THE_CIRCUS.

Jara, René, and Nicholas Spadaccini, eds. *Amerindian Images and the Legacy of Columbus*. Minneapolis: University of Minnesota Press, 1992. 1–95.

Jitrik, Noé. *Esteban Echeverría*. Buenos Aires: Centro Editorial de América Latina, 1967.

Kaethler, Frieda Siemens, and Alfred Neufeld. *Nikolai Siemens der Chacooptimist. Das Mennoblatt und die Anfänge der Kolonie Fernheims: 1930–1955*. Weisenheim am Berge: Agape Verlag, 2005.

Kant, Immanuel. "Determination of the concept of a human race." In *Immanuel Kant: Anthropology, history and education* Edited by Holly Wilson and Günther Zöller, introduced and translated by the editors. Cambridge: Cambridge University Press, 2013, 147–59,

Kelz, Robert. *Competing Germanies: Nazi, Antifascist, and Jewish Theater in German Argentina, 1933–1965*. Ithaca, NY: Cornell University Press, 2019.

Kenny, Robert. "Freud, Jung and Boas." *Notes and Records of the Royal Society* 69, no. 2 (2015): 173–90.

Kittler, Friedrich A. *Discourse Networks 1800/1900*. Translated byMichael Metteer, with Chris Cullens. Foreword by David E. Wellbery. Palo Alto, CA: Stanford University Press, 1992.

Klarer, Mario. "Humanitarian Pornography: John Gabriel Stedman's 'Narrative of a Five Years Expedition against the Revolted N*groes of Surinam' (1796)." *New Literary History* 36, no. 4 (2005): 559–87.

Klein, Marcus. "The Chilean Movimiento Nacional Socialista, the German-Chilean Community, and the Third Reich, 1932–1939: Myth and Reality." *The Americas* 60, no. 4 (April 2004): 589–616.

Klotz, Marcia. "Memoirs from a German Colony: What Do White Women Want?" *Genders* 19 (1994): 154–73.

Kontje, Todd. *Imperial Fictions: German Literature Before and Beyond the Nation State*. Ann Arbor: University of Michigan Press, 2018.

Krause, E. "Abergläubische Kuren und sonstiger Aberglaube in Berlin und nächster Umgebung. Gesammelt in den Jahren 1862–1882." *Zeitschrift für Ethnologie*, vol. 15 (1883): 78–94.

Krimmer, Elisabeth, and Chunjie Zhang, eds. *Gender and German Colonialism: Intimacies, Accountabilities, Intersections*. New York: Routledge, 2024.

Kuder, Manfred. *Die deutschbrasilianische Literatur und das Bodenständigkeitsgefühl der deutschen Volksgruppe in Brasilien*. Berlin: Ferdinand Dümmler, 1937.

Kuhn, Stefan. "Von Bern über Santa Fe nach Buenos Aires. Die Vorgeschichte der Gründung des Argentinischen Tageblatts." *Argentinisches Tageblatt*, April 29, 2009. Nr. 31.716. 1–4.

Kümper, Hiram. "*Nichts als blauer Dunst?* Zigarettensammelbilder als Medien historischer Sinnbildung—quellenkundliche Skizzen zu einem bislang ungehobenen Schatz." *Geschichte in Wissenschaft und Unterricht* 59 (2008): 492–507. In H-Soz-Kult, 08.09.2008, www.hsozkult.de/journal/id/z6ann-103142.

Kuznesof, Elizabeth Anne. "Ethnic and Gender Influences on 'Spanish' Creole Society in Colonial Spanish America." *Colonial Latin American Review* 4, no. 1 (1995): 153–76.

Kuzniar, Alice, ed. *Outing Goethe and His Age*. Palo Alto, CA: Stanford University Press, 1996.

Lagmanovich, David. "Tres cautivas: Echeverría, Ascasubi, Hernández." *Chasqui* 8, no. 3 (May 1979): 24–33.

Lane-Poole, Stanley, and J. D. Jerrold Kelley. *The Story of the Barbary Corsairs*. New York: Putnam, 1890.

Lennox, Sara, and Sara Friedrichsmeyer, eds. *The Imperialist Imagination: German Colonialism and Its Legacy*. Ann Arbor: University of Michigan Press, 2005.

Lessing, Gotthold Ephraim. Lessings *Gesammelte Werke*, 2 vols. Leipzig: G. J. Göschen'sche Verlagsbuchhandlung, 1865. Internet Archive: https://archive.org/details/gelessingsgesam01lessgoog/page/n21/mode/2up.

Lessing, Gotthold Ephraim. "Unter das Bildnis des Königs von Preussen." In *Werke*, edited by Gerd Hillen, with Albert von Schirmding, and Jörg Schönert, Volumes 1–8. Munich: Hanser, 1970. http://www.zeno.org/Literatur/M/Lessing,+Gotthold+Ephraim/Gedichte/Sinngedichte+(Nachlese)/Unter+das+Bildnis+des+K%C3%B6nigs+von+Preu%C3%9Fen.

Lu-Adler, Huaping. "Kant on Lazy Savagery, Racialized." *Journal of History of Philosophy* 60, no. 2 (April 2022): 253–75.

Lu-Adler, Huaping. "Kant's Use of Travel Reports in Theorizing about Race—A Case Study about How Testimony Features in Natural Philosophy." *Studies in History and Philosophy and Philosophy of Science* 91 (2022): 10–19.

Lübcke, Alexandra. "*Welch ein Unterschied aber zwischen Europa und hier.*" *Diskurstheoretische Überlegungen zu Nation, Auswanderung und kulturelle Geschlechteridentität anhand von Briefen Chileauswanderinnen des 19. Jahrhunderts*. Frankfurt a/M: IKO Verlag für interkulturelle Kommunikation, 2003.

Luebke, Frederick C. *Germans in the New World: Essays in the History of Immigration*. Urbana: University of Illinois Press, 1999.

Luh, Jürgen. "Friedrich der Große und Said Ali Aga oder Des Königs Verhältnis zur Sklaverei." *Texte des Research Center Sanssouci für Wissen und Gesellschaft (RECS)* #55. (06.03.2023): https://recs.hypotheses.org/10110.

Lütge, Wilhelm, Werner Hoffmann, and Karl Wilhelm Körner, *Geschichte des Deutschtums in Argentinien*, hrsg. vom Deutschen Klub in Buenos Aires zur Feier seines 100jährigen Bestehens, 18. Oktober 1955 (Buenos Aires: Deutscher Klub, 1955).

MacCormack, Sabine. "Limits of Understanding: Perceptions of Greco-Roman and Amerindian Paganism in Early Modern Europe." In *America in European Consciousness*,

1493–1750, edited by Karen Ordahl Kupperman, 79–129. Durham, NC: University of North Carolina Press, 1995.
Madan, Aarti. "Writing the Earth, Writing the Nation: Latin American Narrative and the Language of Geography." PhD diss., University of Pittsburgh, 2010.
Maler, Anselm, with Sabine Schot. *Galerie der Welt. Ethnographisches Erzählen im 19. Jahrhundert*. Stuttgart: Belser Verlag, 1988.
Mandel, Ruth. *Cosmopolitan Anxieties: Turkish Challenges to Citizenship and Belonging in Germany*. Durham, NC: Duke University Press, 2008.
Mandelbaum, Moran M. *The Nation/State Fantasy: A Psychoanalytic Genealogy of Nationalism*. London: Palgrave Macmillan, 2020.
Martin, Gerald. "Literature, Music and the Visual Arts c. 1820–1870." *A Cultural History of Latin America: Literature, Music, and the Visual Arts in the 19th and 20th Centuries*. Edited by Leslie Bethell. Cambridge and New York: Cambridge University Press, 1998, 3–46.
Masiello, Francine. *Between Civilization and Barbarism: Women, Nation, and Literary Culture in Modern Argentina*. Lincoln: University of Nebraska Press, 1992.
Maschler, Channinah. "Lessing's Ernst and Falk, Dialogues for Freemasons. A Translation with Notes." *Interpretation: A Journal of Political Philosophy* 14, no. 1 (1986): 1–50.
Mayer, Mathias. "Johann Wolfgang Goethe: 'Todeslied eines Gefangenen.'" "Frankfurter Anthologie" section of the *Frankfurter Allgemeine Zeitung*, June 12, 2015. https://www.faz.net/aktuell/feuilleton/buecher/frankfurter-anthologie/frankfurter-anthologie-johann-wolfgang-goethe-todeslied-eines-gefangenen-13644033.html.
Mayo, Carlos A. *Fuentes para la historia de la frontera: declaraciones de cautivos*. Mar del Plata: Universidad de Mar del Plata, 1985.
Mazzari, Marcus V. "Nature or God: Pantheistic Affinities between Goethe and Martius 'the Brazilian.'" *Estudos Avançados* 24, no. 69 (2012): 183–202.
McCall, Leslie. "The Complexity of Intersectionality." *Signs: Journal of Women in Culture and Society* 30, no. 3 (2005): 1771–1800.
McClintock, Anne. *Imperial Leather: Race, Gender, and Sexuality in the Colonial Context*. London: Routledge, 1995.
Mehring, Franz. *Die Lessing-Legende:: Zur Geschichte und Kritik des preussischen Despotismus und der klassischen Literatur*, 2nd edition. Stuttgart: J.H.W. Dietz nachf., 1906.
Mehring, Franz. *The Lessing Legend*. Abridged translation by A. S. Grogan. New York: Critics Group Press, 1938. https://www.marxists.org/archive/mehring/1892/lessing/index.htm.
Meinecke, Gustav. *Aus dem Creolenlande. Erzählungen*. Berlin: Zenker, 1888.
Meinecke, Gustav. *Der arme Sidi Aabderrachman. Eine ostafrikanische Geschichte*. 6. Auflage. Berlin: Deutscher Kolonial-Verlag, 1897.
Meinecke, Gustav. *Deutsche Kultivation in Ostafrika und der Kaffeebau*. Berlin: Carl Heymanns Verlag, 1892.
Meinecke, Gustav. *Die Deutschen Kolonien in Wort und Bild. Geschichte, Länder- und Völkerkunde, Tier- und Pflanzenwelt, Handels- und Wirtschaftsverhältnisse der Schutzgebiete des Deutschen Reiches*. 2nd expanded edition. Leipzig: Verlag von J. J. Weber, 1901.
Meinecke, Gustav. *Katechismus der Auswanderung. Kompaß für Auswanderer nach europäischen Ländern, Asien, Afrika, den deutschen Kolonien, Australien, Süd- und

Zentralamerika, Mexiko, den Vereinigten Staaten von Amerika und Kanada. 7th ed. Vollständig und neu bearbeitet. Mit 4 in den Text gedruckten Karten. Leipzig: J. J. Weber, 1896.

Meinecke, Gustav. *Zuckeruntersuchungen am Pangani.* Vegatationsbilder von Dr. Otto Warburg. 2nd ed. Berlin: Deutscher Kolonial-Verlag, 1909.

Meyns, Chris. "Anton Wilhelm Amo and the Problems of Perception." In *The Senses in the History of Philosophy*, edited by Brian R. Glenney and José Filipe Pereira da Silva, 169–84. London: Routledge, 2019.

Meyns, Chris. "Anton Wilhelm Amo's Philosophy of Mind/" *Philosophy Compass*, 2019;14:e12571. https://doi.org/10.1111/phc3.12571MEYNS13.

Mignolo, Walter. "Introduction: Coloniality of power and de-colonial thinking." *Cultural Studies* 21, no. 2–3, Globalization and the De-colonial Option (2007): 155–67.

Mommsen, Katharin.a *Goethe und die arabische Welt.* Frankfurt a/M: Insel, 1988.

Mücke, Dorothea von. "Authority, Authorship, and Audience: Enlightenment Models for a Critical Public." *Representations* 111, no. 1 (Summer 2010): 60–87.

Muñoz Sougarret, Jorge Ernesto, and Daniel Silva Jorquera. "La modernidad viste de capa española: la utilización de mano de obra infantil arrendada y presidiaria durante la conformación de los mercados laborales en Osorno en la segiunda mitad del siglo XIX." *Espacio Regional: Revista de Estudios Sociales* vol. 1 no. 7 (2010): 87–105.

Museu do Homem do Nordeste. Catalogue. Brazil: Banco Safra, 2000.

Nafziger, Tim. "A window into Antisemitism and Nazism among Mennonite in North America, Part 1." Posted July 30, 2007. http://www.themennonite.org/bloggers/timjn/posts/A_window_into_Antisemitism_and_Nazism_among_Mennonite_in_North_America_Part_1. Accessed August 17, 2014.

Nandy, Ashis. *The Savage Freud and Other Essays on Possible and Retrievable Selves.* Princeton, NJ: Princeton University Press, 1995.

Naranch, Bradley. "Introduction: German Colonialism Made Simple." In *German Colonialism in a Global Age*, edited by Bradley Naranch and Geoff Eley, 1–18. Durham, NC: Duke University Press, 2014.

Nathans, Eli. *The Politics of Citizenship in Germany: Ethnicity, Utility and Nationalism.* Oxford: Berg, 2004.

Neumann, Gerson Roberto. "'Os dois vizinhos. Cenas de colônia', de Wilhelm Rotermund." *Revistas Contingentia* 4, no. 2 (November 2009): 42–59.

Nietzsche, Friedrich. *Also sprach Zarathustra. Ein Buch für alle und keinen.* Projekt Gutenberg Ebook. http://www.gutenberg.org/files/7205/7205-h/7205-h.htm#chap78.

Nietzsche, Friedrich. *Thus Spoke Zarathustra: A Book for All and None.* Edited by Adrian del Caro and Robert B. Pippin. Translated by Adrian del Caro. Cambridge: Cambridge University Press, 2006.

Nisbet, H. B. "On the Rise of Toleration in Europe: Lessing and the German Contribution." *Modern Language Review* 105, no. 4 (October 2010): xxviii–xliv.

Nitsche, Robert Lehmann. *Ulrich Schmidel. Der erste Geschichtsschreiber der La Plata Länder 1535–1555.* Munich: M. Müller & Sohn, 1912.

Noyes, John K. *Colonial Space. Spatiality in the Discourse of German Southwest-Africa 1884–1915.* Chur: Harwood Academic Publishers, 1992.

Obermeier, Frana. *Brasilien "für die Jugend und das Volk": Kinder- und Jugendliterator aus und über Brasilien vom 18. Jahrhundert bis in die Mitte des 20. Jahrhunderts*, Christian-Alberts-Universität zu Kiel, 2016. Published online: https://macau.uni-kiel.de/servlets/MCRFileNodeServlet/macau_derivate_00000404/JugendliteraturBeide.pdf.

O'Donnell, K. Molly. *The Servants of Empire: Sponsored German Women's Colonization in Southwest Africa, 1896–1945*. Oxford: Berghahn, 2023.

O'Donnell, Krista. "Poisonous Women: Sexual Danger, Illicit Violence, and Domestic Work in German Southern Africa, 1904–1915." *Journal of Women's History* 11, no. 3 (1999): 32–54.

O'Donnell, Krista, Renate Bridenthal, and Nancy Reagin, eds. *The Heimat Abroad: The Boundaries of Germanness*. Ann Arbor: University of Michigan Press, 2005.

Oduro-Opuni, Obenawaa. "Modes of Transnationalism and Black Revisionist History: Slavery, The Transatlantic Slave Trade and Abolition in 18th and 19th Century German Literature." PhD dissertation, Arizona State University, 2020.

Oguejiofor, Josephat Obi. Wilhelm Amo Symposium, "The Significance of Anton Wilhelm Amo on Contemporary African Philosophy," December 9, 2021, University of Ghana. https://www.ug.edu.gh/mias-africa/content/anton-wilhelm-amo-lecture-symposium.

Okafor, Uche Onyedi. "Mapping Germany's Colonial Discourse: Fantasy, Reality and Dilemma." PhD dissertation, University of Maryland, 2013.

Oldendorp, C. G. A., and Johann Jakob Bossart. *Geschichte der Mission der Evangelischen Brüder auf den Caraibischen Inseln St. Thomas, St. Crux und St. Jan*. Leipzig: C. F. Laux, 1777.

Oloukpona-Yinnon, Adjaï, ed. *Gbêhanzin und die Deutschen. Politische Korrespondenz zwischen dem Königreich Danhomê und dem Deutschen Riech (1882–1892). Deutsch-französische Dokumentation*. Berlin: Edition Ost, 1996.

Oloukpona-Yinnon, Adjaï Paulin. *Unter deutschen Palmen. Die "Musterkolonie" Togo im Spiegel deutscher Kolonialliterature (1884–1944)*. Frankfurt a/M: IKO—Verlag für Interkulturelle Kommunikation, 1996.

Otterness, Philip. *Becoming German: The 1709 Palatine Migration to New York*. Ithaca, NY: Cornell University Press, 2004.

Overhoff, Jürgen. "Preußens verborgene Sklaven." *Die Zeit* online, August 19, 2020. https://www.zeit.de/2020/35/kolonialismus-preussen-afrikaner-sklaven/komplettansicht#print.

Pataky, Sophie. *Lexikon deutscher Frauen der Feder*. Eine Zusammenstellung der seit dem Jahre 1840 erschienenen Werke weiblicher Autoren, nebst Biographieen der lebenden und einem Verzeichnis der Pseudonyme. *Erster Band A-L* (Berlin: Carl Pataky Verlag, 1898; Deutsches Textarchiv [DTA].

Penny, H. Glenn. *German History Unbound: From 1750 to the Present*. New York: Cambridge University Press, 2022.

Penny, H. Glenn. *In Humboldt's Shadow: A Tragic History of German Ethnology*. Princeton, NJ: Princeton University Press, 2021.

Penny, H. Glenn. *Kindred by Choice: Germans and American Indians since 1800*. Chapel Hill, NC: University of North Carolina Press, 2013.

Penny, H. Glenn. "Unbinding Germans' Transnational Histories." Public Lecture. Zoom. September 14, 2021.

Penny, H. Glenn, and Matti Bunzl, eds. *Worldly Provincialism: German Anthropology in the Age of Empire*. Ann Arbor: University of Michigan Press, 2010.

Philippi, Bernhard E. *Süd-Chile in einer esten Beschreibung* (J. E. Wappäus: Göttingen 1969 [1846]). Mit einem Vorwort von Federico Saelzer Balde.

Piderit, Theodor. "Briefe aus Chile." *Deutsche Klinik. Zeitung für Beobachtungen aus deutschen Kliniken und Krankenhäusern*. Edited by Alexander Göschen. Volume V. Berlin: Georg Reimer Verlag, 1853.

Piderit, Theodor. *Briefe aus Valparaiso (1851–1859)*. Edited and commentary by Ernst Christian Hengestenberg. Munich: Selbstverlag, 2007

Pinto, Patricio Bernedo. "Historia de las estrategias periodísticas del periódico Valdivia's Deutsche Zeitung: 1886–1912." *Historia* 33 (2000): 5–61.

Pomeranz, Kenneth, "Not Just Peanuts: One Crop's Career in Farm and Factory." http://glo baltrademag.com/not-just-peanuts/. Accessed August 30, 2014.

Praktiken und Präsentationsformen in Goethes Sammlungen, vol. 3. Series editors Johannes Grave, Wolfgang Holler, Christiane Holm, and Cornelia Ortlieb, Bundesministerium für Bildung und Forschung. Dresden: Sandstein Verlag, 2020.

Pratt, Mary Louise. *Imperial Eyes: Travel Writing and Transculturation*. London: Routledge, 2008 [1992].

Press, Steven. *Blood and Diamonds: Germany's Imperial Ambitions in Africa*. Cambridge, MA: Harvard University Press, 2021.

Purdy, Daniel. *Chinese Sympathies: Media, Missionaries, and World Literature from Marco Polo to Goethe*. Ithaca, NY: Cornell University Press, 2021.

Quijano, Aníbal. "Coloniality and Modernity/Rationality," *Cultural Studies* 21, no 2: 168–78.

Quijano, Aníbal. "Coloniality of Power, Eurocentrism, and Latin America." Trans. Michael Ennis. *Neplanta: Views from South* 1, no. 3 (2000): 533–80.

Quijano, Aníbal. Keynote, III Congreso Latinoamericano y Caribeño de Ciencias Sociales, August 25, 2015, Quito. FLASCO Ecuador. https://www.youtube.com/watch?v=OxL 5KwZGvdY.

Quintero Herencia, Juan Carlos. "Los poetas en la Pampa y las 'cantidades poéticas' en el *Facundo*." *Hispamérica* 62 (1992): 33–52.

Raisbeck, Joanna. "Race and Colonialism around 1800: Herder, Fischer, Kleist." *Publications of the English Goethe Society* 99, no. 2 (2022): 140–56.

Ramachandran, Ayesha. *The Worldmakers: Global Imagining in Early Modern Europe*. Chicago: University of Chicago Press, 2015.

Ramadani, Zana. *Die verschleierte Gefahr: Die Macht der muslimischen Mütter und der Toleranzwahn der Deutschen*. Berlin: Europa Verlag, 2017.

Ran, Amalia, and Jean Axelrad Cahan. "Introduction: Rethinking Jewish Identity in Latin America." In *Returning to Babel: Jewish Latin American Experiences, Representations, and Identity*, edited by Amalia Ran and Jean Axelrad Cahan, 1–14. Leiden: Brill, 2012.

Ran, Amalia, and Jean Axelrad Cahan, eds. *Returning to Babel: Jewish Latin American Experiences, Representations, and Identity*. Leiden: Brill, 2012.

Ravenstein, Ernst Georg, *Martin Behaim: His Life and His Globe*. London: G. Philip & Son, Ltd., 1908.

Red Haircrow, dir. *Forget Winnetou! Loving in the Wrong Way: A Documentary Film* (2018). https://forgetwinnetou.com/trailer/.
Regier, James Peter. "Mennonitische Vergangenheitsbewältigung: Prussian Mennonites, the Third Reich, and Coming to Terms With a Difficult Past." *Mennonite Life* 59, no. 1 (March 2004): n.p. https://mla.bethelks.edu/ml-archive/2004Mar/regier.php.
Reidy, Michael S. "Mountaineering, Masculinity, and the Male Body in Mid-Victorian Britain." *Osiris* 30, no. 1 (2015). https://doi.org/10.1086/682975.
Rice, John A. "Opera at the Court of Frederick the Great: Graun's *Montezuma* as Royal Autobiography." Expansion of a colloquium talk at Princeton University (October 2009), the University of Pittsburgh (February 5, 2010), and the University of Iowa (May 2010); updated April 2014. https://www.academia.edu/7135439/Opera_at_the_Court_of_Frederick_the_Great_Grauns_Montezuma_as_Royal_Autobiography.
Richter, Julius Wilhelm Otto (Otto von Colmen). *Deutsche Seebücherei. Erzählungen aus dem Leben des detuschen Volkes für Jugend und Volk. 14. Band. Die brandenburgische Kolnie Groß-Friedrichsburg und ihr Begründer Otto Friedrich von der Groeben.* Altenburg: Stephan Geibel Verlag, 1907.
Ried, Aquino. *Deutsche Auswanderung nach Chile.* Valparaiso: July, 1847.
Rinke, Stefan. "Germany and Brazil, 1870–1945, a Relationship between Spaces." *História, Ciências, Saúde—Manguinhos* 21, no. 1 (Jan.-March 2014): 1–16. https://doi.org/10.1590/S0104-59702014005000007.
Rinke, Stefan. "Las relaciones germane-chilenas 1918–1933." *Historia* 31 (1998): 217–308.
Riobó, Carlos. *Caught Between the Lines: Captives, Frontiers, and National Identity in Argentine Literature and Art.* Lincoln: University of Nebraska Press, 2019.
Robinson, Cedric. J. *Black Marxism: The Making of the Black Radical Tradition.* London: Zed Press, 1983.
Rohland-Langbein, ed. *Alemanas en la Patagonia: narraciones de Bertha Koessler-Ilg, Ella Brunswig y Christel Koerte: Cuadernos del Archivo DIHA* Año 1, nr. 2 (2017).
Rosa, Luis Othoniel. "Luisa Capetillo and the Pedagogy of Unruliness." *S/X* 69 (2022): 84–97.
Rotermund, Wilhelm. "Das Glück." *Kalender für die Deutschen in Brasilien.* Rotermund-Kalender. São Leopoldo: Rotermund Verlag, 1882, 29–39.
Rotermund, Wilhelm. "Das Glück." *Südamerikanische Literatur.* Vol. 15. *Gesammelte Schriften von Dr. Wilhelm Rotermund* vol. 2. Sao Leopoldo: Rottermund Verlag, s/d., 65–80. Text transcribed from Gothic by Zuleica L. Kraemer.
Rotermund, Wilhelm. *Kalender für die Deutschen in Brasilien.* São Leopoldo: Rotermund Verlag, 1882.
Rotermund, Wilhelm. *Kalender für die Deutschen in Brasilien.* São Leopoldo: Rottermund Verlag, 1883.
Rotermund, Wilhelm. *Kalender für die Deutschen in Brasilien.* São Leopoldo: Rotermund Verlag, 1897.
Rotermund, Wilhelm, and Reinhard Heuer. *Fibel für deutsche Schulen in Brasilien.* Neubearbeitet von R. Heuer. 5. Auflage. Ausgabe 1: Deutsche Schrift. São Leopoldo: Verlag Rotermund, 1927.
Rotermund, Wilhelm, and Reinhardt Heuer. "Vorwort zur 3. Auflage." *Fibel für deutsche Schulen in Brasilien.*

Rotker, Susana. *Cautivas. Olvidos y memoria en la Argentina*. Buenos Aires: Ariel/Espasa-Calpe, 1999.
Ruíz-Tagle, Daniel Piedrabuena. *Los Lísperguer Wittemberg: una familia alemana en el corazón de la cultura chilena: Identidad y esplendor de la primera familia colonial de Chile. Los protegidos del César*. Vol. 2. Asturias: Booksideal, 2014.
Saint-Pierre, Castel de. "Europe: A Project for Peace." In *The Idea of Europe: Enlightenment Perspectives*, edited by Catriona Seth and Rotraud von Kulessa, translated by Catriona Seth et al., 12–14. Open Book Publishers, 2017.
Sammons, Jeffrey. *Friedrich Spielhagen*. Tubingen: Niemeyer, 2004.
Sarmiento, Domingo F. *Facundo: Or, Civilization and Barbarism*. Introduced by Ilan Stavans. London: Penguin Reprint Edition, 1998.
Sarmiento, Domingo Faustino. "Inmigracion en Chile." In *Obras de D. F. Sarmiento*, vol. 22, edited by A. Belin Sarmiento, 55–146. Buenos Aires: Publications of the Argentine Government, 1899.
Sarmiento, Domingo Faustino, and Johann Eduard Wappäus. *Deutsche Auswanderung und Colonisation*. 2 vols. Göttingen: Universitätsdruckerei, 1848. Nabu Public Domain reprint.
Sassen, Saskia. *Expulsions: Brutality and Complexity in the Global Economy*. Cambridge, MA: Harvard University Press, 2014.
Schäffer, Ritter von. *Brasilien als unabhängiges Reich in historischer, mercantilischer und politischer Beziehung*. Altona: bei J. F. Hammerich, 1824.
Schiebinger, Londa. "Agnotology and Exotic Abortifacients: The Cultural Production of Ignorance in the Eighteenth-Century Atlantic World." *Proceedings of the American Philosophical Society* 149, no. 3 (2005): 316–43.
Schiebinger, Londa. *Secret Cures of Slaves: People, Plants, and Medicine in the Eighteenth-Century Atlantic World*. Palo Alto, CA: Stanford University Press, 2017.
Schiller, Friedrich. "Was heisst und zu welchem Ende studiert man Universalgeschichte? Eine akademische Antrittsrede." In Friedrich Schiller, *Werke und Briefe in 12 Bänden*. Edited by Harro Hilzinger et al. Vol. 6, "Historische Schriften und Erzählungen," edited by Otto Dann. Frankfurt: Deutscher Klassiker Verlag, 1988–. Vol. 6: 411–31.
Schiller, Friedrich. "What Is, and to What End Do We Study Universal History." Translated by Caroline Stephan and Robert Trout. In *Friedrich Schiller: Poet of Freedom* Vol. II. The Schiller Institute, https://archive.schillerinstitute.com/transl/Schiller_essays/universal_history.html.
Schneider, Sylk. *Goethes Reise nach Brasilien. Gedankenkreise eines Genies*. Weimar: Weimarer Taschenbuch Verlag, 2008.
Schüller, Karin. *Die deutsche Rezeption haitianischer Geschichte. Ein Beitrag zum deutschen Bild vom Schwarzen*. Cologne: Böhlau, 1992.
Schulze, Frederik. *Auswanderung als nationalistisches Projekt. "Deutschtum" und Kolonialdiskkurse im südlichen Brasilien (1824–1941)*. Cologne: Böhlau, 2016.
Schulze, Frederik. "German Immigrants (Brazil)." *1914–1918-online. International Encyclopedia of the First World War*. Ed. Ute Daniel, Peter Gatrell, Oliver Janz, Heather Jones, Jennifer Keene, Alan Kramer, and Bill Nasson, issued by Freie Universität Berlin, Berlin 2014-10-08. https/doi.org/10.15463/ie1418.10456.

Scott, James C. *Domination and the Arts of Resistance: Hidden Transcripts*. New Haven, CT: Yale University Press, 1992.
Seume, Johann Gottlieb. *Gedichte von Johann Gottlieb Seume*. Leipzig: Reclam, 1801, 1804, 1809.
Sifford, Elena FitzPatrick. "Disseminating Devotion: The Image and Cult of the Black Christ in Mexico and Central America." PhD dissertation, City University of New York, 2014.
Simpson, Patricia Anne. "Colonising the Play World: Texts, Toys and Colonial Fantasies in German Children's Stories around 1900." In *Jahrbuch der Gesellschaft für Kinder- und Jugendliteraturforschung* (2019): 133–44.
Simpson, Patricia Anne. "Farming Frontiers: The German Woman Pioneer." In *Gender and German Colonialism: Intimacies, Accountabilities, Intersections*, edited by Elisabeth Krimmer and Chunjie Zhang, 29–48. New York: Routledge, 2024.
Simpson, Patricia Anne. "From Miracles to Miscegenation: Enlightening Skin." In *Colonialism and Enlightenment: The Legacies of German Race Theory*. Edited by Daniel Leonhard Purdy and Bettina Brandt. London: Oxford University Press, forthcoming.
Simpson, Patricia Anne. *The Play World: Toys, Texts, and the Transatlantic German Childhood*. University Park: Penn State University Press, 2020.
Smith, Justin E. H. *Nature, Human Nature, and Human Difference: Race in Early Modern .Philosophy*. Princeton, NJ: Princeton University Press, 2022.
So, Fion Wei Ling. *Germany's Colony in China: Colonialism, Protection and Economic Development in Qingdao and Shandong, 1898–1914*. London: Routledge, 2020.
Sommer, Doris. *Foundational Fictions. The National Romances of Latin America*. Berkeley: University of California Press, 1993.
Sosnowski, Saúl. "Esteban Echeverría: el intelectual ante la formación del estado." *Revista Iberoamericana* 47, no. 114–15 (January–June 1981): 293–300.
Soto Rojas, Salvador. *Los Alemanes en Chile 1541–1917*. Valparaiso: Imprenta Victoria, 1917.
Spielhagen, Friedrich. *Deutsche Pioniere. Sämtliche Werke* VIII. Elibron Classics. Facsimile edition. Berlin: Otto Ranke, 1870.
Steinmetz, George. "Decolonizing German Theory: An Introduction." *Postcolonial Studies* 9, no. 1 (2006): 3–13.
Steinmetz, George. *The Devil's Handwriting: Precoloniality and the German Colonial State in Qingdao, Samoa, and South Africa*. Chicago: University of Chicago Press, 2007.
Stoler, Ann Laura. *Duress· Imperial Durabilities in Our Times*. Durham, NC: Duke University Press, 2016.
Stoler, Ann Laura. "Imperial Debris: Reflections on Ruin and Ruination." *Cultural Anthropology* 23, no. 2 (2008): 191–219.
Stölting, Walter. *Baumanns siedeln in Argentinien*. Leipzig: Franz Schneider Verlag, 1934. An exhibit at the Ibero-Amerikanisches Institut in Berlin featured literature for children and young adults. Curated by Ulrike Mühlschlegel and Ricarda Musser, November 13–30, 2006.
Stört, Diana. *Goethes Sammlungsschränke. Wissensbehältnisse nach Maß*, in cooperation with Katharina Popov-Sellinat, Parerga und Paratexte. Wie Dinge zur Sprache kommen. Vol. 3 Dresden: Sandstein, 2020.

Sully, Jess. "Challenging the Stereotype: The *Femme Fatale* in *Fin-de-Siècle* Art and Early Cinema." In *The Femme Fatale: Images, Histories, Contexts*, edited by H. Hanson and C. O'Rawe, 46–60. London: Palgrave Macmillan, 2010.

Sutherland, Wendy. *Staging Blackness and Performing Whiteness in Eighteenth-Century German Drama*. London: Routledge, 2019; New York: Ashgate, 2016.

Tautz, Birgit, ed. *Colors: 1800/1900/2000: Signs of Ethnic Difference*. Amsterdamer Beiträge zur Neueren Germanistik 56. Amsterdam: Rodopi, 2004.

Tautz, Birgit. *Reading and Seeing Ethnic Differences in the Enlightenment: From China to Africa*. London: Palgrave Macmillan, 2007.

Tautz, Birgit. *Translating the World: Toward a New History of German Literature Around 1800*. University Park: Penn State University Press, 2017.

Tepp, Max. *Arboles y Arbustos de la Cordillera Patagónica*. Buenos Aires: Del Umbral Argentino, 1936.

Thiesen, John D., and Theron F. Schalbach. *Mennonite and Nazi: Attitudes Among Mennonite Colonists in Latin American, 1933–1945*. Kitchener, ON: Pandora Press, 1999.

Tirpitz, Alfred von. *Erinnerungen*. Leipzig: Koehler, 1919.

Todorov, Tzvetan. *The Conquest of America: The Question of the Other*. Translated by Richard Howard. New York: Harper Collins, 1984.

Truettner, William H. *Painting Indians and Building Empires in North America 1710–1840*. Berkeley: University of California Press, 2010.

Trüper, Ursula. *The Invisible Woman: Zara Schmelen: African Mission Assistant at the Cape and in Namaland*. Translated by Loretta Carter and Bettina Duwe. Basel: Basler Afrika Bibliographien, 2006.

Tünaydin, Pelin. "Pawing through the History of Bear Dancing in Europe." *Frühneuzeit-Info* 24 (2013): 51–60.

Uphoff, Dörthe. "A história do ensino de alemão no Brasil: Panorama geral e perspectivas de Investigação." (2011). https://edisciplinas.usp.br/pluginfile.php/4490536/mod_resource/content/1/ppt%20DaF%20in%20Brasilien%20R%C3%BCckblick.pdf.

Valko, Jennifer M. "Transnational Mercenaries as Agents of Argentine National in Moritz Aleman's Immigration Propaganda (1874–1908)." *German Studies Review* 40, no. 1 (February 2017): 41–60.

Valko, Jennifer Margit. "Expressing Patagonia: Sightseeing, Journalism, and Immigration in Argentina." PhD dissertation, University of California, Davis, 2005.

Van der Heyden, Ulrich. *Rote Adler an Afrikas Küste. Die brandenburgisch-preußische Kolonie Großfriedrichsburg in Westafrika*. Berlin: Selignow, 2001.

Van Gent, Jacqueline. "Rethinking Savagery: Slavery Experiences and the Role of Emotions in Oldendorp's Mission Ethnography." *History of the Human Sciences* 32, no. 4: 28–42.

Villas-Bôas, Luciana. "A German Mamluk in Colonial Brazil?" In *A New History of German Literature*, edited by David Wellbery et al, 246–50. Cambridge, MA: Belknap, 2004.

Virchow, H. "Review: Piderit, Theodor: Mimik und Physiognomik, 3. Auflage. Detmold 1919." *Zeitschrift für Ethnologie*, Heft 4–6 (1919): 310–11.

Voigt, Bernhard et al. *Deutsch-Südwestafrika. Land und LeuteEine Heimatkunde für Deutschlands Jugend und Volk*. Ed. Kaiserliches Gouvernement von Deutsch-Südwestafrika. Stuttgart: Strecker und Schröder, 1913.

Volberg, Heinrich. *Deutsche Kolonialbestrebungen in Südamerika nach dem Dreißigjährigen Krieg*. Cologne: Böhlau-Verlag, 1977.

Wagner, Florian. *Colonial Internationalism and the Governmentality of Empire, 1893–1982*. Cambridge: Cambridge University Press, 2022.

Walther, Daniel. "Creating Germans Abroad: White Education in German Southwest Africa, 1894–1914." *German Studies Review* 24, no. 2 (May 2001): 325–51,

Walther, Daniel J. "Sex, Race, and Empire: White Male Sexuality and the 'Other' in Germany's Colonies, 1894–1914," *German Studies Review* 33, no. 1 (February 2010): 45–71.

Wappäus, J. E. *Panama Neu-Granada Venezuela Guayana Ecuador Peru Bolivia und Chile geographisch und statistisch dargestellt*. Leipzig: J. C. Hinrichs'sche Buchhändlung, 1871.

Wegener, Zacharias. *A Short Account of the Voyage of Mr. Zachary Wagener, Perform'd in Thirty Five Years, through Europe, Asia, Africa and America*. In A Collection of Voyages and Travels. Some now first printed from original manuscripts, others translated out of foreign languages, and now first publish'd in English : to which are added some few that have formerly appear'd in English, but do now for their excellency and scarceness deserve to be reprinted : with a general preface, giving an account of the progress of navigation, from its first beginning to the perfection it is now in, &c. Vol. II. London: Awnsham and John Churchill, 1704.

Weil, Bruno. "Südamerika der künftige Einwanderungskontinent." *Argentinisches Tageblatt* Nr. 18.562 (July 10, 1947): 5.

Wellbery, David E. et al. *A New History of German Literature*. Cambridge, MA: Belknap, 2004.

Werman, David S. "Freud's 'Narcissism of Minor Differences': A Review and Reassessment." *Journal of the American Academy of Psychoanalysis* 16, no. 4 (1988): 451–59. https://doi.org/10.1521/jaap.1.1988.16.4.451.

Weß, Mechthild. *Von Göttingen nach Valdivia. Die Chileauswanderung Göttinger Handwerker im 19. Jahrhundert*. Münster: Waxman, 2004.

Wildenthal, Lora. *German Women for Empire, 1884–1945*. Durham, NC: Duke University Press, 2011.

Wildenthal, Lora. "Race, Gender, and Citizenship in the German Colonial Empire." In *Tensions of Empire: Colonial Cultures in a Bourgeois World*, edited by Frederick Cooper and Ann Laura Stoler, 263–83. Berkeley: University of California Press, 1997.

Wimmer, Andrew, and Nina Glick Schiller. "Methodological Nationalism and Beyond: Nation-State Building, Migration and the Social Sciences." *Global Networks. A Journal of Transnational Affairs* 2, no. 4 (October 2002); cited from online research depository, http://www.columbia.edu/~aw2951/B52.pdf.

Witt, Marcos A. *Em busca de um lugar ao sol: Estratégias políticas. Imigração alemã Rio Grande do Sul–Século XIX*. São Leopoldo: Editora Oikos, 2015.

Witt, Marcos A., ed. *Fontes litorâneas: Escritos sobre o Litoral Norte do Rio Grande do Sul*. São Leopoldo: Editora Oikos, 2012.

Worthington, David. "Sugar, Slave-Owning, Suriname and the Dutch Imperial Entanglement of the Scottish Highlands before 1707." *Dutch Crossing: Journal of Low Countries Studies* 44, no 1 (2020): https://doi.org10.1080/03096564.2019.1616141.

Wulffen, Bernd. *Deutsche Spuren in Argentinien: zwei Jahrhunderte wechselvoller Beziehungen*. Berlin: Ch. Links Verlag, 2010.
Young, Robert J. C. *Colonial Desire. Hybridity in Theory, Culture and Race*. London: Routledge, 1995.
Zabrodski, Sarah. "Germany's Game of Colonies." Blog entry: https://primo.getty.edu/primo-explore/fulldisplay?vid=GRI&docid=GETTY_ROSETTAIE1540602&context=L.
Zantop, Susanne. *Colonial Fantasies: Conquest, Family, and Nation in Precolonial Germany, 1770–1870*. Durham, NC: Duke University Press, 1997.
Zedler, Johann Heinrich. *Grosses vollständiges Universal-Lexikon aller Wissenschafften und Künste*. 64 volumes. (1731–1754; Graz 1961).
Zhang, Chunjie. *Transculturality and German Discourse in the Age of European Colonialism*. Evanston, IL: Northwestern University Press, 2017.

INDEX

Note: Page numbers in italics refer to the illustrations.

abolitionism: Battle of Boonville, 169; slave plays, 66–67; transatlantic revolutions, 94–95
absolutism: enlightened colonialism and, 20–21, 51–52; Lessing's critique of tyranny, 61, 64–66
Adelung (Staden), 105–107
Africa, 2–3, 253–258; *Aus dem Creolenlande*, 226–230; "Christian Afrikaner," 26–27, 216–225; European mercantilism, 34–35; Kpando site, 45–46, *47–49*; Meinecke on East Africa's cultural politics, 254–258; Meinecke's *Katechismus*, 232; praise of Maria Leopoldine, 96; religious conversion, 220–221; sites of eighteenth-century expansionism, 113–114. See also Brandenburg expansionism; German Southwest Africa
agriculture: American frontier immigrants, 168–169; asserting German identity through children's instructional materials, 143–145; farming-fighting connection, 173; German immigrants in Chile, 182; linking German national destiny to, 190–191; Meinecke on East Africa's cultural politics, 256–258; Schäffer connecting slavery to labor productivity, 101–102; Schäffer justifying Brazil's enslavement, 102–104; Schäffer justifying slavery in Brazil, 103–104; Schäffer on Brazil's wilderness and savages, 98; success of German immigrants in Chile, 181; sugar production in East Africa, 254; white masculinity and nationalist entitlement, 170

Aichele Hörz, Magdelene Barbara, 25, 177–178, 190–194
Albrecht, Christian, 222–223
Albrecht, Elias Kruger, 141
Alcmann (Also Allemann), Ernesto, 297–298
Algeria: Meinecke's *Katechismus*, 232
Allemann, Johann, 278, 278n11
Allemann, Moritz, 278
American Indians: German pioneers in New York, 167–171
Amerindians: German immigrant legitimacy in Chile, 175–176, 180–181; German presence in Chile, 181–182; Goethe's Brazilian poems, 89–90; Hartsink's portrayal of Guyana, 105–106; Hellemeyer's *Erlebnisse eines Mädchens*, 135–136
Amo, Anton Wilhelm, 14–15, 18–19
anarcho-feminism, 247–248
The Anatomy of Blackness (Curran), 78
Anderson, Benedict, 204
Andes mountains: Pideret's transformation, 184–187
Anmerkung (Leiste), 72–73
Appadurai, Arjun, 27, 247
Argentina: "captive" paintings, 152–155; constructing the pioneer identity, 151–165; German nationalist discourse, 173;

323

Argentina (*continued*)
immigrant identity, 24–25; immigrants' embrace of pluralism, 219; postwar immigration, 278–282; pushback against German barbarism, 297–298; rapid German migration, 158–159
Argentinisches Tageblatt newspaper, 158–159
arts: artistic expressions of resistance, 58–60; Benin Bronzes, 296; depicting enslaved whites, 82–84, *83*; *El rapto de la cautiva* and the pioneer identity, 152–155; Frederick's self-presentation, 67–68; Lessing's opposition to tyranny, 61–62; statue of the Great Elector, 21, 31–32, *33*; sugar sculpture of Pedro II and Tereza Cristina, 112
assimilation: Brazilian-German antiassimilation politics, 141; German imperial identity resisting, 207; Missouri Saxon Germans resisting, 114–115; North American perceptions on race and immigration, 139–140
Aus dem Creolenlande (Meinecke), 226–230, 249, 262–269
Aus der Neuen Welt (Bodenstedt), 161
Auslander, Leora, 7, 114
Aus Morgenland und Abendland (Bodenstedt), 161–162
Auswanderung als nationalistisches Projekt (Schulze), 118–119

Balmaceda, José Manuel, 195n29
barbarism: African belief systems in *Aus dem Creolenlande*, 230; "captive" painting recapitulating, 155; "Christian Afrikaner," 222–223; ethnic identifiers and epistemologies in *Aus dem Creolenlande*, 228; German and Dutch critiques, 221–222; German farming-fighting connection, 173; 1930s pushback against, 297–298
Barbary States and Barbary Corsairs, 83–87

Behaim, Martin, 1–2, 2, 3–6, 282–283, 286, 289, 292–293, 298–299
Béhanzim, Bénzim, 44
Benin Bronzes, 296
Berlin: botanical garden, 228; expositions and fairs, 203–205
Beschreibung von Guiana oder der wilden Küste in Südamerika (Hartsink), 104–105
"Beyond Words" (Auslander), 7
Biehl, João, 145
Blackbourn, David, 3, 5
Blackler, Adam, 293
Black people, 138–140; Cramer's brutality toward Black women, 239–240, 244–245, 245n64; E. L. Cramer's childhood reminiscences, 289; Hellemeyer's *Erlebnisse*, 133; in the Prussian court, 53, 55; racist distribution of labor in the Americas and Africa, 9; Ragamuffin rebellion, 146–147; settler colonialism-immigration overlap and conflict, 226–227. *See also* enslaved people; race and racism; slavery
Blumen-Flores, Bartolomé, 175–179, 213
Boas, Franz, 121
Bodenstedt, Friedrich, 150, 160–165
Boers, 284
Bolivia, 195–196
Boonville, Missouri, 169
Bötticher, Georg, 127
bourgeoisie: immigration as manifest destiny, 200
Bowersox, Jeff, 35
Brandenburg African Company (BAC), 35–38
Brandenburg expansionism, 21, 32–35, 40–45
Bräunlein, Peter, 283
Brazil, 111–112, 171; building a cohesive national identity, 115–120; constructing the settler identity in southern Brazil, 120–121; German entitlement, 95–97; Goethe's cross-cultural borrowings,

Index

106–107; Goethe's perspective on Brazil, 88–90; Hellemeyer's *Erlebnisse*, 127–129; immigrants' postwar political alliances, 275–277; Lessing's critique of colonization, 62–65, 73–74; missionary outreach, 216n8; North American perceptions on race and immigration, 139–140; preserving German racial integrity in Brazil, 141–143; recruitment to whiten the population, 239; Schäffer's population divisions and characterizations, 97–104; white enslavement, 82
"Brazil" (Goethe), 90–91
Breuer, Joseph, 133–134
Brewer, Max, 151, 169–170
Briefe aus Valparaiso (Piderit), 183–189
"Brilhantine" (Rotermund), 118
British colonialism: Bülow's envy of, 263–264; Cramer's brutality toward Black women, 240; *Deutschtum* in South America, 199–200; expositions and fairs, 203–204; Farmersfrau trope, 217; German critique of civilizing rhetoric, 200–201; German immigrants' resistance to, 284–285; Germans' loss of land, 290; inter-European colonial competition in Africa, 43–44; missionary interventions in Africa, 220–221; portrayal in Meinecke's *Der arme Sidi Abderrachman*, 264–265
Broomhall, Susan, 152
Brunberger, Hans, 156–157
Buck-Morss, Susan, 13, 65n23, 84
Bülow, Frieda von, 215, 263
Bunzl, Matti, 19, 187
Burmeister, Hermann, 156

Cadena de Vilha, Pedro, 73
Campo, Estanislao de, 163
Canada: Seume on wilderness and civilization, 74–77
cannibalism, 22, 45–46, 89–92, 94, 104–107, 130, 293
Canning, Kathleen, 219
Cão, Diego, 1, 273, 283

Cape Colony (Cape Town), 224–225, 282
"captive" painting, 152–155
Caribbean territories: missionaries, 50–51; small states' colonial aspirations, 56
Carlyle, Thomas, 56–57
Casa Grande e Senzala (Freyre), 99
Casco, José Arturo Saavedra, 269–271
Catholic Church: Catholic-Protestant friction in Africa, 220–221; depictions of enslaved whiteness, 83–84
Chaco region (Argentina), 156–157
childbirth: Piderit's medical practice, 184
children: Cramer's Farmersfrau trope, 241–242; Cramer's paternal and punitive view of Black children, 284–286; Cramer's racist *Kinderfarm*, 272–273; E. L. Cramer's reminiscences, 289; Hellemeyer's *Erlebnisse*, 127–129, 136; racism and patrimony in children's curricula in Brazil, 142–143. *See also* play and games
Chile: Aichele's racial typography on Chilean people, 191–194; Balmaceda's election and leadership, 195n29; "captive" painting, 154n10; citizenship as German destiny, 194–195, 201; constructing a colonial immigrant identity, 213–214; contextualizing the pioneers' national identity, 213; expos and fairs, 203–204; gendered identity of nineteenth-century immigrants, 190; legitimacy of German immigration, 25; Pideret's medical practice, 183–189; postwar political alliances, 275, 277; racial and language identity of German immigrants, 175–183
"Christian Afrikaner," 26–27, 216–225
Ciarlo, David, 226, 275
cigarette packages and cards, 274–275, 276, 279–280
circus performances, 137–138, 148
citizenship: as German destiny, 194–195, 200–201; German immigrants in the North American frontier, 169; Germans as global citizens, 252–253; national identity of German immigrants in Chile, 178

Civilization and Its Discontents (Freud), 121–122
civilizing influences, 216; African belief systems in *Aus dem Creolenlande*, 230; "captive" painting recapitulating, 155; "Christian Afrikaner," 222–223; ethnic identifiers and epistemologies in *Aus dem Creolenlande*, 228; German and Dutch critiques, 221–222; German critique of British rhetoric, 200–201; German farming-fighting connection, 173; German immigrants in Chile, 177, 180–181; Hellemeyer's *Erlebnisse eines Mädchens*, 129–138; Meinecke on the savages of Europe, 254; Seume on wilderness and civilization, 74–77
class. *See* social class
climate: colonial administrators, 256; colonies in tropical regions, 232; intersecting imperial power, 58; Kant on skin color, 79; limiting settling in East Africa, 268; Meinecke on the tropics, 252–253; Meinecke's *Katechismus* covering the GSA colony, 232–234; Meinecke's racial and gender encodings, 249; theories of skin color and, 78–80
Cody, William F. "Buffalo Bill," 137
coffee production, 256
colonial competition, 11, 113–114, 129; constructing the settler identity in southern Brazil, 118–120; establishing *Deutschtum* in South America, 199–200; games as visuals for, 292–293; German assertions of global superiority, 208; German immigrants in Chile, 182; Goethe's cultural landscape, 88–94; immigrant identity in competing European communities, 24–25; inter-European competition in Africa, 42–45; invisibility of Germans, 5; religious conversion in Africa, 220–221; small states, 52
Colonial Exhibition (Berlin; 1896), 231
Colonial Fantasies (Zantop), 11
colonialidad de poder (Quijano, coloniality of power), 7–8, 14–15, 21, 65n23; Lessing decentering imperial power, 73
colonialism, enlightened. *See* enlightened colonialism
colonial rule, forms of, 4–5
competing colonialisms. *See* colonial competition
conflict. *See* war and conflict
Conrad, Sebastian, 4–5, 213
conversion, religious, 55–56, 216; conversion of enslaved souls, 78–79; as racial redemption, 218–225; West Indies, 77. *See also* missionaries
Conway, Christopher, 154, 154n10
countercolonial stories, 178
Cramer, Ada, 26–27, 217, 225–226, 236–247, 274, 284
Cramer, Ernst Ludwig, 28, 217, 246, 272, 274, 283–289, 287–288, 290–291
Cramer, Helmut, 217, 290
Cramer, Ludwig, 239–240, 244–245, 245n64, 246
Cramer, Otto, 238–239
Crenshaw, Kimberlé, 8
Creoles, 226–230
crime and punishment, economy of, 258–262
critical theory, 9–10
cultural missionaries, 248–249
cultural models: cultural Europeanisation, 19–20
cultural nationalism, 298
cultural pioneers, 213–214, 225–230
cultural politics, Meinecke on East Africa's, 255–258
Curran, Andrew S., 78

dancing bears, 69–70, 75, 148
Danhomê, kingdom of, 43–44
Danish colonies, 76–77
Das deutsche Kolonialreich (Meyer), 273
"Das Glück" (Rotermund), 118
deforestation: Brazil, 104
De Jure Maurorum in Europa (Amo), 15

Index

de las Casas, Bartolomé, 35
democracy, Chile's, 195–196, 275, 277
Denmark: Danish-Caribbean contact zone, 51
"Der alte Landmann an seinen Sohn" (Hölty), 291
Der arme Sidi Abderrachman (Meinecke), 248–251, 262–269
"Der befreite Sklave" (Hölty), 84–85
"Der Fall des Alamos" (Meinecke), 226–227
"Der Tanzbär" (Lessing), 69–70, 148
Descartes, René, 15–16
despotism, 64, 66
destiny: Chilean citizenship as German destiny, 194–209; German immigration and colonization as, 25, 239, 252
Deutsche Auswanderung (Wappäus), 190
"Deutsche Diamanten" (Brewer), 151, 169–170
Deutsche Kolonien (Heffter), 282
Deutsche Kolonien in Wort und Bild (Meinecke), 258–262
Deutsche Kultivation in Ostafrika unter der Kaffeebau (Meinecke), 254–255
Deutsche Pioniere (Spielhagen), 164–170
Deutscher Pionier newspaper, 158–160
Deutsche Zeitung newspaper, 194–197, 199–200
Deutschland's Kolonien-Spiel, 250, *251*, 292–293, *294*
Deutschtum, 177, 190, 199–200, 209, 264–269
diamonds, 89, 92, 107, 151, 169–170
Dias, Camila Loureira, 63–64
diaspora, discourse on, 199, 224
"Die beiden Nachbarn" (Rotermund), 115–116, 119–120, 122–125, 138–140, 142
"Die Deutschen von Boonville" (Schneider), 169
Die Kinderfarm (E. L. Cramer), 28, 217, 246, 272–275, 284–289, 287
Die Kinderfarm-Briefe (E. L. Cramer), 28, 286–289, *287*–288, 291

"Die kleine Urwälderin" (Hellemeyer), 127–129
Die Mätresse (Lessing), 86
Dorfgeschichte (Village story) genre, 119
Dutch colonialism: Brandenburg expansionism, 36; Caribbean Islands, 57; German alliances in the North American frontier, 169; German critique of, 221–222; inter-European competition in Africa, 44; Meinecke's criticism of, 254–256; missionary accounts of "Christian Afrikaner," 220; Spielhagen's frontier story, 166–167

East Africa: Bülow's envy of British colonialism, 263–264; Heffter's incentives for German settlement, 282; Meinecke on East Africa's cultural politics, 254–258; Meinecke's economy of crime and punishment, 258–262, 271; Meinecke's *Sidi Abderrachman*, 249, 262–269; satirical verse, 46, 48
Echeverría, Esteban, 152, 154
Eckart, Anselm, 73
education: dismantling colonial institutions, 296; German support of emigration, 175; intellectual migration, 114–115; maintaining German culture through migration, 252; maintaining German language in Chile, 215; Piderit's medical training, 183–184; preserving German racial integrity in Brazil, 141–143; reflecting German imperialist aims, 293
El rapto de la cautiva (Rugendas), 152–155, *153*, 154n10
Emilia Galotti (Lessing), 61–62, 65–66
Emma-Adamah, W. Abraham V. U., 19
enlightened colonialism, 20–23, 50–77; Caribbean expansion, 57–58; enlightened absolutism and, 51–52; global circulation of knowledge, 63; Lessing decentering imperial power, 73

Enlightenment thought and discourse, 21–23, 173; Amo's contributions and perspectives, 15–16; conversion of enslaved souls, 78–79; exported forms of German identity, 19; Friedrich's opposition to slavery, 60–61; German civilizing influences in Chile, 177; racialized discourse about African peoples, 233

ennobled farmer trope, 246

enslaved people, 20–21; enslaved whiteness, 78–79; Frederick's imperial aspirations, 52; German narratives of coloniality, 48–49; German view of postwar loss of land, 281–282; Goethe's Brazilian works, 94; racialization of freedom, 13–14; religious conversion of enslaved souls, 78–79; Wagener's focus on enslaved Africans, 152; West Indies, 51n3. *See also* race and racism; slavery

enslaved whiteness, 82–87

Erdapfel (globe), 1–2, 2, 3–6, 282–283, 289, 291–292, 298–299

Ernst und Falk (Lessing), 64–65, 71–73

Eschwege, Wilhelm Ludwig von, 74, 92

Eurocentrism, 11–12; Brandenburg expansionism, 34; coloniality of world power, 7–11; decolonial projects, 18; the German as export, 247–248; methodological nationalism, 213; pioneer identity in Argentina, 160–161

Europeanisation, 19–20

European powers: Berlin's status, 68; Chile's influx of immigrants, 201–202; competing national identities, 71–73; small states' colonial aspirations, 55–57; transatlantic revolutions, 94–95; white slave trope, 82–84

exotic novels, Meinecke's, 249, 264–269

expansionism. *See* land appropriation and ownership; territorial expansion

explorer/adventurer trope, 250

expositions and fairs, 203–205

Fabri, M. J. E., 104–105

Facundo: Civilización y barbarie (Sarmiento), 151–152

fairs and expositions, 203–205

fairy tale tropes, 127–129

farmer-settlers, 216, 236–247; Aichele's observations replicating the German experience, 191–194; American West, 111; Christian Afrikaner as symbol of resistance, 26–27; conflating settler identity with enslavement, 25; constructing the settler identity in southern Brazil, 120–122; Farmersfrau trope, 26, 217, 236–247

Farmersfrau trope, 26, 217, 236–247

fatherland. *See* homeland

Fausel, Erich, 139

Faust (Goethe), 162–163

Fausto (Campo), 163

Feder, Ernst, 73–74

feminine: Farmersfrau trope, 26, 217, 236–247; Germanness as, 249; *Naturvölker* and *Kulturvölker*, 136; the toxic feminine, 244–245

Fibel für deutsche Schulen in Brasilien, 141–144, *143–144*, 148

Figel, Sara Eigen, 120–121

Fitzler, Mathilde August Hedwig, 170–173

Flores, Agueda, 176–177, 179

Flores, Bartolomé, 175–179, 213

Flores, Elvira, 176–177

France and French colonialism: German alliances in the North American frontier, 168–169; German disparagement of immigrants in Chile, 202; German immigrants in New York, 168; inter-European colonial competition in Africa, 43–44; Lessing's critique of absolutism, 66; Meinecke's *Katechismus*, 232; Seven Years' War, 57

Frankenthal colony, Brazil, 97–104

Frankfurt School, 9–10

freedom: Hegel's racialization of, 13–14; Schiller's message of absolute freedom, 80–81; universal availability, 78–79

Index

freemasonry, 71, 125
Freud, Sigmund, 121, 133–134, 136–137, 137n48
Frey, Johannes, 194–195
Freyre, Gilberto, 99
Friedrich II of Prussia, 6, 21–23; artistic expressions of resistance, 58–60; bartering the Caribbean islands, 57; imperial aspirations, 51–52; Lessing's critique of tyranny, 64–68; opposition to slavery, 60–61
Friedrich III, 31–32
Friedrich Wilhelm, 21, 31–32, 33, 37, 39–40, 48, 53, 54, 67–70, 120–121, 275
friendship and trade agreement (German-Chilean), 195
Fritz, Simon, 63–64

Gallero, Maria Cecilia, 116
Gambia, 79n4
"Ganymed" (Goethe), 91–92
gauchos, 163–164
gender: "captive" painting, 152–155; colonial transmission of cultural patrimony, 141–143; colonizing and German masculinity, 237–238; constituting "wildness," 23–24; constructing a national immigrant identity, 213; Farmersfrau narrative, 26, 241–245; feminine depictions in Hellemeyer's *Erlebnisse*, 137; Meinecke's fiction themes, 262, 264; persecuted heroism trope, 226–228; Piderit's observations of Chilean peoples, 188–189
gendered identities, 150–151; racial typography on Chilean women, 191–192
genealogy: Meinecke's racialized discourse, 233
genocide, 4, 164–165, 170, 208, 238; *Montezuma* opera, 58–60
geographical exploration: Goethe's interest in, 93–94; mapping cannibalism onto distant locations, 105; marketable, 151–152; Meinecke's racialized discourse, 233; Missouri Compromise and the geography of slavery, 218
geological exploration, Goethe's interest in, 90, 93–94, 107
German-centricity in migration, 250–251
German Colonial Congress (1902), 174–175
German History Unbound (Penny), 4
German Southwest Africa (GSA), 6; Cramer's *Kinderfarm*, 272–275; decolonializing African resistance and rebellion, 270–271; Farmersfrau trope, 217, 236–240; Herero Wars, 170, 208, 235–236, 238; language politics, 215; Meinecke's *Katechismus* covering, 232–234; religious conversion, 216–217; symbols of resistance, 26–27
German Women for Empire (Wildenthal), 20, 263
Germany in The World (Blackbourn), 5
Gewald, Jan-Bart, 235
Ghana, 39, 45–46. See also Groß-Friedrichsburg (fort)
Glèlè (king), 33, 43
global citizens: Germans as, 252–253; Schiller on enslaved souls, 80–82
global history, 213
globes and maps, 8–9; Behaim's *Erdapfel*, 1–2, 3–6, 282–283, 289, 291–292, 298–299; colonial rights to conquered regions, 63–64; defining imperialist ambition, 1–3; global vectors of German empire, 45; Lessing researching place names, 70–71; reflecting political vectors, 292–293
Gobineau, Arthur de, 139
Goebbels, Joseph, 291
Goethe, Wolfgang von, 6, 22; Bodenstedt's poetry, 162–163; Brazilian poetry, 89–94; cross-cultural borrowings, 106–107; engaging with the transatlantic world, 73–74
Gold Coast, Africa's, 36–37
Grashof, Otto, 184–186
Graun, Carl Heinrich, 21, 58–60

Great Elector (statue), 21, 31–32, *33*
Grimm, Hans, 280–281
Groß-Friedrichsburg (fort), 33, 36, 38, *39–41*, 42–44, 49
Groß-Friedrichsburg (von Festenberg), 33, 42
"Gumbo" (Meinecke), 227
Guyana, 104–107

Hagenbeck, Carl, 137
Haiti: decolonial revolutions, 8, 13
Hanseatic League, collapse of, 200, 208–209
harem: Meinecke's *Der arme Sidi Abderrachman*, 264–265
Hartsink, Johann Jakob, 104–105
Heffter, Heinrich, 275, 279–280, 282
Hegel, G. W. F., 10, 17, 17n52, 84
Heimat (homeland). *See* homeland
Hellemeyer, Maria, 23–24, 112, 115, 127–129, 129n44, 138–140
Helmar, W. *See* Hellemeyer, Maria
Herero Wars (1904–1908; Herero and Namaqua Genocide), 170, 208, 235, 238
Herrnhut Moravian Archive, 77
Hesse, Volker, 89–90
heteronormative behavior: feminine depictions in Hellemeyer's *Erlebnisse*, 137
Hölty, Christoph Heinrich, 22, 84–86, 92, 291
homeland, German: Bodenstedt's New World tropes, 161–162; Cramer's repatriation, 286–291; exporting imperialist Germanness abroad, 174–175, 199; German entitlement to Brazil, 95–97; German struggle for legitimacy and supremacy, 170–171; Hellemeyer's *Erlebnisse eines Mädchens*, 132–133, 136–137; immigration and citizenship as German destiny, 196; lack of interest in the colonies, 215–216; Meinecke's moral patriotism, 249–252; Piderit's departure as rebirth, 184–185; preserving racial and cultural integrity in Brazil, 141–143;

rancor over lost German territory, 208–209; remigration from Brazilian wilderness to, 112; settler identity in southern Brazil, 119–120
Homestead Act (US; 1862), 111, 237
hooks, bell, 262
Horkheimer, Max, 9–10
Hörll, Albert (also Hoerll), 195, 197, 207–208
humanitarian pornography (Klarer), 95, 155
human rights: Schäffer on treatment of Brazil's slaves, 99–104; transatlantic revolutions, 94–95
human trafficking, 84. *See also* slave trade
Humboldt, Alexander von, 151–152
Hunsrückisch dialect, 119
hunting, 257
hysteric (neurosis in women), 136–137

identity, national, 292; constructing a colonial immigrant identity in Chile, 203, 213–214; constructing the settler identity in southern Brazil, 118–119; dismantling colonial institutions, 296; ethnic identity of South American Germans, 198–199; European national identities, 71–73; exported forms of German identity, 19; expositions and fairs, 203–205; Farmersfrau trope, 240–241; German civilizing influences in Chile, 177–178; German pioneers' entitlement in Argentina, 155–161; ideological and material considerations, 112–114; immigrant identity in competing European communities, 24–25; immigration as manifest destiny, 200; imperialist bent of Germans in the Americas, 129–130; importance of language in, 213–215; naturalization of German immigrants, 196–197; Piderit's professional and German identities, 183–184; Piderit's subjective study of Indigenous Chileans, 187–188; pioneering identity in Rio de la Plata, 152–155; preserving German racial integrity in

Index

Brazil, 141–143; racial and language identity of German immigrants in Chile, 175–183; Rotermund mapping political and politicizing spaces, 125–126; Spielhagen's pioneer literature, 164–170; Togo colonization, 44. *See also* legitimacy of land appropriation
identity, racial and ethnic, 247–248; "Christian Afrikaner" asserting religious and ethnic identity, 220; conflating settler identity with enslavement, 25
identity, regional, 125–126
identity, religious, 55–56; building a cohesive national identity in southern Brazil, 114–118
Imagined Communities (Anderson), 204
imperial formations, 52
imperialism, 2–3; *Deutschtum* as cosmopolitan agency, 209; *Deutschtum* in South America, 199–200; empire transcending territorial boundaries, 45–48; German critique of British civilizing rhetoric, 200–201; German identity as imperial citizens, 197–198; German identity as world citizens, 215–216; German intervention in Brazil's colonial politics, 171; interconnectedness of thoughts and things, 10; maps, globes, and games as visuals for, 292–293. *See also* homeland, German
Inaugural Dissertation on the Impassivity of the Human Mind (Amo), 15–16, 16n49
Inca Empire: German legitimacy in Chile, 177
"In den Prairien" (Spielhagen), 164–165
indentured servitude as slavery, 81–82
India, British colonial conquest of, 201
Indigenous peoples: Bodenstedt's pioneer literature, 164–165; Brandenburg slave trade, 34–35; commodification of the ungovernable, 248; contextualizing the pioneers' national identity, 213; Cramer's brutality toward Black women, 244–245, 245n64; Cramer's Farmersfrau trope,

217, 240–242; cultural appropriation in *Aus dem Creolenlande*, 229–230; European co-optation of Indigenous epistemologies, 48; German alliances in the North American frontier, 168–169; German disparagement of immigrants in Chile, 207; German linguistic borrowing, 213–215; Goethe's "Brazil" lyrics, 90–91; Hellemeyer's *Erlebnisse eines Mädchens*, 130–131, 133; Lessing researching place names, 70–71; Lessing's critique of Brazilian colonization, 72; Meinecke's economy of crime and punishment, 258–262; Meinecke's racialized discourse on African peoples, 233–234; Piderit's museumification, 187; Piderit's observations of Chilean peoples, 188–189; pioneers' displacement in Argentina, 156; racial typography of Chilean women, 191–192; racist distribution of labor in the Americas and Africa, 9; Ragamuffin rebellion, 146–147; Rotermund's "Die beiden Nachbarn," 115–116, 119–120, 122–125, 138–140, 142; Schäffer justifying Brazil's enslavement of, 102–104; Schäffer's characterizations of Brazil's populace, 97–104; Seume on wilderness and civilization, 74–75; uniting colonials in GSA, 236
industrialization, 239, 249–250
industriousness. *See* work ethic
industry: sugar production in East Africa, 254
isolationist practices: Missouri Germans, 218–219
Italian immigrants: German disparagement of immigrants in Chile, 202, 207

Jesuit history, 63–64, 67, 73
Jewish identity: Jewish presence in Latin America, 156
Jung, C. J., 121

Kalender für die Deutschen in Brasilien (Rotermund), 115

Kansas-Nebraska Act, 218
Kant, Immanuel, 19, 52, 78, 270; interventions on race, 79–82; perpetual peace, 86–87; the sublime in his Third Critique, 184–186
Katechismus der Auswanderung (Meinecke), 231–234, 236, 249–250, 252, 252n9
Keller, Gottfried, 122–124
Kenny, Robert, 121
Khokhoi people, 221, 234
Kinder-Lust series, 218–219
Klein, Marcus, 277
Kleist, Heinrich von, 220
Klotz, Marcia, 244–245
knowledge expansion, 39–40, 63, 94
König, Anton Friedrich, 69
Kopper, Simon, 241
Kops, Reinhard, 298–299n10
Kpando site, Togo, 45–46, *47–49*
"Krambambulli," 46
Kulturvölker, 136

labor hierarchies, 58
land appropriation and ownership, 66n28; African coast, 37–38; Aichele's immigration, religion, and marriage in Chile, 193; Cramer's Farmersfrau trope, 241; defining the reach of, 120–121; feuding neighbors, 122–123; German-Chilean friendship and trade agreement, 195; German entitlement and legitimacy in Chile, 176–177, 190–191, 205–206; German entitlement in Brazil, 98–99; German rancor over lost territory, 208–209; incentivizing emigration to Chile, 203; justifying the claim to Argentina, 155–158; Lessing's critique of absolutism, 66–67; settlers in the American West, 111; violence in the opening of Argentinian territories, 152–153. *See also* territorial expansion
Land und Leute (Voigt), 273
language, German, 6–7; Bodenstedt's New World poetic tropes, 161–162; constructing a national immigrant identity, 213; constructing the settler identity in southern Brazil, 119–120; decolonial projects and discourse, 17–20; German support of emigration, 175; immigrant identity in Chile, 198–199; importance in constructing identity, 213–215; intellectual migration, 114–115; Lessing's critique of coloniality of power, 73; master-servant exonyms, 244; Missouri Germans preserving, 218–219; neighbors, 120–121; Piderit's professional and immigrant identities, 189; pioneers imposing on Indigenous peoples, 164–165; preserving racial integrity in Brazil, 141–143, 148; the struggle for cultural identity, 25
Latin America, 9
Ledóchowska, Maria Theresa, 220
legitimacy of land appropriation, 237; African coast, 37–38; colonial rights to conquered regions, 63–64; German entitlement to Brazil, 95–97; German immigrants in Chile, 175–177, 205–206; justifying ancestral claims to Argentina, 155–161
Leiste, Christian, 63, 67, 72–73
Lessing, Gotthold Ephraim, 65n23, 86–87; competitive colonialism, 87–88; critique of Brazilian colonization, 62–65, 72; critique of despotism, 21–22, 52, 61–62, 67–68; dancing bear, 69–70, 148, 256; engaging with the transatlantic world, 73–74; European national identities, 71–73; place names, 70–71; praise poems to Frederick II, 67–70
Lessing, Karl Gotthelf, 86
"Lessing entdeckt Brasilien" (Feder), 74
Lessing-Legende (Mehring), 65–66
"Liebeslied eines amerikanischen Wilden" (Goethe), 89–93
Litran, Guiherme, *147*
London Missionary Society, 220–221

Index

Los Alemanes en Chile 1541–1917 (Flores), 176–180
Lübcke, Frederick C., 191–192, 218–219
Lutheran American states, 26
Lutherans. *See* Rotermund, Wilhelm

Machiavelli, 57–58
Madan, Aarti, 151–152
Maji Maji war (1905–1907), 270–271
maps. *See* globes and maps
Marañón River, Brazil, 64, 67, 72–73
Maria Leopoldine, empress of Brazil, 95–97, 112
maritime exploration, 32–33, 37, 41–42
marketable geography, 151–152
marriage, 227; Aichele's immigration, religion, and marriage in Chile, 193; German legitimacy in Chile, 176–177; Hellemeyer's *Erlebnisse eines Mädchens*, 132, 134–137; Meinecke advocating marriage for German immigrants, 263–269; Piderit's search for a wife, 187; Rotermund's "Die beiden Nachbarn," 122–125; strategic, 55
Martin, Gerald, 163–164
martyrdom: Cramer's Farmersfrau identity, 240–241, 245–246
masculinity, 245n64; E. L. Cramer's *Kinderfarm*, 274; farmer-settlers and German masculinity, 237–238; gender role reversals in *Aus dem Creolenland*, 226–230; Germanness as, 249; German pioneer mascot in colonized New York, 168–169; Goethe's poetry, 91–92; Meinecke's erotic novella, 264–269; military, 131–132, 135–136, 148–149, 170; Piderit's emigration experience, 185, 189; race and gender in German immigration to Chile, 177–178; savage masculinity in pioneer identity, 151
material culture, 7; Brazilian sugar sculpture, 112–113; cigarette packages and collectible cards, 274–275; Great Elector statue, 21, 31–32, 33; return of stolen and purchased objects, 296; Volta Regional Museum, 46. *See also* arts
maternalism: Farmersfrau trope, 217, 241–243, 245–246
Mazzari, Marcus, 107
Mbandero uprising, 241
medical practice, Piderit's, 183–189
Mehring, Franz, 65–66
Meinecke, Gustav Hermann, 252n9; critique of Dutch colonialism, 254–256; *Der arme Sidie Abderrachman*, 248–251, 263–269; dissuading emigration, 236; economy of crime and punishment, 258–262; farmers and the Farmersfrau, 236–237; German legitimacy and entitlement, 5–6; Kpando site, 45; nationalization of immigration and colonization, 248; "professional colonists," 226–230; race, gender, and African belief systems, 230; social inequalities, 296; sugar production in East Africa, 254; Swahili, 270; the tropics, 252–253; worldwide communications, 231–234
Mein Rechnenbuch (Rotermund), 141–142
mercantilism, 34
methodological nationalism, 213
Meyer, Hans, 273
Mignolo, Walter, 9
military masculinity, 131–132, 135–136, 148–149, 170
mining and mineral wealth, 92, 96–97, 99, 101–102, 107, 182, 195, 260
miscegenation, 95, 264; Kant on skin color, 79
missionaries, 216, 216n8; the civilizing influence of conversion, 218–225; colonial remnants, 46; Cramer's brutality toward Indigenous women, 245; cultural, 248–249; Herero conflict, 235; slavery in the West Indies, 50–51; study of Swahili poetry, 269–270. *See also* conversion, religious
Missouri Compromise, 218

Missouri Germans: global colonial networks, 117; landownership intersecting citizenship, 169–170; Lutheran Ohio-Missouri synod, 26, 218–219; resistance to assimilation, 114. See also Rotermund, Wilhelm
mobility, social and geographical, 4–8, 23–26, 84–87, 150–151, 177, 217–218, 228, 262, 264
modernity: coloniality of world power, 7–8
modernization: German immigrant identity in Chile, 195–198, 207–208
Montezuma (opera), 21, 58–60
morality: allegorical Afrikaner and frontier morality, 218–225; Cramer's Farmersfrau trope, 241–242; E. L. Cramer's claim to the high ground, 291–292; Meinecke on the savages of Europe, 254
Moravian Brethren, 50–51
motherland. *See* homeland, German
Mugge, Miqueias, 145
museum collections: Piderit's contributions, 187; return of stolen and purchased objects, 296
Muslim faith: Casco's work, 269–271
Mutterland. *See* homeland, German

Namibia, 218, 235. *See also* German Southwest Africa
narcissism of minor differences, 121–122
Nathan der Weise (Lessing), 61–62
nationalism: Meinecke's ideology, 248–251
National Socialist ideologies and values, 270–271; collectible cigarette packages and cards, 279–280; Cramer's racist *Kinderfarm*, 272–275, 290–291; Cramer's repatriation, 286–287; Cramer's repatriation and embrace of, 290–291; Farmersfrau trope, 217; identifying with American Indians, 166; immigrants' postwar political alliances, 275–277; legacy of African empires, 49–50; portrayal of postwar victimization, 281–282
naturalization, 194–196, 205, 207

Naturvölker, 136
Navarro, Samuel, 159
Nazi-era imperialism. *See* German Southwest Africa
neighbors, 115–116, 119–125, 138–140, 142, 147–148
neonationalism: southern Brazil, 117
"Neueste Erlebnisse aus Ost Afrika," 46, 48
Neumann, Gerson Roberto, 115, 119
New York: eighteenth-century German immigration, 167–171
Nisbet, H. B., 65
noble wanderer trope, 250
North America: Friedrich's engagement with, 58; German identity narrative, 44–45; perceptions on race and immigration, 139–141; Seume on Canada's wilderness and civilization, 74–77; Spielhagen's pioneer literature, 165–170. *See also* United States

Obermeier, Franz, 128
Oduro-Opuni, Obenewaa, 66–67
Oguejiofor, Josephat Obi, 19
Ohio-Missouri synod, Lutheran, 26, 218–219
Oldendorp, Christian Georg Andreas, 50–51, 77
Oloukpona-Yinnon, Adjaï Paulin, 38, 43
"On the Different Races of Human Beings" (Kant), 79
opera: expressions of resistance, 58–60
Orlam Afrikaners, 224
Ovaherero people, 233–235, 241
Overhoff, Jürgen, 53
overpopulation, 174–175

Pacific territories: European mercantilism, 34–35
Paraguay, 278–279
Patacho people, 97–98, 103
patrimony: German immigrant identity in Chile, 176; Goethe's and Schiller's works, 173; material culture, 114; racial

Index

profiling, 19; transmission through the *Fibel*, 141–142
patriotism, emigration as a form of, 249–252
peace, perpetual, 51–52, 62, 86–87
Pedro I, 125
Pedro II, 112, *113* , 153
Penny, H. Glenn, 4, 19, 166, 187, 213
Peru, 195–196
Pesne, Antoine, 53, *54*
Phenomenology (Hegel), 17, 17n52
Philippi, Bernhard E., 180–181
Piderit, Karl Theodor, 25, 177–178, 183–189, 191–192, 194
Pienaar, Petrus, 224
pioneers: Bodenstedt's pioneer literature, 164–165; "captive" painting, 152–155; "Christian Afrikaner" asserting religious and ethnic identity, 220; Farmersfrau trope, 217; German pioneers' entitlement in Argentina, 155–161; immigration to Argentina, 151–165; Spielhagen's *Deutsche Pioniere*, 164–170
plantation economy: Brazil, 99, 104
play and games: adventure stories about play, 127–130; Deutschland's Kolonien-Spiel, 250, *251*, *294* 292–293; noble wanderer trope, 250; transmitting military paternity through, 134–136
plural citizenship, 206–207
poetry: Bodenstedt's New World tropes, 161–163; "captive" painting, 154; German Americans in Missouri, 169; Germans' proprietary relationship with Chile, 205–206; Goethe's cross-cultural borrowings, 106–107; Goethe's "Liebeslied," 89–93; Lessing's critique of tyranny, 64–65; Lessing's tributes to Frederick II, 68–70; Piderit's Andean journey, 186; praise of Maria Leopoldine, 96; Seume on wilderness and civilization, 74–77; slavery as metaphor, 84–86; Swahili narrative poetry, 269–271; transnational colonial geographical boundaries, 46,

48; white military masculinity and entitlement, 169–170; "whitening" of enslavement, 22–23
political space: German-language immigrants in southern Brazil, 116–117
political stability: German presence in Chile, 181–182
population demographics, 174–175
pornography, humanitarian, 95, 155
Portugal and Portuguese colonialism, 9, 22, 62–63; Meinecke on East Africa's cultural politics, 256. *See also* Brazil
postcolonialism, 11, 206; African legacy of German colonialism, 21; Chile's legacy of German colonialism, 25; coloniality of power, 8–9; Goethe's Brazil, 94; *Groß-Friedrichsburg* critique, 33–34; Meinecke's racist revisionism, 234–235
power, 20–21; European co-optation of Indigenous epistemologies, 48; inter-European competition in Africa, 42–45; Lessing's critique of absolutism, 65–66; Prussian crafting of perpetual peace, 51–52; weapons of the powerless, 24–25
Pratt, Mary Louis, 18, 113
precious metals, 99
print media: Aichele's racial typography on Chilean people, 191–194; Chilean newspapers, 194–195; constructing a colonial immigrant identity in Chile, 214; correspondence from Blacks in the West Indies, 76–77; crossing transnational colonial geographical boundaries, 45–46; expos and world's fairs, 204; fostering community, 139; German entitlement in Argentina, 158–161; German recruitment to Chile, 182–183; global German presence and superiority, 208; globally connecting German-speaking subjects, 45–46; Meinecke's coverage of the German world, 231–232; Pideret's medical practice in Chile, 183–189; postwar political shifts, 275, 277; recruiting immigrants to Argentina, 278–279;

print media (*continued*)
reinforcing Germans' sense of superiority, 199; reports of West Indies slavery, 50; Rotermund's German publications in Brazil, 115
professional colonists, 226
"Prometheus" (Goethe), 91–92
Prussia: the colonial unconscious, 53–61; connecting rights and privileges in Brazil, 102–103; crafting perpetual peace, 51–52; expansionist wars, 55–57; Frederick's expansion wars and imperial aspirations, 51; Gold Coast colonialism, 36–37. *See also* Brandenburg expansionism; Friedrich II

Quijano, Aníbal, 7–10, 12–13, 18–19, 65n23, 296

race and racism, 16–17; American racial wars, 218; Amo's contributions to Enlightenment thought, 15–16; attributing to nature, 164–165; Bodenstedt's New World tropes, 161–162; "Christian Afrikaner," 26–27, 216–225; colonial interpretation of resistance, 269–271; coloniality of power, 7–8, 14–15, 21, 65n23; constructing a national immigrant identity, 213; Cramer's *Kinderfarm*, 272–275, 284–289; decolonial projects and discourse, 17–20, 23; dismantling colonial institutions, 296; ethnic identifiers and epistemologies in *Aus dem Creolenlande*, 227–228; Farmersfrau trope, 217, 240–244; German assertions of global superiority, 208; German colonial space and identity in Brazil, 112; German immigrant legitimacy in Chile, 175–176; Hegel's racialization of freedom, 13–14; Hellemeyer's writings for immigrant children, 131; inter-European colonial competition, 43–44; Kant's interventions on race, 79–82; linking German national identity and destiny to, 190–191; Meinecke on East Africa's cultural politics, 254–258; Meinecke's economy of crime and punishment, 258–262; Meinecke's exotic novella, 264–269; Meinecke's *Katechismus* covering the GSA, 232–234; *Montezuma* as expression of resistance, 58–60; Nazi-era supremacism, 27–28; Piderit's observations of Chilean peoples, 188–189; postwar settlers in Brazil, 146; preserving racial integrity in Brazil, 141–143, 148; religious conversion, 55–56, 78–79, 218–225; roots of scientific racism, 19–20; Rotermund's race theory, 139–141; Schäffer's divisions of Brazil's populace, 97–104; Spielhagen's frontier story, 167; transatlantic revolutions, 94–95; transcending territorial boundaries, 45–48. *See also* slavery
radicalism, Black, 235
rape, 134; "captive" painting, 154–155
Raule, Benjamin, 37
Ravenstein, Ernst Georg, 282–283
refugee crisis, 296
Reidy, Michael, 185
Reisescizzen und Tagebuchblätter aus Deutsch-Ostafrica (Bülow), 263, 263n32
religion and spirituality: African belief systems in *Aus dem Creolenlande*, 226–230; Aichele's immigration, religion, and marriage in Chile, 193; building a cohesive national identity in southern Brazil, 114–118; constructing a national immigrant identity, 213; Hellemeyer's *Erlebnisse eines Mädchens*, 133; manifestations of tyranny, 61–62; Meinecke's racialized discourse on African peoples, 233–234; religious discourse and intellectual migration, 114–115; religious identity, 55–56; settler colonialism-immigration overlap and conflict, 226–227; Witbooi's history, 235. *See also* conversion, religious; Rotermund, Wilhelm

remigration, 25; from Brazilian wilderness to German civilization, 112; constituting "wildness," 23–24; E. L. Cramer's return to Germany, 286–289; Hellemeyer's *Erlebnisse eines Mädchens*, 131–137 resistance, 13, 216–217; anarcho-feminism as, 247–248; artistic expressions of, 58; Christian Afrikaner as symbol of, 26–27; colonial interpretation, 269–271; counternarratives opposing colonial expansion, 3–4; decolonial revolutions, 8; defiance of accused Blacks, 262; interconnectedness of thoughts and things, 10–11; Lessing's writings, 61–62; multiple forms of, 6; Ragamuffin rebellion, 146–147; South Cone pushback against German barbarism, 297–298; transcripts of the disempowered, 216; weapons of the powerless, 24–25; whitewash of colonial oppression in GSA, 234–235
revisionist histories, 45–46, 234–235
Rice, John, 58–59
Richter, Otto, 41–42
Rinke, Stefan, 142
Rio de la Plata, Argentina, 151–165
Rohrbach, Paul, 248
Rojas, Salvador Soto, 176–181
Romanticism, Latin American, 152
Romeo und Julia auf dem Dorfe (Keller), 122–124
Rosa, Luis Othoniel, 247–248
Rosales, Vincente Pérez, 195
Rose, Sony, 219
Rotermund, Wilhelm, 23, 112, 114–120, 122–125, 138–149
roture, 65–66, 66n28
rubber trade, 38
Rugendas, Johann Moritz, 152–155, *153*, 154n10
rural-urban divide: internecine conflicts, 147–148; Piderit's observations in Chile, 189; Rotermund's "Die beiden Nachbarn," 115–116, 119–120, 122–125, 138–140, 142

Saint-Pierre, Castel de, 52, 55
San people, 238
Sarmiento, Domingo Faustino, 151–152, 159–160, 278
savages and savagery: Enlightenment philosophies, 22–23; Freud's narcissism of minor differences, 121–122; Germans' disparagement of Chileans, 202; Hartsink's portrayal of Guyana, 105–106; Hellemeyer's *Erlebnisse eines Mädchens*, 129–138; Meinecke on the savages of Europe, 254; Schäffer's divisions of Brazil's populace, 97–104; slavery in the West Indies, 50–51. *See also* slavery
Schäffer, Georg Anton Ritter von, 22, 95–104, 112, 146
Schaumann, Caroline, 185
Schiller, Friedrich, 78, 80–81, 86, 93, 126, 260
Schlüter, Andreas, 231
Schmidt, Gustav, 205
Schmiedel, Ulrich, 156, *157*, 170–171, 173
Schneider, Emil, 169
Schulze, Frederik, 118–119, 119n22, 275
science: attributing racist agency to nature, 164–165; German immigration to Chile, 180; Goethe's love of Brazil, 88–89, 92–94; Hellemeyer's *Erlebnisse eines Mädchens*, 132–133; Piderit's medical practice, 183–184; scientific racism, 19–20
Scott, James, 216
Seidenfaden, Johann, 222–223
Sembritzki, Emil, 42–43
settlers. *See* farmer-settlers
Seume, Johann Gottlieb, 74–77
sexual relations: Hellemeyer's *Erlebnisse eines Mädchens*, 136; Meinecke's exotic novels, 249, 264–269; promiscuity of female "otherness," 137n48; sexualizing German land ownership in Argentina, 155–156; treatment of slaves, 95
Sklavenstücke (slave plays), 66–67
slave plays, 66–67

slavery: Bodensted's romanticization of language, 164–165; coloniality of power, 9; conflating settler identity with enslavement, 25; European displacement to Africa, 43–44; Friedrich's opposition to, 60–61; frontier morality and the allegorical Afrikaner, 218–225; German immigrants in New York, 168–169; Kant on skin color, 79; Lessing's critique of tyranny, 64–65; literary "whitening," 22; Meinecke on East Africa's cultural politics, 255–258; Meinecke's economy of crime and punishment, 258–262; Meinecke's racial and gender encodings, 249; Missouri Germans' opposition to, 218–220; national settler identity, 126; pirate as trope, 84–86; Prussian-era expansionism, 31–34; reports of West Indies slavery, 50–51; Rotermund's "Die beiden Nachbarn," 126; Schäffer's description of wild Brazil, 97–104; Schiller's message of absolute freedom, 80–81; transatlantic revolutions, 94–95; white slavery, 78–79, 82, 82n10, 100–103, 126, 152–155, 154n10. *See also* enslaved people; race and racism

slave trade, 20–21; Brandenburg expansionism, 32–33, 36; Goethe's global landscape, 88–89; Groß-Friedrichsburg, 42–43; in Meinecke's *Der arme Sidi Abderrachman*, 264–269; Prussian involvement, 53; Schäffer's argument against, 99–104; Schiller on, 81–82; start and progress of German colonialism, 21; white slave trope, 82–84, 82n10, 87

Smith, Justin, 12, 14

snakeskin belt, 89, 92–94, 106–107

social class: coloniality of power, 7–8; constructing a national immigrant identity, 213; immigrants' self-identification with the elite, 198–199; Piderit's observations of Chilean peoples, 188–189; revisionist whitewashing of colonial oppression in GSA, 235

social justice movements, 296

social mobility, 24–25

souls, enslaved, 79–82

South America: cannibalism, 104–107; constituting "wildness," 23–24; German identity narrative, 44–45; Lessing's critique of European "possessions," 62–65; sites of eighteenth-century expansionism, 113–114; small states' colonial aspirations, 56. *See also* Argentina; Brazil; Chile; Southern Cone

Southern Cone: defining, 145. *See also* Argentina; Chile

sovereignty: German lack in European colonies, 172–173

Spain and Spanish colonialism, 9; artistic expressions of resistance, 58–60; *Deutschtum* in South America, 199–200; German disparagement of immigrants in Chile, 202, 207; German immigrant identity in Chile, 176, 178–179; German intervention in Brazil's colonial politics, 171; Lessing researching place names, 70–71; Meinecke on East Africa's cultural politics, 256; *Montezuma* opera, 21–22; Piderit's observations of Chilean peoples, 188–189. *See also* Argentina; Chile

Spielhagen, Friedrich, 24–25, 150–151, 164–170

Staden, Hans, 105, 156

Stedman, John, 95

Steinmetz, George, 12, 248

Stoler, Ann Laura, 12, 45, 52

sublime, Kantian, 184–186

sugar production, 254, 256

sugar sculpture, 112, *113*, 113

Suriname, 62–63, 95

Sutherland, Wendy, 86

Swahili narrative poetry, 269–271

Sweden: colonial aspirations, 56

The Taboo of Virginity (Freud), 121–122

"Täuschungen" (Rotermund), 117–118

Tautz, Birgit, 93

Tereza Cristina, 112, *113*

Index

339

territorial expansion: Brandenburg expansionism, 21, 32–36, 40–45, 55–57; Chile's northward expansion, 195–196; eighteenth-century theories of power and sovereignty, 51–52; emigration as patriotism, 251–252; factors driving German migration, 249–250; farmer-settlers and race wars, 236–237; German struggle for legitimacy and supremacy, 170–171; Germany's discontinuous colonial path, 14–15; Herero conflict, 235; imperialist hegemonic politics of empire, 174–175; as literary entertainment, 166–167; maps and globes representing global ambitions, 1–4; religious and cultural rights to conquered regions, 63–64; South America and Africa, 113–114; strategic colonization of conquered territories, 57–58. *See also* land appropriation and ownership
Thaler, Andreas, 278–279
theft: portrayal in *Die Kinderfarm*, 284–285
Therbusch, Anna Dorothea, 67–68
Tirpitz, Alfred von, 209
Tjarks, Hermann, 158
tobacco production, 256
Tobago, 56–57
"Todeslied eines Gefangenen" (Goethe), 89–91, 93
"Todeslied eines Wilden" (Goethe), 107
Togo, 44–46
toxic feminine, 244–245
trade: association with empire, 39–40; economy of crime and punishment, 258–262; Meinecke on East Africa's cultural politics, 255–258; Prussian-era expansionism, 31–34. *See also* slave trade
Transculturality and German Discourse in the Age of European Colonialism (Zhang), 11
transculturation, 113–114
Translating the World (Tautz), 93
travel writings, 104–107; Bodenstedt's poetry as, 161–162; focus on enslaved Africans, 152; German entitlement in Latin America, 156–158; Lessing's assessment, 70–71; writing for immigrant children, 127–129
tropical frontiers, 225–230, 252–253
tyranny, 73; Lessing's critique of, 61–62, 64–65; Portuguese tyranny in Brazil, 102–103

Ulloa, Antonio de, 70–71
Ulrich, Anton, 76, 77
ungovernables, 284–289
United States, 193–194; Americanization of immigrants, 189; German critique of expos and world's fairs, 204; Homestead Act and westward expansion, 111, 237; Kansas-Nebraska Act, 218; language politics, 215; Lutheran American immigration, 26; Meinecke's literary settings, 262; Missouri Germans, 218–219
universality, 13, 22, 78, 81–84, 89–94, 106–107, 173
unruliness, pedagogy of, 247–248
Utenzi (Swahili literary genre), 269–271

Valdivia, Chile, 194–195, 202–203
Valdívia, Pedro de, 176
Valko, Jennifer M, 151
Van Gent, Jacqueline, 50–51, 152
vaterland. *See* homeland, German
Versailles treaty, 209
violence: Cramer's brutality toward Black women, 239–240, 244–245, 245n64. *See also* war and conflict
Voges, Carlos Leopoldo, 123
Voigt, Bernhard, 273
Volberg, Heinrich, 57
Volk ohne Raum (Grimm), 280–281
Voltaire, 51, 59–60
Volta Regional Museum, 46
Vom Urwald zur Kultur: Erlebnisse eines Mädchens (Hellemeyer), 23–24, 112, 127–140
Von der Groeben, Otto Friedrich, 35, 38, 44

von Festenberg, Hermann, 42–43
voodoo, 226, 230

Wagener, Zacharias, 152
Wagenseill, Johann Christoph, 282–283
Wagner, Florian, 256
Walther, Daniel, 273
Wappäus, Johann Eduard, 190
war and conflict: American racial wars, 218; competitive colonialism, 87–88; European national identities, 71–73; farmer-settlers and race wars, 236–239; German recruitment to Chile, 182–183; Hartsink's portrayal of Guyana, 105–106; Maji Maji war, 270–271; Meinecke's racialized discourse, 234; Prussian expansionist wars, 55–57; racial violence in "Christian Afrikaner," 223; Ragamuffin rebellion, 146–147; remigration in Hellemeyer's *Urwald*, 131–132; transatlantic revolutions, 94–95; violence in the opening of Argentinian territories, 152–153. *See also* colonial competition; resistance
Weiduschadt, Patricia, 141
Weiß oder Schwarz (Cramer), 26–27, 217, 236–237
"Weltliteratur" (Goethe), 106–107
Werman, David S., 121–122
West Indies: competing colonialism, 256; enlightened colonialism and Black agency, 76–77; slavery in, 50–51
white masculinity, 122–127, 170, 236–237, 269
whiteness, 35–36, 150–151; Brazil's efforts to whiten the population, 239; Cramer's Farmersfrau discourse, 245–246; defining Brazil's postwar structures, 145–146; Hellemeyer's *Erlebnisse eines Mädchens*, 135; Schäffer on Brazil's labor and slavery, 101–102; the whitening of Brazil, 127–129
white slavery, 78–79, 82, 82n10, 126; "captive" painting, 152–155, 154n10; Schäffer on Brazilian slave conditions, 100–103
white supremacy, 27–28; multiple forms of racism, 296
"wild" and wilderness, 23–24, 118, 237; "Christian Afrikaner," 222–223; constructing the settler identity in southern Brazil, 118–119; Hellemeyer's *Erlebnisse eines Mädchens*, 127–138; as a return to culture, 111–112; Schäffer's characterizations of Brazil's populace, 97–104; settler identity in Brazil, 126–127; Seume on wilderness and civilization, 74–77
Wildenthal, Lora, 20, 132, 263
Wilhelm II, 44, 174–175, 208–209
Witbooi, Hendrik, 217, 234–236, 241, 270
Witt, Marcos Antônio, 118
women: analysis of Meinecke's novella, 260–269; Cramer's brutality toward Black women, 239–240, 244–245, 245n64; Farmersfrau trope, 217, 236–247; single immigrants in Chile, 177–178. *See also* gender; marriage
work ethic, German: Cramer's Farmersfrau trope, 243; German educational superiority, 150–151; German entitlement to land in Chile, 182–183, 190–194, 202; German literary tradition, 162–163; German superiority to enslaved peoples, 103–104; Missouri's German Americans, 169–170; noble wanderer narrative, 250–251; Piderit's bias toward German settlers, 188–189
World War I: Germans in Chile, 176–177; postwar German-Brazilian relations, 142–146; postwar political shifts, 275, 277; rancor over lost German territory, 208–209
World War II: German migration, 175

Zantop, Susanne, 11, 34–36
Zhang, Chunjie, 11
Ziensis, Johann Georg, 67–68